ALSO BY MARK HONIGSBAUM

The Fever Trail: In Search of the Cure for Malaria

VALVERDE'S GOLD

VALVERDE'S
GOLD

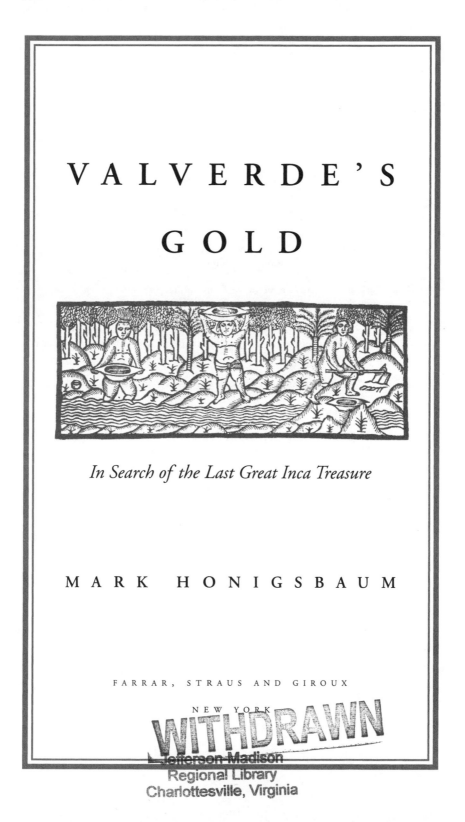

In Search of the Last Great Inca Treasure

MARK HONIGSBAUM

FARRAR, STRAUS AND GIROUX

NEW YORK

Farrar, Straus and Giroux
19 Union Square West, New York 10003

Copyright © 2004 by Mark Honigsbaum
All rights reserved
Originally published in 2004 by Macmillan, Great Britain
Published in the United States by Farrar, Straus and Giroux
First American edition, 2004

Grateful acknowledgment is made to the following for permission to reproduce the images in their possession: Fotografía copyright © Jorge Anhalzer, for the image of the Cerro Hermoso; copyright © 2004 Loren McIntyre / LAM@gscottm.com, for the image of Commander Dyott; copyright © 1956, 1974 by Harold Wilkins, a Citadel Press Book, published by arrangement with Kensington Publishing Corp., all rights reserved, for the image of Harold T. Wilkins's map.

Library of Congress Cataloging-in-Publication Data
Honigsbaum, Mark.
    Valverde's gold : in search of the last great Inca treasure / Mark Honigsbaum.
        p. cm.
    Includes bibliographical references and index.
    ISBN-13: 978-0-374-19170-2
    ISBN-10: 0-374-19170-0 (hc : alk. paper)
    1. Ecuador—Description and travel. 2. Treasure-trove—Ecuador. 3. Incas—Antiquities. 4. Honigsbaum, Mark. I. Title.

F3716.H66 2004
986.6—dc22   2004001744

Designed by Debbie Glasserman

www.fsgbooks.com

1 3 5 7 9 10 8 6 4 2

For Naomi and Frank

I have been a child in fact, but I have been on a quest for buried treasure only in supposition.

—HENRY JAMES, "The Art of Fiction" (1884)

Here is, indeed, a wilful paradox; for if he has never been on a quest for buried treasure, it can be demonstrated that he has never been a child.

—ROBERT LOUIS STEVENSON, "A Humble Remonstrance" (1884)

MAP of the MOUNTAINS of LLAN

by Don Ata

To illustrate a Pap

Pub.ᵈ for the Journal of the Royal Geograp

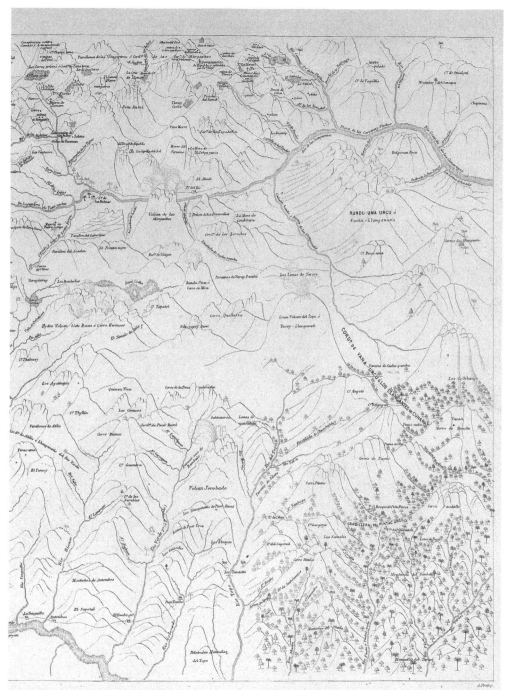

LLANGANATI, IN THE QUITONIAN ANDES.

...anasio Guzman.

...r by Richard Spruce Esq.re

...hical Soc.y by J.Murray Albemarle St.e, London. 1862.

[⅔ of Scale of Original.]

CONTENTS

PRELUDE   3
PROLOGUE   6

PART ONE: THE HOOK   11
  1. The Bearded Man   13
  2. A "Trustworthy Document"   19
  3. The *Derrotero*   32

PART TWO: THE TREASURE SEEKERS   43
  1. An Unexpected Invitation   45
  2. "A Story to Astound the World!"   71

PART THREE: THE LABYRINTH   113
  1. A Literary Gold Mine   115
  2. An Invaluable Manuscript   129
  3. Insight in the Gold Room   140
  4. Conversations with an Orchidist   149
  5. Audience with a Priest   159

PART FOUR: ZUNCHU-URCU   175
  1. Where I Show Blake's Maps to Roland
    and His Opinion Thereof   177
  2. Where I Travel to Píllaro and Meet the
    Famous Don Segundo   186
  3. The Ascent of Mesa Tablón and Don
    Segundo's Story About a "Red-Haired
    Explorer"   194
  4. The Ranges at Last and a Decision
    Reached   206

PART FIVE: "THE ALMOST UNBELIEVABLE
HISTORY OF THE ENGLISH"   211
  1. Dead Ends   213
  2. Seville   236
  3. "Gold, Ghosts, and Commander Dyott"   248

PART SIX: BEYOND THE RANGES   269
  1. Roland and Andy Redux   271
  2. Oro Es Trabajo   294

EPILOGUE   325

Appendix   329
Further Reading   333
Acknowledgments   337
Index   339

VALVERDE'S GOLD

PRELUDE

Around seventy million years ago a fissure opened in the earth's crust near the equator. The fissure was just forty miles long and ran east from what would later become the Ecuadorian Andes. Judging by the subsequent folding and buckling, it possessed tremendous force.

To the south it sent metamorphic rock from deep within the earth crashing against a thick layer of limestone deposited in central Ecuador by the flow of the Amazon to the Pacific. Elevated above the surface of the water, the limestone became scored with subterranean tunnels and chambers. Then, as the collision of the Nazca and South American plates gathered pace, the tectonic forces upended the tunnels and lifted them some thirteen thousand feet above sea level, coming to rest as vertical sinkholes on top of a layer of gneiss and schist.

Volcanism did the rest.

As molten magma rushed to the surface, mineral-rich fluids insinuated themselves into the fissures and cracks to form sparkling veins of galena (PbS), pyrite (FeS$_2$), copper (Cu), silver (Ag), quartz (SiO$_2$), and gold (Au). In section, the latter resembled sticks of rock: milky on the outside, yellow on the inside, as though shot through with sunlight.

Forty million years passed, geologic time; then came the uplifting of the mighty Andean cordillera. Now the great river that had flowed east across South America was dammed. With no outlet to the west, the Amazon became a vast inland lake. As the Antarctic ice cap shrank and the earth warmed, billowing clouds pregnant with humidity drifted west across the young continent. It was on the Andes, and the smaller, more ancient mountain range in its shadow, that they spilled their loads.

In many ways the clouds were the making of the ranges: their rains scoured the paramos—*the high, treeless moorlands—filling the extinct volcanic craters, and they seeped through the bedrock, exposing the quartz reefs with their hidden lodes. But in other places the water had nowhere to go. Instead, it collected in pools, forming wild morasses and muddy lakes covered in mattresses of* pajonal *grass* (Calamagrostis intermedia) *that seemed to shudder and quake with every underground tremor.*

No one knows when the first gold seekers arrived or how long they stayed. Perhaps they came as early as two thousand years ago, when Indians on the coast of Ecuador mastered the art of forging delicate pectorals and brooding funerary masks from gold and platinum. Or perhaps they came fifteen hundred years later, when the Incas invaded the Ecuadorian highlands from Peru, integrating the local tribes into their colonial system of mitimaes.

For the Incas, gold was literally the sweat of the sun, silver the tears of the moon—holy rather than monetary things. In search of the hidden reefs, Indian metallurgists scoured the four corners of the Inca empire, Tahuantinsuyo, panning riverbeds for granular deposits washed downstream by the force of the water. Having identified a lucrative seam, they built artificial pools to separate the gold from the ore and improvised guayras—*furnaces—for smelting the precious metal. But while in Peru and Bolivia the descents to the mines were rapid and dramatic, in Ecuador the journey was fraught with difficulties.*

The reason was the ranges. Bruised, black, and uncompromising, they protruded from the Andes like angry knuckles. Even in the supposed "dry" season, crossing them was treacherous. On the paramo *the wind was fierce, the rain constant. To traverse these frigid wastelands, a man needed to be hardy and fleet of foot. Then, as he descended to the forest, he faced new obstacles: fields of dwarf bamboo* (Neurolepis aristata), *known as* flechas *in Spanish because of their sharp, arrowlike tips, which could take out an eye with a flick of their stems; sheer, mud-slickened slopes on which it was easy to slip and twist an ankle; shuddering bogs and narrow ravines blocked by massive boulders. When the mist lifted, however, there was also much to admire: spectacled bears* (Tremarctos ornatus) *feeding on the sweet heart of the achupalla plant* (Puya hamata); *Andean tapir* (Tapirus pinchaque) *whistling for their young; mountain lions* (Puma concolor) *stalking the beaches for rabbits; bright orange* chuquiraguas *and pink and purple gentians; mauve club mosses and exquisite orchids patterned like butterflies. And every now and again a valley full of* frailejones (Espeletia pycnophylla)—*a tall, palmlike plant with a shaggy trunk topped by a spray of velvety leaves.*

Most spectacular of all was the view. To the west and north lay an avenue of steaming volcanoes, to the east the Amazon, and in between a series of jagged ridges and turreted crags.

The profiles of these mountains had peculiar, shifting forms. Viewed from a certain angle, one resembled a castle; another a sleeping woman; a third, which the Indians called Topo or Tupu, the point of a needle.

But there was one that intrigued men above all others. Seen from a distance, it appeared to have seven openings. The early Spanish explorers who came here drawn by the legends of gold christened it the Volcán de Siete Bocas—the "Volcano of Seven Mouths"—a rumor that the nightly electrical storms that fizzed about its peaks did little to dispel. But the mountain, which the Indians considered beautiful, never erupted. Instead, it bided its time, waiting for the treasure seekers to surmount its summit. Only then did they realize that it wasn't a volcano at all but a granite mass scored with limestone sinkholes as deep and unknowable as the earth that had spawned it.

SHORTLY AFTER CHRISTMAS 1886, AN AMERICAN MERCHANT SHIP WEIGHED anchor at Callao, the port of Lima, and drifted into the cool waters of the Humboldt Current. The current swept the vessel into the Pacific and northwest along the slanting coast of Peru toward Ecuador. Bound for the steamy port of Guayaquil, the four-masted schooner had already called at Buenos Aires and Valparaíso. Guayaquil was to be its last stop before rounding Cape Horn once more and setting sail for Boston and home.

That, at least, was the plan. But as the ship inched up the Ecuadorian coast early in 1887, disaster struck. A navigational error had brought the schooner perilously close to shore. Alerted to the danger too late by his pilot, Captain Barth Blake attempted to heave his vessel back into open waters. But near the Gulf of Guayaquil the ship grazed an underwater reef—perhaps the very same reef that had claimed the Spanish treasure ship *La Capitana* 232 years before—and the rudder shattered on a rock. As the schooner listed in the shallows, Blake frantically ordered his men to cut the rigging. But before they could do so, a high wind caught the ship's mainsail, snapping the mast in two.

Fortunately, the Guayaquil port authorities heard the schooner's distress signals, and the ship was pulled free from the reef before it suffered further damage. But the crew's hopes of being back in Boston by the summer were gone. It would be several months, Blake was told, before Guayaquil's overworked shipyards could repair his boat.

For most sailors the thought of spending three months in Guayaquil was grim. The equatorial seaport was hot and humid and had a reputation for breeding mosquitoes and disease. But for Blake and his second in command, Lieutenant George Edwin Chapman, the accident couldn't have been better timed, for in their knapsacks they carried secret documents purporting to reveal the location of a lost Inca treasure—a treasure believed by many to be the greatest in the world.

Legend had it the treasure had been collected by the Indians to pay the ransom demanded in November 1532 by the Spanish for the release of the uncrowned Inca chief Atahualpa. But when, eight months later, in a brutal act of betrayal the Spanish murdered Atahualpa in Cajamarca, Peru, Atahualpa's loyal generals hid the gold in caves and tombs throughout the Andes. Many of these *huacas* had since been uncovered by treasure hunters, but the whereabouts of the Ecuadorian hoard remained a mystery. This was the mystery Blake and Chapman had sailed around Cape Horn to solve.

The two mariners had first heard about the treasure from a young English colleague in the Royal Navy. The sailor, a nephew of the distinguished English botanist Richard Spruce, had described how in 1857 his uncle had traveled from the depths of the Peruvian Amazon to Baños, a small town in the eastern Ecuadorian Andes. There, Spruce had stumbled upon a *derrotero*—an ancient Spanish treasure guide composed by a former conquistador named Valverde. Tradition had it that Valverde was a poor Spanish soldier who had fallen in love with an Indian princess from the region. Valverde had so impressed the princess's father with his kindness to the Indians that one day the Indian chieftain had taken the Spaniard to one side and revealed the location of Atahualpa's hoard. The gold, he said, was buried in a lake in a cave behind three triangular peaks to the northeast of Baños. Known as the Cerros Llanganatis, the peaks were a dark, wet, and desolate place draped for nine months out of twelve in rain and frigid mists. Many a Spaniard had died or lost his way in the ranges, victims, it was rumored, of Atahualpa's curse.

With the chieftain's help, however, Valverde succeeded in entering the mountains and locating the hoard. But he took only as much gold as he needed to support his bride, and on his deathbed in Spain he left the King detailed instructions as to how to proceed to the treasure lake. This was Valverde's *derrotero*. In 1861 Spruce had published the guide in the *Journal of the Royal Geographical Society* in London. But the guide was cryptic and confusing, and so far no one who had studied it had been able to follow all its sinuosities.

As Blake and Chapman bade goodbye to their shipmates, however, they were quietly confident of success. The reason was that hidden in their leather backpacks they also carried another document: Valverde's map. Spruce had discovered the map during his sojourn in Baños but, unlike the guide, had kept its existence secret. Now in his seventies and confined to a cramped cottage in North Yorkshire, Spruce hoped that with the mariners' help the map would make him a wealthy man.

At first everything went according to plan. Armed with Spruce's information, Blake and Chapman crossed the western cordillera of the Andes, passing over the southern shoulder of Chimborazo, one of the highest volcanoes on earth. At Ambato, a busy commercial town in the sierra, they bought provisions for their expedition—in all probability maize, tinned beef, barley meal, potatoes, and beans. They then rode north, following the winding gorge of the Río Patate until they reached Píllaro, a tiny market town perched just below the Llanganatis range at nine thousand feet. They were now on the *paramo*—a cold, high-altitude moorland peppered with muddy morasses and menacing Andean vegetation. It was here that, abandoning their mules, they walked to the summit of a hill above the village and first glimpsed the three *cerros* peeping through the mist.

Valverde's guide instructed them to look for a mountain "all of *Margasitas*"—pyrites*—and contour around it in a particular direction, indicated in the text by a hieroglyph, until they came upon a straight passage running between two mountains, the Way of the Incas. From here they would be led to a *socabón* (tunnel) "in the form of a church porch,"

---

*Iron disulfide (FeS$_2$), a crystalline mineral whose pale yellow color is commonly mistaken for gold, hence its nickname "fool's gold."

at the end of which they would find a cascade falling into a *tembladal*, a quaking bog. So far every explorer who had followed the guide had foundered on the cryptic symbol; no one could decide whether it indicated you should contour around Margasitas Mountain to the north or to the south. But with the help of Spruce's secret map, Blake and Chapman succeeded in deciphering the riddle and entered the treasure cave.

As their eyes grew accustomed to the dark, they had to pinch themselves to make sure they weren't dreaming. Piled all about the cave were exquisite Incan and pre-Incan artifacts—according to Blake, "the most beautiful goldsmith works" imaginable. These included "life-size human figures made out of beaten gold and silver; birds, animals and corn stalks made out of silver with golden corn ears; gold and silver flowers; pots full of the most incredible jewellery; golden vases full of emeralds and other beautiful stones; gold goblets; and a thousand other artefacts."

Blake and Chapman selected eighteen of the best pieces—as much as they could fit in their small leather backpacks—and exited the cave, aiming to return once they had raised more men and equipment. But rather than retrace their steps, the mariners decided to plot a direct compass course west across the *paramo* to Píllaro.

It was a mistake. As they set off, a mist descended, and they were soon lost in a *neblina*—a freezing white fog. For days they wandered aimlessly through quaking bogs and tangled, razor-sharp vegetation. Their provisions began to run low. Then Chapman, who according to Blake was suffering from a tropical malady, suddenly fell ill and died. Blake buried him on the spot, marking his grave with a pile of rocks and a small wooden cross.

Blake finally emerged from the mountains toward the end of April. Rather than remain in Píllaro, however, he hurried back to his ship— which had been repaired in his absence—and set sail for North America. At Panama he posted a card to Spruce, informing him that he had found the treasure. But by now Blake had started to worry that his shipmates were suspicious—presumably they had not believed whatever story he had told them about Chapman's death and his long absence— so when he reached Boston, he arranged for the maps to be delivered to an old seafarer friend, a captain named Albertson. In a letter to Albertson that accompanied the maps Blake wrote:

It is impossible for me to describe to you the wealth that now lies in that distant cave marked on my map but I could not remove it alone, nor could a thousand men . . . I have to go back to sea for a while, and I beg of you, to take good care of my maps and papers.

Blake returned to England, where he had the pieces appraised by the British Museum, and presented his findings to Spruce. Then, in 1892, he set sail for North America with the aim of selling the gold and emeralds to raise money for a second, better-equipped expedition. This time he planned to take Captain Albertson with him. But Blake never made it. Somewhere off the coast of Halifax he fell overboard and was lost at sea. According to the ship's log, Blake had been drunk and had lost his footing in a storm. But others suspected a more sinister explanation. In his last letter to Albertson, shortly before leaving England, Blake had written:

Even now there are rogues looking at me through the window . . . If something should happen to me and you decide to go and search for that hidden cave marked on my map, look for the Reclining Woman and all your problems are solved.

Part One

THE HOOK

"It's a queer story, Mr. Quatermain," said Sir Henry.
"I suppose you are not hoaxing us? It is, I know,
sometimes thought allowable to take
a greenhorn in."

—H. RIDER HAGGARD, *King Solomon's Mines*

1

THE BEARDED MAN

I FIRST HEARD BLAKE'S STORY WHEN I VISITED BAÑOS IN THE SUMMER OF 2000 to research a book on malaria. I had come to Ecuador looking for insights into Spruce's state of mind during 1858–64, when, having arrived in Ecuador from Peru, he was entrusted by the British government with the task of gathering seeds and plants of the cinchona tree, the source of quinine and then the only known cure for the malarial fevers raging in India. My aim was to retrace Spruce's journey from Ambato to a ridge in the western Andean cordillera where he had harvested the cinchona trees for the Indian plantations. Although I did not know it at the time, I would be following the same route as Blake and Chapman but in reverse, circumnavigating the volcano Chimborazo's glacier from east to west before crossing the shoulder of the mountain and descending to the cinchona forests overlooking the Pacific.

Nestling the foot of another volcano—Tungurahua—Baños is a charming if slightly unnerving place in which to relax ahead of a major expedition. Famous for its thermal waters, the town is a popular weekend holiday destination. It boasts five public baths, a spectacular waterfall, and a Gaudi-esque gray basilica. But though the town's prosperity depends on the heat of the volcano, Tungurahua is also a constant threat. The volcano has erupted four times in the last three hundred years, most spectacularly in 1773, when it showered the town in ash and lava. The autumn before my arrival, fearing that the mountain was about to erupt for a fifth time, the authorities shut the road from Ambato and evacuated the town. But worried that the military would loot their homes, the Baneños had reclaimed the town after only a few months, and by the time I arrived in June, you would hardly have known there had been a crisis.

To my surprise, however, the subject on most people's lips was not the volcano but Valverde's gold. A few months before, the Ecuadorian Air Force had dropped paratroopers into a sinkhole on the summit of Cerro Hermoso, the highest mountain in the Llanganatis range, in the belief (false as it turned out) that it was Blake's legendary treasure cave. Recounting the air force's exploits on the ride to my hostel, my taxi driver informed me that his uncle had also sponsored a number of missions to the Llanganatis and was planning another next year.

"He is obsessed with those mountains, señor. He says the treasure is one of the world's last great mysteries."

At that time I didn't know how to spell "Llanganatis" let alone how to pronounce it—the Ecuadorians say "Jan-ga-natis," pronouncing the double *l* or "ele" as a hard *j* rather than the softer *y* sound favored by Spaniards—but as I already knew quite a bit about Spruce, I was highly skeptical of his connection to Blake. A plucky and famously inquisitive collector, Spruce had spent fifteen years in the Amazon and Andes. During his travels he had made the first botanical study of the *Hevea* rubber tree, found the source of the Indian hallucinogen ayahuasca, and amassed the largest collection of mosses and liverworts in the world. Indeed Spruce's passion for bryology had taken him through some of the densest jungles and over some of the most treacherous terrain in the Americas. If Spruce had really stumbled upon such a valuable map and guide in Baños, wouldn't he have attempted to retrieve the treasure himself? Indeed, the more I thought about Blake's story, the more it struck me as a pirate tale, a confection of fact and fantasy that had been allowed to take root in the wilds of South America but would hardly stand scrutiny in the more skeptical north. What, for instance, was Blake, a former Royal Navy marine, doing in charge of an

American schooner, and how could he just abandon his crew to set off into the Llanganatis? Moreover, why, having found the treasure cave, didn't he return immediately for the rest of the gold?

But though there were many anomalies and discrepancies—in one version I later heard, for instance, Blake was described as a Dutchman—I couldn't get the story out of my mind. What if, as with many pirate tales, it had a basis in fact? What if Spruce really had stumbled upon a treasure map in Ecuador and passed the secret to Blake and Chapman?

The dates certainly fitted. In 1887, Spruce, then aged seventy, had been living in a small cottage in the village of Coneysthorpe near Castle Howard in Yorkshire. In 1864 he had lost his entire savings in a banking collapse in Guayaquil and since his return to England had been forced to subsist on a government pension of just £100 a year. He thus had both the incentive and the time to meet with Blake and, on the mariner's return from South America, receive a report from him about the treasure cave.

If Valverde's guide existed, I reasoned, the place to look was the Royal Botanic Gardens, Kew. The library there had one of the few extant copies of *Notes of a Botanist on the Amazon and Andes*, Spruce's epic two-volume narrative of his travels in South America. It was also the sole repository of Spruce's original leather-bound notebooks and journals. If Spruce had stumbled upon an ancient Spanish treasure guide and map in Ecuador, then Kew was where I would find it.

On my return to Britain, I made an appointment with Kew's archivist Sylvia Fitzgerald. A shrewd woman, with curly brown hair and inquisitive eyes that flickered from behind forbidding spectacles, Fitzgerald was a long-standing admirer of Spruce. Some years before, in an effort to afford the Yorkshireman the acclaim he had been denied in life, she had organized an international symposium in his honor. Academics from as far afield as Harvard and Quito had traveled to York to deliver talks recalling Spruce's scientific achievements. But though there were papers commemorating Spruce's contributions to bryology, his pioneering explorations in the Amazon, and his role in transporting cinchona to the government plantations in India, there was no mention of Valverde's guide or of the lost Inca treasure.

However, as Fitzgerald informed me when I mentioned my interest in Spruce's notebooks, this was not the first time she had received an inquiry about the *derrotero*. Some years before, she said, a man had turned up unannounced at the entrance to the Royal Gardens and asked to be directed to the library. Fitzgerald could no longer recall his name but remembered that he had had a thick beard and had been "extremely animated."

The man explained that he was not a botanist but a geologist. For many years he had worked for multinationals in Central America prospecting for oil, but he was now tired of the business and was looking for something with a bit more adventure. One day, he had read of a lost Inca treasure hidden in a mysterious and inaccessible mountain range in eastern Ecuador. He had heard that the treasure—or rather a map and guide indicating its whereabouts—had first come to light when Spruce had arrived in Baños bedraggled and exhausted after an epic, hundred-day journey from the depths of the Peruvian Amazon. Now he wanted to consult Spruce's notebooks and journals to see if there was any truth to the story.

"In fact," said Fitzgerald, "he asked to see everything Spruce had ever written."

Now, normally archivists recoil at the mention of the word "treasure." Treasure hunters are a notoriously amoral and untrustworthy breed. It doesn't matter how many times they promise to use a pencil and respect the regulations governing the handling of precious documents. If they stumble across a treasure map or some other clue to the location of a lost hoard, they are apt to tear the pages straight from the book.

In the case of the Bearded Man, however, Fitzgerald decided to make an exception. Something about his passion was compelling. If the reports of the size of the hoard were accurate, he enthused, then it would amount to "the greatest treasure trove in history." If he succeeded in finding it, he told Fitzgerald, he planned to build himself a small hacienda in Ecuador—"nothing too fancy"—and give the rest to charity.

"Of course, I'll also take care of you," he added conspiratorially.

"Well, I told him that that was utterly out of the question," Fitzgerald told me. "The rules on archivists' accepting gratuities at Kew are very strict, you know."

Nevertheless, against her better judgment Fitzgerald allowed the Bearded Man access to Spruce's precious manuscripts. For several days he pored over the journals, frantically scribbling notes and excitedly muttering to himself. Then, having apparently found what he was looking for, he bade Fitzgerald goodbye and left for Ecuador. That was the last she saw of him.

I asked Fitzgerald if she could bring me the same notebooks he had consulted, and after a brief delay she returned with three cardboard boxes bound with red ribbon. I undid the ribbon and removed the brown leather journals from their protective casing, taking care not to damage them as I did so.

The first journal was the diary of Spruce's arrival in South America in 1849 and his journey up the Amazon to the Orinoco River basin in Venezuela. It was the size of a small paperback and opened lengthways with a tiny brass locking clasp at one end. Paper had been a precious commodity to Spruce, and he had recorded his daily travails and discoveries in a cramped script, writing on one side of the page before turning the notebook over and continuing his thoughts on the reverse. Although Spruce had used a faint pencil, his words and phrases were clearly legible. Helpfully, at the front of the book, he had also provided a table of contents.

I scanned the entries, looking for a reference to Valverde or *derrotero*, but there was nothing. The second notebook was the same, recording Spruce's continuing journey from Brazil to Peru in 1857.

Then I turned to the third notebook. It was slightly larger than the others and opened width-ways in the conventional manner. On the inside front page, a librarian had written "Misc. Notes (presented by M B Slater Esq, executor to Mr R Spruce, 1908)." After this there was a gap of some thirty pages, followed by a series of entries in Spruce's hand headed "Uses of Amazon plants." Then another gap of several pages, followed by the heading "Miscellanea" and a table of contents of the subsequent entries.

I ran my finger down the list, skipping over those that did not interest me.

"1. Larva of Ecuador," "2. Superstitions of the Quitenian Andes," "3. Indian Languages," . . . "6. Names of Birds," . . . "26. Etymology of Names in the Quitenian Andes."

"Derrotero de Valverde" was listed at twenty-nine.

Next to the entry, somebody—presumably the same librarian—had written in parentheses "Map of Guzmán" and the reference "page 191."

I hurriedly flicked forward to the page in question. There, at the top, twice underlined, was the heading "Derrotero de Valverde" and, immediately below it, in a hand I now recognized as Spruce's, the following comment:

> The copy of the Original Document now before me was made on 14 of Aug. 1827, and the introductory remark, or title (not in very choice Castilian) is that of other copyist.

On the left-hand page Spruce had copied the Spanish into his notebook, while on the right-hand and subsequent pages he had provided a simultaneous English translation. By way of a preface to the *derrotero* Spruce had written:

> Guide, or Route, which Valverde left in Spain, when death overtook/ seized him, having gone from the mountains of the Llanganati, which he entered many times and carried off a great quantity of gold; and the King commanded the Corregidors of Tacunga and Ambato to search for the treasure: which order and guide are preserved in one of the offices of Tacunga.

2

A "Trustworthy Document"

WHEN I WAS TEN, MY FAMILY RENTED A HOUSE ON THE WILD NORTH coast of Cornwall. The house was called Atlantis and overlooked a seething bay—what the Cornish in their charming West Country tongue call a cove. Even though the cove was some two hundred feet below the cliff on which our house was perched, from Atlantis's leaded seaward windows we could clearly measure the waves breaking on the rocks protruding from its narrow skirt of sand. The sight of those green breakers, coupled with the saline taste of the sea, never failed to awaken our young imaginations, and as soon as the car was unloaded, my friends and I would scatter, disappearing down the steep trail that wound down the cliff face toward the beach.

The game would begin the moment we reached the bottom. Leaping agilely from rock to rock, we would make for the caves that peppered the cove, rooting for the smuggling places of old. This part of Cornwall had once been overrun with buccaneers and excise officers—a history reflected in such evocative place-names as "Rumps Point" and "Ligger Bay"—and in our minds the rose-tinted quartz that littered the beach was precious jewels, discarded booty that, once found, belonged to us.

It was around this time that my parents gave me an illustrated edition of Robert Louis Stevenson's *Treasure Island* for my birthday. The book soon became popular with all my friends. The artist had devoted an entire page to Skeleton Island, coloring its swamps a mossy brown and Spye Glass Hill a sunset orange, as though to imply that Captain Flint's treasure lay within easy reach of its summit, and it wasn't long before we were taking the parts of Jim Hawkins, Squire Trelawney, and the old sea dog who checks into the Admiral Benbow with a mysterious sea chest smelling of salt and far-off coral islands. The book fueled our childish obsession with pirate treasure and lost hoards, and as our games became more complicated, the quartz caves beneath Atlantis took on the exotic allure of the Spanish Main.

I grew out of it of course, as children eventually do. But in my heart I never stopped being a treasure hunter, and now, as I turned the pages of Spruce's notebook, I couldn't help but recall our trepidation as the blind man arrives at the Admiral Benbow clutching the dreaded black spot, and our counterfeit elation on unlocking our improvised sea chest and discovering the brightly colored treasure chart we had painstakingly prepared the night before.

"Placed in the town of Píllaro, ask for the farm of Moya, and sleep (the first night) a good distance above it," read the first lines of the *derrotero*. "And ask there for the mountain of Guapa, from whose top, if the day be fine, look to the east, so that thy back be towards the town of Ambato, and from thence thou shalt perceive the three Cerros Llanganati, in the form of a triangle, on whose declivity there is a lake, made by hand, into which the ancients threw the gold that they had prepared for the ransom of the Inca when they heard of his death."

"The mountain of Guapa." Was this the hill Blake and Chapman had climbed outside Píllaro, the hill from which they had first spied the three peaks and plotted their course across the *paramo*?

"From the same Cerro Guapa thou mayest also see the forest, and in a clump of *Sangurimas*, standing out of the said forest, and another clump which they call *Flechas* (arrows), and these clumps are the principal mark, for which thou shalt aim, leaving them a little on the left hand."

"*Sangurimas*"? "*Flechas*"? The words were foreign and intriguing. Sharp, jagged plants to judge from Spruce's translation, but what were their correct botanical names? I imagined Spruce had asked himself the same question. Was this what had first attracted him to the *derrotero*, why he had translated the guide? And if so, where was the map that came with it?

The table of contents had referred to a "Map of Guzmán," but though Spruce had devoted several pages of his notebook to its analysis, the map itself was not there. Was this Valverde's map, the map Spruce had bequeathed to Blake, or some other map? And was its absence from Spruce's notebook confirmation that Blake's story was more than a pirate tale?

I asked Fitzgerald if she had heard the name Guzmán and knew what had become of his map. She paused, flicking through her mental Rolodex as she recalled the papers presented at the Spruce symposium. Then she reached up to the shelf above her desk and handed me a copy of the second volume of *Notes of a Botanist on the Amazon and Andes*.

"Have you tried looking in here? I seem to remember a map somewhere toward the back."

I quickly turned to the last chapter. Headed "A Hidden Treasure of the Incas," it was some thirty pages long and was prefaced by a brief introductory note from the zoologist Alfred Russel Wallace, Spruce's friend and colleague who had edited the journals after his death. "The following narrative," began Wallace, "forms one of the most curious pieces of genuine history in connection with the never-ceasing search for buried treasure in the territory of the Incas."

> We owe to the persevering exertions of Richard Spruce the discovery and the translation of one of the few remaining copies of the official order of the Spanish king to search for the treasure, with the accompanying detailed "Guide" to its locality. Still more are we indebted to his generally esteemed character and ingratiating manners for obtaining permission to copy the unique map of the district containing the treasure, and for undertaking the considerable labour of copying in the minutest detail so large and elaborate a map, without which both the "Guide" and the story of the search for the treasure would be unintelligible.

I closed the volume and reopened it from the back. There, bound in with the end papers, was one of the most extraordinary maps I have ever seen. The first thing that caught my eye was the erupting volcano of Cotopaxi in the top left-hand corner. Then, the bright red line meandering through a strange landscape of jagged crags, lofty lakes, and exotic tropical vegetation. In his effort to combine a vertical with a horizontal elevation, the artist, an Ecuadorian botanist whom Spruce identified as "Atanasio Guzmán," had lovingly sketched the profiles of every mountain as they might appear from the ground while rendering the lakes in relief. Now and again Guzmán could not resist adding churches and houses, coloring their roofs with the same Indian red ink pen he had used to mark the treasure trail. The overall effect was cartoonish and almost childlike in its simplicity—like something you might find in C. S. Lewis's *Narnia* books or J. R. R. Tolkien's *Lord of the Rings*. Indeed, had the map contained a bright red *X* and the legend "buried treasure here," I might have dismissed it altogether. But there was no *X*, just a crucifix inscribed with a morbid and intriguing legend: *"Muerte del Padre Longo"* (Death of Father Longo). The line itself continued far beyond this point, branching in three directions. One fork led due east, twisting and turning past a series of volcanoes marked "Margasitas," "Zunchu Urcu," and "Topo." Another rounded the northern shore of a large lake, Yana Cocha, before ending abruptly at a point inscribed with the legend *"Sublevación de los Indios—Salto de Guzmán"* (Revolt of the Indians—Guzmán's Leap). But the longest led northeast, past the Volcán de los Mulatos and through a region peppered with copper, iron, and silver mines. It terminated in the top right-hand corner near the *"mina de crystals"* and a spot marked *"Discordia y Consonancia con Guzmán,"* indicating that at this point there had been some sort of quarrel and reconciliation with Guzmán.

IN H. RIDER HAGGARD'S CLASSIC ADVENTURE STORY *KING SOLOMON'S Mines,* Allan Quatermain and his companions Sir Henry Curtis, Captain John Good, and the Zulu Ignosi set out to locate the legendary mines of Solomon armed with only a three-hundred-year-old guide compiled by a sixteenth-century Portuguese treasure seeker, José da Silvestra. Quatermain explains that one of da Silvestra's descendants entrusted the guide to him with his dying breath after stumbling out of the desert that guards the entrance to Solomon's Mountains, and that

the original was scrawled on a piece of linen by da Silvestra using a cleft
bone and his own blood as ink. But when Quatermain comes to show
the guide to Curtis, he can only produce an "English rendering" from
his pocketbook—a copy, in fact, much like Spruce's translation of
Valverde's *derrotero*.

At first Curtis and Good suspect Quatermain is trying to hoax them.
But through his evident indignation at being doubted, coupled with his
reluctance to entertain an expedition to the mountains—a sure way of
hooking any treasure seeker—Quatermain soon convinces them.

Having crossed a vast expanse of desert and hauled themselves over
two freezing mountaintops known as Sheba's Breasts, Quatermain and
his companions seek shelter in a cave, only to discover in the morning
that they are seated next to the perfectly petrified remains of the deceased Portuguese explorer.

"There he sat, the dead man, whose directions, written some ten
generations ago, had led us to this spot," says Quatermain, pausing for
reflection, ". . . a sad memento of the fate that so often overtakes those
who would penetrate into the unknown."

As you can imagine, I was not keen to end up the same way, especially not for a treasure that in all probability had never, or no longer,
existed. Before being drawn deeper into the labyrinth, I needed to take
a sounding, to find out who else had investigated the legend and what
they had made of it. I decided to consult the eminent Inca historian
John Hemming. Hemming is a formidably intelligent man with flowing gray hair and a long patrician nose, and his response should have
told me all I needed to know.

"The Llanganatis treasure is a chimera, a trap," he explained firmly
but courteously. "Do you think that if the treasure had existed the Indians would have been able to keep it secret from the Spanish? Of
course not. It's a myth, like El Dorado."

According to Hemming, the Incas did not attach artificial value to
gold and silver, admiring the metals for the way they shone and reflected light but prizing other attractive objects, such as pink mollusk
shells and textiles, just as highly. It was extremely unlikely, he said, that
the Inca generals who knew where Atahualpa's gold was hidden would
have resisted torture until death rather than reveal the whereabouts of a
consignment of metal objects they considered worthless. Also, he very

much doubted that such a large cache could have lain undiscovered for hundreds of years without someone stumbling upon it.

"The Andean Indians know every inch of their homelands. If the treasure had existed, they would certainly have come across such an enormous find. If I were you, I'd leave it well alone."

But of course I couldn't. Instead, I delved deeper into Spruce's notebooks in search of evidence that would confirm Hemming's verdict and lay my wanderlust to rest. But the indisputable, damning proof wasn't there. On the contrary, Spruce believed the *derrotero* was an authentic document; and the more I read, the more I found myself being persuaded by his arguments.

ALTHOUGH HE DID NOT KNOW IT AT THE TIME, SPRUCE'S FIRST SIGHT OF the Llanganatis came on May 23, 1857, as he was working his way up the Bobonaza River to Baños. Two nights before he had stopped at a small village, Puca Yacu, perched on a ravine high above the surging river. To prevent his boats being swept away by the current, his Indian porters had secured them to the riverbank by means of vines overhanging the cliff. But in the night there had been a violent storm, and the waters had risen alarmingly, threatening to snap the vines and wash away the canoe carrying Spruce's precious botanical papers. The porters clung to the vines all night, and only in the morning had the raging waters subsided sufficiently to enable them to unload the boats and haul Spruce's sodden possessions up to the village. "Wearied to death," Spruce spent the whole day and following night recuperating. Then, on the twenty-third, he walked to the plateau above the village. At his feet stretched the valley of the Bobonaza, to the north and west lay the deep gorge of the Pastaza, and rolling away from it "the lofty cordillera . . . in cloudless majesty."

From his new vantage point Spruce, who had never set foot in the Ecuadorian Andes before, was able to make out four volcanoes: Sangay, Altar, Tungurahua, and Chimborazo. But it was only when he reached Baños in July, and heard the legend of the lost treasure for the first time, that he realized he had also been staring at the densely wooded ridges of the Llanganatis.

It was from the villagers of Baños that Spruce first heard the story of how the Incas had supposedly deposited "an immense quantity of gold in an artificial lake on the flanks of one of the peaks" and took a note of the name Valverde, "a Spaniard who from being poor had suddenly become very rich."

According to the villagers, the treasure had been part of the ransom collected by the Incas to buy the freedom of Atahualpa, whom the Spanish had captured and imprisoned in Cajamarca. But when in July 1533 the conquistador Francisco Pizarro reneged on his promise to release Atahualpa and had him executed instead, loyal Inca troops from Atahualpa's northern territories in Ecuador, who were on their way to Cajamarca with the gold, took a detour into the Llanganatis.

Legend had it the hoard was immense—seventy thousand llama-loads of gold and silver weighing some five thousand tons. Having hidden this vast hoard in a lake in the mountains north of Baños, Rumiñahui, the Inca general in command of the gold convoy and Atahualpa's half brother, swore his men to secrecy. Rumiñahui was later captured and tortured by Pizarro's general, Sebastián de Benalcázar, but Rumiñahui refused to reveal the treasure's location and, in his anger, Benalcázar ordered him burned at the stake. Seeing Benalcázar's fury and that his greed had not been sated, the Indians reportedly removed a kernel from a pile of maize and taunted the conquistador: "This grain is what Atahualpa has given you from his treasures and what remains is the other."

Then some years later—perhaps fifty, perhaps longer (no one could recall the exact date)—Valverde had turned up in Píllaro, a village forty miles north of Baños on the western edge of the Llanganatis range, and fallen in love with the daughter of the local chieftain. It was this chieftain who had revealed where Rumiñahui had hidden the gold.

In the years that followed, Valverde and his princess bride ventured into the mountains many times and grew extremely wealthy. But there was more gold than they could possibly carry out, and on his deathbed in Spain Valverde had left the *derrotero*, the written guide giving the King of Spain precise instructions on how to proceed to the treasure lake.

At first Spruce was unsure what to make of the story. Although Baños was a town in the grip of gold fever—every week a new party of treasure hunters would set off into the mountains in search of the hidden cache—Spruce wrote that he found the legend "so improbable that I paid little attention to it." Instead, he went to work collecting flora from the slopes of Tungurahua. Then, in September 1858, he took a trip to Cotaló, a small village on a plateau in front of the volcano. It was there that on a rare cloudless moonlit night Spruce had his second view of the mountain range he had glimpsed four months before from the Bobonaza River.

Sandwiched between the Andes and the Amazon, the Llanganatis are a mysterious and unforgiving place. The Ecuadorians refer to the ranges as *la ceja del mundo* (the eyebrow of the world). There are no roads and few paths, just a series of *paramos* covered in sinewy vegetation, treacherous bogs and glassy black lakes. From February to October it rains continuously, veiling the ranges in an impenetrable white fog—the *neblina* in which Blake and Chapman lost their way. As if that were not bad enough, the mountains are prone to earthquakes and are scored with deep ravines and quaking bogs that have a reputation for sucking men and mules into their depths.

There is no good time to go. Even in the so-called dry months of November, December, and January, weeks can go by without the sun ever penetrating the clouds. When the *neblina* does lift, however, the view is well worth the wait. Were you to stand, as the *derrotero* instructs, on the top of Guapa Mountain looking east, you would see not only the Cerros Llanganati but, a little to the south, the forbidding peaks of Cerro Hermoso, at 13,500 feet the highest point in the Llanganatis. It is on the slopes of this peculiar geological formation—the result of a massive uplifting of limestone sediments caused by the convergence of the Nazca and South American plates in the late Cretaceous period—that many believe the treasure, and possibly Atahualpa himself, lie buried.

No one knows if Spruce ever looked for the gold, but the story certainly piqued his curiosity sufficiently for him to make a determined search for the guide. After lengthy inquiries he learned that the original had been deposited in the archives of a nearby town, Latacunga, along with a *cédula real*, the official order of the Spanish King. Spruce wrote that he obtained "indisputable evidence" that the recipients of the *derrotero* and *cédula real* were the governors of Tacunga and Ambato—Tacunga being the ancient name for Latacunga—and that the documents contained instructions from the King of Spain "commanding those functionaries to use every diligence in seeking out the treasure of the Incas." One expedition had been commanded by the governor of Tacunga in person, accompanied by a friar, Padre Longo, "of considerable literary reputation"—presumably, the same Longo whose death was recorded on Guzmán's map. Spruce continued:

> The *derrotero* was found to correspond so exactly with the actual localities, that only a person intimately acquainted with them could have drawn it up; and that it could have been fabricated by any other person who had never been out of Spain was an impossibility. This expedition had nearly reached the end of the route, when one evening the Padre Longo disappeared mysteriously, and no traces of him could be discovered, so that whether he had fallen into a ravine near which they were encamped, or into one of the morasses which abound all over the region, is to this day unknown.

According to Spruce, after searching for the Padre for some days, the governor gave up and the expedition returned empty-handed. Spruce does not give the date of the governor's expedition, nor does he say how he obtained this information. All he says is that the *derrotero* and *cédula real* were deposited in the archives of Latacunga and disappeared around 1840. "So many people were admitted to copy them that at last someone, not content with a copy, carried off the originals," he comments.

All that remained was the copy seen by Spruce, with the prefacing remarks "not in very choice Castilian," dated August 14, 1827. Unfortunately, no one could remember the date of the original documents—hence Spruce's difficulty in placing the *derrotero* in the reign of Charles I, Philip II, or some later Spanish monarch.

Spruce also made inquiries about Guzmán, discovering that the botanist had resided for some time in Píllaro, the village where Valverde had met his bride, and had made several expeditions to the Llanganatis in search of the gold—expeditions whose paths could be traced on his map. Spruce had devoted several pages of his notebook to an analysis of the map—an analysis he subsequently reproduced almost word for word in a paper to the Royal Geographical Society.* According to Spruce,

---

*"On the Mountains of Llanganati, in the Eastern Cordillera of the Quitonian Andes," *Journal of the Royal Geographical Society*, 31 (1861), 163–84.

Guzmán's original map consisted of "several small sheets of paper pasted together," measuring three feet ten and a half inches by two feet nine inches and "painted with a fine pencil in Indian ink." Spruce had obtained the map from a collector in Ambato, but the man would not part with the original, allowing Spruce only to make a copy. Spruce wrote that Guzmán's original had been "so thoroughly used that it is now much dilapidated, and the names, though originally very distinctly written, are in many cases scarcely decipherable." In order to make sense of the map and place-names—many of which were in Quichua—Spruce had consulted local people familiar with the mountains and language, but in tracing his own copy, he found that Guzmán's scale was misleading. The Spanish botanist had taken no compass readings, and his attempt to combine a vertical with a horizontal projection had produced "some distortion and dislocation." With his simple view of the country, for instance, Guzmán had intended to represent the "actual outline of the mountains" as they appeared from the ground. But Spruce found that "the heights [were] much exaggerated, and consequently the declivities too steep," resulting in positional errors "both absolute and relative." Spruce also called into question the accuracy of the southern portion of the map, in particular Guzmán's decision to show curlicues of smoke issuing from the mouths of Cerros Hermoso, Margasitas, and Zunchu-Urcu and the Gran Volcán del Topo, or Yurag Llanganati (Quichua for "White Llanganati"). "I have conversed with people who have visited the Llanganati district as far as forty years back, and all assure me they have never seen any active volcano there."

Despite his doubts, however, Spruce concluded that the northern portion of the map was broadly accurate. Here Guzmán had recorded the position of haciendas and mines in great detail, suggesting he had repeatedly traversed the region. Indeed, when Spruce questioned the locals more closely, he was told that the legends marked on the map referred to events that had transpired during Guzmán's many expeditions to the mountains. It appeared that Guzmán and his companions had been searching not only for a concealed Inca treasure but also for an abandoned Indian gold mine. But though they had discovered the mouths of several silver and copper mines, and ascertained the existence of iron, lead, and pyrites, both the treasure and the gold deposit had eluded them.

At first Guzmán and his companions worked the silver and copper mines "with ardour." But their enthusiasm soon gave way to disillusion, "partly in consequence of intestine quarrels, but chiefly because they became disgusted with that slow mode of acquiring wealth when there was molten gold supposed to be hidden close by."

No one could recall the exact date of Guzmán's mining venture, but Spruce believed it must have been in the first years of the nineteenth century, since in 1802 Guzmán had reportedly met the German naturalist-explorer Alexander von Humboldt when Humboldt had been passing through Baños on his way to Peru (Humboldt apparently told people that Guzmán had shown him his sketches of the local flora and fauna). Then four, or possibly six, years later, Spruce discovered Guzmán had died in a bizarre accident at a small farmhouse near Patate in the valley of Leytillo, about ten miles east of Ambato. "He was a somnambulist, and having one night walked out of the house while asleep, he fell down a steep place and so perished. This is all I have been able to learn, and I fear no documents now exist which can throw any further light on the story of his life."

I looked again at the map at the back of *Notes of a Botanist on the Amazon and Andes*. Beside the Volcán de Margasitas I noticed that Guzmán had drawn a narrow ravine marked "Chuspi Pongo" (Quichuan for "Mosquito Narrows") and another cross, Peñón de las Discordias (Rock of Discord). Was this the record of another quarrel, the point at which Guzmán and his colleagues had foundered in their search for the treasure? And if so, how had Blake and Chapman succeeded in rounding Margasitas Mountain and finding the Way of the Incas? Had they taken Guzmán's map with them, or had Spruce also discovered another map, a map he had shared only with the mariners?

I felt sure I would find the answer in Spruce's journals covering his six and a half years in Ecuador. Throughout his previous nine years in South America, Spruce had kept a detailed record of his thoughts and experiences. It was these journals—covering the period from his arrival in Brazil in 1849 to his departure from Peru in 1857—that had enabled Wallace to reconstruct the narrative of Spruce's travels and plant discoveries in the Amazon. Imagine my surprise, then, when I asked for Spruce's Andean journals and Fitzgerald informed me they did not exist—or at least that Kew had no record of them. The only journals they possessed were the three before me now. These had been entrusted to Kew's care by Matthew Slater, the executor of Spruce's estate—hence the notation by the librarian on the inside frontpage of his miscellaneous notebook—but, unfortunately, Spruce's Ecuadorian journals had never been found. In 1906, in preparation for editing the narrative of Spruce's travels in South America, Wallace had written repeatedly to Slater, urging him in increasingly exasperated tones to renew his searches for the journals among Spruce's papers. Wallace was convinced that Slater must have overlooked them when he had taken an inventory of Spruce's possessions at the cottage in Coneysthorpe where Spruce had spent his final years.

"It is most unfortunate that you did not, at the time of Spruce's death, put all his MSS. into boxes by themselves," he reproached Slater at one point. "Cannot you get a strong woman to help your daughter make a thorough search from attic to cellar, in cupboards, boxes and bundles, and everywhere else, till they are found?"

In his desperation Wallace even enlisted a clairvoyant, giving him, via a friend, one of Spruce's manuscripts to handle, the better to attune him to the dead botanist's spiritual vibrations. But though the clairvoyant apparently "saw" bundles of Spruce's papers hidden in a cupboard in the hallway of a house with a "Gothic porch," neither a search of one of Spruce's correspondent's homes in Yorkshire nor the recommended "strong woman" yielded the missing journals. Instead, Wallace had had to reconstruct Spruce's travels in the Andes from letters to his colleagues at Kew and from the reports that Spruce had submitted to various official bodies.

One of the papers Wallace had relied on was Spruce's report to the Royal Geographical Society. Spruce's talk on the Llanganatis had been forwarded by Kew's then director, Sir William Hooker, and read before the society on March 12, 1860—Spruce was in Ambato at the time, planning his expedition over Chimborazo to the cinchona forests on the western slopes of the Ecuadorian Andes, and so could not present the paper in person. To accompany the talk, Spruce had sent the RGS his hand-traced copy of Guzmán's map. But the copy was rough and indistinct, and in preparation for the map's publication in its journal the RGS had commissioned a completely new version by an expert engraver, A. Findlay. The first thing you notice about Findlay's version is that it is nothing like Spruce's. In copying Spruce's map, Findlay reduced the scale to three-eighths of the original, further distorting the vertical perspective and accentuating the drama of such features as Cotopaxi, whose flames literally seem to erupt from the page. In addition, whereas Spruce's map is traced in a faint pencil so that you can barely make out the place-names and legends, Findlay's map has every peak and tree sharply drawn, every hacienda and river precisely indicated. It is as if in Findlay's version a film obscuring the original has been removed, bringing the landscape into sudden and dramatic focus.

However, it is not Spruce's or Findlay's original version that usually hooks readers but the version in *Notes of a Botanist on the Amazon and Andes*. It is here that the meandering red lines—indicating the routes of Guzmán's expeditions in search of the treasure—appear for the first time and that splashes of the same color magically materialize on the roofs of churches and houses.

The lines could only have been added by Wallace. It was also Wallace who came up with the catchy title, "A Hidden Treasure of the Incas," explaining that although he himself had not gone looking for the treasure, were he younger and more vigorous he would be sorely tempted. "I am convinced," wrote Wallace, "that the 'Route' of Valverde is a genuine and thoroughly trustworthy document, and that by closely following the directions therein given, it may still be possible for an explorer of means and energy, with the assistance of the local authorities, to solve the interesting problem of the Treasure of the Incas." In all, two weeks should "suffice for the whole expedition."

If Wallace had ended his commentary there, it would have been encouragement enough, but he could not resist one final mischievous thought:

> I have written this in the hope that some one who speaks Spanish fluently, has had some experience of the country, and is possessed of the necessary means, may be induced to undertake this very interesting and even romantic piece of adventurous travel. To such a person it need be but a few months' holiday.

3

The *Derrotero*

AS I HAVE SAID, I AM BY NATURE AND INSTINCT A SKEPTIC. SHOW ME A cornfield scored with strange whorls and concentric circles, and my response will be to look for the pranksters with the combine harvester in the dead of night. It is not that I doubt the possibility of alien life, you understand, just that I know human nature and consider it improbable that aliens would choose such an obviously fraudulent means of communication.

My attitude toward buried treasure is much the same. I am perfectly willing to admit that treasures may lie hidden for centuries, undisturbed and undiscovered in their mountain and oceanic fastnesses, but ask me whether I think it likely that a person who knew—I mean *really* knew—where one was located would draw up a transparent set of directions for all and sundry to follow, and my answer is no. Furthermore, the idea that someone would deposit such a guide in a public archive, where anyone—deserving or otherwise—would be free to peruse it, is so preposterous as to scarcely warrant consideration. If the governor of Latacunga, or whichever official was charged by the King of Spain with investigating Valverde's *derrotero*, had found the treasure, he would have altered it or, at the very least, substituted a fake. That is, of course, if he ever found the treasure at all.

But there was also another, more profound reason for my reluctance to accept Wallace's cavalier verdict, and that was fear. Not fear of the danger or discomfort that awaited me in the Llanganatis, you understand—although the idea of spending weeks trudging through high-altitude bogs in the rain and freezing fog was hardly a prospect I looked forward to with equanimity—but the fear of being ridiculed for taking the guide seriously.

Nevertheless, I couldn't get Blake and Chapman out of my mind. What if the story was true? What if Spruce really had met the mariners and passed them secret information—information perhaps from his private journals? Was this how they had succeeded in finding the treasure cave? Was this why Spruce's Ecuadorian journals were missing?

By now I had obtained a copy of both the guide and the map, and whenever I had an idle moment in my malaria research I would pore over them, convinced that if I stared long and hard enough at the cryptic phrases and images I would divine where the treasure was hidden. Unfurling Guzmán's map, I imagined myself "placed," as the guide instructs, "in the town of Píllaro," and traced my finger along the meandering red line to the farm of Moya. Sleeping "a good distance above" it, I then rose early the next morning and, like Blake and Chapman, climbed to the top of Guapa Mountain, from where, through the gathering mist, I could just make out the peaks of the Cerros Llanganatis, "in the form of a triangle." Somewhere in a declivity beyond one of those peaks, I told myself, was "a lake, made by hand," containing a king's ransom in gold.

Intoxicated now by the *derrotero*'s archaic terminology and phrasing, I sped onto the next passage, feeling myself being drawn deeper and deeper into the labyrinth. After passing through the clumps of *sangurimas* and *flechas* in the forest, treasure seekers were instructed by Valverde to continue east from Guapa in the same direction:

> and a good way ahead, having passed some cattle-farms, thou shalt come on a wide morass, which thou must cross, and coming out on the other side thou shalt see on the left hand a short way off a *Jucál* [place with reeds], on a hill-side, through which thou

must pass. Having gone through the *Jucál*, thou will see two small lakes called *Los Anteojos* (the spectacles) from having between them a point of land resembling a nose.

I paused to examine Guzmán's map. There were Los Anteojos, exactly where Valverde had said they would be.

> From this place thou mayest again descry the Cerros Llanganati, the same as thou sawest them from the top of Guapa, and I warn thee that thou must leave the said lakes on the left, and that in front of the point or "nose" there is a plain, which is the sleeping-place. There thou must leave thy horses, for they can go no further. Following now on foot in the same direction, thou shalt come on a great black lake . . .

The lake marked "Yana Cocha" on Guzmán's map, I thought.

> . . . which thou must leave on the left hand, and beyond it thou shalt seek to descend along the slope of the hill in such a way that thou mayest reach a ravine, down which comes a waterfall, and here thou shalt find a bridge of three poles, or if it do not still exist thou shalt put another, in the most convenient place, and pass over it. And having gone a little way in the forest seek out the hut which served to sleep in, or the remains of it.

At this point, I realized, Guzmán's party must have become confused, because it was here that the lines branched, two leading around the north side of Yana Cocha, leaving the lake on the right hand if you were proceeding, as the guide directs, in an easterly direction. Indeed, the longest line on Guzmán's map diverged from Valverde's Way just after the Spectacle Lakes, shooting off toward the Volcán de los Mulatos and the northeastern corner of the map. Were these alternate treasure routes, I wondered, or did they record a different saga entirely? Perhaps the other paths had nothing to do with the guide at all, but merely recorded Guzmán's expeditions in search of the lost Inca gold mine.

I decided to ignore the puzzle for the moment and continue along the route recommended by Valverde. There it was, running south around the black lake and continuing parallel to the Desaguadero de Yana Cocha, past the cross marked with the ominous legend *"Muerte del Padre Longo."* The third sleeping place mentioned by Valverde must be somewhere in this area.

> Having passed the night there, go on thy way the following day through the forest in the same direction, till thou reach another deep dry ravine, across which thou must throw a bridge and pass over it slowly and cautiously, for the ravine is very deep . . .

This was surely the gorge marked *"la quebrada honda"* on Guzmán's map just in front of the Volcán de Margasitas?

> . . . that is if thou succeed not in finding the pass by which it may be crossed. Go forward and look for the signs of another sleeping-place, which I assure thee thou canst not fail to see, in the fragments of pottery and other marks, because the Indians are continually passing along there. Go on thy way, and thou shalt see a mountain which is all of *Margasitas* [pyrites] the which thou must leave on the left hand, and I warn thee that thou wilt have to go round it thus:

The hieroglyph gave me pause for thought. It was difficult to take seriously, resembling nothing so much as a flagellating sperm. Its twisting tail seemed to indicate that you should contour around Margasitas to the north, leaving the mountain on the right. Yet the *derrotero* clearly stated that you should leave the mountain on the left. Perhaps the hieroglyph merely meant to direct you back up the slope of the mountain on a winding course, until you reached a point on its southern flank high above the forest.

On this side thou wilt find a *Pajonal* [pasture] in a small plain, which having crossed thou wilt come on a strait passage between two mountains, which is the way of the Inca.

Presumably, either Chuspi Pongo or the Rivera de los Llanganatis on Guzmán's map. I say "presumably" because at this point the path suddenly veered to the north to the cross labeled "Peñón de las Discordias," which indicated that there had been a fierce disagreement, possibly over the meaning of the hieroglyph. From here on, unfortunately, the map and the *derrotero* diverged. At this point Guzmán's map became vague and sketchy, but according to Valverde's guide I should now have been heading in the direction of Guzmán's Gran Volcán del Topo.

From thence as thou goest along thou shalt see the entrance of the *socabón* (tunnel) which is in the form of a church porch. Having come through the passage and gone a good distance beyond, thou wilt perceive a cascade which descends from an offshoot of the Cerro Llanganati and runs into a *Tembladal* [quaking bog] on the right hand; and without passing the stream in the said bog there is much gold, so that putting in thy hand what thou shalt gather at the bottom is grains of gold. To ascend the mountain, leave the bog and go along to the right, and pass above the cascade, going round the offshoot of the mountain. And if by chance the mouth of the *socabón* be closed with certain herbs which they call "Salvaje,"* remove them and thou wilt find the entrance. And on the left hand side of the mountain thou will see the *"Guayra"* (for thus the ancients called the furnace where they founded metals) which is nailed with golden nails. And to reach the third mountain, if thou canst not pass in front of the *socabón*, it is the same thing to pass at the back of it, for the water of the lake falls into it.

The *socabón*. Was this Blake and Chapman's famous treasure cave? If so, why did the guide suggest that the treasure lay in a lake whose waters fell into the *socabón* from a third mountain?

Tillandsia usneoides, or "Spanish moss," a species of bromeliad usually found hanging from tree branches.

These inconsistencies had puzzled Spruce, too. Although in his notebook he had translated *socabón* as "tunnel," in his paper to the RGS he
noted that *socabón* was also sometimes used to denote the mouth of a
mine. "Perhaps the latter is meant by Valverde, though he does not direct us to enter it."

Comparing the map with the guide, Spruce concluded that the Way
of the Inca was the upper part of Guzmán's Rivera de los Llanganatis,
and that if Margasitas was considered the first of Valverde's three *cerros*,
then the *tembladal, socabón*, and *guayra* were to be found in the second
mountain, and the lake where the Indians threw Atahualpa's ransom in
the third.

I studied Guzmán's map again. If Spruce's reading was correct, then
the second mountain ought to be Zunchu-Urcu and the third, the
Gran Volcán del Topo—the so-called White Llanganati. But if so, why
hadn't Guzmán drawn a path there, as he had on the northern sections
of the map? Perhaps the terrain had been too difficult or the quarrel indicated by the legend "Peñón de las Discordias" so serious that Guzmán
had been forced to foreshorten his search. Either that or he had never
gone that way.

In hopes of finding an answer to the riddle, I turned to the last sentence of the guide:

> If thou lose thyself in the forest, seek the river—follow it on the
> right bank—lower down take to the beach, and thou will come on
> a deep ravine such that although thou seek to pass it thou wilt not
> find where; climb therefore the mountain on the right hand and
> in this manner thou canst by no means miss the way.

"In this manner thou canst by no means miss the way." The guide seemed
clear enough. If you missed the turning at Margasitas Mountain, all
you had to do was continue along the right bank of the Desaguadero de
Yana Cocha until you came to a deep ravine. At this point you would
have to leave the beach and climb over a mountain, on the other side of
which you would once again find yourself on the Way of the Incas.

While editing Spruce's notebooks, Wallace made a similarly detailed
study of the guide and the map, concluding that there was "really no
contradiction" between the two. Wallace felt sure that the deep ravine

was Chuspi Pongo—not the Rivera de los Llanganatis, as Spruce believed—and that the beginning of the Way of the Incas was the "Encañado de Sacha Pamba." Either way, he was convinced that the treasure lake was to be found on the Gran Volcán del Topo.

Wallace reasoned that because Valverde mentioned only four sleeping places, the whole journey indicated by the guide could only occupy five days. Since the last sleeping place was just before Margasitas Mountain, Wallace concluded that the whole distance from the final camp to the "lake, made by hand," could not be more than twenty miles—"a distance that would take us to the nearer slopes of the great Topo Mountain." Thus the Topo, or White, Llanganati had to be the third of the three Cerros Llanganatis and the place where the treasure was hidden. Guzmán had failed to find it, Wallace argued, only because he had become diverted by "the superior promise of silver and gold mines." Wallace speculated that he may have been hoping to generate sufficient money from his mining activities to finance an expedition in search of the treasure, but before he could return to the mountains with new recruits, he fell over the cliff and died. Indeed, Wallace felt sure that the only expedition that had made a "serious" attempt to follow Valverde's directions was the one led by the governor of Latacunga and the friar Padre Longo. Subsequent explorers either had been "deceived by Indian guides who assured them they knew an easier way, or went in search of rich mines rather than of buried treasure." Hence Wallace's confident assertion that for an explorer of ability and means a Llanganatis expedition ought to be "but a few months' holiday."

As I have said, I am a reluctant treasure hunter. Instinct and logic told me Valverde's guide was a hoax, a practical joke that over the centuries had acquired credibility far in excess of anything its author could originally have envisaged. Nevertheless, in the months that followed my discovery of Spruce's miscellaneous notebook at Kew, I couldn't get the guide and map out of my mind. Guzmán's impressionistic images of volcanoes and lakes seeped into my dreams, haunting my waking hours. In the middle of studying some turgid botanical text on the taxonomy of cinchona, I would feel my eyes glaze over, and I would find myself staring out the window at the Thames drifting lazily toward Mortlake. Autumn had come and gone at Kew, but the gardens were still choked with unraked leaves. It was too cold to picnic outside, and

I found myself spending more and more of my lunch breaks in the hot-house, admiring the palms and giant ferns as I dodged anxious teachers and their unruly charges. The children seemed to enjoy these outings—for them Kew was still a source of wonderment—but I found their enthusiasm depressing: it reminded me how long it was since I had experienced similar sensations. I longed to be transported elsewhere, to an exotic foreign land where schoolchildren had never heard the words "national curriculum" and the source and destination of rivers were still matters of conjecture. Whether or not the treasure existed, the *derrotero* and map seemed to hold out the promise of just such an adventure.

IN MY SPARE TIME I BEGAN TO DELVE MORE DEEPLY INTO THE HISTORY OF Llanganatis explorations. The first thing I discovered was that none of them had been a "holiday." On the contrary, most had ended very badly.

One of the first to take up Wallace's challenge was Edward C. Brooks. A graduate of West Point, Brooks had served as a colonel in the United States Army during the Spanish-American War and had later been appointed Auditor of Cuba. On his retirement from service Colonel Brooks became the South American representative of the American Bank Note Company of New York and traveled to Ecuador, where he fell in love with and married a local woman, Isabela de Troya. Unfortunately for Isabela, however, her American husband also had another passion: the Llanganatis.

It is not known how Brooks first heard about the lost hoard, but sometime in 1912 he obtained a copy of *Notes of a Botanist on the Amazon and Andes* and became an avid student of the *derrotero*. Presumably, his job with the American Bank Note Company wasn't all that lucrative, or else he pined for the kind of thrills he'd enjoyed in the service, as he was soon planning his own expedition to the Llanganatis.

His first attempt was a dismal failure: he had no idea of the topography or the climate of the region and set off ill equipped during the worst season of the year, returning to Píllaro hungry, wet, and exhausted after only a few days. But rather than dampen his enthusiasm, Brooks's experience only kindled his passion further, and he immediately set about planning a second expedition. This time he recruited eight Indian porters and a Peruvian mestizo and waited patiently for the weather to improve. He must have been confident of success, for when the clouds finally lifted and he set off from Píllaro, Isabela was with him at the front of the line.

At first all went well. Brooks had no trouble finding the farm of Moya and Guapa Mountain, where he stood, as per Valverde's instructions, with his back to Ambato and espied what he thought were the "three Cerros Llanganati, in the form of a triangle," peeping through the clouds toward the Amazon. Having descended Guapa, he marched east past the cattle farms mentioned in the guide and the "wide morass" until he reached Los Anteojos, (the Spectacle Lakes) and, in front of them, the "plain" where the *derrotero* instructed he should sleep the first night. The next morning Brooks continued in the same direction, arriving at the "great black lake"—which he identified as Yana Cocha on Guzmán's map. Leaving it "on the left hand," he then rounded its southern shore to the Desaguadero de Yana Cocha and continued east, eventually reaching what he thought was Valverde's ravine and waterfall—the "Cascada y Golpe de Limpio Pungu" of Guzmán's map, beside which the Spanish botanist had placed the cross indicating the spot where Padre Longo had died.

So far so easy, but from the third day Brooks found that Valverde's directions became increasingly confusing. It wasn't just that it took far longer than the *derrotero* indicated to reach the supposed "sleeping places" but also that there were numerous discrepancies between the guide, Guzmán's map, and the actual topography and geology of the region. There were any number of *quebradas* (deep, dry ravines), and mountains containing *margasitas* with caves and lakes abounded in every valley and ridge. The question was, which was the mountain "all of *Margasitas*," and was it the same mountain as the one marked "Volcán de Margasitas" on Guzmán's map?

By now the delays and confusions had got not only to Brooks but also to his porters. The weather was changing for the worse, and heavy storm clouds were gathering. The porters pleaded for him to return to Píllaro with his wife, but Brooks would not do so. Instead, he cajoled them with promises and threats until they arrived at the rim of a waterfilled crater near what is known today as the Páramo de Soguillas. Brooks was convinced he'd found the "lake, made by hand," into which the ancients had thrown Atahualpa's ransom, and he ordered his men to set up camp near the water's edge.

It was a tragic misjudgment. In the night the rains came, washing down the rim of the crater in torrents and elevating the level of the lake. Alerted by the cries of their porters, Edward and Isabela dashed to the safety of a ledge high on the rim of the crater, where they spent the night exposed to the freezing wind and rain. The dawn revealed the full extent of their plight: what had been a small and inviting pool was now a vast expanse of water, somewhere below the surface of which lay their food and equipment. Worse, Isabela had caught a severe chill from the soaking she'd received in the night.

Their only hope was to abandon the search for the treasure and retrace their steps to Píllaro as quickly as possible. Brooks's Indian porters immediately set off at a fast clip. Unfortunately, by now Isabela had become weak and feverish and could not keep pace. The porters must have seen the writing on the wall, for they deserted in the night, leaving Edward and Isabela to fend for themselves.

Abandoned and hungry, Brooks remained camped on the *paramo*, praying for his wife's recovery. But Isabela grew steadily sicker until, weakened by cold and hunger, she died the following night.

Brooks didn't have time to grieve. If he didn't get off the *paramo* soon and find his way back to Píllaro, he, too, would also soon be dead. Setting off into a snowstorm, with only his compass to guide him, he wandered in a daze. Fortunately, he'd had the foresight to arrange for Isabela's father, Alonso de Troya, to send a relief party in the event of his not returning within a specified time, and it was this that saved his life.

Tired and grief-stricken, Brooks returned to the United States. From time to time he talked of mounting another expedition to the Llanganatis, but in 1922 he died—according to his family, of a broken heart.

I UNFURLED AN UP-TO-DATE MAP OF THE LLANGANATIS THAT I HAD OBtained from Kew's map room. There, in a valley slightly to the east of the Páramo de Soguillas, was a lake marked "Laguna de Isabela Brooks," a tragic epitaph to one man's hubris. Surely with the latest geographical information I could do better.

Unfortunately, the rest of the map was sketchier than I had hoped. There were more rivers than on Guzmán's map, and in place of his erupting volcanoes the artist had put small triangles indicating the summits of Cerro Hermoso (Beautiful Mountain) and two other peaks: Cerro Negro (Black Mountain) and Las Torres (The Towers). But aside from these cartographical nuances, knowledge of the region appeared to have advanced little in two hundred years.

I placed my finger on the Spectacle Lakes and traced the route of Valverde's *derrotero* to the great black mass of Yana Cocha. The drainage of the lake was no longer called the Desaguadero but was labeled "Quebrada del Golpe" and, farther east, "Parca Yacu." Beyond this point to the southeast, in the direction that Brooks and most treasure hunters who had followed the *derrotero* had gone, the swirling contour lines bunched alarmingly. The elevations were dizzying: 10,500 feet, 11,200 feet, 13,800 feet. Breathing heavily, I imagined myself surmounting the near-vertical ridges to the *paramo*. Now there was only treeless moorland, and beyond it . . . Suddenly my finger stopped dead. The next quadrant was completely blank. In place of contour lines the cartographer had written simply *"neblina."*

That's when it struck me: the Llanganatis were that rare and vanishing commodity in our over-explored, over-described world—a terra incognita. I would be undertaking not only a voyage into a physical unknown but what Carl Jung called an "archetypal" journey into a psychological unknown—an exploration, if you like, of the collective antecedents of *all* treasure legends. I had to go there. The question was how, and with whom?

Part Two

THE TREASURE SEEKERS

*There is no getting away from a treasure that once
fastens upon your mind.*

—Joseph Conrad, *Nostromo*

1

An Unexpected Invitation

I HAD NO IDEA HOW TO ORGANIZE AN EXPEDITION TO THE LLANGANATIS, much less what I would do when I got there. Unlike Colonel Brooks, I've never had to fall out for parade at six in the morning, scrub a latrine, or quick-march in the noonday sun with a one-hundred-pound pack strapped to my back. To have any hope of finding the treasure, I needed the help of an expert; in short, I needed a treasure hunter.

Before leaving London, I decided to look on the Internet. In truth, I wasn't expecting very much, but to my surprise and satisfaction the combination of "treasure" and "Llanganatis" elicited several hits on Google. One in particular caught my eye. "Adventures into the unknown," proclaimed a banner at the top of the page. "Be a professional explorer, prospector or treasure hunter: 31 ways you can make over $100,000 a year and live a life of adventure and wealth."

Below it was a photograph of a man with soft white skin gazing wistfully into the distance. "Stan at the summit of a volcanic crater near the equator," read the caption.

The man in the picture didn't look much like a treasure hunter. Dressed in a white T-shirt, sunglasses, and trilby, he appeared too relaxed, too comfortable—there wasn't a speck of mud or sweat on him. According to the accompanying text, however, Stan was the real thing.

"Hi there, my name is Stan Grist . . . I look forward to sharing my life's adventures with you which include the pursuit of gold, raw diamonds, lost cities, buried treasure, [and] ancient tunnels . . . Whenever possible, I try to include supporting photos and documents with most of my stories and projects as, otherwise, they might be hard for some people to believe."

From what I could gather, Stan was more Philip Marlowe than Indiana Jones. A former private investigator and geologist, he'd moved to Ecuador from Canada in the early 1980s to pan for gold and to investigate legends of lost Indian cities and hidden mines. His site was a veritable Aladdin's Cave for the uninitiated. Grist appeared to have trawled every book and magazine article that had ever been written on South America in search of fresh treasure "leads," helpfully organizing the maps and *derroteros* into PDF files for easy download at $15.95 a time. Grist's publications had eye-grabbing titles like "The Seven Lost Cities of El Dorado," purportedly a guide to seven lost Indian gold mines, complete with maps made by Jesuit missionaries in the sixteenth century; and "The Quest for the Secret Chamber of the Ancients"—an underground chamber in southern Ecuador that was said to contain a library full of "metallic" books inscribed with strange hieroglyphs of possibly extraterrestrial origin. More to the point, although possibly no more credibly, Grist also claimed to have discovered a secret tunnel system leading from Baños, under the Río Pastaza, to the Llanganatis and Atahualpa's hoard.

I sent Grist an e-mail explaining my interest in Spruce and my plan to return to Ecuador. It took several weeks for him to reply. He'd been in the Ecuadorian Amazon panning for gold with a Canadian mining company, he explained apologetically, and had only just caught up with his correspondence. He'd be happy to meet me when I arrived in Quito and provided me with an address and telephone number. Grist lived in Leónidas Plaza in the Mariscal district of Quito. I was already familiar with the view from his flat: he'd posted that on the Internet, too.

THE *OXFORD ENGLISH DICTIONARY* DEFINES "OBSESSION" AS "THE ACTION of any influence, notion, or 'fixed idea,' which persistently assails or vexes, esp. so as to discompose the mind." That definition is especially pertinent when applied to treasure hunters, but it doesn't go far enough, for few fixed ideas are as corrosive or as unsettling as the thought of buried wealth.

For instance, in *Nostromo,* Joseph Conrad's psychologically acute novel set in a mythical South American republic, the treasure is a cancer that eats away at the character of the hero, eventually bringing about his downfall. In the "most famous and desperate affair of his life," Nostromo, an Italian stevedore famed for his great honesty and integrity, takes a large cache of silver out to sea to prevent its falling into the hands of revolutionaries. But when he returns to the mainland and discovers that everyone thinks that the boat and the silver have sunk and that no one is concerned about him or his brave deed, he decides to keep the loot. One night, while sneaking around in the dark to get his silver, he is shot by the father of the woman he loves. The tragedy accelerates Nostromo's decline, but the cause lies further back, in his obsession with the treasure. Drained of his integrity and nobility, Nostromo begins to unravel. Finally, just before his death, Conrad has him articulate the cause:

> There is something in a treasure that fastens upon a man's mind. He will pray and blaspheme and still persevere, and will curse the day he ever heard of it, and will let his last hour come upon him unawares, still believing that he missed it only by a foot. He will see it every time he closes his eyes. He will never forget it till he is dead and even then . . . Ha! Ha! . . . There is no getting away from a treasure that once fastens upon your mind.

But boarding my flight to Quito, I was preoccupied not so much by the thought of Nostromo as by another fictional treasure obsessive, the Abbé Faria. In *The Count of Monte Cristo,* Alexandre Dumas's classic novel of betrayal and revenge, the hero, Edmond Dantès, first encounters the Abbé in the dungeons of the dreaded Château d'If. You don't have to be familiar with the book to know that the Abbé presents a fearful sight. In the numerous film and television adaptations of the novel, the Abbé is invariably portrayed as an aging lunatic, with long, unkempt gray hair and dirty fingernails. In the book we first meet him lying on the floor of his dungeon, nearly naked, his clothes in tatters, drawing a circle on the floor with a piece of plaster chipped from the wall of his cell. Dumas has already told us that the Abbé is considered mad. Now, however, the inspector of prisons, who has come to pay him a visit, asks exactly what kind of "folly" grips him.

"A rare one indeed," replies the governor. "He believes himself to be the owner of a vast fortune. In the first year of his imprisonment, he made the government an offer of a million francs, if they would set him free; the second year, it was two million; the third three, and so on upwards. He is now in his fifth year of imprisonment, so he will ask to speak to you privately and offer you five million."

The Abbé does not disappoint, following the script the governor has written for him to the letter. "I am not mad," the Abbé tells the inspector in his frustration, "I am telling the truth. The treasure I mention really does exist and I am ready to sign an agreement with you, under which you will take me to a place that I shall designate, have the earth dug up in our presence and, if I am lying, if nothing is found, if I am mad, as you say, then you can bring me back to this same dungeon where I shall remain for ever."

The only hole the Abbé succeeds in digging, of course, is for himself.

"It's a clever idea," the governor tells the inspector, admiring the Abbé's guile. "If every prisoner was to take his warders on a wild-goose chase for a hundred leagues . . . there is a good chance that the prisoner would manage to take to his heels as soon as he had the opportunity."

Was I also chasing a nonexistent beast, a chimera that would lead me, if not into a dungeon of madness, then into a dudgeon of despair?

I was about to find out.

The plane banked sharply as the pilot described an arc high above the Andes. It was night, and below the wing to my left Quito was lit up like the display window at Tiffany. At the center of this luminescence, as if lit from within by a giant sodium lamp, I could clearly make out the dome and towers of the Iglesia de San Francisco, one of the oldest churches in the Americas. According to my guidebook, some two tons of gold had gone into the construction of its altar. But this was nothing compared with La Compañía de Jesús, another church in the heart of the old town, said to contain "seven tons" of gold and baroque flourishes to rival anything in Rome. For the treasure to have escaped the avarice of the architects of such temples, Rumiñahui's Inca troops would have had to remove the gold as far from Quito as possible. The question was whether after five hundred years of occupation any of it still remained.

I had arranged to meet Grist first thing in the morning at the Casa Sol, an environmentally conscious hostel that boasted organic breakfasts and pictures of indigenous Indians on its walls. Given the cursed history of Llanganatis adventurers, I figured I could use the karma. Besides, the Casa Sol was in the heart of the Mariscal, Quito's backpacking district, and a short walk from Grist's apartment.

Waiting in line at immigration the night before, I had felt alive and exhilarated.

"Business or pleasure, sir?"

"Both," I had been tempted to reply (under "occupation" I very nearly wrote "treasure hunter"). Emerging with a ninety-day tourist stamp, I hefted my backpack onto my shoulders and pushed my way through the throng of placard-waving taxi drivers blocking the exit from the terminal.

The ride to the Casa Sol took just twenty minutes; within another ten I was asleep. But in the middle of the night I suddenly awoke short of breath, and by the time the equatorial sun pierced the thin orange curtains above my bed, I felt as though my head were in a vise.

"Soroche," explained Grist as we shook hands over breakfast. "Altitude sickness. Everyone gets it for a day or so. Just don't move around too much, and drink lots of fluids."

In person Grist looked like a cherub. He had bright button eyes and a way of speaking that seemed to turn every sentence into a declaration of faith—as though he were addressing me from the height of some great revelation.

Grist explained that before coming to Ecuador to hunt for treasure, he'd panned for gold in the western United States and worked as a private investigator in Calgary.

"And before that?" I asked.

"Before that, I was a Mormon," he replied.

According to Grist, he'd been a typical graduate of Brigham Young, traveling the world in a Sta-Prest brown suit, winning converts for the Church of Jesus Christ of Latter-Day Saints. Between assignments he would return to Utah to his wife and kids and the curtain-twitching neighbors.

"It was suffocating. Everywhere I went, the Church was watching."

Then, in the early 1980s, came his deliverance. The Mormons dispatched him to the Brazilian Amazon to win some Indian souls. Instead, Grist made contact with an isolated tribe and ended up embracing their way of life.

"That was it," said Grist. "I severed all contact with the Church, divorced my wife, and moved to Canada."

It was there, while working as a private eye, that Grist had his treasure epiphany.

"I was rummaging in a secondhand bookstore when I came across an old article in a copy of *Argosy* magazine. It was about a British explorer, Erskine Loch, who'd found hundreds of ounces of gold in Ecuador in the 1930s. The explorer had been looking for Inca treasure when he stumbled on an old mine. Well, the article captured my imagination. I just couldn't get it out of my mind."

It took several years for Grist to raise the courage and money to quit his job and fly to Ecuador. To hear him tell it, it was the best decision he'd ever made. Armed with maps, prospecting equipment, and a little Spanish, he headed straight for Tena and the Río Napo, the area where Loch had supposedly struck it rich. To his relief, he found the Indians were no longer hostile; on the contrary, for seven dollars a day they were only too happy to help "a gringo pan for gold."

Not only that, but Grist also found enough geological evidence to persuade a Canadian mining company to lease several pits in the area. By the time I arrived in Quito, the mining concern had been going for two years and had yet to turn a profit. But that hadn't deterred Grist from posting a picture of himself on his Web site grinning like a Cheshire cat beside a pile of gold bars and offering to share his knowledge with other prospectors—for a fee, of course.

Grist's prospecting tips left me cold. More interesting was his claim to have found a secret tunnel running under the Río Pastaza to the Llanganatis. Grist said he'd learned about the tunnel when he was visiting Baños and met an eighty-five-year-old landowner who'd shown him the entrance to the site. Apparently two German explorers had wandered into the tunnel forty years before and had never come out. The entrance had since been blocked by a landslide from the volcano Tungurahua, "but," boasted Grist, adopting the exaggerated drawl of a Texas oilman, "one day I'm going to buy that man's land and open that ol' tunnel up."

I hoped to tease more details out of him over a drink, but at lunch it emerged that Grist was teetotal and disappointingly close-lipped about what he did or did not know about the Llanganatis. Instead, he directed me to a friend of his, Roland Glaser, a German who'd moved to Ecuador sixteen years earlier and who, according to Grist, knew Valverde's *derrotero* "back to front, upside down, and inside out." Apparently, Roland was a geologist and miner by profession. In the course of searching for gold, he'd been into the Llanganatis on more than twenty occasions, plotting the treasure route with rare precision.

"Roland has a system," enthused Grist. "There isn't a river or ravine in those mountains he hasn't explored. Get him to show you his aerial photographs."

Frankly, I didn't know what to make of Grist's claims. I had only just met him, and, as far as I knew, both he and Roland were cranks. There was no getting around that statistic, however. I knew that every year all manner of Andinists and jungle-survivalist types set off into the Llanganatis determined to find Atahualpa's gold, only to emerge mangled and half-starved weeks later. To have made the trip some twenty times and survived beggared belief. If Roland was for real, either he was superhuman or he did indeed have a system. I made an appointment to see him the following afternoon.

VALVERDE'S GUIDE HAS INSPIRED COUNTLESS EXPEDITIONS TO THE LLANganatis, but in terms of sheer endurance Erskine Loch's two expeditions to the mountains in the 1930s have never been surpassed. I didn't have a copy of the *Argosy* magazine article, but, fortunately, before leaving London, I had obtained a copy of Loch's book, together with various research notes, and back in my hostel room that evening I reread them in preparation for my meeting with Roland.

Fever, Famine, and Gold opens in a deceptively buoyant mood in the spring of 1935 with Loch standing on the steps of the New York Public Library in midtown Manhattan, raving about the "vast hoards of gold"

secreted in the mountains (evidently, he had just been reading about
Valverde's cache in a popular 1930s treasure anthology). Walking down
Fifth Avenue, he was struck by the coincidence of the newspaper hoard-
ings emblazoned with headlines such as "Roosevelt and the Gold Stan-
dard!" and "High Price of Gold." Suddenly Loch saw his destiny.

"On that instant came a desire," he wrote, "a sudden determination
to reach those far-off Llanganatis, and find a short route to the Amazon."

Accompanied by a *Boy's Own* crew of adventurers that included a griz-
zled gold prospector, Bill Klamroth, a Parisian "ballistics expert," Georges
Brun, and an elderly Spanish *peón*, Señor Quinteros—known as "old
Q"—Loch set off into the Llanganatis in March, the beginning of the
rainy season and the worst-possible time of year for an expedition. Os-
tensibly Loch's purpose was to forge a new, direct route across the ranges
to the east and make contact with a tribe of wild forest Indians, known
as the "Aucas," who lived along the Curaray and Napo rivers. Backed by
the Museum of the American Indian and the New York Zoological Society, he was also charged with collecting Indian artifacts and "bagging"
specimens of the local fauna, including condors, tapir, and the rare Andean spectacled bear. But no sooner had Loch set out from Píllaro with
a team of Indian porters than he began to regret his decision.

"In the afternoon rain came on," he wrote, "and what a different
rain it was from the warm downpours of the Oriente! Biting, cold, and
in continuous blasts, it penetrated to the bone."

Loch's overriding concerns at this point were discipline and the survival of his party. Although it is just eighty miles from Píllaro to the Río
Napo, the mountains are a forbidding obstacle. Everything necessary
for survival—food, bedding, firewood—would have to be carried by
Loch's *peones*. In theory, each Indian could tote a pack weighing sixty
pounds—enough to provide food for fifteen to twenty days. But since
the porters also had to eat on the return journey, the expedition could
go forward for only seven to ten days before having to turn back.

They spent the first few days trudging cautiously through quaking
bogs—grass islands floating on lakes of mud that shuddered every time
man or beast set foot on them. Eventually Loch reached the fields of tall
juncal reeds, and the expedition slowed to a crawl as he and Klamroth
were forced to cut a path with their machetes. Then they ascended "the
high barren *páramo*-lands"—a series of uninhabited moors rising to ten

thousand to twelve thousand feet and interspersed with more *juncal* reeds and wild morasses. Finally, Loch had to negotiate the first in a series of desolate ice-sheathed passes.

Loch was relying on old Q to lead him to the treasure, or at the very least to a line of palm trees beneath a "mountain crowned with gold" that old Q swore he'd seen on a previous expedition. It was not clear to Loch whether old Q's gold mountain was the treasure lake, an old Inca mine or a figment of his fevered imagination. But Loch thought the line of palm trees might be significant—evidence, as he put it, that "the hand of man had been there before."

There were several false starts. At one point Loch thought he had identified Valverde's Margasitas Mountain only to discover, like many a treasure hunter before and since, that the ridge he was standing on was devoid of pyrites and there was no sign of a *cañon*, let alone the *socabón* and treasure lake. He bore south, looking for the three Cerros Llanganatis "in the form of a triangle." But it was so misty and overcast he could have been camped just beneath the three mountains and not known it. Cursing the *derrotero* and its vague directions, Loch began following tapir trails instead. After seven days he and his men were reduced to a "perpetual diet of lentils" but managed to surmount a "terrific crag" and drop down into "another realm": a hidden valley containing a long, pear-shaped lake—one of the landmarks old Q had told them to look out for. The next morning, the mist cleared and they were treated to a stunning view of Cerro Hermoso, which, without realizing it, they had been circling all this time. Soon after, Loch spotted a rock formation in the shape of a church porch, one of the landmarks mentioned in the *derrotero*, and, nearby it, a lake.

At this point old Q suddenly became vague and reluctant to continue. Loch wondered whether he had forgotten the location of the gold mountain or was obfuscating so as not to have to share the treasure. Loch wanted to believe the latter. After all, old Q's conviction that the gold existed just over the next ridge was now his own. But after dredging the lake and finding nothing but mica, Loch had to face reality. His supplies of food were spent.

Famished and exhausted, Loch returned to Píllaro, where he pondered old Q's sudden befuddlement. Perhaps, Loch conjectured, old Q had been meditating on the treasure, mine, or gold mountain for so long that he really believed he'd seen it. "But when faced by people who, like ourselves, sought to run the dream down rather than talk about it, his conscious mind was forced against a blank wall . . . It was not that he wanted to deceive me, but that he could not face undeceiving himself."

Any sane and rational person would have given up then and there. Loch's expedition had lasted thirty-nine days and nights—"days and nights of almost incessant rain." Old Q was mentally unbalanced, and Valverde's directions were unreliable. There was no sign of a mountain of pyrites or of the "strait passage between two mountains." Worse, the landmarks mentioned in the *derrotero*—the dry *quebradas* and valleys containing lakes fed by cascades—were everywhere, making it impossible to know whether one was on the path indicated by Valverde. Guzmán's map wasn't much use either: with the exception of Cotopaxi and Tungurahua, all the volcanoes in the Llanganatis region were extinct.

But like old Q, Loch could not face "undeceiving himself." Instead, he speculated that the curlicues of smoke Guzmán had shown issuing from Margasitas, Zunchu-Urcu, and the Gran Volcán del Topo were really man-made exhalations. After all, it was well known that the pre-Columbian Indians utilized the natural vents in the rocks for smelting metals; viewed from afar, reasoned Loch, the updrafts from these makeshift furnaces could have been mistaken for volcanoes.

Ignoring his better instincts, Loch recruited seventeen soldiers and more *peones* and launched a second expedition.

At first everything went according to plan. Setting out on June 10, Loch successfully crossed the bogs, then guided the horses over a series of *cuchillas*—steep, knifelike ridges—to the Páramo de Soguillas. Once more they made for Cerro Hermoso, searching for evidence of gold and pyrites. But Loch could find no sign of the gold or of Margasitas Mountain and decided to veer north instead to seek a new route across the ranges to the Oriente.

For days he wandered aimlessly. Walls of rain and sleet impeded the team's progress, and the horses and men grew steadily wearier. Then, just as Loch and Bill Klamroth were about to give up, they awoke to "a beautiful clear day." After marching for three hours, they surmounted a pass and looked out to see "a great indentation" running between the ranges to the east and, looming above them, "three peaks . . . right on the line given by Valverde!"

Scarcely able to contain their excitement, they prepared a hearty meal of duck and arose early the next morning. It was now July 4, but rather than the sunny weather they were used to back home, it was raining harder than ever. Loch made for the indentation, what he thought was Valverde's Way, but each time he hit an impasse.

For days they climbed up and down in perpetual rain. Slowly Loch began to acknowledge reality. The Indian porters had deserted him, his supplies were very nearly exhausted, and only seven of the soldiers were still fit to travel. "No more work could be expected of these men upon the lake regardless of what treasure may be hidden in its deep recesses," he wrote. Instead, Loch decided to make the best of a bad situation. Calling for three volunteers he sent the rest of his party back to Píllaro and made a "direct line" for the Río Napo to the east. Although Valverde's lake was now behind him, Loch had not given up hope of finding gold.

"Even if the ancients had thrown their treasure in a lake in the Llanganatis, they were en route from the mines at the time; and now more than ever I was convinced that if they existed, they must lie farther over the eastern slopes."

Unfortunately, the journey proved the most grueling yet—"seventy days of hell which made all the previous misery seem as nothing."

En route, Georges Brun, the French ballistics expert, was stung by a scorpion; Loch slipped down a ravine and broke two ribs; and "Private Pons," the least able of the army recruits, lost his moorings on a raft one day and was swept into boiling rapids, never to be seen again. By the time Loch, Brun, and the two surviving soldiers crawled into an Indian homestead on the banks of the Río Napo at the end of September, they were broken men.

I closed Loch's book and switched off the bedside light. The only sounds were the wind in the trees and the murmur of backpackers in the courtyard below my room. A group of Canadian schoolteachers was gathered around a table, animatedly discussing their forthcoming trip to the Galápagos. They were planning to spend ten days sailing and scuba diving between the islands. In the evenings they would write postcards home and dine on fresh lobster and sea bass. It sounded enticing. What

was I thinking of contemplating an expedition to the Llanganatis? What
if John Hemming was right and the treasure legend was a lie? Moreover,
what made me think I would have better success attaining such an elusive goal than a man well suited to the task—a man whose obsession
had, to judge by his own account, very nearly driven him mad?

The following morning I awoke early and continued reading, but
the more I learned about Loch, the more I began to doubt my fitness
for the challenge.

Educated at Sandhurst, Loch had been a distinguished infantry officer and veteran of half a dozen expeditions to Africa, India, and South
America. In 1914, during the Cameroons campaign in West Africa, he
had been awarded the Distinguished Service Order for bravery under
fire—going to the aid of a wounded officer and, though injured, carrying him on his back to safety. When World War I ended, Loch resigned
his captain's commission and traveled alone from Takum to Banyo—a
journey no white man had ever undertaken before. Then, in 1932, he
had gone on an expedition to eastern Ecuador in search of the Jivaros—
a tribe with a reputation for shrinking the heads of its enemies.

In all, Loch had spent eight months in the Llanganatis, only nine
days of which had been free of rain. It was, he told a fellow explorer on
his return to Quito, in a phrase that has haunted treasure hunters ever
since, "a land of false promises and crushed hopes."

Loch's book ended on a tantalizing note. He was sitting in his Quito
hotel room contemplating the achievements of his Andes-Amazon expedition when an Ecuadorian—named only as "Señor X"—burst into
his room carrying a package. The package contained three pounds of
gold nuggets, golden fishhooks, and a tiny square of beaten gold.
Where did he find them? demanded Loch. Why, on a site near the Río
Anzú in the east, came the reply. The man said he needed Loch's help,
and money, to finance a more extensive search, for surely the trinkets
were evidence that the fabled mine of the Incas existed after all.

Within weeks Loch had set off on another treasure hunt. This time
he brought an American mining expert. Prospecting pits were dug at
the site, but there was no trace of gold. So Loch widened his search, following the Anzú upstream. Eventually Loch discovered an "ancient"
gravel bed containing gold placers and nearby an overgrown depression. Persuaded the depression marked the location of an ancient dike

and canal system, Loch and his men explored the jungle further. Some of the trees appeared to have been planted deliberately, as though the area was once under cultivation. Then Loch found stone implements, fragments of pottery, and a piece of obsidian—evidence that men *had been* there before them. Convinced he had stumbled upon ancient Inca gold workings, Loch sank more test pits and uncovered several nuggets of gold, the largest of which, at thirty-seven grams, suggested that the vein from which they came could not be far away. But, frustratingly, Loch did not reveal the location of the workings. Instead, he ended his book with a question: "Can it be that my most sanguine hopes are justified at last . . . that here, on the fringe of those Llanganatis Mountains where I stood, is one of the sources of those vast quantities of gold which brought ruin to the Inca empire?"

I laid the book to one side. Loch had completed the manuscript of *Fever, Famine, and Gold* in 1938 at the Explorers Club in New York. The following year he had returned to the Río Anzú and formed Scarloch Mines Incorporated. But although he persuaded an American investor to sink $100,000 into digging several more test pits, Loch's mining company had never turned a profit. Why? Had he really stumbled upon a disused Inca mine, or had it all been a figment of his imagination? And if so, was I wise to follow him?

AFTER LUNCH I WALKED THE FOUR BLOCKS FROM MY HOSTEL TO ROLAND'S apartment. The day before, in heavily accented German-Spanish, Roland had told me to find the headquarters of the Banco de Guayaquil and then "look up."

"It's a large red tower block in the heart of the banking district," he said. "You can't miss it. I'll be waiting for you at reception."

The streets were alive with hawkers. On every corner Indian women wearing traditional embroidered dresses were busy preparing *humitas*—the Ecuadorian snack of ground corn mixed with cheese, sugar, and butter wrapped in corn husks. Young men, dressed identically in baseball caps and English football shirts, worked the waiting traffic, their arms bulging with car aerials, personal organizers, and pens—anything, in fact, that they imagined hard-pressed commuters might discover a need for on their way to work. Meanwhile, waiting and observing in front of every other doorway were the ubiquitous private security guards, their slight frames offset by unnervingly large bulletproof vests and automatic machine guns.

"So you found me okay?" purred Roland when I eventually arrived at his block. "The little *ladrones* didn't give you any trouble?"

As he said this, Roland nodded in the direction of two shoeshine boys loitering suspiciously on the pavement outside. In my preoccupation I had barely noticed them.

"No, no trouble," I replied. "They offered to clean my hiking boots, that's all."

"It is good but you must take care. Quito is no longer a safe city."

As if to emphasize his point, Roland pulled a huge set of keys from his jeans pocket and began grappling with the lock to the lift door. Eventually, after several oaths in what I took to be Old Bavarian, he found the right one and ushered me inside. The doors slid quietly shut, only to reopen seconds later inside another set of security gates on the third floor. Roland extracted another key more easily this time, unlocked the metal grille, and showed me into his apartment.

Crossing the lobby, I had the distinct sensation of entering a time warp. Roland's sitting room was furnished in dark woods and rich burgundy-colored rugs of the kind you might expect to find in the home of a nineteenth-century Prussian plutocrat. On either side of the ornate stone fireplace still lifes jostled with pastoral hunting scenes and Catholic relics. There were wooden crucifixes everywhere: on the walls, on the mantelpiece, on the coffee table. It was like something from the Brothers Grimm. The only thing that spoiled the illusion was the view. One entire wall was taken up by a picture window, through which you could see clear over Quito to the bronze statue of the angel on El Panecillo—the hill that overlooks the city's old colonial center—and, rising behind it, the massive brown hulk of Pichincha. It was a beautiful Andean summer afternoon, and for once the thin meniscus of cloud that clung to Pichincha's summit had dissipated, leaving the lip of the crater silhouetted against a perfect azure sky.

"You've climbed it?" Roland asked.

"No, but I've climbed Chimborazo."

"Did you suffer from, how you say, *soroche*?"

"Altitude sickness. Yes, a little. But only the first night."

"It is good but you must climb it again, and Pichincha, too. If not, you'll never acclimatize to the Llanganatis."

Roland motioned for me to take a seat while he ordered the maid to bring us coffee. Dressed in a loose-fitting white shirt and worn trainers, he exuded an easy, relaxed vigor. I guessed he must have been in his early fifties, but with his neat straw-colored hair and wind-bronzed skin he could easily have passed for a man ten years younger. The only clues to his occupation were his thick tawny beard and his eyes. These were tinted the same shade as the sky and seemed to be gazing off into the distance, as though Roland could see Cerro Hermoso peeping over my left shoulder and was just looking where to plant the next crampon.

"I'm a miner—that's my business," he suddenly declared, falling onto the sofa opposite me. "I'm happy just being in the mountains, panning the rivers, and examining the sediments for gold placers. If I found the treasure, too, that would be a bonus."

Roland opened a nearby cabinet drawer and removed a set of photographs of his most recent expedition. In most of them the landscape was draped in a fine white mist that rendered even the most sharply focused shot a blur. Now and then, however, the *neblina* had lifted, and Roland had been able to capture the Llanganatis' extraordinary isolation and beauty. In one shot, eight Indian porters, dressed in identical yellow rubber jackets and trousers, were gathered around a campfire grilling trout. The men had flat cheekbones, sienna-colored skin, and faintly Asian features. Though obviously wet and cold, they looked to be in their element.

"These are my porters," Roland whispered fondly. "Always I take the same men. They are, how you say, *muy fuerte.*"

"Very strong."

"Jah, they can walk all day with one-hundred-eighty-pound packs, no problem."

"And without packs?"

"Oof! Without packs, my friend, they can reach Valverde's valley—what would take you or me three days' hard walking—in nine hours. Believe me, I have seen it with my own eyes."

Roland paused to consider the difference between the Andean and the European physiognomy. With their stocky frames and barrel-shaped chests, the *peones* had bodies that were perfectly adapted to the harsh conditions of the *paramo*. The Indians had a higher concentration of red blood cells, meaning their bodies transported oxygen to spent muscle tissue far more efficiently than Europeans'. But more important than genes was the fact that they had spent all their lives in the highlands.

"Every day, since they were little children, they have walked to school and to market. For them walking is normal—it's their way of life."

Roland handed me another picture showing what looked like a cactus with a tall phallus-like inflorescence rising from a spray of sharp fronds.

"This is the *Puya hamata*. It's a member of the bromeliad family. They only flower once every few years. Bears love to tear away the leaves and eat the heart."

Next Roland handed me a photograph of a valley full of hairy, palmlike trees topped by what looked like pineapple sprays and whitish flowers.

"And these are *frailejones*.* They're beautiful, no? You find them very rarely."

The final picture Roland showed me was of an emerald green lake— like the one mentioned in the *derrotero*—with mist rising from its center.

"You see that?" said Roland, his eyes growing watery and distant once more. "I'm probably the only person in the world who has seen this lake."

According to Roland, the plants and lakes weren't the only things special about the Llanganatis. The mountains were also one of the last refuges for the spectacled bear, the puma, and the Andean tapir—*danta* in Spanish.

"When I made my first expedition to the Llanganatis fifteen years ago, it was normal to see *dantas* and bears breeding in the mountains near Yana Cocha. Now you have to travel many days to see such a thing."

"Why, what happened?"

"Les mataron." Roland made a slitting motion across his throat. "People hunted them for their skins."

However, Roland explained that some of the wildlife he could have gladly done without.

***Espeletia pycnophylla*. A member of the daisy or sunflower family, *frailejones* are common from northern Ecuador to Venezuela. Their name derives from the Spanish word *fraile* (friar) because of the plant's supposed resemblance to a monk at prayer. Although opinions differ, they are probably the *sangurimas* mentioned in the *derrotero*.

"The ticks are a terrible nuisance, and the mosquitoes. Ach! They don't bear thinking about. But when the *neblina* lifts and you find yourself camped in a valley looking out over a field of *frailejones*, believe me, the Llanganatis are one of the most beautiful places on earth."

I wanted to believe him. Before meeting Roland, I had been worried that he might turn out to be another Grist. But the man sitting opposite me didn't seem to be interested in selling me anything. On the contrary, Roland acted as though he was privy to some great secret, a secret that he was in no hurry to share.

Prior to leaving London, I had managed to procure a full-size copy of Guzmán's map from the Royal Geographical Society. It was far more extensive than the version included in *Notes of a Botanist on the Amazon and Andes*. In Spruce's book, the Gran Volcán del Topo—the most crucial area vis-à-vis the *derrotero*—is lopped off at the midway point, and the Curaray and Llanganatis rivers, some of the richest gold effluents in the region, are not shown at all. By contrast, Guzmán's original map extends another fifteen miles to the east and encompasses not only these features but the subtropical Sacha Llanganatis and the Cordillera de Yana-Urcu (Cerro Negro), too.

The map was supposed to be my trump card, something I could put on the table to establish my credentials and, hopefully, use as leverage to negotiate my passage to the Llanganatis. But now that I was comfortably seated in Roland's living room, it occurred to me that the map might also serve to draw him out.

I wasn't disappointed. Roland fell on the map like a cat reared too long on dried food suddenly presented with a fillet of salmon.

"Where did you get this?" he exclaimed. "I had heard there was another part to Guzmán's map, but this is the first time I have seen it."

I explained how I had come by it and that it was one of only a half-dozen full-size engravings remaining in the society's archives. The original, I added, was larger still and nothing like the engraver A. Findlay's cleaned-up, idealized version.

But Roland wasn't interested. He was already bent over the map, tracing the course of the rivers with his fingers.

"Come," he muttered after a long pause, "I wish to show you something."

I followed Roland through the security gate back to the lift. This time he found the key easily and punched the button for the basement.

The door opened onto a dark, dank corridor crowded with old boxes and loops of rope. A young boy, dressed only in shorts, his stomach distended by hunger, clattered past a lit doorway, pursuing a football. Roland muttered a curse, something about *"los niños"*—I didn't catch it all—and rummaged for his key chain again.

We were now standing in front of a thick metal door, behind which I could hear muffled barking. Roland turned the lock and slid back two long bolts. Daylight suffused the corridor. We were not underground but on the first floor, just above the street. Two huge German shepherds pawed at the windows, straining at their tethers.

"Perros, perros," teased the shoeshine boys.

Roland rapped on the glass and the boys scattered. "Welcome to my center of operations," he said with a grin.

The first thing I noticed was a series of bright blue drums attached to H-frames. Stacked around them, reaching nearly to the ceiling, were several boxes packed with tinned tuna, anchovies, pasta, and rice—enough to feed a small army.

Swathes of blue tarpaulin and khaki-colored bedrolls were spread across the floor in the center of the room, while against another wall were piled several sets of rubber suits—like the ones I had seen Roland's porters wearing in the photograph.

Papers and dog-eared books lay everywhere—on the shelves, on the floor, on a desk. Roland popped a cigarette in his mouth, cleared one of the chairs, and motioned for me to take a seat beside him. Then he gathered a huge pile of maps and photographs in his arms and, spreading them in front of me, began tracing his fingers along the grid references as if they were braille. Every now and again he paused at a cross or circle marked in heavy green pencil and emitted a little grunt of satisfaction. From where I was seated, I could just make out the words "Instituto Geográfico Militar" in the top left-hand corner and "Cerros Llanganatis." Finally, after what seemed like half an hour but was probably only a matter of minutes, he spoke.

"You see this, Marcos," said Roland, pointing to a cross to the left of a large lake marked "Pisayambo," "this is Valverde's first sleeping place. And here, a little to the south, is Guapa Mountain, the point from which you are supposed to see the three Cerros Llanganatis."

Roland's finger strode on around two smaller lakes in the shape of a pair of spectacles—Los Anteojos—until he arrived at another cross in front of what appeared to be a level plain.

"And this is the second sleeping place."

Next Roland pointed to Yana Cocha—the great black lake mentioned by Valverde—and its drainage, the Desaguadero. Following the *derrotero*'s instructions to the letter, Roland rounded the southern shore of Yana Cocha and continued in an easterly direction, keeping the Desaguadero on the left, until he reached the Río El Golpe and the Parca Yacu. A little to the south were a series of tightly packed contour lines.

"Here there is a deep ravine, just like it says in the *derrotero*, and a waterfall. This is where I believe Padre Longo died. But that is not all."

Roland unfurled another sheet—not a map this time, but a faded black-and-white aerial photograph. At first all I could make out was a dense wooded hillside without roads or trails. Roland, however, insisted otherwise.

"Look here," he said, pointing at a faint shadow in the tree line. "Do you see? It's an ancient Inca road. I've walked it many times."

I peered more closely at the photograph. If you tilted it so that it caught the light, there did indeed appear to be a line contouring around the hillside. Was this Valverde's Way of the Incas and the route Blake and Chapman had followed to the treasure cave? I made a mental note to interrogate Roland about Blake and Chapman later. For the moment, he was locked on Valverde's guide.

"The road passes between two canyons, here"—Roland stabbed the map emphatically—"just like the way mentioned in the *derrotero*. And here there are three mountains in the shape of a triangle"—Roland indicated a mountain labeled "Las Torres" and, behind it, two more peaks highlighted in yellow—"and look, here is a lake, and here I found a, how you say, *tembladera*?"

"A quaking bog."

"Exactly. So up to this point the *derrotero* is 100 percent authentic. Whoever wrote the guide knew these mountains well and passed this way many times. There is no other possibility."

The problems, said Roland, began on the fourth day. In order to reach the *socabón* and treasure lake, you must, according to Valverde's guide, find Margasitas Mountain and contour around it in the direction indicated by the hieroglyph. But, unfortunately, the area where Roland had identified the Inca way abounded in hills with pyrites, making it difficult to know which was Margasitas Mountain.

Then there was the puzzle of the hieroglyph itself. Its twisting tail seemed to indicate that you should contour around Margasitas Mountain to the north, leaving the mountain on the right. Yet the *derrotero* clearly stated that you should leave the mountain on the left.

Finally there was the riddle of the three Cerros Llanganatis themselves. According to Roland, from Guapa Mountain you could see triangular arrangements of peaks in at least two different directions.

"Look," said Roland, pointing to a series of broken lines radiating from Valverde's hill. "In the old days Ambato lay farther to the southwest, so that if you stood on Guapa Mountain with your back to the town, you would face in this direction." Roland indicated a group of mountains to the northeast labeled "Roncadores." "This is the region of mines on Guzmán's map. And it is true, if you stand on Guapa Mountain, you can see very well three mountain peaks here."

However, today Ambato was farther to the north, meaning that the Cerros Llanganatis ought to lie due east of Guapa in exactly the area where Roland claimed to have found his triangular arrangement of peaks.

"Unfortunately, they are not very clear," Roland admitted frankly. "To see them, you have to narrow your eyes and use a little imagination."

There were other discrepancies, too, more riddles within riddles. On his map, for instance, Guzmán had shown curlicues of smoke issuing from Zunchu-Urcu and from the so-called Gran Volcán del Topo. But Roland confirmed that with the exception of Cotopaxi and Tungurahua, there were no active volcanoes in the Llanganatis region. Indeed, Roland doubted whether the Gran Volcán del Topo, or for that matter the Volcán de Margasitas, existed.

For these reasons Roland believed Guzmán's map and the *derrotero* could be trusted only so far. Rather than set too much store by the treasure documents, Roland preferred to traverse the Llanganatis, panning the riverbeds for ore, and, when he found a promising deposit, follow the ravines upstream, examining the hillsides above the *quebradas* for auriferous seams. In this way, he explained, he had succeeded in identifying a number of promising mining areas.

"For some people the *derrotero* is an obsession. All day long that is all they think about," explained Roland. "But for me it's different. I am a prospector first and a treasure hunter second."

I studied Roland carefully. I half-expected to see the blood vessels bulging in his neck, his eyes popping with frustration like the Abbé Faria in Dumas's novel. But there was not so much as a furrow. Was he really as methodical and levelheaded as he made out, or was it all an act?

I tried another tack. Stan Grist had already told me that Roland owned a farm near Tena on the Río Anzú. Was he familiar, I wondered, with Erskine Loch and the history of Scarloch Mines?

At the mention of Loch's name, Roland smiled knowingly. Then he turned to the pile of documents on the table and began rummaging until he found another photograph. He handed it to me without comment. To my surprise it showed Roland standing in front of an open pit surrounded by farmhands. Judging by their shovels and picks, the pit was about three meters across.

"You see that," said Roland. "Loch dug it. I have fifteen others just like it on my farm."

It turned out that Roland's farm was on the exact site where Loch had prospected for gold following his return to Ecuador in 1938. Roland had investigated all the pits personally. In one he had found a nugget weighing thirty grams, but unfortunately most of the gravels had proved "uninteresting." However, that hadn't prevented him from leasing several sites to a Canadian mining company. "At this very moment they're digging several new test pits. Who knows? Perhaps the Canadians will prove Captain Loch right after all."

If Roland had such confidence in Loch, what, I wondered, did he make of Loch's claims to have discovered old Inca mine workings in the Sacha Llanganatis?

Once again Roland paused and studied me closely. He seemed to be weighing something in his mind. Then, having reached his decision, he turned once more to the pile of documents on the table and unfolded another map showing the continuation of the Parca Yacu into the Sacha Llanganatis. Judging by the packed contour lines, the Parca Yacu dropped precipitously through several more *quebradas*. Then it slowed and widened before joining another river arriving from the north: the Mulatos. Just beyond the junction of the two rivers, where the

Mulatos turned south and east, Roland had circled a deep valley protected on three sides by forested ridges. The hillsides were scored with streams that drained into a narrow *quebrada*, which in turn fed back into the Mulatos. At around the midpoint of the *quebrada* Roland had drawn a series of neat rectangles and what looked like lines radiating north back toward the Mulatos.

"One day I was cutting a trail through the forest when I suddenly emerged in this *quebrada* here." Roland pointed to the ravine running through the valley. "I couldn't believe my eyes. There were several rectangular pools cut into the rock and, running off from them, a series of, how you say, *canales*?"

"Channels."

"Exactly. The channels were overgrown with trees and vegetation, and in several places the walls had been destroyed by landslides, but you could see that they had once stood several meters high."

"Who built them? What were they for?"

"No one is sure. One theory—and it is only a theory—is that they may have been used for washing gold."

Roland explained that in the floor of one of the pools he had discovered a hollow depression. The pools also had sluices at one end to allow water to drain out of the pool and into the channels. Roland theorized that the Indians had deposited gravels from their gold mine in the pool, then directed water through the sluices. The force of the water had washed the lighter gravels into the channels, leaving the gold ore to collect in the hollow at the bottom of the pool.

"Don't you see? This could be the basis for the legend of the lake made by hand."

Roland pointed out that the Llanganatis abounded in natural lakes. If Rumiñahui had wanted to hide the treasure permanently, there were any number of lakes much nearer Píllaro he could have chosen. But Rumiñahui thought he would expel the conquistadores and return for the treasure at a later date. That is why he needed an artificial lake—a lake that he would be able to drain when the time came for him to reclaim Atahualpa's gold.

"And the *socabón*?"

"Perhaps the *socabón* is a reference to an old mine tunnel."

Roland pointed out that in one passage Valverde describes the *so-cabón* as having an entrance resembling a "church porch"—what could be interpreted as the mouth to a mine. Then, at another point, he says that the water from the lake "falls into" the tunnel. Moreover, the reference in the *derrotero* to the forging of "golden nails" and to a *"guayra"* (furnace) suggested that the tunnel and treasure lake were near where the Indians smelted the gold artifacts. It just so happened that in the same valley where Roland claimed to have identified the constructions, he had found some natural vents in the rocks. He believed these vents could have been used by the Indians as wind chimneys to direct oxygen to their fires in order to achieve the high temperatures needed to make the gold malleable. The porters, he revealed, referred to the valley as "El Mundo Nuevo" (the New World).

"Who knows," said Roland, shooting me a conspiratorial look. "Perhaps if we were to explore the valley, we might find the gold mine *and* the treasure."

Was he serious? Roland had a way of making the most outlandish proposition sound natural. His descriptions of old Inca roads and mines inspired confidence, suggesting that in addition to his other skills, Roland had an appreciation of archaeology and geology. But now from nowhere he had introduced this story about the valley of "El Mundo Nuevo." If he was so certain the pools and channels contained the key to where the treasure was buried, why was he telling a complete stranger about them? And why did he need my help to mount an expedition?

I realized that I still knew next to nothing about Roland and how he came to be living in Ecuador. Even with a team of Indian porters to carry food and equipment, an expedition to the Llanganatis was not something to be undertaken lightly. Had he had any experience of mountaineering in Germany?

"Ach, in Europe it was a hobby," Roland replied, waving his arms dismissively in the direction of the Old Country. "In Germany I was a weekend alpinist, that's all."

"So how did you end up in South America?"

Instead of answering my question, Roland wandered over to the bookshelf and began running his finger along the worn spines. He soon found what he was looking for. It was a bright yellow book by a Polish author. It had only one word on the cover, but I recognized the genre immediately. Each chapter contained maps and diagrams of different treasure legends. Thus there were the stories of buccaneers like Captain Kidd and Lionel Wafer and their fabulous pirate treasures hidden on remote Caribbean islands; the legend of the Oak Island treasure—a deep shaft on an island in Nova Scotia said to contain millions of dollars' worth of gold; and, of course, there was a chapter devoted to Valverde's guide.

I asked Roland to translate the book's title and subtitle for me.

"Gold Waiting to Be Found," he replied.

Roland explained that as a small boy growing up in the Black Forest, he had often dreamed of traveling to South America. Quite where the desire came from he did not know, but one day he happened upon the gold book in his local library. He had never heard of Pizarro or Atahualpa, but the stories in the book struck a chord, and he made up his mind then and there to go in search of gold. Attracted by the tales of abandoned Spanish silver mines in Central America, he first went to Mexico. But the situation there "was not very good for prospecting," and he quickly moved on, working his way south through Guatemala and Panama to Colombia.

In 1985 he arrived in Ecuador. Politically and economically the outlook was uncertain. But the price of gold was at an all-time high, and Roland soon established that the rivers of El Oriente—as the Ecuadorians describe the eastern region of the country—contained many potentially lucrative seams. He collected all his capital, bought a farm in Tena, and began making his first forays into the Llanganatis. It was demanding, dangerous work. One minute he would be standing ankle-deep in a shallow stream, panning for gold; the next moment the stream would be a raging torrent, and he would be struggling with all his strength against the current. On another occasion, he would be cutting a trail to a promising ridge, hauling himself up by an overhanging branch with his free arm, when the branch would suddenly snap and he'd find himself sliding headfirst toward the edge of a slick ravine. Needless to say, he survived these and other challenges and was soon making a good living. According to Roland, it cost him no more than $200 to extract an ounce of gold from the rivers and mountains of El Oriente. Given that in the 1980s gold was trading at more than $600 an ounce, he enjoyed a 200 percent profit. Indeed, by the end of the 1980s Roland had done so well from the business that he was able to open his own mine in Zamora, in southern Ecuador, flying his own drilling equipment by helicopter.

Then came the 1990s and the collapse in the world price of gold bullion. With gold trading at $240 an ounce, Roland's mine was only just breaking even. As his incentive for mining diminished, his thoughts inevitably turned to the treasure. Having been to the mountains many times, Roland agreed with Spruce's view that the *derrotero* could only have been written by a person who was familiar with the Llanganatis and who had traveled through the area. Moreover, he knew that most of the landmarks indicated on Guzmán's map were exactly where they should be. What if there really was a treasure and it was still out there, *waiting to be found*? Yes, others had gone looking for it, but none of them knew the Llanganatis like he did; why shouldn't he be the one to succeed?

As Roland told me: "I've been over every inch of those mountains. I know the location of every lake and ridge. If anyone can find the treasure I can."

I don't know whether it was his halting English, which seemed to turn every expression into a statement of irrevocable fact, or his impressive display of maps and equipment, but I believed him. There was something about Roland that inspired confidence. Grist was right, he *was* systematic. Not only had he made a thorough study of the *derrotero* and Guzmán's map, but he planned his expeditions meticulously. To give himself as much time as possible in the mountains and to maximize his chances of survival, Roland had established a series of camps along Valverde's route. His method was to enter the mountains via Los Anteojos accompanied by ten porters loaded with enough provisions to last him several weeks. The Indians would bring the food to a camp Roland had established just beyond the fourth sleeping place—about four to five days' journey. Then, on the fifth day, they would turn back, leaving Roland to continue on with just three men. In this way, and by supplementing his supplies by fishing—"never hunting, we respect the animals"—he had been able to stay in the mountains for up to six weeks at a time.

"What if you slip or fall down a ravine?"

"Ach, then you have to hope that you don't break your back and that someone can reach you. If not . . ." Roland shrugged his shoulders. His implication was clear: in the Llanganatis it was every man for himself.

Throughout our conversation I sensed that Roland had been keeping something back. He clearly knew, or thought he knew, more than he was letting on. Now, at last, he stopped hinting.

"Listen, I know very well where the gold of the Incas is." Roland stabbed the map with his forefinger. "It's here, near the valley where I found the constructions. I proved it one day when I was out prospecting. A little before the valley there is a narrow canyon, exactly as the *derrotero* describes, and when you come out the other side, you can see three *cerros* very clearly. It takes ten days to get there on foot and then another two days to cross this mountain here."

Roland prodded another concentration of contour lines labeled "Gallo-Urcu" (Spanish and Quichua for "Rooster Mountain").

"In all, it will take three weeks, there and back. What do you say?"

In truth I didn't know what to say. The meeting had already far exceeded my expectations. Roland must have sensed my confusion; before I could open my mouth, he raised his hand to silence me; he didn't expect a reply right away.

By now storm clouds had gathered around Pichincha, and Roland's office had started to get dark. I was happy to walk back to my hostel, but Roland insisted on driving. "*No es seguro*—it's not safe," he growled, as though I were his latest acquisition, a piece of property he was duty-bound to protect.

On the way he told me he wouldn't be leaving for several weeks so I had plenty of time to make up my mind. In the meantime, would I make him a copy of Guzmán's map?

I said I would and we shook on it. As his car sped away from my hostel, I found myself looking anxiously back toward the banking district.

2

"A Story to Astound the World!"

WHEN HEINRICH SCHLIEMANN, THE FUTURE DISCOVERER OF TROY, WAS a young boy, his father told him a story he never forgot. Behind their house, he said, was a small pond from which a beautiful maiden appeared at midnight holding a silver bowl in her arms. Near the pond, the older Schliemann continued, was a hill where in ancient times a robber-knight had supposedly buried his beloved child in a golden cradle. Even greater treasures, he claimed, were waiting to be discovered near the ruins of a round tower in the mayor's garden.

"My faith in the existence of these treasures was so great," Schliemann later recalled in his memoirs, "that, whenever I heard my father complain of his poverty, I always expressed my astonishment that he did not dig up the silver bowl or the golden cradle and so become rich."

In 1873, of course, Schliemann did just that, realizing his childhood dreams by unearthing a vast cache of gold, silver, and copper objects at Hissarlik, in northwest Turkey—a site that he had correctly identified as the location of Homer's Troy. Then, in 1876, while excavating at Mycenae in Greece, Schliemann happened upon one of the greatest

archaeological treasures of all time—the gold death mask of Agamemnon, the ancient Mycenaean king referred to in Homer's *Iliad*.

But if Schliemann, a self-made millionaire who turned to archaeology late in life, enjoyed a surfeit of good fortune, the lot of most treasure hunters has been very different. Sir Walter Raleigh's thirty-year
obsession with El Dorado, for instance, brought him nothing but misery. Having convinced himself that the fabled lost city of gold—or
Manoa, as he called it—was to be found beside a salt lake shaped like a
caterpillar in Spanish Guiana, he launched a desperate expedition in
1616 to find it, only to lose his son Walt in an assault on a Spanish gar-
rison. In 1618, on his return to England, Raleigh paid the ultimate price
for his obsession—imprisonment in the Tower, followed by his execution for treason for failing to keep his promise to King James to steer
clear of Spanish possessions in Latin America.

And so it has continued, decade after decade, century upon century.
Space does not permit me to list all those who have died in pursuit of
some elusive lost city. Suffice it to say that in 1925 the British explorer
Colonel Percy Harrison Fawcett also fell victim to this strange fascination when he disappeared in the Mato Grosso region of Brazil with
two companions while pursuing rumors of "old ruins . . . hidden in the
forests of the Amazon basin." Fawcett, about whom more later, was
never found, and it is now accepted that he and his companions were
probably murdered by Indians to whom they had given some sort of of-
fense.

Usually, though, the treasure obsessive suffers a more mundane fate.
Convinced that he alone holds the key to a centuries-old riddle—
whether that riddle be the location of a lost city, a hidden Indian mine,
or buried pirate treasure—he will mortgage his house and business on
the venture, ceasing only when the banks call in the loan. For evidence
one need look no further than the Oak Island treasure. Located on a remote Nova Scotian island beside an old oak tree, there is a shaft, twelve
feet in diameter, in which treasure hunters have discovered stones
carved with strange symbols that supposedly point to a fabulous pirate
hoard. There is just one problem: the shaft is protected by a succession
of false timber ceilings and booby-trapped tunnels that flood whenever
anyone nears the bottom. As a result, despite the best efforts of a series
of Wall Street syndicates equipped with the latest engineering technology,

so far no one has succeeded in probing the shaft beyond a depth of about two hundred feet. Nevertheless, spurred by the challenge of solving the mystery, a succession of investors with more money than sense have been attracted to the Oak Island treasure, including in 1909 Franklin D. Roosevelt and in 1940 the actor Errol Flynn. To date, six people have died trying to solve the engineering riddle, and more than a million dollars have been sunk into this veritable "money pit"—in all probability, far more than the value of the hoard itself.

Roland didn't strike me as the sort of person to invest time and money in a similarly hopeless cause, but my search of Llanganatis treasure lore on Google had thrown up the name of another treasure obsessive who fit Conrad's psychological profile to a T. His name was Andrés Fernández-Salvador, and from what I could gather from an old article about him posted on the Internet, he was something of a dreamer.

"Fool's Gold: In the Diaphanous Mists of the Ecuadorian Andes, a King's Ransom Lies Buried. Or Does It?" read the rather skeptical headline that accompanied the interview with him. According to the article, Fernández-Salvador, the heir to a bottled-water fortune, had made more expeditions to the Llanganatis than any other treasure hunter alive. A former bodybuilder and world sprint champion, he was also addicted to danger—he'd once crashed a helicopter into Cerro Hermoso and been marooned in the ranges for thirty-three days (apparently, he'd survived by eating tree roots). Though he was now in his seventies and had slowed a little, judging by the interview he had lost none of his passion.

"It's not important that I find [the treasure]," he'd told the interviewer at one point. "I'm a bridge in the quest. It's like the quest for Fermat's Last Theorem or the double helix."

Even more intriguing was that at his ranch in Guayaquil, Fernández-Salvador kept a huge collection of primary treasure documents, including Blake's maps and letters. The journalist had clearly gone there in hopes of prying some of these secrets from him, but as well as being a former track star, Fernández-Salvador was a champion drinker, and the only thing the interviewer had come away with was a sore head.

Nevertheless, I decided it would be worth meeting him. Although I had heard Blake's story many times, I had never seen his maps and letters. If Fernández-Salvador was indeed the keeper of the grail and was willing to share Blake's documents with me, it might help me decide whether Blake had really known Spruce and whether the legend of Valverde's gold was more than just a pirate tale.

FERNÁNDEZ-SALVADOR—OR "ANDY," AS HE WAS SOON INSISTING I CALL him—proved surprisingly easy to find. His father had owned Tesalia, the largest bottled-mineral-water company in Ecuador, and although Andy was no longer the majority shareholder, he still kept a desk at the company's offices in Guayaquil. To my surprise and relief he also spoke perfect English, albeit in a manner I thought had gone out of fashion in the 1950s.

"Ah yes, Richard Spruce," said Andy warmly when I explained what I was doing in Ecuador. "A scholar and a gentleman. I remember the first time my father showed me a copy of *Notes of a Botanist on the Amazon and Andes*. I devoured it in a single sitting."

I told Andy that I had just retraced Spruce's expedition over Chimborazo in search of the cinchona tree and was now hoping to write about his fascination with Valverde's guide—I thought it politic at this point to skirt my meeting with Roland and my own treasure-hunting ambitions.

"I've often thought about writing about my own experiences in the Llanganatis," Andy replied, his voice suddenly becoming hushed and confidential, "but first I have to complete what I set out to do. You know that I'm very close now?"

Andy's question didn't seem to require a reply. It was a line, I suspected, he repeated to himself in his sleep, something he told every would-be treasure hunter.

"Come to my ranch for a chat," he continued, relaxing now into an idiom reminiscent of polo meets, dry martinis, and regattas at the Guayaquil Yacht Club. "I go there every Tuesday. My chauffeur will drive. We can talk on the way."

And so it was that having just grown acclimatized to the thin air of the Quitenian Andes, I found myself boarding a plane for Guayaquil. According to that morning's *El Comercio*, Ecuador's coastal capital was in the grip of an unseasonable low—whether it was a pre–El Niño event or the result of global warming no one knew—and the night before it had rained torrents, overwhelming the sewers. The shantytowns on the edge of the city were the worst hit. Below a picture of a mulatto woman wading through a flooded paddy field, the caption read: *"Epidemias Peligrosas"* (Dangerous Epidemics).

The flight was cruelly short. No sooner had we crossed the western cordillera of the Andes than it seemed the pilot was announcing our descent to Guayaquil airport. Stepping onto the tarmac, I felt as though I were wading through treacle. It was only nine in the morning, but here at sea level the equatorial sun was brutal, and within seconds my neck and forehead were beaded with sweat.

"Just wait until you're crossing the Río El Golpe," I imagined Andy mocking. "And the mosquitoes—oof, like you wouldn't believe!"

I recognized him immediately—a small, vital man with restless black eyes, barking orders into his mobile phone.

"Ah, Marcos," he said with a smile, momentarily breaking off from his conversation. "It's hot, no? Such is life in the tropics," and he let out a triumphant hoot, as though he had just made the greatest joke in the world.

Andy took my bag, and we climbed into the back of his SUV. He was tiny—no more than five feet five. Dressed in jeans, cowboy boots, and a denim shirt, with a fussy ascot tied around his neck, he resembled nothing so much as a Latin Alan Ladd.

To my relief the air-conditioning was on full blast—such are the comforts of the rich—and as we pulled away from the airport, Andy was soon weaving his spell, inviting me to share the confidences of his colorful and—to his mind at least—heroic life.

"Have you heard about the time I equaled Jesse Owens's sprint record? It was 1938. I crossed the line in 10.3 seconds, just behind the Panamanian world champion Lloyd LaBeach. Unfortunately, we didn't have a wind-speed mechanic, so it isn't in the record books, but I can tell you there was no wind that day and we were running on a track with six-inch spikes!"

I checked Andy's face, but he had a thick gray mustache that made it difficult to gauge his expression. I tried to imagine him in his heyday, an Ecuadorian titan breaking records and hearts from Panama to the Côte d'Azur (he told me he'd once held the bodybuilding title "Mr. Ecuador"), but it was no use. Scrunched up on the backseat, he looked wizened and drawn. Loose skin hung from his neck in folds, and his hands were speckled with liver spots. In an effort to camouflage his advancing years, he had dyed his hair jet-black. But the overall effect was less of a former athletics champion than of a seventy-eight-year-old desperate to cheat time.

By now we had left the airport far behind and were zooming through the slums and flooded backstreets. The chauffeur turned hard right, showering water onto a group of mestizo children playing in front of a rotten doorway.

"This is a shortcut," said Andy, momentarily breaking off from his reminiscences. "From here we can pick up the road north and be at my ranch in two hours. I've often wondered how fast I would have run on a modern track with modern shoes."

Fifteen minutes later we had reached the city limits, and the country opened out into a wide, flat vista of flooded paddy fields.

"Imagine," said Andy, taking in the view, "twice Francisco Pizarro landed here and twice he had to return to Panama for fresh supplies. What men those conquistadores were, what determination."

Beside the road Indian women in brightly colored skirts had set up charcoal braziers and were silently roasting pigs—like the thirst for gold, a Spanish import to the New World.

"It was only when Pizarro reached the coast of Peru in 1532 and heard the fantastic reports of the Inca empire that he knew he'd come to the right place," enthused Andy, "but you already know the history, yes?"

I did, but I wanted to hear it again from a Fernández-Salvador, a scion of the Ecuadorian ruling classes and a man who could trace a direct family line to those early Spanish robber-adventurers. And so I allowed Andy to recount the story of the conquest—a story he had told many times before.

"DID YOU KNOW THAT THE INCAS DINED ON PAPAYA FROM THE JUNGLE in the morning and fish from the Pacific in the evening? It was said that the royal runners could deliver a message from one end of the Andes to the other in just five days."

According to Andy, Pizarro was a romantic, gold-hungry rogue who had little idea of the majesty of the empire he had come to destroy. He had just two things going for him: ratlike cunning and luck.

Pizarro's first tentative landing on the coast of Ecuador in 1527 had coincided with the death of the tenth Inca, Huayna Capac, from small-pox, a disease against which American indigenous peoples had no immunity. On his deathbed, Huayna Capac had controversially split the Inca empire between Atahualpa and his half brother, Huáscar—even though Huáscar was the more senior and thus, according to Inca law, the rightful heir to the throne.*

The accommodation proved a disaster. Determined to rule alone, Atahualpa called on his loyal Ecuadorian generals to begin an insurrection against Huáscar, who had dominion over Peru and the south. The civil war lasted five bloody years, but in 1532—the year of Pizarro's return to Ecuador and his march south along the coast to Peru—Atahualpa inflicted a decisive blow against Huáscar at Ambato, defeating a forty-thousand-strong army under the command of one of his brother's leading generals. By the time Pizarro turned east into Peru's mountainous interior in the autumn of the same year, Tahuantinsuyo—the Inca empire, which stretched along the spine of the Andes from Colombia to Chile—had become weak and divided.

"Pizarro's timing couldn't have been better," said Andy. "He arrived in Peru at exactly the right moment!"

Accompanied by just 168 conquistadores—62 on horse, the rest on foot—Pizarro had ridden unopposed up the western cordillera of the Andes to where Atahualpa was camped at Cajamarca. Atahualpa's spies had kept him fully informed of the conquistadores' advance, "and yet," said Andy, "he did nothing to stop them. Incredible, no?"

One reason might have been Atahualpa's fascination with the reports of the bearded white men's horses—an animal unknown to the Incas—and their armor. Having just defeated Huáscar, he probably also considered it inconceivable that a small party of foreigners, isolated and far from home, could pose a threat to his eighty-thousand-strong Indian army. If so, however, he was mistaken.

---

*It is true that Huayna Capac was considering making Quito his northern capital, but in going so far as to say that he wished to divide his empire, Andy may be guilty of repeating a story put about by Atahualpa's supporters after Huayna Capac's death. Modern historians such as John Hemming doubt that this would have been Huayna Capac's intention, and Huáscar's followers in Cuzco certainly did not know of the story or accept it.

"Pizarro was crafty. He liked to fight dirty. Besides, he was crazy for the Incas' gold. He couldn't turn back."

Pizarro had seen several fine examples of Inca gold and silverwork two years previously when his men had intercepted a balsa raft off the coast of Manta. Now he planned to emulate Cortés's victory over the Aztecs in Mexico twelve years earlier and win himself a place in history.

Pizarro's men had ascended the western cordillera of the Andes along a well-trodden Inca trail. But though on their journey they passed numerous terraces planted with maize and cotton, nothing had prepared them for their first sight of Cajamarca. Emerging from the mountains on Friday, November 15, the conquistadores suddenly found themselves in front of a narrow valley. Before them stretched flat, cultivated fields and a series of thatched Indian clay houses built around a central plaza. The most spectacular sight of all, however, was Atahualpa's army.

"The Inca had ordered his men to pitch their tents on the hillside above the town," mused Andy. "Imagine what a sight that must have been, Marcos! Eighty thousand Inca troops, the whole imperial army, spread out before them!"

If the Spanish were fearful, however, they did not show it. Instead, Pizarro rode into Cajamarca and sent his brother Hernando to invite Atahualpa to a meeting. Hernando found Atahualpa camped at some nearby hot springs. The Inca was wearing the royal insignia—a series of cords wound around his head with a fringe of scarlet tassels at the front—and had just begun a fast. At first Atahualpa rejected Hernando's invitation, accusing the Spanish of behaving badly toward some Indians on the coast. But after hearing Hernando's denials, Atahualpa relented and said he would meet Pizarro in Cajamarca the next day.

That night the Spanish stared up at the campfires of the Inca army shimmering on the hillside above Cajamarca like "a star-studded sky" while they plotted an ambush. The square at Cajamarca was surrounded on three sides by long barrack-like buildings, each with twenty openings, perfect for concealing and loosing cavalry. Pizarro told his men he planned to lure Atahualpa into the horseshoe and then, when the moment was right, sound the attack.

"Those conquistadores must have been shitting themselves," said Andy. "Think of the odds. One hundred and seventy men in a strange land far from home and facing an army of thousands!"

The following day Atahualpa broke his fast and celebrated the victory of his forces over Huáscar. As the celebration continued through the morning and into the afternoon, the Spanish became steadily more jittery. When would the Inca come? Would he be bearing arms?

Eventually, late in the afternoon, Atahualpa's entourage began to move slowly toward the town. Hearing that his armies had been victorious in Cuzco and he would soon be crowned Lord Inca, Atahualpa had decided to turn his meeting with Pizarro into a victory parade. Entering the square on a gold-and-silver litter, he was accompanied by just five thousand unarmed men.

It was not so much a battle as a carnage. Armed with steel swords, the Spanish easily overwhelmed the unprepared Indian troops. Some Incas were so terrified of the horses and the conquistadores' bloodcurdling cries of "Santiago" that they fell over one another in a desperate bid to escape, only to be crushed under the Spanish hooves. Others fled to the town limits, knocking down a stretch of wall in hopes of making it back to their encampment. But no sooner had the fleeing Indians reached the open plain than the Spanish cavalry ran them down, spearing and chopping them to the ground. Rather than come to the aid of their fallen comrades, the bulk of Atahualpa's army, watching from the hills, remained rooted to the spot. As a result, by nightfall virtually the entire royal escort lay dead, and Pizarro had taken Atahualpa and his golden throne hostage.

Andy paused, his admiration for Pizarro's audacity mingling with other emotions.

"Can you believe how easily they captured Atahualpa? Pizarro received a cut on the arm, but it was from one of his own horsemen. Those poor Indians, they didn't stand a chance."

What happened next was possibly even more extraordinary. Instead of ordering his army to swamp the Spanish, Atahualpa struck a deal. Knowing the Spaniards' greed for gold, he stood on his tiptoes, reached his hand as high up the wall of the room in which he was being held as he could, and promised Pizarro that in return for his freedom he would fill his cell with gold to the height of the line and "twice as much silver besides."

"I've been inside that room, Marcos! It measures seventeen by twenty-two feet, and the mark is eight feet from the floor."

It took several months for the gold trains to reach Cajamarca from the various points of the Inca empire, but by May 1533 Atahualpa had delivered to Pizarro 1,326,539 gold pesos and 51,610 silver marcos, about 13,000 pounds of gold and 26,000 pounds of silver—a stupendous sum, equivalent to about $22 million at today's values. However, the sight of so much wealth did little to assuage Pizarro's greed. No sooner had the gold objects reached Cajamarca than Pizarro set teams of men to breaking and crushing them in order to maximize the amount the chamber could hold.

"Why do you do that?" stammered Atahualpa incredulously. "I will give you so much gold that you will be sated with it!" But it was never enough.

Andy closed his eyes, as though imagining what the room looked like before Pizarro's wanton vandalism.

"There were goblets and vases of every shape and size," he muttered. "Golden ears of corn with their leaves sheathed in silver; royal headdresses of spun gold; plates of silver; and golden replicas of birds, llamas, and mountain lions—all of them life-size!"

Andy broke off from his reverie. Was he reciting from some half-remembered text—one of the chronicles of the Spanish conquest perhaps—or was he thinking of another treasure hoard entirely?

Andy turned to me, his face red with indignation. "Atahualpa was sure all the gold arriving in Cajamarca would satisfy Pizarro, but he was wrong. Pizarro's greed was limitless"—Andy slammed his hand down hard on the seat between us—"he just wanted more and more!"

What Atahualpa didn't realize was that Pizarro and his brothers were merely the advance party of a much larger invasion force—a force that had already conquered Mexico and was now intent on adding Peru and Ecuador to its New World possessions. Not only that, but Pizarro also faced competition from other conquistadores eager to claim a share of the loot and a governorship.

According to Andy, when Pizarro's partner Diego de Almagro arrived from Panama, Atahualpa's fate was sealed. With rumors that a hostile Indian force—the remnants of Atahualpa's army—was preparing to rescue the Inca, Almagro began pressing Pizarro to execute Atahualpa and march immediately on Cuzco to seize the rest of the gold.

"Pizarro was in a quandary. He genuinely didn't know what to do"—Andy twisted uncomfortably in his seat as though he were Pizarro racked by an identical emotional conflict "he'd come to respect Atahualpa, you see, but the rumor that one of his most loyal generals was coming to his aid scared the pants off him. He couldn't risk leaving Atahualpa alive in Cajamarca."

Andy rapped the chauffeur's seat and ordered him to pull into a roadside cantina. He had been talking so much he was hoarse.

"¡Dos Pilsners!" he barked. An elderly Chinese woman shuffled over to our table with two beers. Meanwhile, the chauffeur took the seat opposite and began distractedly swatting the flies circling a lone soy sauce bottle. The restaurant's specialty was arroz chaufalan—chicken fried rice—but Andy spat with contempt when I suggested we order it.

"Rice is for peasants—here, I eat only noodles."

I wanted to ask Andy what a family of Chinese were doing in the middle of an Ecuadorian cattle town, but his mind was still focused on those distant events in the Peruvian highlands.

"Of course you're familiar with Valverde's derrotero. Well, here's an extraordinary coincidence. Did you know that the priest who signed Atahualpa's death warrant was also called Valverde?"

According to Andy, the priest, Vicente de Valverde, had been present at the ambush in Cajamarca. Indeed, it was Valverde who had provided Pizarro with his pretext for charging, making his way to the foot of Atahualpa's litter as he entered the square and presenting him with his breviary. Valverde explained that it contained the credo of his master, the King of Spain, Charles I, also known as the Holy Roman Emperor Charles V, and bade the Inca to submit. But instead of taking the prayer book in his hands, Atahualpa knocked it angrily to the ground, prompting Valverde to sound the alarm: "Come out, come out, Christians! Come at these enemy dogs who reject the things of God!"

By the time Almagro reached Cajamarca, most of the ransom gold had already arrived from Peru and Bolivia. All the Spanish were waiting for was the convoy from Atahualpa's northern territory, Ecuador, one of the most eagerly anticipated of all because Quito was the seat of Atahualpa's power. However, Ecuador was now under the command of Rumiñahui, whose name in Quichua means "Stone Face." As well as having fought alongside Atahualpa in the campaigns in the north, Rumiñahui was, like Huáscar, a half brother to the captive king and had witnessed first-hand the carnage at Cajamarca. It was he who had led the unarmed

Indian troops from their encampments into the main square. And when Pizarro's cavalry attacked Atahualpa's litter, Rumiñahui was one of the few to make it back to the hills, later fleeing to Quito with the remnant of the army.

Because Ecuador was one of the richest gold-mining regions in the Inca empire, the Spanish fully expected Rumiñahui's tribute to dwarf anything they had seen so far. But on July 26, fearing that Rumiñahui had secret orders to attack the Spanish positions and would never deliver the ransom, Pizarro reneged on his promise to Atahualpa and had him garroted in the same square where he had captured him eight months before.

Once again Father Valverde played a key role. In order to try Atahualpa on the trumped-up charges of fomenting rebellion, Pizarro needed the signature of someone supposedly above the fray. Valverde readily agreed to give his imprimatur, declaring that "the Inca, at all events, deserved death." Then, once Pizarro's tribunal had delivered the desired verdict and Atahualpa was waiting to be burned at the stake, it was Valverde who persuaded the Inca to be baptized, promising him that if he did so he would be spared immolation and instead "enjoy" the Christian death of strangulation. No sooner had Atahualpa been garroted, however, than Valverde reneged on his promise and burned the Inca's corpse. He then had him interred in the newly built church of San Francisco in Cajamarca, performing the funeral obsequies himself over the protests of Atahualpa's wailing wives and sisters.

In Andy's mind the priest's betrayal was further confirmation that the Llanganatis treasure was no myth. He pointed out that Inca tradition demanded that after death Atahualpa be mummified and buried with all the treasure he had accumulated during his reign so that the sun could call him back to another life on earth. Andy reasoned that by tricking Atahualpa into being baptized and then burning and interring his corpse in the newly constructed church at Cajamarca, Valverde was hoping to keep all the gold for the Spanish.

"But Atahualpa's corpse didn't remain in Cajamarca!" Andy suddenly declared. "As soon as Pizarro left for Cuzco, the Indians disinterred Atahualpa and transported his body north to Ecuador and the Llanganatis. Remember that point, Marcos; it could hold the key to the whole mystery!"

Andy pushed his bowl of noodles to one side and leaped to his feet. "*Vamos*—Let's go!"

The chauffeur, who had drifted off to sleep, snapped to attention like an obedient guard dog, sending the soy sauce bottle clattering from the table. I reached out a hand, catching it just in time.

"*Gracias,*" he whispered. But his eyes were more grateful still. Working for Andy must be exhausting. He did everything in a hurry, as if his life depended on it.

I looked up to see that Andy was already at the car and holding the door open—with me, at least, he was the perfect gentleman. He waited for me to take my seat before resuming his narrative. "If only Pizarro had held on, he would have got everything. Rumiñahui had left Quito and was just a few miles from Cajamarca when he heard of Pizarro's treachery."

According to the mestizo historian Garcilaso de la Vega (1539–1616), Rumiñahui's convoy was immense—seventy thousand *cargas* (llama-loads) of gold and silver weighing five thousand tons.* This was undoubtedly an exaggeration. Another late-sixteenth-century chronicler, Gonzalo Fernández de Oviedo, says that Rumiñahui was accompanied by fifteen thousand soldiers and sixty thousand *cargas* of gold and silver—four and a half thousand tons. But Pedro de Cieza de León, a Spanish soldier-turned-chronicler who passed through Peru just three years after the conquest and wrote his history fifty years before Garcilaso, put the size of the convoy at a far more conservative six hundred *cargas*, or forty-five tons. "Even so," said Andy, at current prices that would make the treasure worth "around $25 million."†

"Think of the wealth, Marcos. Incredible, no?"

Andy paused, lost in reverie. The town was behind us now, and we were speeding through prime cattle country past gated haciendas set well back from the road. I tried to visualize the ghostly train of llamas strung out along the length of the Andes, their saddlebags glinting in the sun, but the image wouldn't come. Andy was right, it *was* incredible. Had there really been as many as fifteen thousand soldiers en route to

---

*A Spanish *carga* was equivalent to 75 pounds. Therefore, 70,000 *cargas* would be 5,250,000 pounds.
†To be precise, 600 *cargas* is 45,000 pounds, or 720,000 ounces. At $350 a troy ounce that would give the treasure a value of $25.2 million.

Cajamarca? And if this treasure had been on its way to Peru, why carry it all the way back to northern Ecuador and the Llanganatis? Wouldn't it have been far simpler to hide the treasure along the route?

Andy had read my mind. "There are many rumors about where that gold is buried, Marcos, but no one knows what I do. I am very close now"—that phrase again—"I can feel it. It's only a matter of time."

What information was Andy privy to? He had dropped so many hints that I was desperate to ask him about Blake's maps and letters. But we had only just met, and I didn't want to put him on his guard, so instead I changed the subject.

"It's so much money, Andy. What would you do if you found it?"

"Oh, I'm not interested in the money. In any case, the Ecuadorian government would never allow me to take the treasure out of the country. No, the thing is to find it. Imagine what a story that would be, Marcos—a story to astound the world!"

Andy's declaration left me momentarily speechless. On the face of it, it was a preposterous claim of course: everyone cared about the money. Andy's statement was also misleading in another sense: while the government had vowed to safeguard the Inca artifacts for the nation, legally 50 percent of the hoard belonged to the finder, and the government was obliged to compensate him or her according to the price the items might fetch at auction, which was potentially far more than their weight in gold. Nevertheless, there was something irresistible about Andy's enthusiasm. Whereas if Roland found the treasure I suspected he would try to keep his discovery secret as long as possible, if Andy found it he would broadcast the news far and wide. Being first, that was the real prize. And Andy was right: if he succeeded in finding the treasure, everyone would know his name. No longer would he be the man who had *nearly* beaten Jesse Owens's world record.

For the last half hour the haciendas had been growing more infrequent, the land wilder and more unkempt. Palms and giant bamboos overhung the roadway, forming an arch of steaming vegetation through which a truck would have been hard-pressed to pass. But like a blowdart hurtling toward its target, we shot through the green tunnel at speed, coming to a halt in front of a massive wrought-iron gate.

The chauffeur honked twice, and an Indian girl with tangled black hair and startling blue eyes appeared at the window of the gatehouse, followed by a blond-haired boy: her brother. Andy made a joke about the American construction workers who'd built the highway—something about the nights being long and the local women obliging—and ordered the girl to unfasten the padlock. She moved warily, as if the gates were the bars of a cage and the car a savage animal that might rear up and devour her at any moment. In the background, I imagined animals being hurriedly corralled and grass being clipped as word spread that the *patrón* had arrived.

"This is it," Andy announced. "Pacaritambo—Dawn Inn."

We roared up a rutted mud track to emerge at the crest of a hill in open pastureland. There was no sign of a house, just acre upon acre of rolling green fields.

"When I came here in 1972, this was all jungle," Andy said proudly. "In those days there was no road. I had to walk twenty kilometers from the nearest town and swim two rivers. Now I have 1,800 tropical milking cows and 600 horses. We grow maize, bananas, barley . . ."

He trailed off, a look of genuine contentment spreading across his face. Andy had been born to privilege. He told me his father had acquired a volcanic spring in Machachi in the central Ecuadorian highlands in the 1920s, later bottling and selling the gaseous mineral water by the crate-load under the brand name Guitig—Tesalia, a still mineral water, was added later. The water business had made the family millions, enabling Andy to attend the best schools in Europe and North America. But he yearned to achieve something in his own right, and when the government began offering lots for sale in the jungle, he decided to swap his business suit for jeans and trek out to Pacaritambo.

"In those days there was no law here; this was the Wild West. To make the land mine, I had to defend it by force."

We drove to the edge of the field, and Andy unlocked the first in a series of gates. It seemed to take forever to reach his house. Every now and then a flatbed packed with farmhands rattled by, the truck's axles swinging alarmingly under the weight of the men.

"Well, one day things came to a head," Andy continued. "The squatters refused to leave, and there was a shoot-out."

"What happened?" I asked.

"Well, let's just say they never bothered me again."

I looked at Andy to see if he was joking, but his eyes were as black and hard as obsidian. Was it possible, I wondered, that he'd killed a man?

We had now reached the last gate—the tenth, I think. To the left were a series of low farm buildings and the metal rails of the cattle pens; to the right, the horses' stables and, in front of them, a dusty polo field. On the edge of the field the mangled remains of a light airplane lay nose down in the grass like a squashed fly. Three buzzards circled lazily overhead, their wings spread against the white heat of a tropical afternoon.

"This is my home," announced Andy as we drew into a banana grove.

It wasn't what I had been expecting. The house was raised up on bamboo stilts, with an iron staircase leading from ground level to a teak deck and an ornately carved veranda. Inside, Andy had gone for a colonial feel, with wicker chairs and reproductions of English hunting scenes hung beneath slowly revolving wooden ceiling fans. Next to the main house were purpose-built changing rooms for the polo players and a huge, rusting iron cage. The cage had once contained a baby ocelot, but the cub was long gone and all Andy had left were memories.

He showed me pictures: in one a younger Andy with more lustrous hair but the same urgent expression reared up on a young pony, Stetson held theatrically aloft like the Lone Ranger; in another, a group of Buenos Aires playboy types with white jodhpurs and hairy chests were gathered in a semicircle, leaning seductively on their polo mallets. Every now and again, I caught a glimpse of one of Andy's daughters and a glamorous woman in sunglasses, but the house contained none of the usual family portraits. Later I would learn why: Andy had been married three times and had ten children, but he was no longer on speaking terms with his ex-wives and complained that "even now they are conspiring with lawyers to rob me of the rest of my fortune." ("In this country," he added ruefully, "the best lawyer is the one who buys the conscience of the judge first.")

We sat at a long table on the veranda, and Andy rang a small handbell. Moments later, Andy's chef, a doleful young man with large brown eyes, emerged from the kitchen with two whiskeys, followed soon afterward by a vegetable broth and two plates of grilled chicken. I did most of the eating, Andy most of the talking. He hardly touched his food, ringing the bell only to call for refills of his glass.

Andy explained that although he had grown up in Ecuador, he had first heard about Valverde's gold in 1937, when he read a report in the *Los Angeles Examiner* about Erskine Loch's expedition the previous year. The article fascinated him, but because he was enrolled in a military academy in California at the time, he simply filed it away. To hear Andy tell it, the 1940s were the best years of his life. At the academy he had not only excelled at athletics but been much in demand on the football field. During World War II, he'd served in the U.S. Army and gained a reputation as a crack shot and a top combat instructor. After the war, he returned to California, where—on his vet's salary—he was able to rent a bungalow near the beach in Santa Monica. According to Andy, his neighbors were Tyrone Power and Ronald Reagan—"in those days he was Ree-gan, not Ray-gan," Andy said with a cackle.

He glossed over the next few years. I had heard that he had been a gambler in his youth, and I suspected that much of his time had been spent in casinos or else jetting around the world in pursuit of beautiful women. It wasn't until 1948, when he returned to Ecuador and his father showed him a copy of *Notes of a Botanist on the Amazon and Andes,* that his interest in the treasure was revived. Andy read the book at his father's bungalow beside the volcanic springs at Machachi that were the source of his bottled-water fortune.

"From that moment my mind was fixed on the treasure," he told me. "It was as if the mountains were calling me. Despite everything that has happened to me since, I've never lost that conviction."

He stared at me, his gaze steely and unflinching. Had it really been like that, I wondered, or had the Llanganatis simply been another challenge like the hundred meters, a way of justifying his haute lifestyle and a goal that, having set himself, Andy was unable or unwilling to relinquish? To hear him tell it, those early expeditions were certainly frustrating.

On the first, in November 1952, Andy faithfully followed the directions in the *derrotero*. But just as Brooks had found, after the fourth day Valverde's guide was useless: Andy could not find the "deep dry ravine" that led to the Way of the Incas or the mountain "all of *Margasitas*" that should have lain to the southeast of Yana Cocha.

Convinced that the *derrotero* was wrong—or at least that Guzmán and others had misinterpreted it—Andy decided to clear all preconceptions from his mind and return to first premises. Echoing what Roland had told me, he said that by now he had discovered that in the seventeenth century, Ambato (or Hambato, as it was then known) had lain farther to the south. Standing on Guapa Mountain with his back to the old Ambato, Andy found that the *derrotero* oriented him to the northeast to a region known as the Roncadores. This was the very same region that the northernmost trail on Guzmán's map led through, the region peppered with lead, silver, and copper mines and the perplexing legends *"Muerte de Romero"* and *"Conspiración contra Conrado."*

"Well, it just so happened that there were three peaks in that direction, so off I went," he said.

Like his previous trip, it was a failure, but Andy did find a beautiful green lake. Not only that, but sitting on a rock one day, he slipped his knife into a crevice and removed a small chunk of silver.

"I was convinced that if I kept looking, I would also find gold in those mountains, but we never did. I must have gone back three times in all."

Andy's companions in those days were Guido Boschetti, the son of a famous Italian alpinist who had previously been into the Llanganatis in the 1930s, and Ben Butler, a big Texan with a booming voice who was then a fixture of the expatriate scene in Quito. When they limped back to Quito after weeks of pounding rain and chilling fogs, it was Butler who, seated around a bar, put flesh on their exploits and turned them into the stuff of legend.

"Ben used to say," Andy adopted a Texas drawl, "'It's so windy up thyaar you need four men to hold on to yure hat and when you open yure mouth yure pants blow off.'"

Andy slapped his thighs and laughed with glee. It sounded like a well-rehearsed line. But not all his anecdotes were so amusing.

"You know the Indians believe the treasure is cursed," he interjected at one point. "They call the Llanganatis a *tierra encantada*—a bewitched land. They believe there's a *duende*—a little man like a leprechaun— who wanders around up there and drives you mad."

On one expedition Andy and his party of Indian carriers had reached a wide gorge. It was fifteen feet across, and everyone took turns jumping it: Boschetti first, followed by Andy and the porters. Eventually it came to the last man, an Indian who had started the expedition full of spirit but had become gradually more lethargic and listless as the days had worn on. Andy screamed at him to follow, but the man stood rooted to the spot, as though in a trance.

"Eventually, without warning, he threw his machete across and we all had to duck. Then, without tying the safety rope around his waist, he leaped."

The Indian fell against Andy, and then toppled backward, pulling Andy down with him into the gorge.

"He wouldn't let go of me—he kept whispering, 'Come with me, come with me, we both die.' Just as we were about to slip over the edge together, I pushed him away. I had to, to save myself."

Andy saw the Indian grab a tree branch on the way down, and then fall headlong into the river. Afterward, he climbed down to look for him, wading into the freezing water until it was dark, but it was useless and he had to return to Píllaro without him. According to Andy, a year later the Indian's body was found intact wedged between two huge boulders. The cold had preserved him in perfect condition.

Andy dismissed the curse. "Like all superstitions, the curse affects you only if you believe in it," he said. But later, when the drink had got the better of him, he returned to the story, morbidly replaying the moment he had had to let go. "That man wanted to die, *he wanted to die!*" he told me.

Between 1956 and 1962 Andy didn't make any expeditions to the Llanganatis. The family water company was taking up more and more of his time, and as soon as he finished at the office, he would take off for his ranch to check on his cattle and make sure the settlers weren't encroaching. Then, in 1963, armed with "new information," he leased a helicopter from the Ecuadorian military and flew over Cerro Hermoso.

Andy was reluctant to tell me what his new information had been— "Later, Marcos, we have plenty of time"—and once again I found myself wondering if it had something to do with Blake's letters and maps. In general, treasure hunters had given Cerro Hermoso, which lay far to the south of Valverde's Way, a wide berth. Indeed, Guzmán had erroneously labeled it the "Hydro Volcán de Siete Bocas" (the Volcano of Seven Mouths), an error that was not corrected until 1873, when a German geologist, Wilhelm Reiss, climbed to the top (seventy-five years later, Reiss's findings were confirmed by another German geologist, Walther Sauer, who declared it to be a massive granite extrusion that had been forced from the earth millennia before by the collision of the Nazca and South American plates). But I sensed that this wasn't the moment to interrogate Andy about Blake and Chapman. Fueled by the whiskey and the memory of his death-defying flight to Cerro Hermoso, he was already flying high over El Oriente.

"We caused quite a stir when we landed in Baños," Andy said, chuckling. "The village children had never seen a helicopter before—few people in Ecuador had."

Accompanied by a young Indian pilot straight out of flying school and another explorer, Andy took off from Baños on February 8. The helicopter was a Cessna, one of the only models the company, better known for its light airplanes, ever made and a prototype that had been rejected in the United States as unsafe.

For the first ten minutes they followed the gorge of the Río Pastaza east, overflying the Shell Mera trucks bringing oil up the dirt road from Puyo. Then, at the point where the Río Topo joined the Pastaza, they swung north, following the Topo's drainage until they reached Cerro Hermoso.

In all, the flight took thirty minutes. Andy's idea had been merely to pass over the mountain and check out his information before returning later to make a proper investigation on foot. Besides a little water, they had no provisions and no equipment.

Unfortunately, as they swung in low over the mountain to take a sight line—later Andy would reveal the significance of this maneuver—they were buffeted by winds, and the rear rotor jagged on the side of a cliff. The blade shattered instantly, and the helicopter plunged downward, spinning toward a small island in the middle of the river. Fortunately, a bog on the island cushioned their fall, halting the rotation of the helicopter. Thick foliage prevented them from sinking further, but they were now stuck, and when they turned the engine over, a spark from the exhaust ignited the tall grasses. Andy threw himself to the ground, thinking the gas tank was about to blow, but by now the pilot had seen what was happening and had grabbed an extinguisher.

"Thank God for that quick-thinking Indian," said Andy. "Otherwise, we would almost certainly have been goners."

The helicopter was now badly charred, and they had no parts to repair the damaged rotor. Not only that, but the radio was shot, and as theirs had been the only serviceable helicopter in Ecuador, there seemed little hope of an air rescue.

Figuring it would take several days for a land-based search party to find them, Andy went ashore to look for food. But they were trapped in a gorge beneath the sheer walls of Cerro Hermoso. The only way out was to climb to the shoulder of the summit some three thousand feet above the river.

His hands tearing on the jagged rocks, Andy struggled up the near-vertical cliff face, using the trunks and branches of trees for leverage. Then, just when he was thinking of turning back, he reached a ledge and hauled his body onto it.

Andy was now standing high above the Río Topo, looking straight down at the island and the marooned helicopter. Above him the granite walls of Cerro Hermoso continued inexorably upward.

With renewed heart Andy continued to climb, pacing himself this time. The rocks were peppered with cavities and small openings that trapped the rainwater, and in a number of places Andy was intrigued to see that the water had worn tunnels in the rock. Then, about halfway up, he stumbled upon an opening that was deeper than the rest. Thick vines, dripping with moisture, overhung the entrance, behind which lay a platform of level rock and a receding wall containing another, smaller entrance. Parting the mossy vegetation, Andy crawled through to find himself inside a tunnel maybe thirty meters deep. It was so dark he couldn't see to the end of it, but it seemed to lead into the heart of the mountain.

Andy inched his way along the passage on his hands and knees, listening as the sound of running water grew louder. Suddenly he stopped dead. Instead of touching a floor of solid rock beneath him, his hand grasped empty air. The tunnel had become a vertical shaft, down which a cascade of ice-cold mountain water was rushing. Recalling the lines from the *derrotero*, Andy could barely contain his excitement:

And to reach the third mountain, if thou canst not pass in front of the *socabón*, it is the same thing to pass at the back of it, for the water of the lake falls into it.

Could this be the entrance to Valverde's famous tunnel? The entrance certainly resembled a church porch, just as Valverde had described it. But if so, where was the gold? Perhaps Andy had approached the *socabón* from the wrong side, and the treasure lake and *guayra* where the Indians had smelted the metal lay above him, on the opposite side of the mountain.

Andy explored the opening as best he could. After the shock of the crash and the imperatives of survival, he had all but forgotten the treasure; now his enthusiasm came surging back. Unfortunately, it was already very late, and he had to return. Convinced that his information had been good and that he had been right to scout Cerro Hermoso, Andy descended to the river, determined to return to the mountain when and if he ever reached Baños again and could organize a proper expedition. But when, toward nightfall, he found his companions, he saw the situation was grave. They had had no food, and the pilot looked ill. Not only that, but there had been no response to their distress signal.

The next four days passed in a dream. To keep his team's strength up, Andy collected berries and any other plants he thought might be edible. But the plants gave them diarrhea, and the pilot contracted pneumonia. Then, on the fifth day, when they had all but given up hope, they heard a loud buzzing in the distance. Looking up, they saw a Helio Courier, a small plane designed to fly at low speeds without stalling, coming toward them from below the clouds.

"We couldn't believe it. The next thing we knew a man's voice came over the radio asking if we needed any help."

The voice belonged to a pilot from the Summer Institute of Linguistics, a missionary group that combed the Amazon looking for new tribes to whom it could bring the word of God. Andy told the pilot they'd crashed and needed a new rotor blade, and the missionary radioed back to say he would see what he could do.

A few days later, the pilot returned. "He had bad news and good news. The bad news was that no one was coming to rescue us. The good news was he had a package for us."

The next moment a parcel came hurtling out of the sky. "It contained food, medicine, and three Bibles." Andy paused, laughing at the missionaries' sense of priorities. "I think I still have my copy somewhere around here."

Over the next few weeks the pilot continued making regular drops while the air force sent to Miami for a replacement rotor and for instructions on how to install it. ("My Indian pilot had only three hundred hours of flying time," Andy explained, "and none of us were mechanics.") Eventually the new blade arrived, but when it came time to drop it, the package landed in mid-river. Fortunately, it wedged between two boulders, but the parachute threatened to drag it downstream, and Andy had to saw through the cables with a sharp rock to stop its being swept away.

Having recovered the package, the pilot patiently set to work, but no sooner had he repaired the rotor than they realized they needed new batteries and had to radio for another drop. By now they had spent nearly a month on the island, and the snow on Cerro Hermoso and other peaks was starting to melt. If they didn't leave soon, the river would begin to rise and the island—together with their hope of escape—would be gone.

Day after day it continued foggy and overcast. The visibility was so poor they couldn't risk a takeoff. Then, on the evening of the thirty-third day, the clouds suddenly parted and a small patch of blue appeared above their heads.

"Quickly," Andy shouted, "this is it!"

The helicopter shuddered free from the bog, then soared toward the blue hole. Flying on instinct, they continued up, glad to have escaped from the island and the cursed mountains. Then, with night nearly upon them, Andy spotted the lights of the Shell Mera trucks glimmering on the horizon. He ordered the pilot to plot a course toward them, and they followed the trucks all the way back to the air force base at Puyo. "No one could believe it; everyone had given us up for dead."

The next day a colonel from the air force showed Andy a telegram he'd received from one of the army's jungle outposts. It read: "We discovered the remains of a helicopter in the jungle. Two men are crazy and naked in a tree."

Andy paused, his eyes focused off into the distance. I studied him more closely. It was late and his eyes were puffy from the heat and the alcohol. Resuming his story, Andy said his diet of tree roots and river water had left him weak and emaciated for months. But although he didn't feel up to returning to Cerro Hermoso in person, he sent others in his stead. Their reports convinced him that the cave he had discovered was significant. For years afterward, he said, he had been fixated on the mountain.

By now I had become desperate to ask him what had led him to Cerro Hermoso in the first place. Before I could say anything, Andy excused himself from the table and disappeared into his bedroom. I assumed he had gone to the toilet—we had now been drinking for several hours, and he had not relieved himself once—but after waiting several minutes and hearing no sound, I got up and knocked on the door.

There was no answer.

Tentatively I entered his room, nearly tripping over a huge animal-skin rug—the remains, I later learned, of a jaguar Andy had shot on the ranch in the 1970s. The TV was tuned to CNN, but no one was watching; instead, there on the bed lay Andy, fully clothed and snoring. Above his head a holster containing his pistol dangled casually from the bedstead.

THE FOLLOWING MORNING I AWOKE AT SEVEN TO FIND ANDY ALREADY seated at the table, drumming his fingers impatiently. He was eager to inspect the ranch and suggested I drink my coffee quickly so that we could saddle up. Andy had selected for me a young mare—what he described as a "trotting horse"—with a long, unkempt mane that he said I should grab on to if she got too frisky, and after he'd shown me how to hold the reins, we set off across the fields accompanied by his farm manager and an assistant.

At first everything went smoothly. The sky was heavy, presaging rain. But the rain never came, and despite having awoken with a hangover, I kept close to Andy, gently egging on my horse with a sharp heel whenever she threatened to fall behind.

Andy was inordinately proud of his ranch. "Farming is in my blood," he explained. When his father had been a young man, the government had also given him a tract of land in the jungle. Like Andy, he had set out to tame it, importing tropical milking cows and his own ice-making machine. But Andy's father never mastered the science of breeding cows in the tropics, and after a series of floods washed away his crops, he abandoned the farm and decided to concentrate on his more lucrative water business.

Andy, however, had studied animal husbandry and served on the Ecuadorian cattle ranchers association. In the 1980s he had negotiated generous credit terms with the World Health Organization for the importation of foot-and-mouth vaccine, with the result that the disease had virtually been eradicated from Ecuador. His own herd, he boasted, had once numbered five thousand. But for various reasons—whether fatigue or the demands of his ex-wives and his children Andy was unclear—he had since been forced to reduce his holdings considerably.

We stopped by the pens and watched the farm manager corral the cows and inject them with antibiotics. Every now and then Andy would wander over to the cattle bars and lay his hands reassuringly on a Jersey. Later, at the stables, he demonstrated the same concern for the horses, and I was reminded of a picture he had shown me the day before in which he had been cradling the ocelot cub in his arms. With his employees and people in general Andy was fierce and combative, but animals seemed to bring out his tender side. However, with Andy, such moments could pass in a flash.

At around the midpoint of our tour we reached a hill overlooking a deep gully, and Andy galloped straight down, his men following nonchalantly behind. Cautiously I pulled the reins tight, restraining my mount.

"Let the horse be," he snapped irritably, "she knows what to do."

At the bottom we tethered the horses to a tree trunk and waded across a bog to inspect a cornfield on the other side. But my poor equestrian skills had been noted, and for the rest of the day I was treading on eggshells.

After we returned to his house, lunch began as it had the day before—amicably and with whiskey aperitifs—but this time the food never arrived. I began by asking Andy the question that had been nagging me since the previous night: what was the new information that had so excited him in 1963? In order to understand that, he replied, he first had to go back to 1958, when he was working for his father and traveling frequently between Quito and the coast. One day, as a favor, he had stopped at Santo Domingo de los Colorados, a subtropical mountain village about two hours from Quito, to deliver some letters to a friend of his father's. The friend was Commander George Miller Dyott, a former flier in the Royal Naval Air Service and a legendary explorer. Then in his seventies and retired, Commander Dyott—as he was known—had enjoyed enough adventures to fill several lifetimes.

Born in New York in 1883, Dyott had started life as an electrical engineer and had once held out hopes of a business partnership with Thomas Edison. When Edison rejected him, he turned to plane design. He claimed he was present at Kitty Hawk in 1903 when the Wright brothers had launched the first powered airplane, and by 1910 he had begun designing and building his own monoplanes at Hempstead Plains in New York. When World War I broke out, he joined the Royal Naval Air Service as a wing commander, gaining a reputation as a daring night flier and designing and building the Dyott Battleship, a bomber-cum-aerial-survey-plane that was later used to carry out geological explorations in Africa.

Following the war he traveled widely, popping up in locations as diverse as the Yucatán peninsula, Peru, and Bengal. In India he was known as a crack shot both with a camera and with a gun, once stalking a man-eating tiger that had become a nuisance to a local maharaja. And in Peru he pioneered the flight corridors over the Andes that are still in use today.

Dyott's lifelong love affair with Ecuador began in 1924 (he settled permanently in the country in 1935), when he visited the Andes on a photographic assignment for *National Geographic* magazine and became the first non-Indian to climb the volcano Sangay. Next he went in search of head-hunting Indians in El Oriente—an expedition that resulted in a book, *On the Trail of the Unknown in the Wilds of Ecuador and the Amazon*, and a series of vivid photographs that consolidated his reputation as an explorer. But the escapade that made his name and fixed him firmly in the public's imagination was his hunt for Colonel Fawcett in 1928.

A retired British army officer turned explorer, Percy Harrison Fawcett had gone missing in Brazil's Mato Grosso with his son, Jack, and a friend, Raleigh Rimmel, three years before. Fawcett had become obsessed with the stories of a lost city of gold—a city he referred to only as "Z" and that he believed lay somewhere along Brazil's unexplored jungle frontier with Bolivia. Now Lloyd's of London and the North American Newspaper Alliance wanted to establish the truth and commissioned Dyott to retrace Fawcett's route.

Dyott spent several days surveying Mato Grosso by air. Then—accompanied by sixty-four bullocks, twenty-six men, and four huge folding canoes—he trekked into Mato Grosso on foot. The expedition lasted several weeks, but though Dyott recovered an identification tag from one of Fawcett's trunks and encountered a peculiar race of pygmies, he could find no trace of the missing colonel.

In his subsequent book, *Man Hunting in the Jungle*, Dyott argued that Fawcett had almost certainly been killed by wild forest Indians, and, while the book didn't endear him to Fawcett's family, he was soon inundated with other assignments, including a request to undertake an expedition to the Llanganatis.

Whether it was the whiskey or the time of day I don't know, but Andy seemed to mellow visibly as he recalled his meetings with Dyott. On his way to and from the coast Andy would stop regularly at Dyott's ranch, and over dinner the septuagenarian explorer gradually revealed the mission and information that had brought him to the Llanganatis.

"Dyott had gone into those mountains in '47, and again in '48, but on the last occasion he hurt his knee so badly he had to quit," Andy recalled wistfully. "I think he was looking for someone younger to take up the cause."

According to Andy, Dyott loved mysteries. It was rumored that following World War I, he had been the head of intelligence for the British security service in India and during World War II had run Allied spying missions against Nazis in Bolivia. "The treasure appealed to Dyott's love of cloak-and-dagger," said Andy. "It was a puzzle he just couldn't leave alone."

In 1945 Dyott had received a letter from a woman in Philadelphia—Andy didn't mention her name—containing a series of letters and two maps. The maps had been disguised so as to make it difficult to identify the region they described, but the letters indicated that they referred to an Inca treasure hidden in the mountains of eastern Ecuador and purported to reveal the location of both the treasure cave *and* a lost Inca gold mine.

Blake's letters and maps, I thought.

The documents had come to light in a peculiar way. Some years before, the woman had inherited a house beside the sea from her grandfather, an old sea captain known familiarly as "Uncle Sammy." The summer house was located in New England, near the coast of Maine—Andy wasn't sure exactly where—and overlooked a small island. One day, the woman's husband was browsing Uncle Sammy's bookshelf when he came across a copy of his King James Bible. Inside was a note telling him to look inside another book, *Knapsack and Rifle*. But though her husband searched everywhere for the book, he couldn't find it and consigned the intriguing message to the back of his mind.

Then, about a year later, the couple's sons were rummaging in the attic when they came across an old box full of books. Inside was an adventure story set during the American Civil War. Its title was *Knapsack and Rifle*. When the boys began turning the pages, a sheet of paper fell from the binding. On it were written the words: "All about the Inca treasure in Ecuador in the hollow tree on the island."

The boys quickly rowed to the island, which they knew well, having played there when they were younger, and found the tree. Attached to one of the branches was a wire, and nestled in the hollow of the oak at the other end was a flagon of whiskey containing the letters and two maps.

"The maps showed sections of the Llanganatis—though the boys did not know this at the time," said Andy.

"And the letters?"

Andy paused.

"The letters were addressed to Uncle Sammy and signed 'Barth Blake.'"

I held Andy's gaze, not daring to move. I didn't want him to know that I had already heard about Blake, that he and Chapman were the reason I had returned to Ecuador, the reason I was now sitting on his porch drinking whiskey. I wanted him to think he was telling me the story for the very first time.

Andy took a long, deep draft of whiskey and lit a candle. The sun had begun to set behind the banana grove, casting long shadows on the porch. My neck and back were dripping with perspiration, but Andy was oblivious. We had been drinking since lunchtime, and he was now in another place.

He asked if he could borrow a piece of paper, and I ripped a page from my notebook. Andy stared at it for a moment, then traced a line from memory, adding what looked like an X and a phrase that I couldn't make out. He handed the paper back to me.

"This is Blake's first map," said Andy.

Up close I could see that he had drawn a peak in the shape of an inverted *V* with a bump or ledge protruding from one side, and that the *X* was really a cross. Along the bottom he had written, "Look for the cross and 4 to L."

I wanted to ask him what the enigmatic phrase meant, but before I could do so, he held up his hand theatrically and asked for another sheet of paper. He then traced another design and scribbled more phrases before returning the paper to me with a flourish.

"This is Blake's second map," he said.

On it Andy had drawn two mountains, one in front of the other, and at the point where the slope of the smaller mountain intersected with the larger, he had written, "gold in hidden cave here," and, a little to the north, "Location of probably the world's biggest gold mine." Along the flank of the larger mountain he'd also drawn a meandering line marked "Inca path."

Andy closed his eyes and recited from memory: "Everything coincides with Valverde's map except for the Inca path, which is longer than I ever thought."

What did he mean by "Valverde's map"? Was this another fragment from Blake's letters? I was eager for an answer, but Andy wasn't to be interrupted.

"Blake was a sailor from Nova Scotia," he explained eventually. "Dyott thought he may have been a captain in the Royal Navy or possibly the merchant marine—he wasn't sure. Blake and Uncle Sammy had been planning an expedition to the Llanganatis together, which is why Blake had sent him the maps and letters. But their expedition never happened."

In 1886, Andy said, Blake had set sail from the east coast of North America on a schooner bound for Panama and Peru. By November the ship had rounded Cape Horn, and by December it had reached Callao. But on the next leg of the journey to Ecuador it had run aground—in Andy's version of the story only the schooner's rudder was damaged, not the mast as well—and Blake had been forced to put in for repairs at Guayaquil.

"The delay was fortuitous," said Andy. "It wasn't Blake's first time in Ecuador, you see. In one letter to Uncle Sammy he explained that he'd already been here several times looking for Atahualpa's hoard!"

Accompanied by George Edwin Chapman, Blake set off from Guayaquil, riding over the western cordillera of the Andes to Ambato, where they fitted out their expedition. They then made for Píllaro, where they hired porters and mules to take them as far as Los Anteojos.

"Those are the Spectacle Lakes mentioned in Valverde's guide. I assume you're familiar with the guide?"

I nodded.

"Good. But did you know that Blake also had a second document— Valverde's map? That's what he was referring to when he wrote to Uncle Sammy."

So Andy *had* been quoting from one of Blake's letters. By now I was bursting with questions: What was the name of the woman who had sent Dyott the documents in 1945 (Andy still hadn't told me)? How had they come into Andy's possession, and did he still have a copy of Valverde's map? But once again I held my tongue.

It was now March 1887, Andy continued, and the start of the rainy season. At first Blake and Chapman followed the classic route of the *derrotero*, rounding the southern shore of Yana Cocha so as to leave the black lake on the left before continuing east into the Llanganatis range along the right bank of the Parca Yacu. But instead of turning south when they reached the area where Guzmán had shown the Volcán de Margasitas and the cross marking the death of Father Longo, the mariners continued east, past Chuspi Pongo and the Rivera de los Llanganatis, to a narrow ravine—the Cascada de las Tundas.

"At this point Blake and Chapman suddenly veered north," declared Andy triumphantly. "Valverde's map contained different information from the guide, you see, information about a lost Inca gold mine." Andy jabbed at the legend on Blake's second map. "That's what Blake means when he writes 'location of probably the world's biggest gold mine.'"

So Roland and Loch weren't the only people who believed there was a gold mine in the mountains; Andy believed it, too.

However, according to Andy, Blake and Chapman had no interest in working the mine. Spruce had simply directed the mariners to the Cascada de las Tundas because it was from there that Valverde's map indicated they could identify the "strait passage between two mountains" mentioned in the *derrotero*—a passage that, according to Andy, led them back across the Parca Yacu toward the Páramo de Soguillas, the high, treeless moor where Colonel Brooks was to lose his way two decades later. It was here that Andy thought Blake had picked up Valverde's Way of the Incas—a way that, if his letter to Uncle Sammy was to be believed, had proved "longer" than the line drawn on Valverde's map.

"That path led directly to the treasure cave, Marcos! They entered it in early April."

Andy closed his eyes and recited once more from memory: "It is impossible for me to describe to you the wealth that now lies in that distant cave marked on my map but I could not remove it alone, nor could a thousand men."

In the next sentence Blake informed Uncle Sammy he had to go back to sea for a while and asked him to take "good care of my maps and papers." Andy then quoted verbatim apparently from the rest of the letter, recalling Blake's description of the "incredible" silver and gold figures that had shone at him from the gloom of the treasure cave. "Maybe you cannot believe me when I tell you. There are thousands of gold and silver pieces of Inca and pre-Inca handicraft, the most beautiful goldsmith works you are not able to imagine."

Andy suddenly stopped reciting and grabbed my arm. "Think of the wealth, Marcos! A king's ransom in gold—more than fifteen thousand men could carry on their backs!"

I forced a smile between clenched teeth: Andy may have been in his seventies, but he still had a grip like steel.

"Blake wrote that it was only by the merest chance that he found the cave," he continued, relinquishing my arm. "Imagine, Marcos. Hundreds of golden idols encrusted with the finest emeralds in Ecuador!"

To hear Andy describe it, it was almost as if *he* had been inside that cave. At this point I couldn't resist interrupting his narrative.

"So that means Blake found Valverde's *socabón* and removed the treasure?"

Andy raised a hand imperiously.

"Patience, Marcos, I'm coming to that. Yes, Blake removed eighteen of the best artifacts and a handful of emeralds, but he had to leave the bulk of the treasure behind. It was four days back to Píllaro, and he and Chapman still had all their food and equipment to carry."

According to Andy, it was difficult to tell from Blake's map—the second map, that is—where exactly Valverde's treasure cave lay. Some thought it was on Cerro Hermoso, but others—including Dyott—thought it lay farther north on the slopes of Cerro Negro or Las Torres. If it was on Cerro Hermoso, then, to return to Píllaro, Blake and Chapman would have had to head northwest, contouring along the knife-edge ridges and buttresses of the Jaramillo range—"Farallón y Precipice de Yana Rumi" on Guzmán's map. If it was on Cerro Negro, they would have had to cross the Páramo de Soguillas—the high, treeless moor where Isabela Brooks met her death—to emerge somewhere in the vicinity of Zunchu-Urcu, known on modern maps as Cerro Pan de Azúcar (Sugarloaf Mountain).

"But Chapman never made it," Andy suddenly declared. "Somewhere in those godforsaken mountains he succumbed to illness and died, hence the cross on Blake's first map."

Dyott believed the cross marked the spot where Blake had buried his companion after they had become lost in the *neblina*. But according to Dyott, the cross didn't merely mark Chapman's grave; it was also a clue to where the treasure was hidden.

"Blake wrote, 'Look for the cross and 4 to L.' In other words, look for Chapman's grave, then four degrees to the left, and you will be directly in line with the treasure cave. At least, that was Dyott's theory . . ."

Andy trailed off, lost in thought. If Blake's maps were so valuable, I wondered, why was he sharing them with a complete stranger? Why wasn't he off looking for the treasure himself or, if he no longer had the strength and energy, sponsoring someone to look on his behalf?

"Blake eventually stumbled out of the Llanganatis in early May," Andy continued. "He was weak and exhausted, but he wrote immediately to Uncle Sammy, describing the contents of the cave and enclosing the first map—the map with the cross."

When Blake reached North America, Andy said, he wrote again to

Uncle Sammy, enclosing the second map, in which he gave the location of both the gold mine and the cave. He then returned to England.

"Don't you see, he sent the maps to Uncle Sammy for safekeeping. His plan was to return when he had raised enough money for a second expedition. But Blake never made it. Five years later, on his return to North America in 1892, he was lost at sea—in all probability, pushed overboard off the coast of Halifax." His last words to Uncle Sammy were, "If something should happen to me . . . look for the Reclining Woman and all your problems are solved."

I pulled a face. Andy had told the story well, adding many details I had never heard before, such as the location of the Inca gold mine, but the whole thing still struck me as most improbable. How had two British sailors—if indeed they *were* British—succeeded in crossing the *paramo* and finding both the gold mine and the treasure cave without the aid of Indian porters? Moreover, what had become of the artifacts Blake had removed from the cave? Had these also fallen conveniently overboard?

Then there was the message in Uncle Sammy's Bible and the discovery in "the hollow tree on the island." It sounded like something from the pages of Haggard or Stevenson. Finally there was the question of how Blake had come by a document as precious as Valverde's map. Were he and Chapman in league with Spruce? Had the botanist passed Blake the map in the hope that it would make them rich?

Despite the whiskey and the heat, the story struck me as a fantasy— just the sort of tale an old man would make up for the amusement of his grandsons. Andy sensed my skepticism. He said that, like me, Dyott had doubted the story at first. To make sure he wasn't being hoaxed, he'd traveled to Philadelphia to interview the woman and examine Blake's letters to Uncle Sammy and his copy of the King James Bible. That's when he made another startling discovery. Holding the Bible up to the light, Dyott noticed tiny pinpricks under certain letters in the Book of Judges. When he put the letters together, they spelled out the phrases "Atahualpa's gold in the lake of Marcasitas [*sic*]" and "treasure in dead volcano by extinct lake." The woman also showed Dyott a telegram sent from Los Angeles to New York via Western Union and dated June 1897. The telegram, which did not record the name of the sender, read: "Tell John that Atahualpa's hoard has been found in a cave in a mountain next to an extinct lake."

The woman had no idea who John might be, but Dyott quickly established that Uncle Sammy had never been to South America and didn't have the detailed knowledge of Ecuadorian place-names that would have allowed him to forge Blake's letters. That left just two possibilities—either Blake had made the whole thing up or his letters and maps were genuine.

"Can I see the letters and maps?" I asked suddenly.

"I'm afraid not," said Andy. "You see, Dyott never gave them to me."

Andy explained that Dyott had kept Blake's letters and maps in an envelope at his ranch. During their talks he would sometimes fetch a document from the envelope and show it to Andy. But he would not allow him to examine the document for very long, and when their conversation was over, he would return it to the envelope for safekeeping.

Coming at the end of such a long and detailed explanation, Andy's claim perturbed me. Was he telling the truth? After all, if Dyott had never allowed him to make a copy of the letters, how did he know he was quoting Blake accurately? And how, if Dyott had never allowed him to examine the letters, did he know that Dyott hadn't simply made the whole thing up?

There was also a further possibility. What if Blake was, like the sea captains of pirate fiction, a practiced spinner of yarns? What if he had been leading Uncle Sammy up the garden path for his own amusement?

Andy shot me an irritated look. He was on his fifth whiskey and wasn't in the mood to be questioned. "My memory's perfect," he barked. "Besides, I kept notes of all our conversations."

He reached into a drawer and pulled out a frayed folder containing a sheaf of typewritten pages and a dog-eared blotter. Opening the pad, he ran his finger along the lines, muttering and grunting contentedly.

"Listen to this," he said finally, "Wednesday, 22 October 1947: a nice quiet day with no discordant notes . . ." Andy paused, chuckling over the Commander's turn of phrase (he appeared to be reading from Dyott's journal). "Sometimes I give up hope of being able to do anything worthwhile in this *cursed region*. Not the singlest description which I have read gives the slightest idea of the nature of the country and Loch's account is the most misleading of all."

"Dyott hated Loch," Andy interjected. "He thought he was a fool. Listen, here's another entry: 'I have set into some curious quests in my time but this is certainly by far the most strange.' This from a man who'd been into Mato Grosso on the trail of Fawcett!"

Andy slammed the blotter triumphantly shut and threw himself onto the floor. I thought he'd passed out with elation, but when I looked across, I saw that he was positioned facedown with his arms stretched above his head and the weight of his body resting on his fingertips.

"Let's see if you can do this," he said, tensing his fingers and raising his body off the ground. Obediently, I stretched out beside him, adopting the more conventional push-up position. "No, like this!" Andy yanked my arms straight and spread my fingers as though forming a bridge for a pool cue. "Now try it." I tensed my arms but nothing happened. I felt like a fish floundering on a beach. "You see, no one is built like me," he declared. "I'm unique."

He glared at me hard. Then, as if as an afterthought, he added: "I've been into those mountains 150 times. Nobody knows them like I do. I'm number one!"

There was real fury in his eyes now—the frustrated sprinter was daring me to challenge him. I tried to distract him by returning the conversation to Dyott. It was obvious Andy had obtained a detailed record of his two expeditions to the Llanganatis, but I still knew next to nothing about them. Had Dyott succeeded in deciphering Blake's maps, and if so, where did he think the treasure cave was located? Was it on the slopes of Cerro Hermoso, and was this why Andy had gone there in 1963? Or was it on some other mountain—Zunchu-Urcu perhaps, or Guzmán's mysterious Gran Volcán del Topo?

But Andy was not in the mood to answer questions. Until now, we had skirted the subject of my own treasure-hunting ambitions. As far as Andy was concerned, I was simply a writer after a story. But as the sun sank behind the banana grove and evening turned to night, he gave full vent to his suspicions.

"How can I talk to you about the Llanganatis?" he goaded. "You've never even been there."

Without mentioning Roland, I pointed out that I had already climbed Chimborazo and was hoping to make my first expedition in a few weeks.

"Hah! Chimborazo is nothing. You think you can just walk into the mountains and take the treasure out? I've been trying for fifty years. Believe me, I've seen the way you ride a horse. You won't survive a minute."

Hoping to deflect him onto a more conciliatory path, I asked him to describe the Llanganatis, but it was too late: the whiskey was speaking for him.

"Jan-ga-natis, with a hard *j*"—Andy spat the words with real venom—"hard, like the rocks and terrain you will find there. It's a barren, forlorn place—as Dyott put it, 'utterly devoid of noise.' When you're in those mountains, it rains continuously. And the mud, it gets everywhere—in your boots, under your nails. Trust me, you'll be cursing every second."

The subject of my book riled him even more.

"You write your book, and tomorrow I'll write a better one. No one knows what I do!"

Was this how Dyott had kept Andy at his table all those years? Was I now to be cast in the role of supplicant, gratefully accepting any scraps the old treasure hunter threw me?

I saw my life draining into a whiskey bottle as Andy plied me with a succession of ever more fantastic stories. His hunger was limitless. He was no longer the charming raconteur who had collected me at the airport, but Nosferatu. The evening would end only when he had sucked the last drop of vitality from me.

I longed for a mahogany crucifix or a shaft of bright sunlight, anything to break the spell. But it was late and I had no wish to antagonize Andy further, so I nodded meekly and made my excuses. It was a discussion we could resume in the morning.

That night I slept fitfully. I dreamed that I was suspended high above the Río Topo, clinging to the walls of Cerro Hermoso. The river was in full flood, and the rain came in sheets. Above me, through the fog, I could hear Andy's voice spurring me on. But each time I hauled myself up to the next foothold in the expectation of finding him waiting for me, he was gone. Eventually I reached a ledge and clambered over—much, I imagined, as Andy had done in 1963. But instead of emerging onto level ground, I discovered I was now perched on a pinnacle in front of a deep ravine. On the other side, his hand outstretched, Andy was beckoning me to jump.

"Come on, Marcos. It's safe. I've found the *socabón*."

I wanted to believe him, but I was paralyzed by indecision. What if it was too far and I slipped or pulled Andy down into the ravine with me?

"Marcos, Marcos!" he kept calling.

I had to jump. If I didn't, Andy would think me a coward.

Suddenly, just as I was about to leap, there was a knock on my door and I awoke with a start. Rubbing my eyes, I stumbled onto the veranda to find Andy already seated at the table, quietly sipping coffee.

"Sorry about my behavior last night," mumbled Dr. Jekyll contritely. "It's the whiskey, I shouldn't have drank so much."

I accepted his apologies. "No harm done," I replied—but it was a lie. Andy had allowed me to glimpse his demons; our relationship could never be the same again.

The first hour of the drive back to Guayaquil passed in an uneasy silence. There was still so much I needed to know. If I was to make sense of Dyott's two expeditions to the mountains and the clues on Blake's maps, I needed to persuade Andy to let me examine Dyott's journals. I also needed to know the name of the woman in Philadelphia who had written to him. But drained by the previous night's performance, Andy seemed to have temporarily lost his powers of speech.

Slowly, eased by the motion of the car and the familiar sight of the haciendas, he regained his voice, but the name on his lips this time wasn't Dyott but that of another treasure hunter, his son-in-law Diego Arias.

In Ecuador, Diego's passion for the Llanganatis was well known. A sinewy fifty-year-old with a long white ponytail, Diego had liked nothing better than to hike into the mountains in his trademark British army pith helmet, rooting for clues. Andy had recruited him to the quest in the early 1970s after Diego's marriage to his daughter Monica and had loved him like a son. But in 1998, while driving home from a party in Tumbaco one night with another of Andy's daughters, there had been a tragic accident and Diego had been killed.

Andy showed me a picture of him and Diego embracing on the ranch. They were roughly the same height, but whereas Andy cut a brutish and vital figure, Diego seemed slight and insubstantial beside him. This shortcoming was accentuated by Diego's droopy eyelids and pensive, equine features. Next to Andy he looked more like a poet than a treasure hunter. How, I wondered, had he survived in the Llanganatis?

From what I could gather, Diego was the willing apprentice every aging treasure hunter needs. Like Andy, he was partial to drink, and when
they weren't striding across the *paramo* together, Diego would hang out
at the ranch, turning over the riddle of Blake's maps and letters late into
the night. By the 1980s the symbiotic relationship between father and
son-in-law had become too much for Monica, and she and Diego had
divorced. But though the separation was acrimonious, Diego never left
the ranch. Instead, Andy gave him his own head of cattle to manage,
and when Andy was too busy or too tired to venture into the Llanganatis to check out a new nugget of information, he would send Diego
in his place.

Shortly before Dyott's death in 1972, Andy and Diego had visited the
commander, and, Andy said, Dyott had shared "more details" of his investigations. Andy refused to be drawn on the specifics but hinted that
Dyott had considered the discovery of the coded message in Uncle
Sammy's Bible significant—particularly the pinpricked phrase "treasure
in dead volcano by extinct lake." Like Andy, Diego had initially concentrated on Cerro Hermoso but after that meeting his attention had
shifted to Zunchu-Urcu. Dubbed the "gateway" to the Llanganatis because of its prominent position overlooking the ranges, Zunchu-Urcu
is no longer volcanic (the name is actually Quichuan for "Mica Mountain"). However, the mountain is notable for a huge black stone that
was probably forced to the surface during the formation of the ranges
more than twenty-five million years ago, and its base is peppered with
small tunnels—probably the remains of ancient volcanic chimneys.
The mountain also overlooks two lakes—known as Los Cables—that
could be mistaken for the remains of ancient volcanic craters. But
according to Andy, Diego was attracted as much by the beauty of
Zunchu-Urcu as by its history and would often spend days camped by
the mountain just enjoying the view. "He used to say to me, 'Andy, it's
so peaceful up there, there's no one to disturb you.'"

In 1990 he set up a foundation dedicated to the preservation of the
Llanganatis' unique flora and fauna and began lobbying the Ecuadorian
government to declare the Llanganatis a national park—a goal that was
finally achieved, four years later, in 1994. But by now Andy had begun
to suspect that Diego's obsession with the mountains was a way of evad-

ing his other responsibilities. Without telling Andy, Diego sold off the cattle Andy had given him as a gift, frittering the money away in drinking and gambling. Then, when a bar he owned in Quito went bankrupt, Andy cut him off.

"I told Diego that he still had an ex-wife and his children to take care of, but he wouldn't listen. All he thought about was the treasure."

Despite everything, though, I sensed Andy missed him. After the accident Andy had hiked into the mountains with Diego's ashes.

"I scattered his remains on Zunchu-Urcu. It was what he would have wanted," he told me.

He paused. We had now crossed the Río Daule and were reentering the suburbs of Guayaquil. I knew Andy didn't believe in curses—traffic accidents were a common occurrence in Ecuador; nevertheless, I couldn't help thinking that once again the life of a treasure hunter had been cut tragically short. First Blake and Chapman, then the Indian who had toppled into the gorge, now Andy's son-in-law. And I wasn't even counting Isabela Brooks or Padre Longo, the priest mentioned on Guzmán's map. Was there a lesson here?

Once again Andy appeared to have read my mind. In the late 1990s, he said, another friend of his, an American geologist named Bob Holt, had hiked to Cerro Negro looking for Blake's treasure cave—Andy did not explain why he had picked this mountain, but I got the impression it had something to do with Dyott's journals. Rather than hire a team of Indians, however, Holt—a strapping Vietnam vet and experienced mountaineer—took just one porter, a young Indian boy, to carry his food and equipment.

At first everything went well. Holt hiked to Zunchu-Urcu, then crossed the Páramo de Soguillas, contouring around its sharp ridges until he reached a valley with a misty lake surrounded by *frailejones*. But it wasn't the *frailejones* that interested Holt so much as the sight of the mountain towering above them.

Cerro Negro is aptly named. A dark granite mass aligned north-south across the ranges, the mountain resembles nothing so much as the hump of a brontosaurus. Viewed from below, its sheer walls appear to form an endless chasm, while its ridge-like peaks, rising as high as 12,500 feet, are rarely visible, being draped in continual cloud. Together

with Las Torres a little farther to the north, Cerro Negro presents a formidable barrier—the last palisade before the dazzling descent of the
Llanganatis to the Amazon.

For whatever reason, Holt was determined to climb the mountain.
But as he ascended the cliff face, he lost his footing and slipped, impal-
ing himself on a tree trunk. According to Andy, the young Indian porter
rushed to the bottom, but there was nothing he could do. Holt had
broken his back and was unable to move.

The boy had no choice but to retrace their steps to Píllaro. It took him
four days. By the time he reached the village, he was "beside himself."
He quickly explained the situation, and the villagers put together a rescue party, but by the time they returned to Cerro Negro, Holt had died.

We were now pulling into the airport, and Andy's chauffeur was getting ready to hand me my rucksack, but Andy hadn't finished his story;
there was a postscript. The villagers had wanted to carry Holt back to
Píllaro so that his family could bury him, but Holt was over six feet and
weighed 250 pounds, and they couldn't budge him.

"In the end the army sent in commandos," said Andy. "The mission
was so hard they were all given a month's leave afterward."

I envisaged the commandos—small, tough men raised, like Andy, in
the rarefied air of the equinoctial Andes—struggling under the weight
of the American. It seemed a ridiculous waste of men and resources,
and once again I found my sympathies lay with the Ecuadorians—a
people who had endured so much from foreigners treating their country like a playground. But if Andy had any regrets about his role in
sending Holt to his death, he didn't show them. Instead, like a restless
cyclist, he'd already switched to another gear.

"Dyott was very English, very proper, you know. He always insisted
we put on a jacket and tie before dinner."

Andy handed me my rucksack.

"Ah, there's your gate. If you're quick, you should just make the
flight . . . 'Andy,' he used to say, 'you know why we make such good explorers? Because we're small. We can duck under the trees without getting snagged on the branches.'"

Andy let out a deep guffaw and pushed me toward the departure
gate.

"Give me a call to let me know where you're staying in Quito. You never know, I might look you up."

I thanked Andy profusely and pushed my way to the front of the check-in desk. By the time I had my seat assignment and turned around again, he was gone.

Part Three

THE LABYRINTH

*The library was full of secrets, and especially of books
that had never been given to the monks to read.*

—UMBERTO ECO, *The Name of the Rose*

1

A Literary Gold Mine

THERE IS A LONG TRADITION OF WRITERS GOING IN SEARCH OF BURIED treasure and, conversely, of treasure hunters who, frustrated at their failure to find some hidden cache, have spun their adventures into literary gold. Indeed, to the extent that both require a fertile imagination and the ability to suspend disbelief—if not on your own part, then at least on your readers'—treasure hunting and treasure writing may simply be flip sides of the same coin.

When you also consider that the writers of the greatest treasure narratives drew their inspiration directly from the exploits of real-life piratical characters—buccaneers with such novelistic monikers as Bowlegs and Quelch—it is hardly surprising that over time and in the retelling the genres have tended to become blurred. It is well known, for instance, that Stevenson drew the inspiration for *Treasure Island* from the legends surrounding Cocos Island.* Similarly, Haggard—inspired by the success

---

*A Pacific island four hundred miles northeast of Ecuador that is said to be littered with pirate caches, including the fabulous "treasure of Lima." Cocos first appeared on a map in 1541, but its exact location remained in doubt for a long time. With an abundance of fresh drinking water and coconuts, it soon became a favorite spot for pirates to rest and careen their ships ahead of fresh raids on Spanish shipping.

of Stevenson's novel to write his own "tale of adventure for boys"—based the character of Allan Quatermain on the real-life journals of the Rhodesian big-game hunter Frederick Courteney Selous, whose *A Hunter's Wanderings in Africa* had struck a chord with bored Victorian readers eager for tales of derring-do from the far-flung empire.

But Stevenson's and Haggard's real genius was their ability to entertain a child's-eye view of the world, to enter into and bring to life the boyish realm. For instance, Stevenson began writing *Treasure Island* for the amusement of his twelve-year-old stepson, Lloyd Osbourne, whom he had discovered one day painting an imaginary island; within seconds Stevenson picked up the paintbrush and began elaborating his own details. Similarly, Haggard was able to incorporate into *King Solomon's Mines* half-remembered tales from his own childhood—notably a story told to him by a retired sea captain about the discovery of a mummy's tomb.

The story obviously left an impression on Haggard; years later, he tracked down the last extant artifact from the dig—a mummy's gold ring.* But it was the source of another key element in Haggard's fictional narrative that really intrigued me. The only clue Quatermain and his companions have to the location of King Solomon's mines is the map left by the deceased Portuguese explorer. As treasure maps go, it is extraordinarily simple, showing a dotted line leading across the desert to Sheba's Breasts and Solomon's royal road. From there the parchment instructs the treasure hunters to proceed in a straight line until they reach the base of three mountains known as the "Three Witches." It is behind these mountains that, Haggard writes, Solomon's mines lie.

> The mountains, or rather the three peaks of the mountains, for the whole mass evidently consisted of a solitary upheaval, were, as I have said, *in the form of a triangle* [my italics], of which the base was towards us, one peak being on our right, one on our left, and one straight in front of us. Never shall I forget the sight afforded by those three towering peaks in the early sunlight of the following morning.

---

*See Morton Cohen, *Rider Haggard: His Life and Works* (London: Hutchinson, 1960). Cohen argues that Haggard drew on the details of the mummy and the ring for his description of Quatermain's entry into the tomb of the king of the Kukuanas.

Haggard gives no clue as to where he obtained this intriguing detail, but I found its inclusion in his narrative unsettling—Valverde's *derrotero* contained exactly the same phrase. Had Haggard read Spruce's famous paper to the Royal Geographical Society, or had he recalled the details from somewhere else? Was he acquainted with the *derrotero*, or were the three *cerros* simply an archetypal image, a common fixture in treasure stories, no more real than the Portuguese explorer and his faded parchment?

If this was the only parallel between Haggard's life and work and Valverde's *derrotero*, I might have dismissed it, but there was another. In 1891, after stopping in New York to field reporters' questions about the success of *King Solomon's Mines*, Haggard had set off for Mexico with his wife, Louisa. The ostensible purpose of his trip was to do research for a new novel he was writing based on the life of the Aztec emperor Montezuma. But Haggard's interest had also been piqued by his mining engineer friend John Jebb, who claimed to have uncovered important new information about the hiding place of Montezuma's lost treasure. Legend had it that Montezuma's nephew Cuauhtémoc had hidden the treasure—which included a solid-gold head of the late emperor and eighteen jars full of precious stones—in a pit somewhere on the shores of Lake Tezcuco. For years speculators had tried to discover the location of the cache, torturing the Indians to betray the secret, all to no avail. Now, however, as in the story of Atahualpa's hoard, an Indian cacique living beside the lake had revealed the pit's location to a Mexican descendant of the conquistadores, and the Mexican in turn had confided the secret to a Cuban geologist named Don Anselmo.

To cut a long story short, Don Anselmo and the Mexican formed a partnership, excavated the pit to a depth of sixty feet, and uncovered a great stone bearing a carved owl—the totem of Cuauhtémoc—behind which they discovered another passageway and steps leading up to a solid wall. But before they could dynamite it, the pit was sold to an official of the Mexican government, and, fearing the treasure would be taken from them, Don Anselmo and the Mexican filled in the shaft and approached Jebb for help.

By the time Haggard reached Mexico City, Jebb had concluded negotiations with the official and had obtained permission to dig for "antiquities" on his land. But by now the Mexican had died, and Don

Anselmo had disappeared. Then, just as Haggard was about to set off, he received a telegram announcing the sudden death of his beloved son, Jock. Grief-stricken, Haggard set off for Chiapas state, where Jebb said he knew of another interesting silver mine. But by now Haggard had lost all heart for the quest, and the trip was a disaster. There was no gold or silver, and on the way back Haggard was attacked by brigands, mosquitoes, and dysentery. Nevertheless, recalling the episode years later in his autobiography, *The Days of My Life*, Haggard wrote that the existence of the treasure was "not to be doubted." He had little confidence, however, that the golden head of Montezuma or the jars of precious stones would be recovered because "the Aztecs buried them deeply, having time at their disposal."

Before embarking on an equally challenging and possibly demoralizing journey to the Llanganatis, I needed to be sure I wasn't being led into a similar cul-de-sac. The legends of Montezuma's and Atahualpa's hoards shared many of the same narrative elements: the extraordinary effort to hide the gold from the Spanish, the refusal of the Indians to reveal its location under torture, then the sudden and inexplicable decision years later by an Indian chieftain to share the secret with a descendant of the hated conquistadores. The difference was that in the case of the Llanganatis, there was a map and a guide. Unfortunately, these raised more questions than answers.

Who was Valverde (and when had he lived)? Did he know Guzmán, and what relation, if any, did Guzmán's map bear to Valverde's guide? Clearly, both documents were the work of people who knew certain parts of the Llanganatis well, but at crucial points both the *derrotero* and the map became vague and imprecise, as if the author or authors had suddenly lost their way, or else deliberately set out to confuse. Furthermore, what was the meaning of the meandering trails and curious legends marked on Guzmán's map, and what was the result of the expedition commissioned by the King of Spain and led by the governor of Latacunga in which Padre Longo had mysteriously died—a death perplexingly recorded on Guzmán's map but not referred to in the *derrotero*? Perhaps the treasure had been taken out of the mountains long ago, and explorers like Andy had been chasing shadows ever since. Or perhaps, like the Aztecs, the Incas had buried it so well and so deeply it would never be found.

Finally, how did Atahualpa and Rumiñahui fit into the story? Neither Spruce nor Wallace mentions the Inca ruler or his Quitenian general by name, referring only to the "treasure of the Incas." Was Rumiñahui's involvement known to the Spanish chroniclers of the conquest, or was it smuggled into the narrative at a later date?

Before being drawn deeper into the labyrinth, I needed to be certain that I wasn't making a fool of myself, that there was a possibility that Valverde and the Cerros Llanganatis really existed and that his guide was, as Spruce claimed, an "authentic" document. In short I needed to conduct a different sort of treasure inquiry—an inquiry into the documentary sources.

I began by visiting Quito's Catholic University—a sprawling complex opposite the U.S. Embassy on Avenida 12 de Octubre. The librarian looked surprised to see a gringo and hesitated over my ID—an old British paper driver's license. But when I explained that I wanted to read the classic histories of the conquest—books like Garcilaso de la Vega's *Royal Commentaries of the Incas*, Pedro de Cieza de León's *The Discovery and Conquest of Peru*, and William H. Prescott's *History of the Conquest of Peru*—he helped me fill out the slips himself. They arrived in less than half the time it would have taken at the British Library—a rare example of efficiency in a country crippled by corruption and the dollarization of its currency.

The books were filled with descriptions of the incredible wealth of the Inca empire—descriptions that echoed Andy's vision of the gold awaiting us in Blake's treasure cave. They spoke of Coricancha, the magnificent Temple of the Sun in Cuzco, with its golden altar adorned with the image of the sun, around the foot of which were arranged the mummified remains of the Inca kings seated on golden daises; of the thick gold chain commissioned by Huayna Capac to commemorate the birth of his first son, Huáscar—a chain that was said to have stretched the length and breadth of the great square at Cuzco and that was so heavy that "two hundred Indian warriors had difficulty in lifting it"; and of the royal Inca gardens with their delicate reproductions in gold and silver celebrating the cornucopia of the New World. According to Prescott, the articles in the gardens consisted of "goblets, ewers, salvers," and vases of "every shape and size" as well as "curious imitations of different plants and animals." The passage continued:

Among the plants, the most beautiful was the Indian corn, in
which the golden ear was sheathed in its broad leaves of silver
from which hung a rich tassel of threads of the same precious metal.
A fountain was also much admired, which sent up a sparkling jet
of gold, while birds and animals of the same material played in the
waters at its base.

Prescott's references to golden goblets and golden ears of corn reminded
me of the phrases Andy had recited from Blake's letter.

I looked at the date Prescott's book had been published—1847, just
forty years before Blake had set sail for Ecuador. Was Blake familiar
with Prescott's history? Had he read these passages during his voyage
around Cape Horn, and had he inadvertently, or perhaps deliberately,
drawn inspiration from them?

Prescott's images were certainly vivid. Having lost his eyesight in a
bizarre accident at Harvard (he was hit in the left eye with a bread roll),
Prescott became a Spanish scholar, using his formidable memory and
imagination to tell the story of the rise of Spanish power in the Americas. For inspiration, he turned to the eyewitness accounts of the priests
and soldiers who had been present at the conquest or, where these
proved insufficient, the accounts of chroniclers—such as Garcilaso—
who had written about the events in Peru a few decades later.

A literary detective now, I turned to Garcilaso, mining for sources.
He had also lingered in the Royal Gardens. "The beard of the maize
husk was done in gold and the rest in silver, the two being soldered together. [The Inca] made the same distinction in dealing with other
plants, using gold to copy the flower or anything else of a yellow tint
and silver for the rest," he wrote. Some of these artworks had been destroyed by the Spanish, melted into gold ingots when they defiled the
Incas' temples, but the majority had suffered a very different fate. In a
passage that stopped me dead, Garcilaso had written:

Most of these riches were buried by the Indians as soon as the
Spaniards arrived thirsting for gold and silver, and they were so
carefully concealed that they have never been found, nor is it likely
that they will be found unless they are come upon by chance, for

it is clear that the Indians of today do not know the places where these treasures are.

This verdict echoed Haggard's opinion on the Aztec treasure. Surely Garcilaso didn't mean the Llanganatis hoard? If so, then my quest was pointless.

My faith shaken, I pressed on with my reading in the increasingly forlorn hope of finding some—any—confirmation of Valverde's story.

The first thing I discovered was that although Cieza disagreed with Garcilaso's and Fernández's estimates of the size of Rumiñahui's convoy, he was adamant that the ransom gold from Quito was larger than any of the tributes the Spanish had received for Atahualpa from other parts of the Inca empire. According to some accounts, Cieza heard Rumiñahui took the gold to a lake and "threw it into its deepest part." According to others, he "buried it in great crags among heaps of snow," and then killed the men who had carried it on their backs so they would never reveal its location. Cieza continues, "And although they themselves later died in torture, strangely they did not want to reveal what they knew, but wanted to die believing that they would be going to live forever with the Incas, their sovereign lords."

Cieza's reference to a lake made me pause. Was this the famous "lake, made by hand," mentioned in the *derrotero*? Did "great crags among heaps of snow" refer to the glaciated peaks of the Llanganatis? And what of the passage describing the Indians' courage under torture? One reason John Hemming had dismissed the *derrotero* as a fabrication was that the Spaniards were experts at torture.

"If the treasure existed, and Rumiñahui knew where it was, he would have revealed the secret rather than endure further suffering," he had assured me.

Yet here was Cieza, one of the most respected chroniclers of the conquest, a soldier-historian who had visited South America ten years after the events in question and who said that he would rather ignore hearsay than "include even a single word of what did not happen," writing the exact opposite.

Still, it was pretty thin. Rumors of treasure in lakes abounded in the years following the conquest. Similar rumors had sent Pizarro's partner

Francisco de Orellana over the eastern cordillera of the Ecuadorian Andes and down to the Amazon in search of the fabled El Dorado. Moreover, I knew that the Peruvians and Bolivians had long been convinced that Atahualpa's gold lay hidden within their own borders. Indeed, the Bolivians had spent many years draining a lake near Sorata in the belief that it contained one of Atahualpa's missing convoys, while, writing in 1910, Sir Clements Markham, the respected Inca historian and former president of the RGS, reported that the Peruvians believed some eleven thousand *cargas* of gold were hidden in the mountains of Azangara, just north of Lake Titicaca.* Indeed, if Cieza's report had been the only confirmation of the Llanganatis legend, I might have abandoned my search for the treasure then and there. But there was more.

Valverde makes no reference to Rumiñahui, and neither does Spruce. But the deeper I delved into the history of the Spaniards' pursuit of Rumiñahui, the more apparent the connections between Atahualpa's general and the Llanganatis became.

In the spring of 1534 Pizarro had completed the sacking of Cuzco and was ready to turn his attention to Quito. But by now Rumiñahui had had nearly nine months to hide Atahualpa's gold and organize the resistance. To further complicate matters, another Spanish raiding party, led by the governor of Guatemala, Pedro de Alvarado, had recently landed in northern Peru and was reported to be on its way to the Ecuadorian capital. Fearing that unless he acted quickly the Quitenian treasury would slip from his grasp, Pizarro dispatched one of his most trusted commanders, Sebastián de Benalcázar, to hunt Rumiñahui down. Aided by his commander, Zope-Zopahua, Rumiñahui elected to fight a classic guerrilla war. Crack troops were sent on ahead of the main battalions of his northern army to ambush Benalcázar on the royal road between Cuenca and Riobamba. Then, at Riobamba, Rumiñahui ordered his men to dig a series of pits in hopes of entrapping and neutralizing the

---

*See Sir Clements Markham, *The Incas of Peru* (London: Smith, Elder, 1910). Markham writes that the location of these secret *huacas* was still known to a few select Indians as late as the nineteenth century. Indeed, during a visit to Cuzco in 1852, Markham interviewed the wife of an Indian resistance leader who remembered her husband's returning home in 1815 laden with artifacts from a secret *huaca* on the Huatanay River. She said her husband had been led to the cache blindfolded and was permitted to take only as much gold as he needed to buy arms to equip his troops.

conquistadores' horses. But Benalcázar had cleverly allied himself with the Canaris, a tribe of Indians in southern Ecuador hostile to the Incas, and his Indian informants were able to alert him to the traps so that he could take evasive action. As a result, by the time Benalcázar reached Riobamba in May 1534, Rumiñahui's army was in retreat.

At this point Benalcázar enjoyed another stroke of luck. A considerable army—some fifty thousand Indian troops—still lay between the Spanish and Quito. But at this precise moment the volcano Cotopaxi, lying just off the royal road between Riobamba and Quito, erupted. The nearest town to the eruption was Latacunga—the very same town from which, several years later, the *corregidor*, on the orders of the Spanish King, would set off with the *derrotero* in search of Atahualpa's treasure. As fire, ash, and rocks rained down on Rumiñahui his troops took it as an omen. According to Cieza, the Indians believed that "when a volcano or mouth of fire near Latacunga erupted, foreign people from a faraway land would come to wage war on them, and they would become so powerful that they would become their masters."

It was at this point that Rumiñahui's own legend as an uncompromising and ruthless resistance leader was born. Many of the chiefs wanted to negotiate with the Spanish, but Rumiñahui refused, arguing that the conquistadores' offer of an armistice was a trick to get their hands on the treasure. When Benalcázar sent a messenger to reiterate the peace offer, Rumiñahui called his troops together and roused them with the words "Look at the ruses with which they want to deceive us and with what words they want to convince us, so they can take away from us the treasure they think is in Quito . . . God forbid we should trust these people who neither told the truth nor will tell it; let us rather die by their hands and their horses so that they do not oppress and force us to willingly follow their excesses and fulfil their pretensions."

To underline his determination, Rumiñahui then had the messenger executed, and he retreated to the outskirts of Quito, where he tried to keep the Spanish from entering the city by fortifying his troops behind the walls of a rugged ravine. But Benalcázar stormed the fort, and Rumiñahui had to retreat once more—this time to Quito itself. Fearing the Spanish were about to take the city and its treasure, Rumiñahui gathered all the gold together and offered the *yanaconas*—the cloistered virgins who waited on the Inca in the Sun Temple—a stark choice:

either flee with him or risk rape by the Spanish. In fact, it was no choice at all. When three hundred of the *yanaconas* said they preferred to take their chances with the Spanish, Rumiñahui accused them of being prostitutes and executed them. He then razed the city.

As a result, when Benalcázar reached Quito on June 22, not only was the city in flames, but the temples and shrines were bare of ornaments. It was then that, seeing the Spaniards' despair, the Quiteños delivered their famous taunt, comparing the treasure Atahualpa had delivered to Pizarro to a grain of maize beside the much larger pile that was outstanding.

Enraged, Benalcázar launched a series of frantic raids on nearby towns, then ordered one of his captains to hunt Rumiñahui down. The place the Spanish found him, it seems, was the Llanganatis.

I say "seems" because at this point the chronicles once again become vague. Cieza's fourth manuscript, dealing with the Quitenian campaigns, is missing, and Garcilaso's and Fernández's accounts are sketchy. The best account we have is the one left by Antonio de Herrera, the official chronicler in chief of the Indies, which is cited by John Hemming in his excellent modern history, *The Conquest of the Incas*.

Herrera—who according to Hemming almost certainly copied his very detailed description from Cieza's lost work—writes that after mounting one further desperate attack on the Spanish in Quito at night, Rumiñahui had fled to a fortified retreat near Píllaro, the village to the west of the Llanganatis where Valverde would later fall in love with and marry his Inca princess. A long, hard battle ensued, at the end of which his supplies of missiles and ammunition were exhausted. At that point, being "without arrows, lances or battle-axes," most of his men surrendered. But once again Rumiñahui fled. There is no record of where he went, but very possibly it was into the ranges to the east— the very same ranges where he may have earlier secreted Atahualpa's gold.

All we know for certain is that Rumiñahui was captured at Panzaleo, a point midway between Píllaro and Latacunga. He had been attempting to cross a snow-covered pass above the village in order to rejoin Zope-Zopahua, who had taken up a defensive position on a nearby hilltop. According to the officer sent to capture him—again cited in Hemming's book—Rumiñahui was discovered "through a short cut that led to a lake . . . beside a small hillock, leaning against a tree," and, after another fierce skirmish, taken into custody.

We know what happened next. Benalcázar threatened Rumiñahui with being burned at the stake, then tortured him. But neither Rumiñahui nor Zope-Zopahua, who by now had also been captured, would reveal the treasure's location, and Benalcázar had no choice but to send them to their deaths, executing them in the main square in Quito in the first days of December 1534.

And that was it. The chroniclers make no further mention of Atahualpa or of Rumiñahui. Instead, the Spanish set off in other directions—to Colombia, Peru, and Bolivia—chasing reports of "golden indians" and hidden mines that seemed to offer a better chance of return. As far as the early Spanish historians were concerned, the trail had gone cold.

FOR NEARLY THREE HUNDRED YEARS NO ONE SPOKE OF ATAHUALPA'S hoard again, but the obsession had not died; it was merely dormant. Spruce and Wallace revived it. Then adventurers like Brooks and Loch took up the challenge. Gradually, as news of their expeditions spread, a new generation of writers became hooked. Some of these had been treasure hunters themselves. Others simply saw a good story. They consulted the old books, noted the chroniclers' descriptions of the room in which Atahualpa had been held and the reports of the missing convoys, and—ignoring any evidence to the contrary—re-spun the legend for a new generation weaned on the fiction of Stevenson and Haggard.

By the 1930s authors like Alpheus Hyatt Verrill, a onetime treasure hunter who claimed to have been personally acquainted with Brooks, were making astonishing statements. In *Lost Treasure: True Tales of Hidden Hoards*, published in 1930, Verrill estimated that the room in Cajamarca in which Atahualpa had been held prisoner could have held 248 tons of gold. Subtracting the amount the Spanish had actually obtained for the Inca's ransom, Verrill came up with a missing figure of more than half a billion dollars, "surely the greatest hidden treasure in the world!"

Six years later in *They Found Gold: The Story of Successful Treasure Hunts*, Verrill revised his estimate down considerably. Now Pizarro had secured nearly $20 million worth of gold as a portion of Atahualpa's ransom, "yet fully ten times more"—or $200 million worth—"was being brought to buy the freedom of the captive Inca."

To arrive at either of these figures, Verrill had had to lump together all the gold convoys that were presumed to be on their way to Caja-marca when Atahualpa was murdered. But interestingly, Verrill considered only the convoys from Peru and Bolivia "Atahualpa's treasure." The gold convoy from Ecuador was, he argued, "not the treasure of the betrayed and murdered Inca [but] . . . far more probably, a treasure that was being moved from some deserted and 'lost' city in the trans-Andean jungles to Quito or elsewhere, and was hastily concealed when word reached the carriers that the Spaniards were invading the land."

In Verrill's version of the legend only Valverde figures; there is no mention of the Llanganatis, Píllaro, or Rumiñahui. But while Verrill seems to have gleaned most of his information from Spruce, new "facts" have been added. Thus Verrill's Valverde is a "poor" Spanish soldier who had definitely taken part in the conquest. His army service over, he settled down and married an Inca princess, but his marriage did not win him the respect of his peers, who continued to "scoff at" his poverty and shun him. Eventually his bride could take his morose moods no more and revealed the secret that would make him "the richest Spaniard in the country and the envy of all men." Leading Valverde over peaks, ridges, and canyons, she brought him to "the crater of an extinct vol-cano," in the center of which was a turquoise lake and, soaring above it, "three snow-capped pinnacles." Having crossed the lake, they entered an arched cleft in the mountain in the shape of "a church door." The opening led to a narrow tunnel, at the end of which, writes Verrill, was a "great cavern" full of gold.

> The cave was piled high with golden statues and idols, plates and vessels of solid gold, bundles of thin gold plumes and sheets of beaten gold, ingots of gold and bags of gold nuggets and dust, golden ornaments, and models of birds, animals and other objects wrought in gold and silver; golden ears of corn with husks and silk of silver; coronets and head ornaments, ceremonial utensils and

armlets of gold ablaze with gems, and massive bars of silver . . .
countless tons of precious metals, millions in treasure.

Verrill provides no source for this supposed eyewitness account, and I
wondered whether, like Blake's description of the treasure cave, it wasn't
another rhetorical flourish, a fiction inspired by—or culled from—
Garcilaso's descriptions of the royal Inca gardens in Cuzco. Their imaginations fired by the immense size of the missing hoard and the paucity
of information surrounding Valverde's life, other authors were soon in-
venting even more outlandish "facts."

In *Modern Buried Treasure Hunters,* Harold T. Wilkins, a Cambridge
linguist turned treasure hunter, reported that in 1933 an Ecuadorian
lawyer had found Atahualpa's gold buried in a tomb at Nizac, near
Chimborazo, together with the headless body of the dead Inca king.
The head itself, wrote Wilkins, was to be found in the Trocadero museum in Paris—though how it had got there (presumably Rumiñahui's
ghost dug it up after his own demise) he did not elaborate.

Not content with repeating such easily disprovable nonsense,
Wilkins decided to fictionalize Spruce's account, bestowing the fore-
name "Juan" on Valverde and illustrating his story with a map, bearing
the legend *"El Derrotero de Tesoro del Yngas,"* obtained—he informs
us—"from a very rare MS. copy of the original guide." It must have
been very rare indeed since neither Spruce nor Wallace in fact mentions it, though Wilkins claims they both had examined it. In all likeli-
hood Wilkins copied the chart from Guzmán's map—which of course
was unearthed by Spruce—as it exhibits many of the botanist's characteristic sketches of trees as well as several of the trails he followed in
search of mines.

Wilkins drew another map, however, that *did* cause me concern. In
Mysteries of Ancient South America, published in 1945, he posited the
existence of a hidden tunnel system running from Lima to the Atacama
Desert in Chile with spurs east to Cuzco. In an elaborate hand-drawn
map accompanying the text, Wilkins indicated that the key to this tunnel
system, or *socabón*, was a rock near Ilo on the Peruvian coast carved with
alien hieroglyphs. According to Wilkins, these hieroglyphs contained a
coded message pointing to a hidden door behind Los Tres Picos (The

Three Peaks) a few miles inland. According to the map, these in turn led to a vast hoard hidden in Peru's eastern cordillera, though whether this hoard was the missing Ecuadorian treasure, another of Atahualpa's gold convoys, or the fabled lost city of Paititi, Wilkins is unclear.*

Like his claims to have discovered Valverde's chart, Wilkins's map of the secret tunnel system struck me as an elaborate fantasy. The question was, how had those three mountains lodged themselves in his imagination? Despite his fictional flights of fancy, Wilkins was also a scholar. Before writing *Mysteries of Ancient South America*, he had spent twenty-five years patiently translating old Jesuit maps and documents in the British Library. What if triangular arrangements of mountains were a common feature of all *derroteros*? In other words, what if the Cerros Llanganatis were a tried-and-tested arrangement of topographical points, a psychic trigger, so to speak, for all treasure narratives?

---

*Wilkins drew his inspiration for the map from the writings of the Russian theosophist Helena Blavatsky. During a visit to Peru in 1850 Blavatsky claimed she met a "gentleman in Lima" who showed her the entrance to the tunnel system and guided her to a massive stone slab—"The Tomb of the Inca"—on the border between Peru and Bolivia. Blavatsky was told that on the death of Atahualpa, the tomb had been ordered sealed by the "Inca queen," who then committed suicide. Although Blavatsky's account is riddled with factual errors (not least the correct location of the Bolivian border), some scholars believe the source of the legend may be a massive rock, the Morro de Arica, in northern Chile, where in 1983 archaeologists uncovered the remains of nearly one hundred mummies of the Chinchorro people. Dating back more than seven thousand years, the Chilean mummies are the oldest ever discovered.

2

AN INVALUABLE MANUSCRIPT

THE FOLLOWING MORNING I WAS AWOKEN EARLY BY THE SLAM OF HAIL-stones in the courtyard outside my room. Through my bedroom window I could see that a ferocious black cloud had gathered about Pichincha, disgorging sheets of icy rain and sleet onto the streets below. In short it was a typical day in Quito. By the time I had breakfasted, I calculated, the sun would have turned the cloud to steam and Pichincha would be framed by a rainbow. If I hadn't been planning to spend the whole morning in the library again, it would probably have been a good day to get in some climbing practice.

In the course of my interview with Roland he had made fleeting references to another treasure hunter, an Ecuadorian named Luciano Andrade Marín. Like Roland, Andrade was a geologist who had prospected the Llanganatis many times for gold in the company of an Italian alpinist, Tullio Boschetti (Tullio was the father of Guido, the climber who had gone with Andy on his expeditions to the mountains in the 1950s). More important, Andrade had made a scholarly investigation of the *derrotero*, uncovering new information about its probable age as well as about other early expeditions to the ranges.

"It is a fascinating book, perhaps the best investigation of the treasure legend ever," Roland had told me.

Unfortunately, he didn't have a copy. No one did. Andrade's book had long been out of print, and first editions were "like gold dust." However, Roland thought I might be able to find one at the Banco Central del Ecuador.

"They have their own archive, you know."

Ordinarily I would have laughed at the irony, but in a country where banking was as uncertain and as changeable as the weather, it made a kind of sense. After all, what better place for the most valuable book ever written about the Llanganatis—a book that might hold the key to the location of the greatest treasure in the world—than in the vaults of Ecuador's central bank?

I set off for the archive directly after breakfast, crunching the hailstones beneath the soles of my hiking boots as I walked south toward the city center. The Banco Central occupied a ten-story glass tower block next to the Hilton Colón—a well-known downtown landmark and, in the past, a popular meeting place for treasure hunters. Once again I was asked for an ID—my passport this time—and was shown into the reading room. The archivist, a gray-haired man wearing a white smock, nodded knowingly when I wrote the name Andrade and disappeared behind the stacks, reemerging moments later with not one but two small white paperbacks.

I turned them over and studied the covers. Both were illustrated by an intricate, labyrinthine design with the word "Llanganati" written across the top in lurid Gothic script. The first had been published in 1937, the second thirty-three years later, in 1970. However, in both cases the title on the frontispiece was the same: *Viaje a las misteriosas montañas de Llanganati* (Voyage to the mysterious Llanganati Mountains).

Roland was right. Andrade described himself as a geologist and a geographer. His first book, *El Ecuador minero*, was a study of old Inca and pre-Inca mines. Then, in the early 1930s, he had come across Valverde's *derrotero* with its intriguing description of a bog containing "grains of gold" and the furnace for smelting metals. Whether or not there was also a treasure in the Llanganatis, it seemed to support the theory that the region had been an important source of gold and silver for the original Indian inhabitants of Ecuador.

In 1933 Andrade decided to see the ranges for himself. Accompanied by Boschetti, another climber, Humberto Ré, and twenty-five Indian porters, he set off from Píllaro in December. The expedition lasted a little over five weeks and was every bit as harrowing as Loch's was two years later. Instead of rounding Yana Cocha and following the Desaguadero as per Valverde's instructions, Andrade set a direct compass course across the *paramo*, contouring Zunchu-Urcu, Cerro Negro, and Las Torres until he arrived at the banks of the Jatun Yacu, an affluent of the Río Napo. By the time his party arrived back in Píllaro in February 1934, they were unrecognizable. Only eleven of the original twenty-five porters lasted the expedition, most of them having deserted on the Jatun Yacu rather than endure another crossing of the mountains. The weather had been awful, and they had quickly exhausted their supplies of food; by the time they reached Píllaro again, their clothes hung from their bodies in rags. Andrade writes: "It was the most terrible geographical adventure that it is possible to realize in Ecuadorian territory . . . without doubt maps of the region should carry a warning, 'uninhabitable forever!'"

Despite these travails—or perhaps because of them—Andrade's book was an instant success. According to a note to the 1970 edition, the Mercantil Press of Quito could not print copies fast enough. Within days of its publication in 1937 it "had virtually disappeared from Ecuador"—most of the editions ending up abroad in the collections of American and European treasure enthusiasts.

What made Andrade's book such a valuable commodity—what made his manuscript stand out from the rest of the treasure pack, so to speak—was its scholarship. Like every treasure hunter before and since, Andrade was convinced that the *derrotero* could have been written only by someone familiar with the Llanganatis who had traveled through the ranges many times. The conundrum was that just when the treasure seeker thinks he is on the correct trail, the hieroglyph appears and the *derrotero* is suddenly transformed from "a serious document, truthful and methodical, into a modernist drawing, full of incomplete figures and contradictions."

Determined to get to the bottom of the riddle, Andrade decided to ask the questions no one else had: What was the derivation of the word "Llanganati"? Who was Valverde? When did he write the *derrotero*? And what was the result of the expedition commissioned by the King of Spain and led by the governor of Latacunga in which Padre Longo had mysteriously died?

Andrade was nothing if not tenacious. His investigations didn't end in 1937 but continued into the second, 1970 edition. This sold as briskly as the first—justifiably, as it contained important new information about the various expeditions in search of the treasure. Alarmingly, these investigations suggested that while Valverde may have been a real person and his guide authentic, the *derrotero* had almost certainly been altered after his death and the treasure removed long ago!

Andrade's initial inquiries focused on the word "Llanganati" or "Llanganate," as it is more commonly written in Spanish. Where did the word come from, and when was it first applied to the mountain range?

Spruce believed the source was the Quichua word *llánga*, meaning "to touch," and indicated that the group of mountains by that name touched on the sources of the rivers all around, hence the names "Llanganatis del Río Verde" and "Llanganatis del Topo" that appear on Guzmán's map. The *ll* would originally have connoted the French *j* sound, indicating the Quichua pronunciation "Jan-ga." But in Castilian *ll* also connotes *y*, and over time the preferred Spanish pronunciation became "Yan-ga-natis."

Andrade disagreed. Flatly contradicting Spruce, he argued that *llánga* in Quichua signified "workshop of mines" or "factory of metal smelting" and that the ending *ati* referred to the Atis—the Indian families who had ruled the Píllaro region before the arrival of the Spaniards, *ati* being the Quichua word for "victorious one." According to Andrade, Rumiñahui was probably the grandson of an Ati from Píllaro and an Ati himself. Thus a more accurate translation of Llanganatis would be "factory of metal smelting for the victorious ones" or, more simply, "the mines of the Atis."

The first written reference to the mountains appears on a map of Quito dated 1750, where the spelling is given as "Llanganate," the un-accented terminal *e* having been added by Spanish speakers to indicate the shorter Quichua *i* sound. Then, in a historical dictionary of the Americas published in 1789 the Llanganatis are described as an area "rich in gold mines."

A few years later, in 1793, a curate from Píllaro named Mariano

Enríquez de Guzmán mounted what appears to have been the first expedition to the Llanganatis. Was this curate, who lived in Píllaro between
1784 and 1797, related to Spruce's "Atanasio Guzmán," the Spanish
botanist whose map would provoke so much interest? Andrade was
unable to find a connection. It appeared to be just another historical
coincidence—like the one between Vicente de Valverde, the Dominican friar who had been present at Cajamarca, and the *derrotero* writer
Valverde. However, Andrade did discover that Enríquez de Guzmán
had also drawn a map of his expedition—a map that clearly indicated
that in 1793 the curate had been armed with a copy of Valverde's *derrotero* and that it had been a *different* one from Spruce's. Andrade in-
ferred this from the fact that on the curate's map Cerros Llanganatis are
placed to the north of the Desaguadero de Yana Cocha in the Mulatos
region and not to the south of the Desaguadero as both Spruce's copy
of the *derrotero* and Guzmán's map seemed to indicate. There were
other curious anomalies, too. Neither the curate's map nor the accompanying documents made any reference to the death of Padre Longo.
Instead, they simply described the expedition as an exploration aimed
at "the discovery of the problematic Cerros Llanganates of the town of
Píllaro and the route to the Province of Mines."

Next Andrade turned to the vexed question of Valverde's identity. As
with the Guzmáns, he discovered that plenty of people in the region
had the same name. A Jerónimo de Valverde had been received by the
corregidor of Latacunga as early as 1650. Andrade also found records for
Joaquín, Isidoro, and Felipe de Valverde in Latacunga dating back to
1750. However, the only Valverde he could find who had been alive at
the time of the conquest was a Pedro de Valverde recorded as having
been present in Quito in 1538.

Intriguingly, Andrade discovered that Spruce had also made inquiries about Valverde and Guzmán and had drawn similar blanks. In
1863, shortly before returning to England from Peru, Spruce had written to a botanist friend in Ecuador asking for help with various facts
and dates. Did he know when Humboldt had met Guzmán? Had
Guzmán practiced botany in Quito? Had he exercised the same profession in Píllaro? Did anyone remember Valverde and in which town he
had lived? Most fascinating of all, Spruce wrote: "There are some who
say that Valverde was a deportee or a criminal exiled to America for his

crimes who, in order to escape being handed over to the authorities when he returned to Spain, fabricated his account of gold of the Llanganati. How can we establish whether there is any truth in this?"

After making his own inquiries, Spruce's botanist friend reported that he'd found several drawings by Guzmán and that Humboldt had considered him "superior to Linnaeus," but that was all the information he could find.* Spruce never got an answer to his questions about Valverde, and, frustratingly, his writings contain no clue as to where he may have heard the rumors about Valverde's criminal past, since, of course, his journals from Ecuador are missing.

Nevertheless, from his research Andrade was able to reach a number of tentative conclusions: namely, that the *derrotero* had probably arrived in Ecuador sometime toward the end of the eighteenth century; that there had been more than one copy; and that the original had almost certainly been adulterated, so the copy found by Spruce was only accurate for the first three days. But although that would have placed the *derrotero* firmly in the reigns of Carlos III or Carlos IV, Andrade was still no closer to knowing who Valverde was, when the expedition led by the governor of Latacunga had left Píllaro to look for the treasure, and what had caused the sudden death of Padre Longo. Like Spruce one hundred years before him, Andrade appeared to have hit a brick wall.

After the publication of the first edition of his book Andrade continued to delve. He discovered that in 1812 General Toribio Montes, president of the Audiencia of Quito, had also organized an expedition to the Llanganatis. However, the papers relating to the expedition had been bought by a Swedish count named Moerner—one of the growing band of Llanganatis enthusiasts—and he wouldn't agree to share them. Andrade also discovered that Guzmán had left a number of scientific papers and that these, together with his maps, were now in the collection of a famous Jesuit historian and archaeologist, Jacinto Jijón y Caamaño. Once again, however, there was no chance of gaining access to them.

Then came an astounding breakthrough—or so it seemed at the time. On October 28, 1965, the Quito evening newspaper, *Ultimas Noticias*,

---

*Carolus Linnaeus, the Swedish naturalist and so-called father of botany who invented the system of plant taxonomy still used today.

published an article headlined "Fabulous Treasure," claiming that three families in Lima were on the point of inheriting 23 billion sucres that had been deposited in the Royal Bank of Scotland in Edinburgh in 1803 by the governor of Latacunga, a certain Antonio Pastór y Marín de Segura, also known as the Marqués de Llosa. Claiming to be directly related to the governor via the "Puga Pastór" branch of the family in Guayaquil, the descendants had begun judicial proceedings in Lima to recover the inheritance. The article continued:

> The fortune is valued at 460,000,000 pounds sterling and originally sent by the ship *El Pensamiento*, which embarked from the port of Lambayeque under the command of Captains John Doigg and John Fanning. The cargo contained various crates of gold and silver bars, a great quantity of emeralds, other precious stones, gems, gold powder, gold Inca necklaces, masks, and vases. The deposit was made by Sir Francis Mollison in accordance with the authorization given him . . . Don Antonio Pastór y Marín de Segura was born in Cartagena, Spain, in 1772, and his parents were Don Bartolomé Pastór and Doña Rosa Marín de Segura. His godparents were King Carlos III and the Queen. He came to America as the *corregidor* of Latacunga in 1794. Later he held public offices in Chile and Lima . . . Following his marriage to Doña Narcisa Martínez he had one son and later seven grandsons . . . The *corregidor* died in 1804. His will requested that his great fortune be divided between his descendants in the fifth generation, several of whom reside in Ecuador and others in Peru.

That wasn't all. In a follow-up article on November 8, *Ultimas Noticias* gave further details, reporting that the fortune had been deposited in the name of Narcisa Martínez and that more than eighty people had attended a meeting in Quito in which they had produced documents seeking to prove their relationship to the governor's wife.

So there it was, the answer to the question that Andrade and every other Llanganatis obsessive had been seeking. If the article was to be believed, the name of the governor mentioned by Spruce in his famous paper of 1861, the man who had led the first expedition to the Llanganatis, was Don Antonio Pastór y Marín de Segura. What is more,

Pastór had found the treasure and smuggled it out of the Americas without apparently having to pay any dues to his patron, the King of Spain.

The implication of these revelations was potentially shattering. If it was true that the treasure had been removed in the early nineteenth century and deposited in the Royal Bank of Scotland, what on earth was the point of continuing to look for it?

The *Ultimas Noticias* article must have sent Andrade into turmoil. For all his protestations that the main purpose of his expedition had been scientific and that he was first and foremost a geologist, the extent and depth of his researches suggested that he was now obsessed with the treasure. But if the story in the newspaper was true, it had all been for nothing.

In the weeks and months that followed the newspaper's bombshell, Andrade found plenty more reasons for gloom. He confirmed that a Don Antonio Pastór y Marín de Segura had indeed been living in Ecuador in 1794. According to records held in Quito, he had served not as governor of Latacunga but as administrator of tributes in Ambato. Nevertheless, he had later added the collection of rents in Latacunga to his official duties, so the newspaper was broadly correct. Even more intriguing, in 1793 he had started a cinnamon-export business, harvesting the aromatic bark from the forests of Canelos to the east of the Llanganatis. Could the cinnamon business have been a cover, wondered Andrade, a ruse to enable him to venture into the Llanganatis and smuggle the treasure out without arousing the suspicion of the King's spies?

It certainly looked that way. With the exception of one or two dates and details, the information in the newspaper article struck Andrade as spot on. All his previous research pointed to the *derrotero*'s having appeared in Ecuador for the first time in the early 1790s. Now it transpired that Pastór had been exploring the Llanganatis at exactly that time.

Andrade's conclusion was unequivocal. Pastór must have been dispatched to Ecuador by Carlos IV with the express purpose of investigating Valverde's guide and establishing whether it was a true document. To keep Pastór honest, the King had also sent a priest—the Padre Longo mentioned by Spruce—to accompany him on the expedition. But on the way back Pastór murdered Longo to keep the discovery secret and substituted an adulterated copy of the *derrotero* in the archives at

Latacunga. This was the copy that Guzmán and subsequent treasure hunters had referred to, and it explained why, after the third day, all of them had lost their way. The only thing missing, argued Andrade, was Pastór's last will and testament—that and proof that the money had actually been deposited in the Royal Bank of Scotland of course.

Interestingly, while Andrade was happy to accept most of the newspaper's claims, he was adamant that on this last point the governor's descendants were mistaken. Pastór couldn't possibly have deposited £460 million worth of gold in the bank, because that would have meant he'd removed *all* of the treasure. According to Fernández, Rumiñahui had needed fifteen thousand men just to transport the treasure into the Llanganatis, so, reasoned Andrade, Pastór would have needed at least as many to remove it. But Pastór didn't have anything like that many men at his disposal, and, even under the cover of his cinnamon-export business, he wouldn't have been able to deploy them without arousing suspicion.

In other words, the newspaper's revelations changed nothing: the bulk of the treasure was still there. The key, argued Andrade, was to find the original version of the *derrotero*. Since the *cédula real* was issued in Spain, another copy—unadulterated by Pastór—must have been placed in the official records. It was simply a matter of sending a researcher to Spain and trawling the files of the Archivo General de Indias in Seville until it was found. Indeed, in a tantalizing endnote to the second edition of his book, Andrade wrote that a "distinguished" Ecuadorian—whose name he had been sworn not to reveal—had discovered Valverde's original *derrotero* in exactly this way. The researcher— a man "known for his seriousness, intellectual ability and for his great authority and prestige in the matter of historical documents"—had come across the guide by chance while examining other historical records in Seville. Unfortunately, he had subsequently misplaced the guide among his personal papers. Nevertheless, Andrade concluded that if the researcher was telling the truth, then the *derrotero* would "cease to be a mere matter of tradition and legend" and ought to be considered an authentic document.

That was not the only late addition to Andrade's book. In a further addendum headed "Another Mysterious Case of Llanganati Explorers," Andrade also became the first writer to set down the story of Blake and Chapman's expedition. Oddly, he made no mention of Blake's connection to Uncle Sammy or of Dyott's commission from the family in Philadelphia. Instead, Andrade claimed that the information about Blake's maps and letters had come to light when Dyott had been contacted by Spruce's grandson.

According to Andrade, Spruce's grandson had introduced himself to the commander one evening at the opera in London and had invited him back to his house. There he had shown Dyott a card Blake had supposedly posted to Spruce from Panama after he had emerged from the mountains. In the card Blake had informed Spruce that the map he had lent him was "completely correct," except for one or two minor details, and that he had found Valverde's treasure cave. But unfortunately, Spruce never read the card; by the time it reached him in England, he was dead (Spruce died in 1893, some six years after Blake's expedition: Andrade does not explain the delay, and one can only assume that the card was lost in the post).

Soon after, Blake himself was killed on the voyage from England to North America (in Andrade's version he fell overboard near New York rather than Halifax). Only when Spruce's grandson went through his grandfather's possessions did he discover Blake's maps and letters. Offering to put up the money, the grandson asked if Dyott would be willing to undertake an expedition on his behalf.

Dyott readily agreed, making his two expeditions to the Llanganatis. Andrade does not say whether Dyott succeeded in deciphering the clues on Blake's maps, only that after his second expedition in 1947 he contracted a severe gastrointestinal infection and had to spend several weeks recovering in a hospital. Andrade writes that, believing that he "could live more happily and peacefully" without the treasure, Dyott never went in search of it again.

Intriguingly, Andrade does not say who told him the story, claiming once again that his informant wished to remain anonymous. Nevertheless, he insisted the story was authentic and that his informant had interviewed Dyott at his ranch in 1960. Andrade also added one further intriguing detail: only Chapman had been in the Royal Navy; Blake was Dutch.

. . .

I CLOSED ANDRADE'S BOOKS AND RETURNED THEM TO THE LIBRARIAN. My head was swimming. The chroniclers' accounts of Rumiñahui's role in secreting the treasure and his subsequent capture by the Spanish had been encouraging. Andrade's analysis of the etymology of the word "Llanganati" and his discovery of the curate's expedition to the Llanganatis in 1793 had provided further reassurance of the *derrotero*'s authenticity. Moreover, his conclusion that the *derrotero* uncovered by Spruce had probably been adulterated accorded with my own prejudices, for why would anyone leave a genuine treasure guide in a public archive? Now, however, I didn't know what to think.

The first issue was the discrepancy over how Dyott had obtained Blake's maps and letters—Andrade's version, that Dyott's commission had come from Spruce's grandson, was completely at odds with Andy's story about the King James Bible and the "hollow tree on the island." Second were the questions raised by the revelations in *Ultimas Noticias*. Who were Captains Doigg and Fanning, and had anyone checked to see whether there were any records proving the existence of their ship, *El Pensamiento*, or the deposit in the Royal Bank of Scotland?

Finally, there was the question of why, having been told by a supposedly unimpeachable source that Valverde's guide was to be found in Seville, Andrade hadn't gone looking for it. Couldn't he afford the airfare, or was he reluctant to make the journey lest in turning over one more stone he discover that there was nothing there at all?

The more I thought about it, the more convinced I became that Roland's method was the only one that made sense. The *derrotero* took you only so far. Even the most diligent and levelheaded researcher soon became lost in a maze of conflicting facts and false leads every bit as perilous as the quaking bogs in the Llanganatis. The only way forward was to make a thorough survey of the mountains in the hope that somewhere between Píllaro and the *paramo* faith in the *derrotero* would be repaid. In other words, Valverde's gold wasn't like a story by Haggard or Stevenson, where you know from the beginning that the hero is going to get the loot. In the case of the *derrotero* you had to inch toward revelation step by treacherous step.

3

Insight in the Gold Room

I EMERGED FROM THE LIBRARY LOST IN THOUGHT. IT WAS NOW THE evening rush hour, and the buses were spewing greasy clouds of diesel onto the sidewalk. In hopes of avoiding the fumes, I began following one of the elevated walkways that winds around the university complex toward the Parque El Ejido—one of Quito's rare green oases. From my vantage point I could see clear over the city to the winged figure of the Angel of Quito on the summit of El Panecillo and, nestling in its shadow, the gilded domes and spires of the colonial quarter. I had read somewhere that Quito boasted an astonishing eighty-six churches— more than any other city in Latin America. The Iglesia de San Francisco, a huge church and convent built by the Franciscans on the ruins of Huayna Capac's royal palace, was said to be the most magnificent of all. But for the moment I wasn't interested in these monuments to Christian avarice. Instead, as I wandered above the traffic, trying to collect my thoughts, I found myself drawn to a building of a more recent vintage.

Built in 1995, Quito's Archaeological Museum dominates views of the downtown. A huge circular building clad in mirrored plates, it has a long, sloping roof that from a distance could be mistaken for the prow of an abandoned tanker. Once inside, however, one gets a very different impression. Divided into five interconnecting *salas* arranged over two floors, the interior is airy and spacious. From the marble-tiled atrium one is led past a series of panels depicting Ecuador's prehistory to emerge in a vast, open room packed with precious pre-Columbian sculptures and ceramics. Shaman-like jaguar figures with sharp, snarling mouths and lascivious tongues lick at the glass cases while, beside them, the contented faces of priests, their cheeks bulging with quids of coca, peer comically from urns. On the second floor these pagan images give way to the more conventional Christian relics from the colonial period and, finally, a series of vast canvases depicting the birth of the republic.

But I hadn't come to the museum for a lesson in archaeology or history. I had come to see and, if possible, to touch gold. After reading the chroniclers' vivid descriptions of the artifacts in the Temple of the Sun and hearing Andy describe the golden idols awaiting us in Blake's cave, I wanted proof that not all treasure was legendary, that on occasion a *huaquero* had succeeded in prying an artifact from the black Ecuadorian earth, and that my quest wasn't in vain. In the Sala de Oro—the museum's gold room—I had been told I would find two of Ecuador's most valuable artifacts. The first was a haunting gold funerary mask with platinum-alloy eyes; the second an exquisite, wafer-thin solar diadem with a mythic face sprouting dozens of twisted rays tipped by hissing serpents. The diadem was the most famous piece in the museum's collection—its Medusa-like image featured on the cover of nearly every guidebook to Ecuador—yet neither it nor the mask was of Inca origin. Instead, archaeologists attributed the pieces to the Tolita culture, which had thrived on the Pacific coast of Ecuador between 600 B.C. and A.D. 400, some one thousand years before the Incas, and then the Spanish, had conquered the highlands.

A party of Ecuadorian schoolgirls preceded me into the gold room. Dressed in identical blue-pleated skirts, with white socks and blouses, they trudged dutifully behind their guide—a professorial-looking woman with steel-rimmed spectacles. The first objects we came to were a series of delicate earrings and pectorals in the shape of cats, ducks, and monkeys. Although many of the pieces were no larger than my thumbnail, the Tolita goldsmiths had rendered the anthropomorphic images entirely naturalistically, with hinged parts that mimicked the articulation of wings and claws. Next came a series of golden conch shells and spiral-motif earrings—the work of the Bahía, a people who had occupied the coast of Ecuador at around the same time as the Tolita—and a series of gold breast and nose plates engraved with the images of human heads. Like the Tolita earrings these objects illustrated the Bahías' mastery of filigree and repoussé. But only when I turned a corner and came face-to-face with the Tolita funerary mask did I realize just how sophisticated the Indian goldsmiths had been.

To fashion the mask, the Tolita had had to develop a special technique for heating the obdurate platinum grains contained in the gold-bearing gravels of the rivers that drained from the mountains of southern Colombia and northwestern Ecuador. The Tolita discovered that when the gravels were heated over a charcoal brazier to 2,000 degrees Fahrenheit, the gold liquefied and bonded with the particles of platinum, forming a molten mass that, after cooling down, could be alternately hammered and reheated to become a malleable material—a technique not fully mastered by the Spanish until the eighteenth century.

However, viewing the mask now, I was impressed not so much by the techniques necessary to forge it as by its symbolism. To the Spanish, gold represented wealth and power—a passport to a better life on earth—but for the Tolita and Inca goldsmiths it was the exact opposite. The value of the hammered-gold face lay not in its weight but in its golden color—a color that enabled the high priest or king who wore it to partake of the sun's immortality.

This point was brought home to me when I rounded the next corner and nearly tripped over the schoolgirls. Sitting cross-legged on the floor in front of the diadem, they were listening in rapt attention as the guide explained the significance of the artifact.

"What does it remind you of, children?"

A plump girl with long dark tresses shot her hand up.

"The sun."

"That's right, child, the sun, because the sun brings light and heat. Do you know how the Incas regarded gold, children?"

The girls looked at one another blankly.

"They called it the sweat of the sun."

The guide turned to another display case, containing a polished silver plate.

"And silver, what do you think silver represented, children?"

Again no one dared to venture a guess.

"Why, the moon of course. The Incas believed that when the sun slept, the moon shed tears for the loss of its golden light—tears that fell to earth as silver. A beautiful idea, no?"

The girls nodded, their mouths gaping with appropriate awe.

It was indeed a beautiful idea. John Hemming was right to say these objects had no monetary value for the Incas, but their symbolic value had been incalculable. The Incas worshipped the metals not for what they could buy but for their proximity to divinity. That is why Atahualpa had been so incredulous when Pizarro had begun smelting the artifacts rifled from the Sun Temple in Cuzco into gold ingots, and why it had been so important for his followers to take to his grave as much of the gold he had accumulated during his reign as possible.

The point had not been lost on Andy. He'd hinted as much during the drive to his ranch. Why else had Vicente de Valverde, the Dominican friar who had baptized Atahualpa, been so eager to inter the Inca in Cajamarca? The implication was obvious: find Atahualpa's tomb and you might stumble upon the great treasure of Quito, too. Was this what Andy had been looking for on Cerro Hermosa, the piece of the puzzle he'd omitted from his serpentine narrative? And what if the message in Uncle Sammy's Bible and the Western Union telegram addressed to "John" was true? What if Blake had found the lake and treasure cave in the Llanganatis but had only succeeded in removing a portion of the hoard? Wouldn't it be worth studying Blake's maps and letters to find the rest?

The more I thought about it, the more convinced I was that I should take Roland up on his offer and join his expedition to the Llanganatis. Even if Andrade's suspicions proved correct and the treasure had been removed by the governor of Latacunga in the eighteenth century, it still ought to be possible to identify the remains of Inca roads and the pools and channels Roland had seen in the Sacha Llanganatis. And if Roland and I found Valverde's *socabón* nearby the mining constructions, well, it would be a pretty good story. Not necessarily one to "astound the world," as Andy had put it, but one that might convince skeptical historians that Blake and Chapman really had been onto something, that Atahualpa's hoard really had been buried in the Llanganatis after all, and that the guide Spruce had uncovered all those years ago in Lata-cunga was authentic. By the time I exited the museum, I had made up my mind. I would telephone Roland and tell him I wanted to join him.

On the way back to the hostel I stopped at an Internet café and di-aled Roland's number. Now I had made my decision I couldn't move quickly enough. In my mind I was already crossing the *paramo*, my backpack bulging with all the necessaries for survival. But there was no answer at Roland's office. I dialed again to make sure I hadn't made a mistake, and when there was no reply a second time, I tried his apart-ment. This time his housekeeper answered.

"El señor Rolando no está aquí," she muttered. *"Se fue a la costa."*

Then I remembered it was Saturday. Quiteños always fled to the coast on weekends. Even at the height of summer the nights in Quito could be surprisingly cool. But at the beach, just five hours away, you were in another country: the tropics, with the heat and humidity to match.

With mounting resignation, I asked for the number of his beach house.

"Lo siento, señor," came the predictable reply. *"En la hacienda no hay."*

So that was it, Roland was incommunicado for the weekend. At a loss as to what to do, I checked my e-mail. My in-box contained several concerned messages from family and friends worried that I had already left for the Llanganatis. There was also a message from Stan Grist apol-ogizing that he wouldn't be able to meet me again because he had to fly to El Oriente to prospect for gold. The most interesting message, how-ever, was from an American botanist friend, Lou Jost.

An orchid specialist, Lou had lived for many years in Baños and, like me, was an aficionado of Spruce. He was also something of an expert on Valverde's guide and had spent many hours puzzling over Andrade's theories. But though Lou, like Roland, had recommended I read An-drade's books, we had never discussed his findings in detail. Imagine my surprise, then, when I clicked on his message and read the following:

> Welcome to Ecuador! I tried calling you at your hotel several times, but without success . . . almost forgot to tell you, a friend told me about a friend of his family, Padre Moreno, who is a prominent Ecuadorian historian. This historian spent a lot of time in Europe studying the archives, and he stumbled across the treasure account

in the Archives of Seville. He has a copy of it here. If it differs
from the account published by Spruce this would tend to confirm
Andrade Marín's theories and could even lead to the treasure . . .
This priest says he is too old to go look for it himself.
Take care, Lou

I blinked and reread Lou's message to make sure I had understood it
correctly. Did he mean the original copy of Valverde's *derrotero*, the one
supposedly buried in the Archivo General de Indias in Seville?

I tried dialing Lou's number, but all the lines to Baños were busy. Frustrated, I turned to that morning's *El Comercio*. There on the front page
was a picture of Tungurahua with a dense cloud of gas and ash issuing
from its crater. According to the article, the volcano had gone from yellow to orange alert, and the authorities might have to evacuate Baños.

I opened my map and traced my finger south along the dragon's
spine of the Andes to remind myself of the route. It was a year since I
had visited Baños and first heard the story of Valverde's gold. Baños—
like the Llanganatis—lies in El Oriente. There it was winter, and the
nights would be cooler and damper than in Quito. But at least I would
be heading in the right direction.

That evening I loaded a few clothes into my backpack—enough for
two or three days—and went to bed early, awaking the next morning at
sunrise.

The bus station lay on the edge of Quito's old town. To get there, I
had to catch a tram north for several blocks, then walk down a steep
flight of stone steps. Campesinos—their skins scorched ocher by the
sun and sierra winds—pushed past me, their stocky frames bent double
under the weight of potatoes and grains bound for market. Every few
yards I would pass an Indian woman—a wailing infant hidden in her
layered skirts—stirring a cauldron bubbling with the entrails of some
unidentifiable mammal. Cow, chicken, guinea pig: there was no telling
what went into the mix. *"Bienvenido al Terminal Terrestre,"* declared a
sign above my head. "Welcome to the End of the Earth," I thought, or
at least the end of life as I knew it.

After being closeted in the library, I was looking forward to experi-
encing the people and country for myself. The road to Baños headed
due south along the Pan-American Highway—a route that would give

me a prime view of some of the highest and most active volcanoes in the world. Usually on your right, leaving Quito, you had a good view of Pichincha and, on a clear day, to the left or east, Antisana. Then, after an hour, came the perfect conical peak of Cotopaxi, followed, an hour later, by Chimborazo—the so-called monarch of the Andes.

Today, however, clouds the size of humpback whales swam across the horizon obscuring the peaks from view. After half an hour of twisting my head uselessly from side to side in hopes of spotting one of the Andean colossi, I gave up and contented myself with reading about them instead.

According to my guidebook, each volcano has its own cycle. Three years previously, in October 1999, Pichincha had erupted with the force of a small nuclear warhead, sending a spectacular mushroom cloud of smoke and ash rising nine miles above Quito. The last comparable eruption had been in 1660, when the sky, according to an eyewitness at the time, had turned dark "for nine days." However, in the case of Cotopaxi, the next volcano en route to Baños, the cycle was considerably shorter—once every one hundred to two hundred years. Thus Cotopaxi had erupted at the height of the Spanish conquest in 1534 and again in 1768 and 1877. Vapor was last seen issuing from the crater in 1975, and in recent years volcanic "episodes" had become increasingly frequent, suggesting that another big event was imminent.

The volcano that intrigued me most, however, was Tungurahua— whose name in Quichua means "little hell." Towering 16,500 feet above Baños, Tungurahua has no discernible cycle: it erupted in 1773, 1797, 1886, and yearly from 1916 to 1920. Then, in September 1999, Ecuador's Instituto Geofísico recorded a sudden increase in seismic activity inside the crater and declared an orange alert. The following month, magma reached the surface, sending incandescent rocks spilling from the crater in a spectacular display clearly visible from the surrounding mountainsides. It was amid fears that the cone was about to collapse and cause a river of mud and lava to flow down the mountain that the authorities had evacuated Baños. One of those caught up in the mayhem was Lou.

Raised and educated in Texas, Lou had moved to Baños in the late 1980s in order to explore the forested and still largely unexplored slopes above the town and along the corridors of the Río Pastaza. Although he'd studied physics at university, his first love was nature. For a time he'd worked as an ornithologist, pointing out different species of cloud-forest birds to tourists. His specialty, however, was epiphytes—exquisite orchids, many of them no bigger than a thumbnail, that mimic the colors and markings of butterflies and bees. Interestingly, these orchids abound in the same cool, dank forests as the mosses and liverworts that had fascinated Spruce. When Lou learned that Spruce had spent several months collecting in and around Baños in 1858, he naturally turned to *Notes of a Botanist on the Amazon and Andes* for clues as to where he should conduct his own researches. It was there that Lou, like me, read for the first time the story of Valverde's *derrotero*. But what interested Lou more was the enigmatic trails recorded on Guzmán's map. Lou suspected the topography and climate of the Sacha Llanganatis were perfect for orchids, but it appeared, from the lack of detail on Guzmán's map, that the Spanish botanist hadn't visited the region. Only madmen like Loch, and perhaps the treasure seekers that followed him, had gone *that* far.

Skeptically, Lou began collecting all the information he could on the Llanganatis and making his own tentative forays into the forested valleys along the Río Topo northeast of Baños. By 1998 he had amassed more than forty "type" orchids—unique specimens never before seen by any other collector. Lou took photographs of them and forwarded them to colleagues in the United States for classification. But he kept the best examples in a makeshift greenhouse on the roof of his house in Baños, the better to be able to care for them and admire their distinctive patterns and colors.

Then came the evacuation. Lou, along with twenty thousand Baneños, was given only a matter of hours to pack his bags and leave. In desperation, he made museum specimens of his most precious orchids—several of which were the only known examples of their species—and clambered into a truck, leaving the water pump on his greenhouse running in the hope that it was a false alarm and he would soon be allowed back. But by now the military had sealed the main road into town. In their panic, people were prostrating themselves before Nuestra Señora del Rosario de Agua Santa—a gaudy neon-lit icon in the town's basilica, which, it was believed, had miraculously protected the faithful from previous eruptions.

For weeks Tungurahua spluttered and boomed, but the feared cataclysm did not materialize. Then, shortly after Christmas, rumors began circulating that rogue soldiers had gone on a looting spree. On January 2, 2000, some five thousand townspeople armed with shovels and rocks stormed the military roadblock and reclaimed their homes. But it was too late for Lou. Although the military had left the town's electricity supply running, Lou's makeshift greenhouse required weekly attention, and without anyone to regulate the humidity his orchids had died.

At first the thought of returning was unbearable, and Lou remained in Quito. But by February agencies had begun offering tours to Baños again, and Lou decided it was time to pick up the pieces of his former life. Gathering his maps and botanical papers, he rented another apartment in the town and began constructing a new, improved greenhouse. By the time I arrived for the first time in Ecuador the following July, he had already been living there six months.

4

CONVERSATIONS WITH AN ORCHIDIST

THE EXTRAORDINARY THING ABOUT BAÑOS IS THAT YOU DON'T SEE THE town until the last moment. The road from Ambato drops sharply, following a narrow, twisting course dictated by the flow of the Río Patate and then the Río Pastaza to the Amazon. On one side the view is blocked by the sheer walls of Tungurahua, on the other by huge boulders and mist from the river's churning waters far below the roadway. Then suddenly the bus swings sharply to the left and you are crossing the Vascun bridge. If you look up hard to the right now, you might just catch a glimpse of Tungurahua's smoking crater. The next moment you skirt around a wall of solid rock and you're in Baños.

The first sight of the town is spectacular. To the right a sheer hillside rises up eight hundred yards, its face scored by a dramatic waterfall that seems to fall directly onto the soaring spires of the basilica. A white stairway winds up one side of the cliff to a mirador looking out on the crater, while far below it to the left lies the Pastaza. The gorge is like a Hoover, sucking the heat of the jungle toward the sierra. But long before the humid jungle air can reach the Andes, it cools into billowing white clouds that condense on the lush, forested hillsides below Baños.

You can observe those ghostly, drifting forms all day. They are a source of endless fascination, a reminder that the only thing separating you from a similar fate is Providence.

This ever-present threat of destruction gives Baños a miraculous ambience. Stepping from the bus, I instinctively opted for a roundabout route to Lou's apartment via the basilica. On entering the church, I was astonished to see a series of huge tableaux depicting not the usual apostolic scenes but extraordinary and faintly comic acts of salvation by the town's patron saint. Thus one painting showed a salesman whose car had plunged into the Pastaza dangling from a cable strung high above the river, while another depicted villagers taking shelter in a tiny chapel during the eruption of 1773. At the bottom of each tableau was a long and involved legend explaining how in each case it was *"Nuestra Señora"* who had prevented calamity. Indeed, it was thanks to Baños's patron saint that no one had perished in the eruptions of either 1793 or 1797—events that both occurred on February 4, a miracle that Baneños commemorated every year with a procession in the town square.

Leaving the basilica, I realized that it was exactly this sense of mystery and magic that I loved about Ecuador. In the North the idea of a lost treasure beggars belief. To mention it in polite society is to risk being labeled a crank or a dreamer. But in Ecuador, where miracles are still possible, no one doubted the treasure's existence. It was as tangible as the halo on Nuestra Señora.

I found Lou's apartment on the second floor of a travel agency near the main square. There was no bell, so I crossed to the opposite pavement and shouted his name. Seconds later a mop of unruly brown-blond hair emerged from a half-open window, followed by a pair of wire-rimmed glasses.

Dressed in white jeans and black rubber boots, Lou looked as if he'd just returned from an expedition. He was taller than I remembered—about six foot two—with pale, translucent skin that spoke of too much time in the cloud forest. Apologizing for the chaotic state of his apartment, he led me upstairs past a maze of pipes and guttering that seemed to defy the laws of physics. Inside, boxes and half-unpacked suitcases lay spread around the room, spewing their contents onto the floor. Week-old pasta pots and plates clogged the sink, while scientific papers and teach-yourself Windows programming books occupied the only available desk space. The most remarkable feature of Lou's apartment, however, was the bathroom. In order to get to the toilet, you had to negotiate a jungle of shoots and suckers sprouting from a makeshift herbarium housed in the tub. It was like something out of *The Day of the Triffids*.

"I'm building a new greenhouse on the roof," Lou explained. "The problem is, I still haven't figured out how to hook up the pump." As he said this, he picked up what looked like a part for a nuclear reactor and began grappling with a complicated-looking hose attachment.

Lou was intrigued to hear about my meeting with Andy. A few years before, he revealed, he'd been recruited by an American television production company to make a film about the treasure. Accompanied by Andy's son-in-law Diego Arias and a film crew, he'd retraced Valverde's route as far as the Desaguadero, pointing out the Llanganatis' unique flora while recording interviews for the camera. "They wanted me to tell them the history of Spruce and the *derrotero*—the usual stuff," Lou explained.

But while the documentary crew had abandoned the expedition when the weather turned inclement, Lou had never lost his passion for the Llanganatis *or* for the treasure. Fascinated by the role that botanists had played in the story, he made inquiries about Guzmán and discovered that the papers belonging to the archaeologist Jijón y Caamaño that had been inaccessible during Andrade's researches were now available to the public. As it happened, these papers had already been examined by an archaeologist at the Catholic University named Ernesto Salazar and summarized in his book *Entre mitos y fábulas* (Between myths and fables).

According to Salazar, Guzmán's ambitions and talents had mirrored those of the great German naturalist-explorer Alexander von Humboldt. Setting sail from Cádiz in 1796, Guzmán had written that his aim was nothing less than to "comprehend the three kingdoms of nature." True to his word, on the outward voyage via Montevideo and Buenos Aires, he had made copious drawings of birds, insects, and animals, as well as notes on the geology and botany of the New World. Then, on his arrival in Ecuador in 1797, he'd attempted a classification of the entire flora and fauna of the Guayaquil region. But interestingly, Guzmán's main source of income was cartography—his real name,

incidentally, had been not "Atanasio," as Spruce had written, but Anastacio. Among his personal papers were more than forty-six maps, including
several of the Píllaro region. One of these was a key to all the local farms
and smallholdings, together with the names of the inhabitants, suggesting that Guzmán had been engaged as an official census taker. But frustratingly, nowhere in Guzmán's papers was there a diary of his time in
Píllaro, or any letters explaining his interest in the mines and geology of
the region. Indeed, the only evidence that Guzmán had gone in search
of the treasure was his map of the Llanganatis and a botanical citation,
Ranunculus guzmanii, the name given by von Humboldt to a flowering
plant, "Urcu Rosa," discovered by Guzmán on the *paramo* in 1805 shortly
before his death.

Having exhausted the available textual references, Lou next turned
to the puzzle of the *derrotero* and map. Like Andrade, he agreed that the
guide could only have been written by someone who had actually been
into the mountains. Like Spruce, he also found the references to *sangurimas* and *flechas* significant.

"Spruce wasn't sure what *sangurimas* were," Lou explained, adjust-
ing his glasses bookishly. "The local people told him they were a tree
with 'white foliage.' He thought it might be a species of *Cecropia*, but it's
also a pretty good campesino definition of a *frailejón*. The problem was
that in Spruce's day, *frailejones*—what we now call *Espeletia pycnophylla*,
subspecies *llanganatensis*—had yet to be classified, so he had nothing
to go on."

And *flechas*?

"That will be the dwarf bamboo *Neurolepis aristata*. Very nasty. You
don't want to get too close to their tips—they're as sharp as arrow points,
hence the name. A friend of mine almost had his eye taken out by one."

"But what about Margasitas Mountain and the confusion over the
hieroglyph?" I asked. "No one has ever proved the existence of the
mountain, and those who thought they'd found it became lost."

"You're right, but that's where Andrade's theory comes in. It makes
perfect sense. The *corregidor* found the treasure, killed Padre Longo,
and then altered the *derrotero*."

Lou's reasoning amazed me. Here was a trained physicist and botanist,
someone schooled in the laws of cause and effect and the strict rules of
Linnaean taxonomy, telling me he trusted a faded newspaper story.

I confessed my doubts. I pointed out that the *Ultimas Noticias* article made no mention of Padre Longo or the *derrotero* and that the suggestion that the governor had killed the priest came solely from Spruce. Surely, to infer from this that the governor had altered the *derrotero* and left a forgery in the Latacunga archives was a classic case of two plus two makes five.

But Lou was adamant that Andrade's "insight" was, as he put it, "one of the strongest points in favor of the treasure's existence." In his 1937 book Andrade had already confirmed the *derrotero* probably dated from the late eighteenth century. He, too, had theorized that the governor had killed Padre Longo when he discovered the *derrotero* was a true and accurate treasure guide. Then, in 1965, *Ultimas Noticias* had independently provided the name of the governor and a date that exactly fitted Andrade's chronology for the appearance of the *derrotero* in Ecuador. Lou was clear: "Andrade's research and the newspaper article are two independent threads that both converge on this guy Pastór."

"Okay," I replied. "I grant you the coincidence is curious, but what about Guzmán's map?" I pointed out that while the northern section was broadly accurate, the southern portion was devoid of details and those Guzmán had included were mostly wrong. Contrary to the fanciful curlicues of smoke he had shown issuing from the Gran Volcán del Topo and other peaks, there were no active volcanoes in the region, and both Zunchu-Urcu and Cerro Hermoso were shown in the wrong positions, suggesting that Guzmán had never visited the area.

"In fact, I'm not sure that Guzmán's map has anything to do with the treasure," I said. "It doesn't even mention gold."

To show Lou what I meant, I opened the full-size copy of Guzmán's map I'd brought from the RGS and began tracing the botanist's route through the Mulatos region north of Yana Cocha.

"See, here he marks copper, iron, and silver mines. He's even written, 'Mina de Crystals,' by which I assume he means quartz. But there's nothing about a gold mine."

Lou nodded, acknowledging my points one by one. Then he reached across me and pointed to a river on the far right of Guzmán's map.

"You see this river here, the Curaray. That is probably derived from *curi*, the Quichua word for gold. It flows from the Sacha Llanganatis to the Bobonaza. When Spruce was journeying from Peru to Baños, he came up the Bobonaza and wrote that you had only to dip your hand in the river to find gold ore. The point is, Spruce knew the rivers were rich in gold and believed that the source was probably the Llanganatis."

Next Lou pointed out a series of numerals on the surface of Yana Cocha and Laguna de Soma, a small lake lying just beyond the crystal mine at the top right-hand corner of Guzmán's map. "What do you think the significance of those numbers is?"

Before I could answer, he reached inside a drawer and with great ceremony began reading from Spruce's famous paper to the RGS.

"Along these tracks travelled those who searched for mines of silver and other metals, and also for the gold thrown away by the subjects of the Inca," he intoned. "That the last was their principal object is rendered obvious by the"—here Lou paused for emphasis—"*carefulness with which every lake has been sounded that was at all likely to contain the supposed deposit.*" Spruce's text continued:

> The mines of Llanganati, after having been neglected for half a century, are now being sought out again with the intention of working them . . . the gold of the Incas never ceases to haunt people's memories; and at this moment I am informed that a party of explorers who started from Tacunga imagine they have found the identical Green Lake of Llanganati, and are preparing to drain it dry. If we admit the truth of the tradition that the ancients smelted gold in Llanganati, it is equally certain that they extracted the precious metal in the immediate neighbourhood; and if the socabón of Valverde cannot at this day be discovered, it is known to every one that gold exists at a short distance, and possibly in considerable quantity.

"So, you see," declared Lou triumphantly, "Spruce wasn't worried that Guzmán's map doesn't refer explicitly to the gold or treasure. Everyone in Baños knew there was gold nearby. That's why, when he arrived in Baños in 1857, the town was in such a fever and why he took so much trouble to investigate the story."

While I still had my doubts about the existence of the treasure, I was secretly pleased by Lou's reply. It confirmed my belief that Roland was on the right track and that there might really be a lost Inca mine in the mountains.

By now I was desperate to ask Lou about his new information. If someone had found the original *derrotero*, that changed everything: it meant there was finally a real chance of solving the mystery. So far I hadn't mentioned Lou's e-mail; now the questions came pouring out in a breathless rush: Who was this mysterious Padre? How did Lou's friend know that he had found the *derrotero* in Seville, and did it differ from the original?

"Patience, patience," Lou replied. "I'll tell you everything I know. First, have you heard of the Austrian explorer Paul Thur de Koos?"

I confessed I hadn't.

"Well, it is said de Koos also found Valverde's *derrotero* in Seville."

According to Lou, in 1913, one year after Colonel Brooks's fateful expedition to the Llanganatis, de Koos had also made an expedition to the Soguillas region. Enthused by the treasure story, he then returned to Europe and made a thorough search of the Seville archive.

"De Koos supposedly found Valverde's guide and returned to Ecuador with it. On his last trip to the Llanganatis he brought a large quantity of gold out of a lake. He then went back to Europe to raise capital for a second, better-equipped expedition. But just as he was about to sail from Lisbon with all the necessary diving equipment, he contracted pneumonia and died. If you look at a map of the Soguillas region you'll see there's still a lake there named after him."

"So what happened to *his* copy of the guide? Did he leave it to his family?" I asked.

"No one knows," Lou replied.

There was a pregnant pause. Was Lou trying to prepare me for something? "Okay," he said finally, "now I'll tell you what I know about the priest."

A few months earlier, Lou explained, a writer friend who was researching a guidebook to the province of Tungurahua had come to Baños to interview him about the local flora and fauna. Before long they started talking about the Llanganatis, and the treasure story came up.

According to Lou, his friend casually remarked that he knew someone who had found the original treasure document. Taken aback, Lou pressed him for more details. "That's when he told me his family were friendly with this noted historian, Padre Moreno."

Moreno was a priest at the Iglesia de San Francisco in Quito and a specialist in the history of the Spanish conquest. According to Lou's friend, his sister had been helping Moreno with a research project when she mentioned Valverde's *derrotero* to him. The Padre replied he knew the guide very well. "In fact, he told my friend's sister that when he'd been in Seville conducting historical research, he'd stumbled upon the original in the archives."

"Did he say whether he still had it?"

"I'm afraid I don't know. My friend didn't press him for details, and Moreno didn't tell his sister anything more. But having reread Andrade's book, I now think there's a good chance that Moreno may have been Andrade's mysterious informant."

"You mean the 'distinguished' Ecuadorian researcher Andrade mentions at the end?"

"Exactly."

So that was Lou's nugget. What *was* the connection between the treasure and priests? First Vicente de Valverde, then Padre Longo, now this Franciscan. I paused to consider the implications. If Padre Moreno was Andrade's informant and he was telling the truth, then that would indeed be proof that the *derrotero* was a genuine historical document. Moreover, if it differed significantly from Spruce's version, that would suggest that Pastór *had* doctored the original and that the treasure might still be out there.

Had Lou tried to contact the Padre? Did he have the *derrotero*? Was the original still in Seville?

Lou couldn't answer my questions. He'd never spoken to Moreno, but, if I was interested, it should be easy to find him. "I believe he still presides over Mass at the *iglesia* every Sunday."

After lunch Lou took me on a tour of Baños. The clouds that had enveloped the basilica in the morning had lifted, and it was now a sunny winter afternoon. Beside the church, young boys were energetically pulling *melcocha*—a local toffee made from sugarcane—into long pale gold strips and bagging it for the emerging congregants. Despite the hysterical newspaper reporting, here—in the eye of the volcano—there was little sign of panic. On the contrary, the covered market was groaning with fresh produce, while in the high street the usual groups of old men whiled away the afternoon at sidewalk cafés, sipping tea and clucking at passing backpackers. Every now and then we would pass an agency advertising evening ascents of the volcano by jeep. I couldn't help noticing that they all featured the same picture of the lava erupting orange against the black Ecuadorian night and the identical itinerary: "Departure 10 p.m., cocktails included."

If I ever got into the Llanganatis, it would be a very different experience. Everything I had read about the expeditions in search of the treasure told me that crossing the ranges would be an ordeal. It wasn't so much the tangled *paramo* vegetation and the sapping mud as the weather. Every day in the Llanganatis was the same. How had Loch put it? "Our world of perpetual mists and biting, never-ceasing rains." Was that to be my world, too?

The rest of the weekend passed in a dream. In the late afternoon I walked to the Piscinas de la Virgen, an old municipal pool with flaking blue paint built hard against the cliffs on the edge of town. The thermal waters were an uninviting yellow-brown but seductively relaxing once you slipped beneath their steaming surface. When I could bear the heat no longer, I got out and rinsed off under a set of waterspouts linked by rubber hosing to the waterfall. The water was invigorating and liberating. Staring up at the cliffs and the drifting clouds, I found it hard to believe that on the other side of the ridge just three hours away lay the polluted streets of Quito.

In the evening Lou stopped by my hotel, and together we hiked to the mirador for a view of the volcano, but by the time we reached the viewing platform, the crater had been obscured by cloud. Every now and then there was a muffled boom, and a mushroom of black smoke rose high into the air. But the next moment a bank of clouds would gust in from the east and the fog would turn a shapeless gray.

Luckily, the next day—Sunday—was clear, and after rising early for another swim, I hiked to the mirador on my own. This time Tungurahua's glacier was sharply silhouetted against a cerulean sky. Every three minutes or so the scree-scored walls of the crater would shake, and Tungurahua would belch a perfect mushroom-shaped ash cloud. It was fascinating, like watching a series of mini Hiroshimas. My mind was absolutely focused. Antonio Pastór and the deposit in the Royal

Bank of Scotland. Barth Blake and George Chapman. Padre Moreno and the *derrotero*.

I couldn't possibly pursue all the leads at once. Barth Blake and the Royal Bank of Scotland would have to wait. The key was the *derrotero*. If I could make contact with Moreno, I might be able to save myself a trip to Seville. Not only that, but he might have the document that had so far eluded every other treasure hunter—the original copy of the guide.

It was time to return to Quito.

I found Lou on the roof of his apartment, still grappling with the pump. Inside, his orchids were laid out in neat rows. They were too small to be seen with the naked eye, so Lou handed me a magnifying glass.

"See how this one mimics the markings of a bumblebee—and this could be a butterfly."

Lou was right, the orchids were exquisite. He had no need to go chasing priests. He'd already found his treasure. With regret I told him I had to leave.

He momentarily stopped what he was doing and looked up from his potting trays, a concerned frown playing about his lips. "If you have any questions, or if anything's troubling you, please feel free to run it by me," he offered gently. "The Llanganatis are a labyrinth, you know."

5

AUDIENCE WITH A PRIEST

I ARRIVED BACK IN QUITO LATE ON SUNDAY AFTERNOON AND IMMEDI-ately called a historian friend, Fernando Ortiz. Judging by his muffled yawns, I'd awoken him from a siesta.

"Ah yes, the famous Father Moreno," said Fernando, clearing his throat. "I believe he's a member of the Academy of History, but we've never met."

According to Fernando, Moreno had written several books on the early postconquest history of Ecuador, including a definitive study of Fray Jodoco Rique, the Flemish friar who had founded the Franciscan order in Quito and had supervised the construction of the magnificent church and convent named for the order's patron saint.

"Like all Franciscans, he's *muy cerrado*—very secretive—but I have a student whose father used to work for him."

Fernando passed on the number of his student, Alina Freire, and I called her straightaway. Alina had just returned from the Missouri Botanical Garden and was working on her dissertation at the Catholic University. When I told her of my interest in the Llanganatis and why I wanted to speak to Moreno, she became very excited. "My family is from Baños," she said, as if no other explanation was necessary. "My father knows Moreno well. I'll see what I can do."

Next I called Roland. He was apologetic about not having informed me about his trip to the coast, more apologetic than he needed to be. His mother-in-law had an apartment in Bahía de Caráquez, he explained, and his wife liked to go there on weekends.

I told him I'd considered his offer and was ready to join his expedition. There was a pregnant pause.

"You know, Marcos, those mountains are not such a good place for a city person. Besides, in El Oriente it's now the rainy season."

I said I'd just returned from Baños and the weather there didn't seem so bad.

"Ach! Baños is a holiday village," he scoffed. "On the *paramo* it's completely different. In any case, I don't have the time right now."

Roland explained he'd just bought a plot of land in Los Chillos, a well-to-do suburb of Quito, and his wife was urging him to build her a new house.

"You know how much I've spent until now on expeditions to the Llanganatis? Nearly $100,000. My family thinks I'm crazy."

Roland didn't strike me as the sort of man who would let a little spousal nagging stand between him and a five-hundred-year-old Inca treasure. There was something he was leaving out, I was sure of it.

I realized that I had been lucky to meet Roland when I had. Now, with dread, I sensed my passage to the Llanganatis slipping away. Had he been teasing me the previous week when we had pored over the maps together, or had he simply been caught up in the excitement of the moment—an excitement that had dissipated with the cold light of day?

I didn't know the answer, but I knew I had to forestall a decision, to keep the possibility of our expedition open. I decided not to mention Andy and what he had told me about Blake and Dyott (I didn't want Roland to think I was negotiating with another treasure hunter). Instead, I told him about my meeting with Lou and what he had said about Moreno.

"That could really be something new," Roland agreed, more animatedly. "Ask him if he still has his copy of the *derrotero*, then we could make a comparison."

The next moment I heard a clatter of plates and the urgent murmur of domestic voices.

"Listen, my wife is calling, I have to go. Phone me as soon as you've spoken to Moreno."

And with that Roland hung up.

The next few days passed without any word from Alina, so I spent the time browsing the shops and bookstores along Avenida Juan León Mera, a busy, traffic-clogged artery running through the heart of the Mariscal. The street was buzzing with Internet cafés, tour agencies, and funky organic restaurants offering *comidas vegetarianas*. Four French girls, their hair braided Rastafarian-style with brightly colored beads, were trying to negotiate a discount for a mountain-bike descent of Cotopaxi. The tour guide was explaining that the hire of the jeep and bikes for the day came to $40 per person, or $160 for the group—that was enough to keep an Indian family in meat and grain for a year. The girls were right, it was too much, a gross distortion of the underlying economic reality. The sign above the shop read, "The Biking Dutchman"; the money wouldn't even be going to an Ecuadorian.

I wandered into Libri Mundi, a chic bookstore where they checked your bag at the entrance, and found a book titled *Llanganati*. It was a coffee-table-sized hardback illustrated with stunning black-and-white photographs and potted histories of the various treasure hunters. The author, Jorge Anhalzer, was described as one of Ecuador's premier photographers. According to the accompanying blurb, for many years he'd worked as a guide, leading parties of rich Americans along Valverde's route and photographing the mountains in his spare time from his own light aircraft. The absence of color accentuated the mountains' dreamy, surreal quality. One photograph showed a porter, machete in hand, emerging in a valley of *frailejones*. In another, taken from the air, the sawtooth peaks of Cerro Hermoso protruded from a bed of fluffy white clouds, like the humps of some prehistoric monster. But Anhalzer had not been content merely to record the botany and geology of the Llanganatis; he'd also delved into the psychic geography and etymology of the treasure legend. According to Anhalzer, the origin of the name "Topo" could be a Quichua word, *tupu*, meaning "brooch" or "point of a needle." I was also intrigued to see he'd reproduced the *derrotero* in

large Gothic script in the original Castilian. A few pages later, he'd in-
serted a photograph of the Iglesia de San Francisco together with a picture of the chapel at its side. Taken from the foot of a flight of steps
leading up from the plaza, the photographs made the church and the
chapel seem to be raised above the level of the surrounding buildings.

It was not an illusion. According to Anhalzer, the elevation of the
church was the result of a deliberate decision by the Franciscans to com-
mence construction on the ruins of Huayna Capac's royal palace. There
were also intriguing legends associated with the building's history. One
of these spoke of an Indian stonemason, Cantuña, who had supposedly
sold his soul to the devil. The story went that Cantuña had fallen behind on the construction of the church and had made a pact with the
devil to help him finish the work on time. But on the morning that the
devil came to claim Cantuña's soul, the Indian spotted a small stone
missing from the base of one of the walls of the chapel and was saved.

That, at least, was the Spanish version. But Anhalzer also related the
Indian version, which was somewhat different.

Now Cantuña was an orphan, the child of one of Rumiñahui's officers who had been killed during the sacking of Quito. Burned and
grossly disfigured by the fires lit by Benalcázar, the child Cantuña had
wandered the streets of the ruined Inca city, shunned and ignored, until a kindly conquistador named Hernán Suárez took pity on him and
invited him into his home. There he discovered that despite Cantuña's
disfigurement (it was said he had a face that "resembled a demon"), the
boy was intelligent and had good judgment, so Suárez instructed him
in the Christian faith. But unfortunately Suárez was a poor business-
man and within a matter of months was reduced to such poverty that
he found himself obliged to sell his house. It was at this point that Cantuña took the conquistador to one side and told him that if he made
certain modifications to the foundations of his home, he, Cantuña,
would solve all his financial problems.

Suárez readily agreed, and the conquistador's fortunes were transformed overnight. When Suárez died, Cantuña was declared his heir
and inherited the house. To solidify his place in Spanish society, Cantuña began donating money to the Franciscans—whose new church
and convent were in the same neighborhood—and distributing alms to
the poor. But the priests couldn't understand how a mere Indian had

become so wealthy and compelled Cantuña to give an account of himself. It was then that Cantuña told them he'd made a pact with the devil. The priests wanted to exorcise the demon of course, and when Cantuña refused, saying he preferred to have the money to touch for the rest of his life, they warned him he would be damned forever.

Only when Cantuña died did the Franciscans discover the secret furnace in the basement of his house and, lying beside it, several gold ingots and Inca artifacts. Cantuña had been smelting gold for years.

According to Anhalzer, no one knew where Cantuña had obtained the artifacts. Some said the treasure had been buried under the house all along; others said his father had been one of those "who had been in the Llanganatis with Rumiñahui."

Once again I was struck by the parallels with Valverde. Suárez's kindness to Cantuña seemed to mirror Valverde's kindness to the Píllaro Indians. Suárez had taken Cantuña into his family just as Valverde had taken the Inca princess as his bride. And in exchange both had received a confidence.

This union of victor and vanquished, this joining of Spanish and Indian blood, raised complex cultural and psychological issues—issues that went to the heart of the conflict between Catholic and Inca cultures. Perhaps the real significance of the treasure legend was metaphorical, an example of collective Indian wishful thinking: if you, the Spanish, show us kindness, then that kindness will be reciprocated, and the harmony we used to enjoy in this land will be restored. A more obvious example of this attempted resolution was the syncretism in Indian religious practice. Beside the usual reliquary candles in the chapel of Nuestra Señora in Baños, for instance, were offerings of local vegetables and fruits—symbols of the Inca cornucopia. Similarly, the nave of the basilica was peppered with images of the sun—a common practice in both Ecuadorian and Peruvian churches. An archaeologist friend later informed me that in the case of the Iglesia de San Francisco, the craftsmen recruited by the Franciscans had been cleverer still, carving images of serpents and fruit bowls into the altar and aligning the altar with one of the towers in such a way that on the morning of the winter solstice—December 22—a beam of sunlight was seen to pass directly across the face of God. A similar phenomenon occurred at El Quinche, a church northeast of Quito built, like San Francisco, on a sacred Inca site, except that here the altar was perfectly illuminated by the sunset of the summer solstice—June 21.

I had yet to see the Iglesia de San Francisco and was looking forward to combining my meeting with Moreno with a tour of the church and the old town. But then, on Thursday, came a message from Alina. Her father had called Moreno and he was not available.

"Padre Moreno is leaving for Esmeraldas first thing tomorrow morning and cannot meet you. Besides, he told my father to tell you that he has no interest in the Llanganatis."

"Did your father ask him about the *derrotero*?"

"Yes, he confirms he was in Seville but says he never found it."

I asked if I could speak directly with Señor Freire, and she gave me her father's number in Baños. His tone immediately set me on edge.

"*Sí, patrón,*" said Señor Freire solicitously. "I know the Llanganatis well. How can I help you?"

I didn't need help, I explained, I already had someone who could guide me in the mountains. There was no reason to tell him about Roland's sudden reluctance. I was interested only in knowing whether he had spoken with Moreno and what he'd said about the *derrotero*.

"He didn't find it," replied Señor Freire. "He told me it's a lie."

So what Alina had told me was correct. The priest was saying the rumors that he'd found the *derrotero* were false. Was it possible that Lou's friend had been mistaken and that Andrade's informant had been someone else? But no, Lou had been adamant. Besides, there was something about Moreno's dismissal that didn't ring true. It was too pat, just the sort of thing you would say if you wanted to give a foreigner the brush-off.

I looked up the convent's address in the white pages and rang the number listed. A Sister answered the phone. I asked to be put through to Moreno, and she connected me to the refectory.

"*¡Alo!*"

"*¿Fray Moreno?*"

"*Sí. ¿Quién es?*"

I imagined Moreno wiping soup from his chin.

"*Soy el historiador inglés, el amigo del señor Freire.*"

"*Ah, sí. El buscador de tesoros.*"

So, my reputation had preceded me. I explained my background and my interest in the *derrotero*. Was it possible to see him first thing Friday morning before he left Quito for the weekend?

There was a long pause. "Come to the church at ten o'clock," Moreno replied in excellent English. "We can talk after Mass."

The following morning I caught a tram after breakfast, disembarking at Plaza Grande, the square in the heart of old town where Benalcázar had laid the first foundation stone of the Spanish city. Even at this early hour the streets had an air of desperation. On Chile, a narrow, cobblestone alleyway running east from the plaza, the sidewalk was packed with hawkers selling everything from hair dye to wooden kitchen utensils and clothes brushes. Shoeshine boys, their fingers and faces grimy with boot polish, darted like flies in and out of the crowds. At one point I rounded a corner and was almost knocked off my feet by a toothless woman on a skateboard. I wheeled around, only to realize, to my horror, that the woman had no legs and that the skateboard was actually a rough plank attached to the undercarriage of an old pram.

According to my guidebook, while San Francisco was the oldest church in Quito, it was by no means the richest. That honor belonged to La Compañía de Jesús, a seventeenth-century Jesuit church near Plaza de la Independencia. Begun in 1603 and completed in 1765, just two years before the Jesuits were expelled from South America, La Compañía boasted the most lavish interior of any church in Ecuador—its altar, walls, and ceilings were burnished with seven tons of gold. I recalled Stan Grist's telling me that it was the sight of La Compañía's altar that had convinced him that Ecuador might be a good country for gold mining.

Standing outside La Compañía now, however, I was struck by its uniformly gray exterior—the result of the Indian stonemasons' reliance on volcanic rock. Only when I passed beneath the angels, saints, and cherubs guarding the entrance did the impression change. Grist was right: inside it was gold leaf gone mad. La Compañía's dome, altar, and columns were so richly decorated it was as if the Jesuits had bottled the very essence of the sun. But, oddly, the most memorable feature of the church was not its gaudy interior but a mural to the right of the main door. Depicting gluttons and other miscreants being tortured for their sins, the mural was a vivid portrayal of hell or, as the writer Paul Theroux put it when he passed through Quito on his way to Patagonia in 1980, "pure Bosch." Looking at the tableau now, however, with its gory depictions of greed, I was struck by the hypocrisy: the Jesuits counseling the Indians against a sin they themselves were guilty of many times over.

I hoped Moreno would be different. After all, Saint Francis had been a champion of the poor, a humble workman who had renounced all material possessions. If Moreno had found the *derrotero*, then surely he would see that he had no right to keep it; that the gold was the rightful property of the Indians; and that, as a historian, he had a duty to share his knowledge of it.

I wound up Sucre, a narrow alleyway packed with more cheap haberdasheries. Brushing past the stallholders, I was reminded of the warnings posted in my hostel to beware of con artists operating in the backstreets. A favorite trick, apparently, was to spray *dulce de leche*—a sticky caramel—on your trousers, and then rush up to you with a concerned look and a fistful of tissue paper. While one member of the team helped to clean off the caramel, his accomplice would rifle the contents of your rucksack.

This morning, however, it was quiet, and I arrived at Plaza de San Francisco unmolested. Save for a stray newspaper vendor, the square was deserted. Directly in front of me, rising from the eastern side of the plaza like a pair of rocket launchers, were the church's towers and, to the right, the whitewashed walls of the convent. A group of elderly women were in front of the entrance, blocking the main door. Behind them, deep within the bowels of the church, I could just make out a flickering orange light.

The women were selling incense and rosary beads, and against my better instincts I purchased a candle. My offering must have done the trick because the next moment the women parted like the Red Sea and I crossed the threshold.

Inside, it was standing room only. The nave and lateral chapels were packed. From the Mudejar-inspired choir area, an antique organ was sounding Mass, sending sonorous chords bouncing off the church's huge gilded dome. Looking up at the vaulted ceiling, I realized the windows were too small and too high to admit much light from either north or south. As a result, one's eyes were naturally drawn to the east, along the length of the nave to the magnificent altar and pulpit carved with Inca fruit bowls, serpents, and glowing images of the sun. There, beneath Bernardo de Legarda's famous carving of the Virgin of Quito—the model for the giant bronze statue on El Panecillo—stood Moreno, a slight, gray-haired man resplendent in his white Franciscan robes.

Moreno read a lesson from Saint Matthew; murmured, "Esta es la palabra de Dios"; and kissed the holy book. Then he raised his eyes to heaven and began offering his flock Holy Communion. This last part—the distribution of the wafers and wine—seemed to take forever. The line of congregants stretched the length of the church and out the door.

To kill time, I wandered into a side chapel, where another queue was forming. Judging by their ragged clothes and rough appearance, the congregants here were the poorest of the poor. As my eyes adjusted to the flickering light, I saw that each person grasped a candle and a scrap of paper. On entering the chapel, they would throw themselves in front of a giant wooden crucifix and begin genuflecting wildly. Then they would pin their notes to the cross and, lighting their candles, offer up fervent prayers.

After twenty minutes or so the crucifix was completely covered, and I could take the scene no longer. There was something terribly sad about the way these proud Indian people had been reduced to prostrating themselves before an imported God. It was as if their culture had been utterly sublimated and all they had was the cross and their scraps of paper.

To my surprise, when I returned to the nave, Moreno and the line of worshippers had disappeared. In their place a chorister was offering up out-of-tune "hallelujah"s. The next moment the organ throbbed back to life, and the bars of a familiar theme came floating down the aisle. I couldn't place it at first—Beethoven, Mozart? Then I realized it was music from *The Godfather*. Was someone up there mocking me?

Worried Moreno was about to give me the slip, I hurried next door to the convent and announced myself to the Sister at the front desk—a Joyce Grenfell look-alike with buck teeth and prescription glasses. She nodded enthusiastically—"Padre Moreno is expecting you"—and pointed to a chair. I took a seat and waited, my mind racing.

Why had Moreno told Alina's father that he was leaving the city when he knew he would be in Quito? Was it to throw me off the scent, and if so, why had he agreed to meet me this morning? More important, had he really found the *derrotero* and would he be prepared to share it with me? A few minutes later Moreno appeared at the door and beckoned for me to enter the convent. My wait was over.

Divested of his robes, Moreno was the epitome of an academic. With his razor-cut gray hair and brown woolen suit, he wouldn't have looked out of place on the campus of Harvard or Yale. He shook my hand warmly and showed me to a bench in the cloisters to the left of the door—evidently, the interview would not be taking place in his office.

I began by repeating what I had told him over the phone: how, like him, I was a historian; how I had spent the previous two years reading Richard Spruce's journals and retracing his journeys through Ecuador in search of the cinchona tree; and how, finally, while reading his account of his stay in Baños in 1857, I had become fascinated with Valverde's *derrotero*.

Moreno waved his hand contemptuously, interrupting my flow. "Hah! The *derrotero* is just a story. I don't believe there ever was a soldier named Valverde."

I had expected smoke and mirrors but not this; thrown by Moreno's unexpected dismissal of my premise, I floundered: "But I was told you'd been to Seville, that you'd found the *derrotero*?"

"Whoever told you that is a liar!" snapped Moreno. "It is true I spent some time in the Seville archives, but I never found any trace of a *derrotero* or of a *cédula real*."

Not knowing whether to believe him, I tried a different tack. "But what about the expedition by the governor of Latacunga and the cross on Guzmán's map indicating the death of Padre Longo?"

"Another invention! There *was* no Padre Longo."

"But you must be familiar with Andrade Marín's book? Andrade was convinced there had been a *derrotero* and that the King of Spain had sent it to the governor with express orders that he search for the treasure."

"Yes, yes, I know all about Luciano's *theories*"—Moreno pronounced the word with a hiss—"he and I were once friends, you know."

So he *had* known Andrade. Perhaps Lou was correct and Moreno had been Andrade's mysterious informant after all.

"Did you ever discuss the treasure with him?" I asked, hoping to catch him off guard.

Moreno eyed me warily. Had I been indiscreet? "No," he eventually replied, "we never discussed it. At that point in my life I wasn't interested in the treasure—it was only afterward that I read his book and formed my own opinions."

I could see I wasn't going to get anywhere by pursuing this line of inquiry. If Moreno had found the *derrotero* and had shared it with Andrade, he wasn't about to tell a gringo historian. However, at this point Moreno suddenly volunteered some extraordinary information.

"I'm almost certain I know where the treasure is, and I can tell you it's not in the Llanganatis. Andrade, Loch, Dyott—they were all looking in the wrong place!"

According to Moreno, Lou's friend had misunderstood him: the information he had discovered in Seville was connected with the location of Atahualpa's tomb, not the *derrotero*. Moreno explained that he had spent twenty years in the Archivo General de Indias, sifting through the communications between the conquistadores and their financiers—men like Gaspar de Espinosa, the governor of Panama, and his agent, a priest named Hernando de Luque. It was from this correspondence that Moreno claimed he had identified the Inca's last resting place.

Moreno pointed out that Atahualpa was only three years into his reign when he was executed by Pizarro and would have just begun to amass his fortune. Nevertheless, his hoard had been considerable.

"Rumiñahui brought the llamas loaded with gold to within fifty miles of Cajamarca," said Moreno. "He was just waiting to see what would happen. Would Pizarro keep his promise and release Atahualpa or would he kill him?"

When Rumiñahui learned that Pizarro had broken his promise, he ordered his men to return to Quito with the gold (in Moreno's version there were two thousand llamas, each carrying two *cargas*, making the total weight of the treasure thirty tons). But Rumiñahui remained behind, waiting until Pizarro had left for Cuzco to enter Cajamarca and disinter Atahualpa's corpse. That was in August 1533. Since Benalcázar did not reach Quito until the following June, Rumiñahui had had ten months to embalm Atahualpa—the chroniclers disagree whether this took place in Cajamarca or Quito—and lead his mummy in a slow funeral procession toward Quito. En route Rumiñahui stopped at various points along the royal Inca road so the local caciques could pay their respects. Then, with the obsequies over, he buried Atahualpa and the gold in a location where the Spanish would never find it.

"Even today there are Indians alive who know the secret and won't reveal it," Moreno declared, wagging his finger in the air for emphasis. "They've been hiding it all this time!"

By now I was dying to ask Moreno where he thought Atahualpa's tomb was located. Was it, as Andy seemed to believe, on Cerro Hermoso, or was it on some other mountain? But Moreno had other ideas. "I could sell this information many times over, but the fact is I'm no longer interested," he teased.

All Moreno would tell me is that he had once shared his findings with a colonel in the Ecuadorian Army. The colonel was a cartographer and radar expert, practiced at reading the topography and hydrology of the Andes. Together he and Moreno had identified the mountain where Atahualpa lay buried and had planned an expedition to it. But on the eve of their departure the colonel had suffered a heart attack and died. The next thing Moreno knew the colonel's widow disappeared, taking the precious documents from Seville with her. Moreno claimed the experience had convinced him that the treasure was "cursed." "It is better to leave it where it is," he said.

Moreno's statement seemed to make further interrogation pointless. Even if he was now telling the truth—and it was a big if—it was clear that he had no intention of revealing where he thought the treasure was buried. Nevertheless, in hopes of extracting further confidences from him, I thanked him for his time and asked whether he would meet me for lunch the following day.

At first he demurred. "Why don't you go to Seville and look for the documents yourself?" he suggested slyly. "You're still young, you have plenty of time."

I replied that I fully intended to and would welcome his giving me some tips on where to look. Wrong-footed by my cordiality, Moreno had no choice but to relent—he did not wish to appear unhelpful to a fellow historian: "Come here at noon, and we can resume our conversation."

I left the convent elated. I had not forced a confession, but I had bearded the historian in his den and extracted something almost as valuable. At least that's what it felt like as I emerged from the sanctuary of the convent and bounded down the stairs to the plaza. Only when I reached the tram stop did I realize Moreno had told me nothing of any use. Without knowing the source of his information, I had no way of checking his claim about Atahualpa's tomb, much less of discovering where the gold was buried.

The more I replayed our conversation, the more my sense of unease deepened. In the middle of the interview there had been a sudden commotion at the door of the convent, and a young woman had burst into the cloisters, tears streaming down her cheeks. She had been extremely distraught, and it took several minutes for the nuns to calm her. Eventually she managed to tell us that her husband had left her and that "the demons inside her head" were telling her to kill their children. Grasping Moreno's hands, she fell to her knees and pleaded with him to perform an exorcism. But rather than offering her spiritual comfort, Moreno dismissed her in what I felt was a rather un-priestly manner and suggested she seek the help of a professional psychiatrist.

At another juncture, we had been discussing the testimonies of the great historians of the conquest when Moreno had mentioned the theory that Cieza may have been a *converso*—a Jew who had converted to Catholicism to escape persecution by the Inquisition.* The next thing I knew, Moreno had thrust a business card into my hand bearing the name "Agustín Moreno Proaño."

"Here, I'm known as Father Moreno, but my real name is Proaño," he said. "My ancestors were Sephardic Jews from Toledo. To escape the Inquisition some of my family fled to Amsterdam; the others, well . . ."

Moreno shrugged his shoulders. His inference was unmistakable. If I understood him correctly, here was a Catholic priest, a man who had just sanctified the Body and Blood of Christ, saying that in ethnic terms at least, he was still a Jew! Was this a genuine revelation or an-

---

*The theory is not as far-fetched as it may appear: according to the Dutch archaeologist and historian Victor Wolfgang Von Hagen, Cieza's maternal family were listed as suspected *conversos* in Seville, a town that in the sixteenth century had a large Jewish community; he also points out that Cieza's texts are peppered with suspiciously over-the-top appeals to God and the mysteries of the church. See Von Hagen's introduction to *The Incas of Pedro de Cieza de León* (Norman: University of Oklahoma Press, 1959).

other of Moreno's "confidences," a true story or something that he had
invented to deflect my attention away from the *derrotero*?

Leaving the old town, I felt less certain than ever that I knew the answers to those questions. I was a novice prying open the door to centuries-
old secrets. Nevertheless, I sensed that something significant had passed
between us. Next time we met I vowed I would not allow Moreno to
divert me so easily.

But there was no next time. When I returned to the convent the
following morning, the Sister handed me a note. Written in an old-
fashioned hand with the date inscribed in Roman numerals, it read:

> Dear Mark,
> Sorry, I was called for an urgent meeting at the Academy of His-
> tory at noon. Maybe we will see [*sic*] again in London. Good luck!
> Agustín

I didn't believe Moreno's excuse for a second, but in a way I was relieved. If he had turned up and allowed me to question him, then the
edifice he had so artfully erected the day before might have started to
crumble. This way, he retained his dignity and, perhaps, his secret, too.

I wrote him a note, telling him that I doubted we would meet in
London "or anywhere else" and reminding him that he had a duty as a
historian to share his knowledge with future generations. My hope was
to shame him into publishing the *derrotero* without appearing to preach
or hector. I am not sure I succeeded on either score.

When I returned to the hostel, I called Lou and gave him a blow-by-
blow account of the meeting. I was grateful to find him at his most rational and scientific.

"I suppose Moreno could be telling the truth, but the fact that he
lied about not being in Quito suggests otherwise. He was obviously
hoping to avoid you."

Lou did not know what to make of Moreno's information about
Atahualpa's tomb, but thought that his admission that he had known
Andrade was significant.

"Don't you see, it all fits. He must have been Andrade's secret informant. But from what you've told me, if Moreno has the *derrotero*, he'll never let you see it. You'll have to go to Seville and find it yourself."

I asked him to check whether his friend was sure Moreno had been referring to the *derrotero*. As usual, Lou was happy to oblige, and the following day I received an e-mail saying that his friend was adamant: Moreno *had* been talking about the *derrotero* and had made it clear to his sister that it was a different version from the one that Spruce had found in Latacunga. For good measure, Lou included a copy of their correspondence. In it his friend explained—somewhat charitably, I thought—that Moreno was "one of those old-fashioned historians who doesn't understand the importance of spreading information." After this, by way of a postscript, Lou had added perspicaciously:

I feel certain that the lies and secrecy surrounding this document prove that it is significantly different from the Latacunga version . . . There would be no point in the secrecy otherwise. And that suggests that the treasure really existed and was found by Pastór, else there would be no point in him doctoring the Latacunga copy. This story is getting really interesting . . .

Part Four

ZUNCHU-URCU

Suddenly I heard an exclamation of fear from some one, and turned my head down the cave . . . Sitting at the end of it . . . was another form, of which the head rested on the chest and the long arms hung down. I stared at it, and saw that it too was a dead man, and what was more, a white man.

—H. RIDER HAGGARD, *King Solomon's Mines*

Where I Show Blake's Maps to
Roland and His Opinion Thereof

THERE COMES A POINT IN EVERY TREASURE HUNTER'S APPRENTICESHIP
when the books and maps can be dissected no more and the speculation
has to stop. Short of returning to Europe and making an appointment
with the archivist in Seville, I felt I had read everything I could in
Ecuador about Valverde's gold. The only thing left was the mountains
themselves.

Despite the sudden cooling of Roland's enthusiasm, I was confident
that I could change his mind about our expedition, that with a little more
persuasion and perhaps the right pecuniary incentive I could convince
him that I had what it took to survive in Loch's realm of "false promises
and crushed hopes." Rather than risk another telephone rebuttal, I decided to confront him at home. If Roland didn't think I was up to an
expedition to the Llanganatis, he would have to tell me in person.

I walked from my hostel to Roland's apartment building and pressed
the buzzer. This time there were no shoeshine boys loitering outside.

"Ah, Marcos, how are you?" boomed the familiar Teutonic voice.
"I've been expecting you. The security guard will show you upstairs."

I emerged from the lift to find Roland waiting for me on the first floor. He slipped a protective arm around my shoulder and ushered me into his office. Everything was exactly as I remembered it—the tarpaulin and tanks spread across the floor, the riot of books and maps on the table. There had been just one small change. On the wall immediately to the left of the door, where previously there had been a mirror, Roland had hung a garish new portrait of an Indian warrior. Staring implacably ahead, the warrior's eyes appeared fixed on some distant horizon. As if to emphasize the purity of the Indian's genes, the artist—who had signed himself simply "Gallo"—had given the warrior high noble cheekbones and piercing black eyes.

"Do you like it? Can you guess who it is?" asked Roland.

I furrowed my brow, looking blank.

"It's Rumiñahui. It was painted by a friend of mine, Colonel Gallo."

Roland explained that to the army Rumiñahui was a resistance hero, the greatest general in Ecuadorian history.

"The army believes the treasure is theirs. They'll never let the state take it," he said, showing me to a chair.

Then, lighting a cigar, he changed the subject: "So how did it go with Moreno?"

I gave him a précis of our meeting, describing how the priest had tried to avoid me and our cryptic conversation in the convent. Roland found Moreno's theories about Atahualpa's tomb intriguing but dismissed his claims that Valverde and Padre Longo were fictions.

"Don't believe him. Even now he's probably plotting how to get the gold for himself!"

Just as the army considered the treasure theirs because of Rumiñahui, so the Church thought that it had a prior claim on the gold because of Atahualpa's conversion to Christianity at Cajamarca. Indeed, following the conquest, both the Franciscans and the Jesuits had established mission posts deep in the Amazon. There, under the guise of offering the Indians spiritual salvation, they had kept watch over the Spanish mines and used their influence to try to extract confessions from the Indian slave laborers.

"Those priests were smart. They wrote everything down," said Roland. "Perhaps Moreno was telling the truth when he said he hadn't discovered the *derrotero* in Seville; perhaps he discovered it right here in an old Franciscan archive."

The Iglesia de San Francisco, Quito. The church appears to be raised above the level of the surrounding buildings, a consequence of its having been built on the ruins of Huayna Capac's royal palace.

"If thou lose thyself in the forest, seek the river." Efraín leads the porters along a beach on the Parca Yacu.

"Here thou shalt find a bridge of three poles, or if it do not still exist, thou shalt put another, in the most convenient place, and pass over it." Roland inches along a tree trunk slung across the Parca Yacu. Roland and Don Segundo felled more than eight trees before they found three with which to ford the river.

"Having gone a little way in the forest, seek out the hut which served to sleep in, or the remains of it." This hut belonging to an agricultural cooperative near Yana Cocha now serves as Valverde's first sleeping place.

"Look for the reclining woman, and all your problems are solved." Looking east from the Río Mulatos toward the undulating hills of the Sacha Llanganatis.

Cotopaxi as it appears today. At 19,347 feet, Cotopaxi is the highest active volcano in the world.

LEFT: Don Segundo places flowers at Diego Arias's grave beneath Zunchu-Urcu. Diego used to spend days camped beside the peak, admiring the natural beauty of the ranges. In 1994, his lobbying efforts resulted in the government declaring the Llanganatis a national park.

BELOW: Commander George Miller Dyott.

ABOVE: Richard Spruce, aged forty-seven. The picture was taken in 1864, the year he arrived back in England after fifteen years exploring the Amazon and the Andes.

RIGHT: Roland panning for gold on the Río Mulatos: "I am very close now—I can feel it."

ABOVE: Erskine Loch pictured beside a lake on the *paramo*, dressed in a sheepskin jacket of his own design. The first explorer to cross the ranges from east to west, Loch spent a total of eight months in the Llanganatis, only nine days of which were free of rain. It was, he wrote, "a land of false promises and crushed hopes."

RIGHT: Drawing by Poma de Ayala depicting Atahualpa's execution in 1533. Atahualpa was buried beneath the new church of San Francisco in Cajamarca, only for his corpse to be disinterred by Rumiñahui, mummified, and transferred to a secret location.

Andy inspects a maize field on his ranch. A former president of the Ecuadorian cattle rancher's association, Andy used to keep a herd of five thousand tropical milking cows. Today, his ranch boasts just eighteen hundred.

Olivier Currat examining the "Inca wall" in 1997. Constructed from close-fitting polygonal blocks and built into the hillside at a forty-five-degree angle, the wall appears to serve no strategic purpose. In one place, water from a nearby brook falls over the wall in a wide sheet, "making a sort of artificial waterfall."

ABOVE: The sawtooth peaks of Cerro Hermoso jut through the clouds. It is easy to see why, viewed from afar, the mountain could have been mistaken for a volcano with "seven mouths." BELOW: The M-like profile of Zunchu-Urcu, just as it appears on Guzmán's map.

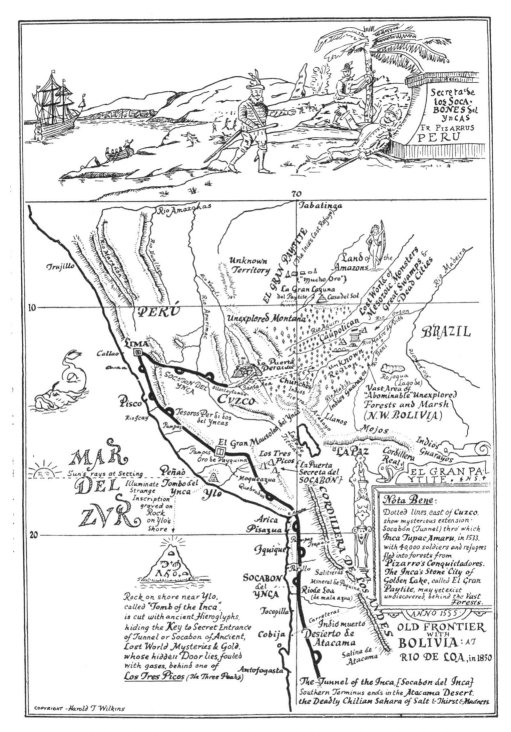

Harold T. Wilkins's curious map of the *Socabón del Inca* ("Tunnel of the Inca").
Running the length of the Peruvian Andes, the *socabón* is said to be approached
via a door behind three triangular peaks. According to Wilkins, the key to the
door is to be found inscribed on a rock near Ilo, but to date neither the
tunnel system nor the rock have been found.

Roland found Moreno's admission that he had known Andrade even more significant. According to Roland, Andrade had been obsessed with a valley behind Las Torres. After the publication of the second edition of his book, he had mounted several expeditions to the valley accompanied by an American treasure hunter. Together they had probed a lake at the foot of a prominent peak and investigated a cave inhabited by a wild puma. Years later one of Andrade's porters had led Roland to the cave. Nearby Roland had found Andrade's abandoned mining equipment, but, except for some rabbit bones discarded by the puma, the cave itself was empty.

Considering the situation now, however, Roland thought it possible that Moreno and Andrade had once been partners. "Perhaps Moreno discovered the location of Valverde's *socabón* and passed the information to Andrade. Perhaps that's why he kept going back to the same valley."

By contrast, Roland thought Moreno's story about the sudden death of the Ecuadorian Army colonel on the eve of their expedition to Atahualpa's tomb was a red herring.

"That's just an Indian scare story. Moreno knows the treasure is hidden in the Llanganatis. He's trying to put you off!"

Had Roland forgotten that only a few days before he'd also tried to dissuade me? This seemed the perfect opportunity to remind him of his offer.

"Look, Roland, I have to get into those mountains. I have to see the Llanganatis for myself."

Roland hesitated, pulling on his cigar.

"Ach, now is not the best time. It's not just the weather, Marcos. My parents are unwell."

According to Roland, his father was eighty-nine and had a heart condition. His seventy-one-year-old mother was too poorly to care for him alone and was pleading with Roland to fly home.

"I am waiting to hear from the doctors, but I may have to go to Germany in the next few days."

I studied Roland carefully. Was this an excuse? Until now I had seen him only as a treasure hunter, an obsessive whose ambition for the gold took precedence over every other feeling. Now, it seemed, Roland was also somebody's son.

With no cards left to play, I decided to tell him about my meeting with Andy. I wanted to know whether Roland had seen Blake's maps and letters and what he made of the clues "Look for the cross" and the "Reclining Woman." Besides, the news that I had been consorting with a potential rival might be just the spur I needed to goad Roland to action.

"*Ah, sí*, you met the famous Señor Fernández-Salvador?" asked Roland with surprise. "I've come across his tracks in the mountains many times, but we've never been introduced."

I gave Roland a summary of my conversations at Andy's ranch, leaving out his phlegmatic outbursts and the air of melancholy that had hung over our encounter. Instead, I played up his vigor and passion for the quest, hinting—without any evidence—that he was planning another expedition to the Llanganatis shortly and had promised to take me with him (a bald-faced lie).

"Be careful! Fernández-Salvador is a risk taker," Roland warned. "If something should go wrong in the mountains, you won't see him for dust. Besides, my impression is he gets one idea into his head and excludes all other possibilities. That is not my way. First I pan the rivers for gold, then I make a geological survey . . ."

It was a speech I had heard before. Roland was probably right about my not being able to depend on Andy, but I was no longer sure that I could rely on Roland, either. Although I had yet to follow Valverde's guide, I knew that the search for the gold could not be reduced to a set of logical propositions. To have made so many expeditions to the Llanganatis, Roland had to be convinced—just as Andy was—that his interpretation was the correct one and that everybody else's was wrong. The question was, which one of them was more likely to lead me to the grail?

I decided to tell Roland about Blake's maps and letters. He knew the Blake and Chapman story of course—everyone in Ecuador did—but he had never seen the maps.

I unfolded the pages Andy had torn from my notebook. In the cold light of day his sketches looked like schoolboy doodles. I handed them to Roland and began translating the legends.

"Here Blake wrote that he found 'probably the world's biggest gold mine,' according to Andy, just to the north of where the Río El Golpe meets the Parca Yacu. And here, a little to the south, he indicates that he discovered Valverde's Way of the Incas and the *socabón*. See, Blake wrote, 'gold in hidden cave here.'"

Roland furrowed his brow skeptically.

"And this map," said Roland, pointing at the first of Blake's maps, "what does it say here?"

"Look for the cross and 4 to L."

"Four to L?"

"Four to the left," I explained, the words sounding ridiculous as soon as I uttered them. "Commander Dyott—you know who Dyott was, don't you?—believed it was a reference to where Blake had buried Chapman's body. Look for the cross—in other words, look for Chapman's grave—then four to the left, and that's where you'll find the treasure cave."

"But what is this mountain he has drawn here?" asked Roland, pointing at the first map. "And what is this ledge to one side?"

"I don't know. Andy hinted that Blake and Chapman had found the treasure cave on Cerro Hermoso and had been returning from there when Chapman fell ill and died, but later he seemed to change his mind. He wasn't very clear."

I didn't say that by this time Andy had in fact been drunk and ranting incoherently.

"There's also a further clue. Blake wrote that if you got lost and couldn't find the Inca Way, then you should look for something he called the 'Reclining Woman' and all your problems would be solved."

Roland paused, lost in thought. Something was clearly troubling him, but he wouldn't say what. He picked up Blake's second map—the one showing the Inca Way—and began tracing his finger along the meandering line. Then he reached over to the pile of papers on the table and opened one of the maps from the Instituto Geográfico Militar.

"You remember the Inca road I showed you the last time you were here?"

I nodded.

"Well, if it's the same road as the one on Blake's map, then it leads this way"—he traced an arc south of the Río El Golpe, around the foot of Las Torres toward the Páramo de Soguillas and Cerro Negro. "If Las Torres is the first peak, then this is the second peak, and this is the third"—Roland indicated the two peaks behind Las Torres that he had pointed out to me at our first meeting. "But if what Andy told you is correct, then that would mean that Las Torres is the first peak, Cerro Negro is the second, and this is the third." He pointed to a mass of ominously bunched contour lines rising to 15,000 feet far to the southeast. "Cerro Hermoso, Beautiful Mountain."

I peered more closely at the map. On the northwestern face of Cerro Hermoso, Roland had marked another cross and, a little bit farther to the east, a small green circle.

"Here I found the remains of a wooden shelter, what could be Valverde's fourth sleeping place," said Roland, pointing at the cross. Then, pointing at the circle, "But on the fifth day it's impossible to get beyond this point. The vegetation is so thick you are always having to cut, cut, cut with the *machetero*."

He swung his arms in an *X* pattern above his head, imitating the action of a machete.

"In one section of the forest it took me eight days to cut a path to the ridge. I have been all over that mountain, and I can tell you, if there's an artificial lake or *socabón* there, I never found it."

"So you don't believe Blake found Valverde's treasure cave?"

"I'm not saying that, just that it couldn't have been on Cerro Hermoso. Now, remind me, what was the other clue Andy gave you?"

"Look for the cross?"

"No, the other one."

"The Reclining Woman?"

"Jah, that's it. I think I know this formation. You can see a woman's head and body very clearly in the profile of this range here"—Roland pointed to the Farallón de Jaramillo—"and sometimes in this mountain, too." He pointed once more to Cerro Negro.

"What about Cerro Hermoso?"

Roland thought for a second, then shook his head.

"It's possible but only if you make, how you say, *una fantasía.*"

"A fantasy."

"Jah. It's like I told you before, the mountains play tricks with your mind. The longer you spend there, the more you start to see these kinds of formations everywhere."

"What about Blake's other clue—'Look for the cross'?"

Roland picked up the first map Andy had drawn—the one with the inverted V-shaped peak and ledge—and mulled over its contours.

"There is a mountain that looks something like this near Zunchu-Urcu, or it could be Zunchu-Urcu itself viewed from below. I'm not sure."

Roland paused, puffing on his cigar.

"Even if it is Zunchu-Urcu, I doubt you'll find a cross there now. It would have been destroyed years ago. Are you sure Blake meant a wooden cross?"

I said I wasn't sure of anything. All I knew was what Andy had told me. Roland looked at me quizzically and turned once more to Andy's second map. "There's something else I don't understand," he muttered. "You say Blake found the gold mine to the north of the Parca Yacu."

"That's what Andy said."

"I'm afraid that's impossible. I've been all over that area, and I can tell you the only rocks you'll find there are pyrites. You know the common name for pyrites, don't you?"

"Fool's gold."

"Exactly."

I was now confused and slightly irritated. I had shared Blake's maps with Roland in an attempt to rekindle his enthusiasm for our expedition, but if Roland was intrigued by Andy's theories, he wasn't prepared to admit it. Instead, his only interest seemed to be in picking holes in Blake's story. Fearing my ruse had backfired, I told Roland that we could discuss Blake's clues for weeks. The only way to make sense of his story was to hike into the Llanganatis and study the maps in situ.

"If you're not interested, then I'll just have to go without you," I told him firmly.

Roland stopped perusing the maps for a moment and smiled.

"Have you ever used a machete, my friend?"

I admitted I hadn't.

"It is not so easy. One lapse of concentration and you can cut yourself here"—he indicated a point just above his left knee where the downward swing of a machete would strike his leg—"or here." He touched the same spot above his right knee. "Besides, how would you find your way?"

"I have the maps. I'd use a GPS."

Roland's smile grew broader, and he shook his head patronizingly from side to side.

"The maps are not so accurate, my friend, and a GPS only works if you can read the landmarks. How will you navigate in a *neblina*?"

"I don't know. I guess I'll have to hope for the best."

Roland's smile turned to a frown. "This is a serious business, my friend. Do you know that on my last expedition a man nearly died?"

According to Roland, the accident had occurred when he had been trying to cross a set of rapids on the Parca Yacu. The porters had improvised a bridge from a series of tree trunks and were inching their way across with the tanks of food strapped to their backs when one of the Indians slipped.

"I reached out my hand and grabbed him here"—Roland indicated the crossbar of one of the H-frames that had been attached to the tanks. "I caught him just in time. One second later and he would have been swept downstream."

Roland looked at me with an intensity I had not seen before. I returned his stare. I wanted him to know that I understood what I was getting into and wasn't about to be put off.

"Look, Marcos," he said finally, reaching a decision, "why don't you begin with a hike up to Zunchu-Urcu? I could recommend one of my men. If, after that, you still want to go with me to the valley of 'El Mundo Nuevo,' then we can discuss it when you get back."

I considered Roland's proposition. Was this a test? Perhaps he wanted to see how I would fare on my own before deciding whether to take me into the heart of the ranges.

"Whom would I go with?"

"I have just the man—Don Segundo. He knows the route to Zunchu-Urcu very well. It shouldn't take you more than four days there and back."

According to Roland, Don Segundo lived in a small village called San José de Poaló, ten miles north of Píllaro. Now in his sixties, he had led countless expeditions to the Llanganatis and knew the mountains like the back of his hand.

"For someone like Don Segundo, Zunchu-Urcu is a walk in the park. Just take care not to show him Blake's maps. If the porters suspect you know where the treasure is"—Roland paused, drawing his hand across his neck in a slitting motion—"you'll end up like Padre Longo."

Was Roland serious, or was he trying to frighten me again? There was only one way to find out.

"Give me Don Segundo's address," I said.

2

WHERE I TRAVEL TO PÍLLARO AND MEET
THE FAMOUS DON SEGUNDO

WISPS OF GRAY FOG CLUNG TO THE SLOPES OF THE RÍO PATATE, GIVING
the boulders that littered the roadway an eerie, ghostly quality. For the
last half hour the commuter bus from Ambato had been stealthily working its way toward the bottom of the gorge, its axles wheezing under its
quotidian load of schoolchildren, machete-toting farmhands, and
women returning from market. On the outskirts of the town a local
football team wearing the blue-red-and-gold uniform of Ecuador's national squad had recklessly added its weight to the throng, testing the
bus's brakes to the limit. Under the circumstances, a six-foot three-inch
gringo backpacker seemed an unnecessary additional burden. I was also
attracting comment.

"Where are you off to?" asked the woman to my right as I squeezed
my backpack under the seat, hoping to make myself as inconspicuous
as possible.

"Píllaro," I replied.

"¡Sí!" she exclaimed. "But why would you want to go there?"

I was prepared for this, too.

"I like to fish. I hear you have wonderful trout in the Llanganatis."

The woman looked at me in astonishment, then whispered something to the man sitting beside her and laughed.

"Come on," she said eventually. "What *really* brings you here?"

Roland had schooled me in the importance of not talking about the treasure. Píllaro, he had warned me, was Ecuador's "Wild East." If the Pillareños got wind of the fact that I was carrying treasure maps and other valuable documents, they would try to rob me.

Heeding his advice, I had concealed Blake's maps in my money belt and brought just $200—enough to pay for Don Segundo's time, a little food for our expedition, and our transport to and from San José de Poaló. Before leaving Quito, I had also taken the precaution of contacting Jorge Anhalzer, the photographer whose book on the Llanganatis I had studied in the Libri Mundi bookstore in Quito. If this was to be my only foray into the ranges, I reasoned, I would need someone who knew the mountains at least as well as Roland and whom I could trust if we ran into trouble. Not only was Jorge a friend of Lou's, but he also had firsthand experience of the Indians' treachery.

In 1986 Jorge had agreed to guide a Wall Street broker and his fiancée along the Río Mulatos. It was supposed to be a relatively easy ten-day expedition. But on their third day in the mountains their porters suddenly deserted in the night, taking much of the food and provisions with them. As they were already several miles downriver, Jorge decided to press on, but over breakfast the broker's fiancée—a beautiful Broadway actress—got a trout bone stuck in her gullet, and Jorge had to perform emergency surgery.

This, however, was to prove the least of their problems.

Rounding a bend in the river, Jorge suddenly discovered the reason for the porters' desertion—the beach had disappeared. In its place was a narrow ravine with rock walls rising steeply on either side. Unable to follow the river, Jorge instructed the broker and his fiancée to remove their rucksacks and begin scaling the rock face. But when it came time to pass their belongings up after them, the rope slipped and one of the rucksacks, containing a chain saw and more precious food, fell into the water. Once on the other side of the ravine, they discovered the forest was so thick that it took them all day to cover just half a quarter of a mile. By the seventh day the broker and his fiancée were begging for a helicopter to airlift them out.

"I took them to one side and explained that this was not Hollywood; unless they kept walking, they would die," Jorge told me.

He eventually brought them out via the Jatun Yacu, in El Oriente, on the seventeenth day. By then they had been without food for six days and had reached the limit of their endurance.

Jorge's experience as a guide had convinced him that the treasure was better left where it was. "The treasure is a curse," he said. "As soon as people believe they are getting close, they become tense and start to fight."

He preferred to concentrate on his photography. Flying high over the Andes in his microlight, Jorge produced stunning images that immortalized an Ecuador of steaming craters, vertiginous green lakes, and forgotten Inca fortresses. One of his most famous photographs, taken at eighteen thousand feet, showed a group of climbers on the summit of Cotopaxi—tiny red pinpricks dwarfed by the swell of the volcano's glacier. Another showed the vestiges of an Inca trail winding into the Llanganatis. Most of these "Ways" had long since been destroyed by earthquakes and landslides, but Jorge believed that in the sixteenth century the existence of a well-maintained network of roads and paths would have enabled the Indians, or a battle-hardened soldier like Valverde, to move rapidly through the Llanganatis with minimum effort.

"You have to remember that the Inca traveled lightly and slept under the stars. When they were hungry, they trapped rabbits and birds. In one day they could cover twenty, perhaps thirty kilometers."

In fact Jorge argued that Wallace had underestimated the distances in Valverde's guide—one day's travel in the sixteenth century being the equivalent of anything from two or three days for a modern explorer. That was why the treasure had never been found. With the exception of Erskine Loch and possibly Luciano Andrade Marín, no one had penetrated the mountains sufficiently deeply.

"The Indians took the gold as far from the Spanish as they could. They knew that the mountains would be their own defense," he declared.

I told him how Roland had a similar theory, how during his geological surveys he had stumbled upon a series of man-made pools and channels in a valley near the Río Mulatos. To my amazement, Jorge replied that during his disastrous 1986 expedition, he had stumbled upon the very same constructions. He estimated that the pools measured five meters by two meters and were as deep as they were wide. Like

Roland, he had also noticed several holes in the nearby rocks—what could be the *guayras*, or furnaces, for smelting metals. Unfortunately, with his food running out, he wasn't able to examine the constructions for very long, his priority being to get the broker and his fiancée to safety as quickly as possible. The following year, 1987, he had returned by helicopter, hoping to locate the constructions from the air. But a series of landslides had transformed the valley beyond recognition, and he was unable to find them. Nevertheless, he hadn't given up hope of returning one day on foot to make a proper archaeological survey.

"Everything fits with the *derrotero*," he explained. "The narrow canyon, the lake made by hand, the *guayras*. The only thing that was missing was the *socabón*."

At another point Jorge opened a drawer and took out a grainy black-and-white photograph of a rock with faint lettering scored in the side.

I asked him for a magnifying glass. To my amazement the letters appeared to be "4 P L."

"What's this?" I asked.

"It's Blake's clue, no? I found it one day when I was exploring an Inca Way above the Mulatos. I didn't believe it myself at first, but the writing is unmistakable—*cuatro por Ele*, '4 for L.'"

I stared long and hard at the photograph. The "P" and "L" were faint, but the "4" was indeed unmistakable. Was it a natural formation, or had Blake scored it in the rock face as some sort of reminder to himself? And why would an English speaker have written "P" for *"por"*? Surely Blake would have written "4 T L"—"four *to* the left"?

Jorge could not explain the discrepancy. Nor could he explain why he had found the formation in the Sacha Llanganatis, and not—as Blake's map seemed to indicate—in the region of Zunchu-Urcu and Cerro Negro. All he knew was what he had seen.

"The camera does not lie," he said. "Zunchu-Urcu is only the gateway—if you want to find the treasure, you have to go down the Río Mulatos into the Sacha Llanganatis."

Patiently, I explained that that was my intention but first I needed to exclude the possibility that Blake had discovered the treasure nearer to Píllaro. Eventually, after much discussion, and seeing that I was fearful of being abandoned in the mountains, Jorge agreed to accompany me. We would rendezvous in Píllaro after I had made contact with Don

Segundo. On the chance of fine weather, Jorge would also bring his assistant, Rómulo, to carry his lenses and camera equipment.

THE BUS ARRIVED IN PÍLLARO SHORTLY AFTER MIDDAY, DROPPING ME BEside a bustling market. Extracting my backpack from beneath the seat, I bade my female inquisitor goodbye and wove my way through stalls piled high with onions and quinoa, the Andean grain that is a substitute for pasta. From behind fedoras and brightly colored ponchos, dark inquisitive eyes registered my progress. Every Indian I passed seemed to have a smile especially for me—a smile that seemed to say, "I know why you're here."

The market smelled of plowed earth and chicken carcasses—a musty, feathery scent that pricked my appetite—and after exploring the stalls for a few minutes, I decided to look for somewhere to eat. But instead of heading for the town center, I took a wrong turn and found myself on a broad avenue leading toward open fields. At the end of the avenue was a roundabout and, in the center, an enormous bronze statue of an Indian warrior. In his left hand he grasped a spear while his right hand was outstretched and seemed to be pointing toward the *paramo*.

Curious, I walked to the foot of the statue for a closer look. The set of the mouth and eyes reminded me of the portrait in Roland's office: it was Rumiñahui all right, but in full battle dress and with a royal sash around his head. I checked the direction of his arm with my compass. Rumiñahui was pointing not toward the Llanganatis but toward Ambato—the direction from which I had just come.

Smiling to myself, I gazed across the plowed fields in the direction he should have been pointing. The earth was coal-black and slick with grease. Where the *paramo* met the horizon, the land seemed to swell and shift to a muddy gray.

I shivered. According to my altimeter, Píllaro was 7,880 feet above sea level—160 feet lower than Quito—but here the atmosphere seemed much colder and thinner. Already I could feel the beginnings of a *soroche* insinuating itself between my temples.

There were only two hotels in Píllaro, so I chose the one nearest the center—a five-story blue-washed concrete block overlooking the plaza. I regretted my decision almost immediately. A bullfight was scheduled for the following afternoon, and pickup trucks decorated with yellow bunting and swaying with gay Andean family groups were already circling the square, sounding their horns. Every now and then the trucks would part, and a brass band, accompanied by a thumping bass drum, would wend its way through the crowd, trailing excited schoolchildren in its wake. As if this cacophony were insufficient, the electrical-goods store opposite had decided to take advantage of the influx of people to stage a last-minute promotion. I watched aghast as the store manager positioned two huge speakers in the street below my room. The next thing I knew he was barking out the prices of fridges and televisions to the accompaniment of Queen's "We Will Rock You."

By nightfall my *soroche* had become a throbbing headache. I took two Alka-Seltzer tablets to deaden the pain and buried my head in the pillow, but the pulse of Queen's chorus was palpable even through the bedsprings.

I awoke early the following morning, my tongue rasping against the roof of my mouth. Although my headache was gone, my nose was blocked, and I seemed to have caught a cold. I dressed as warmly as I could and hurried across the road to the taxi stand. There were only two drivers waiting, making negotiations tricky. Both wanted $30 for the ride to San José de Poaló; after much haggling, I beat one of them down to $25—an extortionate sum even for fiesta time. I was reminded that when Erskine Loch had stopped here to provision his expedition in 1936, he had dubbed Píllaro "the Place of Thieves." "The spirit of old Valverde must haunt the place," he wrote, "for I well believe he has been its principal source of revenue for the last four hundred years."

The plan was to negotiate a contract with Don Segundo, and then return to Píllaro in order to rendezvous with Jorge the following morning. But I had no phone number for Don Segundo and no idea whether I would find him at home. All I had was a letter of introduction from Roland and a map showing the rough layout of the town and the position of his house.

For the first half hour we followed a two-lane cobblestone highway northeast past plowed fields planted with potatoes and beans. Then the road veered to the west, and the highway gave way to a narrow gravel track that rose to meet the *paramo*.

A veil of mist hung across the treeless landscape, giving the *paramo* a haunted, ethereal quality. As the road ascended to 9,200, then 9,800 and 10,500 feet, I strained my eyes in hopes of catching sight of Guapa Mountain. But the ranges were obscured by drizzle, and the only landmark I could make out was the occasional fence marking the limit of a farmer's smallholding. Were it not for the momentary sighting of a campesino toiling in the fields, his poncho pulled tight against the fierce *paramo* winds, we could have been on Dartmoor.

The road continued on, past a dusty schoolyard and a half-constructed church. Then we crested 11,200 feet, and I spotted a *chuquiragua*, a hardy shrub with bright red flowers beloved by Andinists from Peru to Colombia. Somewhere through the mist, I told myself, lay even more exotic vegetation—the dwarf bamboos, or *flechas*, of the *derrotero* and Valverde's exotic *sangurimas*.

The road curved to the west. We passed through a forest and more cultivated fields. Then we dropped to below 9,900 feet again and entered a warm valley planted with maize. In the distance I could just make out a football pitch and, on the slopes rising above it, a series of low bungalows.

"San José," muttered the taxi driver.

I showed him Roland's sketch, explaining as best I could the location of Don Segundo's house. We circled the football pitch twice, then stopped at the *tienda* to ask directions. A truck pulled up behind us, and an elderly couple clambered over the guardrail. Removing two huge sacks of groceries from the flatbed, they hopped over a barred gate and began scrambling up a sheer mud slope toward one of the houses. As they did so, the taxi driver came running out of the shop.

"Don Segundo," he cried.

The man turned slowly, tilting his baseball cap to get a better view. He was already halfway up the hill.

I leaped over the gate, waving Roland's letter of introduction in the air. But as I hurried up the incline, I slipped and lost my footing, falling flat on my face. I hauled myself from the mud to see Don Segundo observing me in silence, an amused smile spreading across his wind-chapped lips. He pointed at his feet and rocked the heels of his rubber boots into the ground.

"*Así*—Like this," he said, bending his knees outward as though mimicking a bowlegged sailor.

I followed his lead, dragging my heels cautiously through the ooze. I couldn't believe how difficult it was. For each two steps forward, I would slip one back, so that after five minutes I had closed only half the distance between us.

Eventually I reached the spot where Don Segundo was standing and thrust Roland's letter into his hands—I was too breathless to speak. Don Segundo stared at the note for a second, then handed it back to me with an embarrassed silence: he couldn't read. I studied his hands: they were rough and calloused, the hands of a laborer. But what fascinated me most was his face. With his high cheekbones, cinnamon-colored skin, and vaguely Asiatic eyes, he could have been Rumiñahui's elder brother.

"*Rolando, el alemán.* I'm a friend of Roland's, the German," I explained.

Don Segundo gripped my hand warmly. Then, balancing the sack of groceries over his shoulder with his free arm, he began dragging me slowly up the slope. Eventually we reached his house—a mud-and-adobe building with a corrugated iron roof—and he showed me to a chair on the porch.

I collapsed, gasping for breath.

"So I guess you're looking for a guide," he said nonchalantly.

I nodded.

"My fee is $15 a day. When do you wish to go?"

"Tomorrow."

Don Segundo thought about this for a second. If he was surprised by my request, he didn't show it.

"Okay," he replied finally, "but in that case you'll have to provide the food."

3

The Ascent of Mesa Tablón and Don Segundo's Story About a "Red-Haired Explorer"

WHEN BLAKE AND CHAPMAN SET OUT FROM PÍLLARO IN THE SPRING OF 1897, there was no road, just a worn mule trail heading east past the Hacienda de Moya and north over Guapa Mountain to Laguna de Pisayambo—the corkscrewing route marked in red on Guzmán's map. Today, however, explorers setting off into the Llanganatis can safely disregard the first part of Guzmán's map and continue directly along the cobbled road from San José. After a forty-minute drive east the road emerges above Pisayambo—now a large reservoir and hydroelectric dam—where it turns into a rutted gravel track. From here you bump and grind over potholes for half an hour until you reach another lake, Laguna del Tambo. A few hundred yards farther on lies a small stream, the Río Milín, and a narrow bridge. It is here that the road ends and the trailhead begins. To go any farther, you must be prepared to rough it in the traditional manner.

If we had been following the classic route set out in Valverde's guide, we would have hiked from here to the plain in front of the Spectacle Lakes—Valverde's first sleeping place. Although the terrain is marshy, there are no sudden rises, and the elevations do not go above 10,500 feet.

But the route to Zunchu-Urcu required us to head in a completely different direction—southwest toward the range marked "Cordillera de Achudivis" on Guzmán's map. There we would have to contour around a mountain known as Mesa Tablón to a pass at 13,000 feet—La Puerta (The Doorway). From here we would have to cross fields of dwarf bamboo and a series of bogs to reach Laguna de Auca Cocha and our first campsite.

After a second day and night in Píllaro I was better acclimatized. Nevertheless, as we set out from the Río Milín in the swirling mist— Don Segundo leading the way, followed by myself, Jorge, and his assistant Rómulo—I was suddenly overcome by apprehension. My only previous expedition experience was the trek around Chimborazo's glacier. On that occasion we had used pack mules to transport our food and equipment. Now, like the rest of the party, I would have to tote a sixty-pound pack containing my tent, sleeping bag, and provisions.

For the first half hour we followed the trailhead east along a gently ascending slope. Every now and then through the drifting mist I would catch sight of an icy stream meandering lazily across a glaciated valley or a small rounded hillock, its sides worn smooth by the rasping *paramo* winds. The landscape was timeless, ancient. In the murky half-light the hollows in the hillocks seemed to cast peculiar anthropomorphic shadows (in one, I swore I could make out the profile of an ape). Somewhere—I couldn't remember where exactly—I had read that they might be old burial tombs. But though a number had been excavated by treasure hunters, no one had ever found any Indian relics.

A light drizzle had been falling ever since we had left the bridge, but now, as we veered southeast across the *paramo* along a barely discernible path, the terrain grew boggier, the vegetation more sinewy and tangled. Falling in behind Don Segundo, I tried to maintain a steady rhythm, mimicking his easy stride as he balanced on the tufty grass islands that dotted the bogs. But in some places only a fragile carpet of lichens and succulents coated the surface, and in one spot I placed my foot in Don Segundo's boot print only to sink up to my knee in slime.

Extricating myself from the mud required the application of seldom-used muscles. I tried adopting a light hopping gait so as not to sink again, but after several paces the effort proved too much, and I was reduced to focusing all my energy on simply moving forward.

Except for the occasional gurgle of an underground brook, the silence was all-enveloping, the only sounds those of my own automation as I huffed and puffed through the sodden flora.

For the first hour I kept pace with Don Segundo. It helped that he was wearing a bright yellow jacket like the one Roland had shown me in the photograph in his office. But by the second hour he had become a misty blur, and I had relinquished my place to Jorge and Rómulo. It wasn't just that Don Segundo and the others moved differently; they also seemed to require less oxygen. Roland had told me how the Andean Indians—with their stocky builds and larger hearts and lungs— were better adapted to high altitudes than Europeans, but it was only now, struggling behind a man twenty years my senior, that I appreciated the difference our physiologies made. No wonder Andy had boasted that it was an advantage for explorers to be small. It wasn't only—as Dyott had put it—that they could slip beneath the tree branches more easily.

We had now been ascending steadily for two hours, and although I couldn't see more than three feet in front of my face, I imagined Laguna de Pisayambo lay far below us. At 11,200 feet we suddenly crested the lip of a hill and dropped down into a forest of dwarf bamboos—the *flechas* mentioned in the *derrotero*. Remembering Lou's warning about the tips springing back and catching my eyes, I walked with my arms outstretched, parting the stems cautiously, like a zombie probing in the dark. Then, after some one hundred yards, the bamboo forest abruptly ended, and we found ourselves in front of another huge marsh. Having crossed it with the usual difficulty, we began corkscrewing up the side of a steep ridge.

The rain had now eased somewhat, and high above our heads I could see the dark granite outcropping of Mesa Tablón and, below it, a narrow pass—La Puerta, the so-called doorway to the Llanganatis. Eager to register our first conquest, we pushed on up into the breathless sky, our lungs screaming against the altitude. The final six hundred yards were excruciating, a resolve-testing battle of muscle and sinew against the sapping mud. Finally, at midday, we hauled our weary bodies through La Puerta and fell against the spur of Mesa Tablón.

We were now perched on a cold tableland at 13,000 feet. An icy northwesterly wind whipped across the *paramo*, freezing our words in mid-sentence. To the south I could just make out the ramparts of the Jaramillo massif, clouds storming like cannon smoke against its black buttresses. Jaramillo's profile corresponded perfectly to the Farallón y Precipice de Yana Rumi of Guzmán's map. Yet he had shown the Farallón far to the northeast of Mesa Tablón (Achudivis on his map), while his distorted scale placed Zunchu-Urcu much too far to the east. More intriguing still was the absence of Auca Cocha; yes, Guzmán had indicated a lake named "Angas Cocha"—Quichua for "Hawk Lake"—but this was shown lying in a depression to the south of the Achudivis, whereas the real Auca Cocha lay due east.

Interested to know what Don Segundo would make of these discrepancies, I handed him Guzmán's map. Removing his black rubber gloves, he took the map gingerly in his hands. Don Segundo had been guiding treasure hunters in these mountains for twenty years. If anyone could make sense of Guzmán's puzzling topographical representations, I figured, he could.

Pursing his lips, Don Segundo traced his finger from Pisayambo to Yana Cocha and then south to the Farallón y Precipice de Yana Rumi and the Hydro Volcán de Siete Bocas—Cerro Hermoso. He seemed fascinated by the curlicues of smoke Guzmán had shown issuing from the mountain and his detailed drawings of farms and haciendas. Just to the left of Hermoso, for instance, Guzmán had drawn another small lake. Don Segundo asked me to read what was written on it.

"Sara Cocha," I said.

He responded that he'd never heard of a lake with that name but that it was the right shape for Auca Cocha. The only problem was that, if that was the case, Cerro Hermoso ought to lie much farther to the south. Also, Don Segundo had never seen smoke or lava issuing from Hermoso. Nor had he ever heard of a Volcán de Margasitas.

Could he explain these anomalies, I asked?

Don Segundo thought for a moment. "Sometimes at night, when it is clear, you see flashes of light in the direction of Hermoso."

"Flashes of light?"

Jorge, who had been following our conversation with interest, interrupted: "He means lightning."

"But most of the time," Don Segundo continued, "when it's cloudy like this, you don't know where you are *or* where you're going."

He stood up and, spreading his arms with a flourish, cried: "*¡Estamos perdimos en la oscuridad!*—We're lost in the darkness!"

It was true. Without Don Segundo we could have walked for days without ever finding the right path. Perhaps that explained the discrepancies on Guzmán's map; perhaps the Spanish botanist hadn't found the trail either but had relied instead on the accounts of Indians who had passed this way—Indians who, unlike Don Segundo, had mistaken the lightning flashes for explosions. Could that be why he had shown Zunchu-Urcu much too far to the east and drawn volcanoes that didn't exist?

From Mesa Tablón it was only an hour to Auca Cocha, and after dipping into our stores of salami and chocolate, we began picking our way across the barren tableland, straining against the wind and rain. Despite my Gore-Tex outer layer, I was now thoroughly wet and miserable. Climbing to La Puerta, I had been sweating so profusely I had been forced to unzip my jacket. Now my fleece lay sodden and heavy against my skin. I recalled how on Loch's expedition to the Llanganatis it had rained nonstop for thirty-nine days—"continuous blasts," he'd written, that had "penetrated to the bone." At last I knew what he meant.

A little after 1 p.m. we reached the lake. Miraculously, our arrival coincided with a brief improvement in the weather. With the sun warming our faces for the first time, we made a clearing in the reeds beside the shore and watched as Don Segundo cast his fishing line over the lake's glassy waters.

The story I had told the woman on the bus had not been a complete fabrication: in the 1940s President Galo Plaza Lasso of Ecuador had seeded all the lakes in the Llanganatis with trout. In addition to his talents as a guide, Don Segundo was an expert fisherman. "With luck you should eat very well," Roland had assured me.

But if there were any trout lurking beneath the surface today, they stubbornly refused to bite, and after casting his line dissolutely in the shallows for several minutes, Don Segundo asked if we wished to continue walking. There was another campsite by Los Cables—the Cable Lakes—he said. If we kept up the same pace, we should reach it well before nightfall.

Jorge conferred with Rómulo for a moment, then looked to see my reaction. Wearing a brown three-quarter-length leather jacket, Rómulo had yet to break into a sweat. Meanwhile, taking advantage of the brief cessation in the rain, Jorge had stripped off his rubber poncho to reveal a loose-fitting white cotton shirt and trousers.

Lulled by their optimism and the waxing light, I agreed to press on. We had not gone more than one hundred meters before I was regretting my decision.

Leaving the lake on our right, we surmounted a shallow depression and began picking our way gently across what appeared to be a wide morass. But all of a sudden the sky darkened and rain lashed down from the heavens, transforming the morass into a seething bog. With the water pooling at our feet, we tried to reclaim solid ground, but the morass gripped and tugged at us with every step. Placing my foot on what I thought was a grass island, I was alarmed to see the surface shudder and ripple. Was this what Valverde had meant by a quaking bog?

By the time I reached the other side, my trousers were caked in mud, but the test had only just begun. Almost immediately Don Segundo plunged into another forest of dwarf bamboos. Stumbling after him, I tried to part the arrow-like tips so that they wouldn't catch my face, but we were now clambering up a slippery one-in-five gradient and all my effort was concentrated on simply maintaining my footing. After some forty minutes we reached the top of the slope and began contouring along a vertiginous ridge. But though the forest had ended, we were now shrouded in the *neblina* I had heard so much about. The fog was all-enveloping, like being wrapped in cotton wool and stuffed inside a refrigerator. To prevent myself from falling, I had to keep my eyes continuously focused on the ground, probing sometimes with only the tip of my boot. The approach to Auca Cocha had been testing enough, but this was ten times worse. The wind swirled and howled from all sides, as though eddying up from some deep pit. One false step and I could find myself plunging into a bottomless chasm, with only the brittle echo of my screams to alert my companions to my demise.

A little after 5 p.m. we reached the first Cable Lake. What should have been a three-hour hike had taken more than four. It was now raining steadily, and after pitching our tents and erecting a tarpaulin to provide shelter for our kitchen, we gathered around the campfire. Despite the damp, Don Segundo had managed to get a flame going using the branches of a local shrub—the resinous *caspivela* (candlewood)—and after a warming soup of pasta and tuna, we retired to bed, cold, wet, and exhausted.

That night I dreamed I was walking with the Bedouin in the Sahel. A white light phosphoresced on the dunes, warming my hands and feet. On the horizon I could see an oasis, its surface shimmering turquoise in the desert heat. But just as we were about to plunge into its cooling waters, the scene suddenly shifted and I found myself trailing behind Don Segundo in the mist. I knew it was him because I could hear the chime of his machete on bamboo, but no matter how hard I tried, I couldn't seem to close the distance between us. Then the scene shifted again, and I was trudging through mud up to my waist. It was an effort to move forward. My feet were no longer warm, but cold and wet.

"*¡Levántate!*" hissed Don Segundo. "Get up!"

It was no dream.

I opened one eye and raised my head from my pillow just in time to see water pooling at my feet.

"Quick, Marcos, the rain!"

Clambering out of my sleeping bag, I pushed my head cautiously through the tent flap. The sky was black and menacing. Where once there had been a reed clearing there was now a bog. Worse, it looked as though the bog was about to become a river.

Grabbing my rubber boots in one hand and my sleeping bag in the other, I scrambled up the slope just in time to see a wave collapse the guy ropes.

"The map!" I cried. "The map! Get my *mochila*." Sticking out a hairy brown arm, Don Segundo grabbed my backpack. The next thing I knew my tent was floating on a brown sea.

Jorge and Rómulo, who had wisely pitched their tent on higher ground, gave us a pitying look.

"In the Llanganatis we have an expression," Jorge said, laughing. "*Buscando el tesoro hay que andar volando*—To search for the treasure, you have to move very fast."

It rained all morning, not warm jungle rain but frigid, viscous droplets that splattered my face and eyes and trickled annoyingly under the lining of my hood. For an hour we huddled forlornly beneath the tarpaulin in the hope that the sky would clear. When it became obvious that it wouldn't, we gathered our tents and backpacks together and set off through the tall *juncal* reeds to the foot of Zunchu-Urcu.

On his map Guzmán had drawn the mountain with a V-like trough in the middle, so that its summit resembled an *M*. But approaching from the *paramo*, I realized that this was an illusion. In fact Zunchu-Urcu was not a mountain at all but a gigantic protrusion of mica, black limestone, and granite. Somehow, during the formation of the ranges, the rocks had fused to form two jagged peaks, at the base of which I could just make out the vents of what appeared to be ancient volcanic chimneys. Viewed from the west, the smaller of these peaks was up-turned and tilted away from the larger peak, giving the mountain the comical appearance of a snub-nosed dog. But as we contoured around the second Cable Lake to the south, the perspective subtly shifted. Gradually the nose of the smaller peak blended with that of the larger one, producing the characteristic M-like profile of Guzmán's map. By contrast, when we began contouring around the foot of Zunchu-Urcu to the north, the smaller peak disappeared behind the larger until it seemed to be merely a ledge—a ledge not dissimilar, in fact, to the one Blake had shown protruding from the mysterious mountain on his first map. Was Roland right? Was Zunchu-Urcu the mountain next to whose summit Blake had drawn a cross?

Until now, I had kept Blake's maps to myself, but after two days of trekking through the mud and rain with Don Segundo, the secrecy suddenly struck me as irrational. If Commander Dyott and Andy hadn't been able to figure out the meaning of Blake's drawings, what chance was there that I would? Besides, Don Segundo didn't appear to be all that interested in the treasure. On the contrary, when we reached the foot of Zunchu-Urcu and I charged off to examine the vents and tunnels at the base of the mountain, he busied himself with clearing a campsite and collecting firewood. When I returned from my probings empty-handed, I discovered him crouched over a makeshift wooden cross, placing flowers in a vase fashioned from an old plastic bottle.

"What are you doing?" I asked.

Looking at me as though I wouldn't understand, he replied that this was where "Señor Fernández-Salvador" had scattered the ashes of his son-in-law Diego Arias. "I knew Diego. He was a good man. Whenever I am passing, I like to pay my respects."

So Don Segundo had known Diego and Andy. Perhaps he knew of their obsession with Blake and Chapman, too.

I unzipped my money belt and handed him the scrap of paper on which Andy had scrawled Blake's first map. Don Segundo studied the sketch for a second, smiled, and pointed to Zunchu-Urcu.

"Diego thought this was the mountain. That's why he spent so much time here."

I asked him if he thought it possible that two mariners could have traveled through these mountains unaided and discovered the gold?

Don Segundo paused, arranging the flowers in the bottle. "It's possible, yes," he replied, "though for many years I refused to believe it."

I pressed him for an explanation: What did he mean, "for many years"? What had made him change his mind? Once more Don Segundo paused, taking his time.

In 1979, he eventually continued, a group of Swedish treasure hunters had arrived in San José and asked him to guide them to Cerro Hermoso. Don Segundo had been to the mountain only once before but was confident of finding the way and agreed to escort them. Just as he had done with us, he led the Swedish explorers across the *paramo* to Mesa Tablón. However, at this point, rather than veering northeast to Zunchu-Urcu, he continued southeast, passing through a valley that lay between the Jaramillo massif and three lakes known as Las Tres Marías.

Convinced that the treasure lay in one of the caves near Hermoso's summit, the Swedes spent several days abseiling into its upended limestone sinkholes. But like every treasure hunter before and since, they found that the caves were empty. Finally, after a week, they had had enough and asked Don Segundo to lead them back to Pisayambo. But en route a *neblina* descended from nowhere, and Don Segundo lost his bearings.

"It was only my second time at Cerro Hermoso. I wasn't sure of the path," he explained apologetically.

For several hours they wandered aimlessly in the mist. Then, all of a sudden, Don Segundo looked up to see a rocky prominence he had noted earlier—the buttresses of the Jaramillo massif. Convinced that if he could reach the summit he would be able to see the way, Don Segundo led the Swedes up a steep slope rising from the valley floor. The ascent was grueling—four hundred yards straight up through driving rain and howling wind.

"It took us four hours of steady climbing to reach the top," Don Segundo told me. "When we got there, the Swedes were exhausted."

Thankfully, the Jaramillo's buttresses provided shelter from the wind, but they were now perched at 13,800 feet and the *neblina* chilled them to the bone. Hoping to find something to burn, Don Segundo left the Swedes to erect the tents and began exploring the recesses in the buttresses for firewood.

"I was hoping to find *caspivela* or, failing that, bamboo, but there was nothing. Then I noticed what appeared to be a tree propped up against one of the ledges."

Don Segundo approached the ledge for a closer look, but as he drew nearer, he got the shock of his life: it wasn't a tree at all but the skeleton of a man.

The skeleton was leaning upright inside the ledge, as though the man had taken shelter there and died on his feet, or else had been deliberately placed in that position. His flesh had long since decomposed—as had his clothes—but one or two hairs still clung to the skeleton's brittle bones. According to Don Segundo, they were red hairs, "the hairs of a gringo."

That was not all. On the ledge beside the skeleton was an old leather backpack of the type explorers had worn in the late nineteenth century.

Spooked by his discovery, Don Segundo retraced his steps and informed the Swedes.

"At first they thought I was joking," he told me. "Then they saw that my hands were shaking."

Don Segundo led them to the ledge and showed them the skeleton and the worn leather backpack. Inside was a roll of tattered bills. The money, said Don Segundo, was of a foreign denomination, though the bills were too decayed to make out which country had issued them.

At that time Don Segundo had not heard about Blake and Chapman and decided that the skeleton probably belonged to a lone gringo explorer who had lost his way returning from Cerro Hermoso. Out of respect for the manner in which the man had died, Don Segundo decided to leave the skeleton exactly as it was.

For several years he thought nothing more of his discovery. Then, at Zunchu-Urcu in the mid-1980s, he ran into Diego, who told him the story of *"los dos marineros."* According to Don Segundo, Diego thought Blake had found the treasure in a cave on either Cerro Negro or Cerro Hermoso. The key, he said, was Chapman's grave. If he could ascertain where Chapman had died—and where the cross had been—he might be able to figure out which mountain they had been exploring and where the treasure lay.

"He showed me a map like yours. He said there was a clue written on it."

"Look for the cross and 4 to L," I translated.

"Yes, but not only that. He said one of the sailors had also mentioned something about a sleeping woman."

For a moment Don Segundo's Spanish threw me. A sleeping woman? Then I realized what he was referring to—the clue in Blake's last letter to Uncle Sammy: "If something should happen to me . . . look for the Reclining Woman and all your problems are solved."

Of course! Hadn't Roland told me that the profile of the Jaramillo resembled a reclining woman? It all fitted. What if Blake and Chapman had lost their way returning from Cerro Hermoso? What if, like Don Segundo, they had taken refuge in the Jaramillo, only for Chapman to die?

According to Don Segundo, that had certainly been Diego's view.

"When I told him about the red-haired explorer, he became very animated. He said it must be Chapman. He pleaded with me to take him to the exact spot."

After considering the matter, Don Segundo agreed. But many years had passed since he had been on the Jaramillo, and when they got there, he couldn't find the ledge or the skeleton.

"Perhaps one of the Swedes came back later and removed it. Or perhaps my memory was faulty. In the fog one ledge looks much like another, you know."

Nevertheless, Don Segundo was adamant that the skeleton of the red-haired explorer had existed and that had he and the Swedes not happened by, it would still be there—undisturbed in its mountain fastness.

"There are no animals up there, nothing. For all we know, the explorer could have been standing in that ledge for a hundred years."

Don Segundo's story gave me pause for thought. The image of the red-haired explorer was almost too fantastic. Once again it reminded me of Rider Haggard. Hadn't it been on their way to Kukuanaland that Quatermain and his companions had stumbled upon the skeleton of the Portuguese explorer José da Silvestra—the same explorer whose map, scrawled in his own blood, had persuaded them to embark on the quest for King Solomon's mines?

Furthermore, if the red-haired explorer was, as Diego had believed, George Edwin Chapman, why had Don Segundo found him standing against a ledge? Blake had said he had buried his friend, marking Chapman's grave with a pile of rocks and a small wooden cross.

Had Blake's story become garbled in the retelling, or had the mariner been lying? What if Blake had murdered Chapman so that he could keep all the gold for himself? What if there never had been a grave or a wooden cross?

Diego had pondered these questions, too, hiking up to Zunchu-Urcu with Blake's maps to turn the riddle over in his mind. According to Don Segundo, these deliberations resulted in his refocusing his attention on Cerro Hermoso.

I could well understand why. If the red-haired explorer had been Chapman, then the discovery of his body in the Jaramillo range would suggest that he and Blake had been returning from Hermoso and not Cerro Negro. But why in that case had Andy steered me away from Cerro Hermoso? Why had he hinted that Dyott thought the treasure lay buried on Cerro Negro, a mountain whose profile, according to Roland, also resembled that of a reclining woman?

The permutations were endless. Clearly, if I was to make sense of the puzzle, I would have to approach Andy again and ask to look at Dyott's journals. But would a man as jealous as he was of his relationship with Dyott agree to share them?

4

THE RANGES AT LAST AND A
DECISION REACHED

IT HAD TAKEN ONLY TWO HOURS FOR US TO WALK FROM OUR FLOODED campsite by the first Cable Lake to the foot of Zunchu-Urcu. Now, with the rain easing, Jorge was eager to trek to the northeastern shoulder of the mountain. Rising 13,800 feet above the *paramo* de Soguillas, Zunchu-Urcu looks directly toward Cerro Negro and the Sacha Llanganatis. When the conditions are right, you can supposedly see clear across the ranges to the Río Napo and the Amazon.

Once again I found myself walking in Don Segundo's boot prints. Although the rain had eased, clouds still steamed about Zunchu-Urcu's peaks, slickening the slope with moisture. Clinging to the shrubs and bushes for leverage, we hauled ourselves up a series of near-vertical inclines to emerge on a broad, rock-strewn ledge. Treading cautiously, we then began contouring in a zigzag fashion toward the summit.

To my right, through the drifting vapor, Zunchu-Urcu's black peaks shifted, then fused into one. In a moment, I told myself, we would arrive at the summit and all the effort would be worthwhile. But when we reached the shoulder of the mountain, the mist was denser than ever.

Somewhere, far below us, we could hear toads croaking, but the fog made it impossible to pinpoint their location.

For an hour, Don Segundo, Jorge, Rómulo, and I sat on the ridge, distractedly casting stones into the chalky brume. At 6 p.m., with the light turning ashen, we retraced our steps to the lake.

There was no sunset that night. Instead, we huddled around the embers of the campfire, blowing on reeds to keep the flame from faltering. Then, a little after 9 p.m., just as we were about to fall asleep, the clouds parted and our camp was lit up by a ghostly white light. Unzipping the tent, I looked up to see a full moon emerging through the clouds. Its ivory beams fell directly on Zunchu-Urcu, illuminating its comic profile and casting an ironic silhouette onto the still waters of the lake. But if the outline of the mountain was remarkable, what I saw next made me gasp. There, to the right of Zunchu-Urcu's "nose," pulsing through the spreading blackness, were four stars in the shape of a cross.

"Quick, Don Segundo, look!"

Don Segundo pried himself from his sleeping bag and joined me beside the lake.

"*La Cruz del Sur,*" he whispered. "The Southern Cross. It's most visible in the spring and early summer."

"But don't you see, that's when Blake was here. As a sailor, he was used to using the stars to navigate. Perhaps his clue is meant to read, look for the Southern Cross, then four *degrees* to the left."

I removed my GPS and measured the declination. Roused by my shouts, Jorge had now joined us beside the water. From our position to the west of Zunchu-Urcu, the Southern Cross lay directly over Cerro Hermoso. Four degrees to the left, however, brought us in line with Cerro Negro and, beyond it, the Sacha Llanganatis.

"You see," said Jorge, rubbing the sleep from his eyes, "it's as I told you. If you want to find the treasure, you have to go east, down into the forest."

That night I had difficulty sleeping. In my mind's eye I could still see the Southern Cross blinking like a flashing beacon above Zunchu-Urcu. It was so obvious I couldn't believe no one had thought of it before. Blake knew how wet and windy it was on the *paramo*. He would hardly have left a wooden marker on Chapman's grave and expected it to remain intact. He *must* have meant the Southern Cross—a constellation that would have been clearly visible to him in late April, the month he exited the ranges. The only problem was that constellations vary markedly from year to year. When Blake had been in the mountains, the night sky would have looked very different. To make sense of his clue today, one would have to know the exact position of the Southern Cross in the spring of 1887.

The following morning we rose before daybreak and hiked back up to the shoulder of Zunchu-Urcu. This time we were in luck. The weather had held, and crimson-tinged altocumulus streaked the lightening sky. Then, as we crested the shoulder of the mountain, the first rays of sunlight fell across the ranges from El Oriente.

We inched onto the ridge from which, in a fit of boredom, we had cast stones the day before, astonished by both its narrowness and the precipitousness of the drop on either side. Far below us to the right, in the direction from which we thought we had heard the toads croaking, lay a sparkling emerald green lake; to the left, a series of crystal-clear waterfalls. But this was nothing compared with the stunning panorama of volcanoes, mountains, and jungle that stretched all around. Previously I had only been able to imagine the Llanganatis from Roland's and Jorge's photographs and the distorted topography of Guzmán's map. Now, at last, those lofty lakes and precipitous gorges had depth and color.

Behind us, on the horizon, ash and pyroclastic material billowed from the crater of Tungurahua in a vast funnel of cloud that seemed to have been dropped from the sky. Next, to the northwest, came the dark mirror of Yana Cocha and, rising behind it on the horizon, the inverted ice-cream cone of Cotopaxi. A little to the right, another volcano, Antisana, was followed by the castle-like ramparts of Las Torres and, directly to our east, blocking our view of the forested slopes below it, the massive black hump of Cerro Negro. Finally, over our right shoulders to the southeast, lay Cerro Hermoso, its sawtooth peaks jutting through the frothing clouds like the spine of some fearful dragon.

However, it wasn't Cerro Hermoso or Cerro Negro that held my attention so much as the ranges beyond them. Lower and less jagged than the peaks that towered over them, the Sacha Llanganatis seemed to stretch on forever. Here and there, in their shadowy recesses, I could just make out the flash of a lake and a twisting ribbon of water. Then, at the point where the sun met the horizon, the mountains abruptly sank into steaming jungle.

We spent two hours on Zunchu-Urcu. It was only later, trekking back to Pisayambo through the mist, that I realized I had not spotted anything that resembled an Inca Way, much less three *cerros* "in the form of a triangle." Nevertheless, it was a view that few explorers had been lucky enough to see, and I felt extraordinarily privileged. Surveying Guzmán's valleys and rivers at last, I longed to plunge into those forests and make a concerted effort to find the treasure. But at the same time part of me hesitated. The ranges were so wild and untouched it could take you all year just to explore one peak.

By the time we reached the trailhead and regained the road, however, I knew I couldn't leave it there. I had to probe the riddle of Blake and Dyott and Valverde's map, even if it meant disillusion and despair.

Part Five

"THE ALMOST UNBELIEVABLE HISTORY OF THE ENGLISH"

And here let me warn all prospective treasure
hunters to beware of charts, maps, written directions
or similar documents purporting to reveal the
precise spot where some hoard has been cached.
Nine times out of ten these are faked, or if genuine
they were purposely made misleading, the owners
of the treasures being the only persons who
could understand them. In other words,
they are a sort of code.

—ALPHEUS HYATT VERRILL, "HINTS FOR TREASURE HUNTERS,"
They Found Gold

1

DEAD ENDS

A TUNGSTEN SKY HUNG OVER HEATHROW, LOW AND IMMUTABLE. EMERG-
ing from the cabin of the Iberia Boeing, I felt as though someone had
suddenly flicked the switch labeled "Panavision" to the off position. If
I closed my eyes, I could still see the outline of Tungurahua's crater
erupting on the horizon, but when I opened them again, the sky was
gray and lackluster.

On previous returns from abroad I had been able to rationalize this
sense of impending gloom as a purely physiological phenomenon, the
understandable declension of the spirit that accompanies the sudden
absence of sunlight. But this was more than a temporary case of sea-
sonal affective disorder. This time it felt as though another light had
been extinguished, too.

There was nothing for it but to resume my routine as quickly as possible. It wasn't as if I didn't have plenty of leads to pursue. Top of my list
was the story in *Ultimas Noticias*. What made everyone so certain that
the governor of Latacunga had found the gold? And even supposing
Pastór had deposited it in the Royal Bank of Scotland, what had become of his descendants' claims to the treasure?

No sooner had I unpacked my bags than I began delving into the bank's history. The first thing I discovered was that although the Royal Bank had been founded in Edinburgh in 1727, its growth coincided with the decision in 1783 to open a branch office in Glasgow in order to service the burgeoning trade in tobacco from the West Indies. That trade had made the bank's name well known throughout the Caribbean and Latin America. More important, from the point of view of the governor of Latacunga and Marqués de Llosa, Antonio Pastór y Marín de Segura, the bank did not owe an allegiance to Charles IV, the King of Spain. On the contrary, Spain and Britain were on the brink of war (hostilities were announced in 1804). Thus, assuming Pastór had spirited the gold and precious stones from Atahualpa's hoard out of Ecuador without Charles's knowledge, the Royal Bank would have been a logical hiding place. Was this why, in 1803, Pastór had approached the banker Sir Francis Mollison and asked him to deposit the treasure at the bank's Edinburgh branch?

I decided to write directly to the Royal Bank. It was the first time I had tried to set the story down on paper. I was reminded of its vast historical sweep—the extraordinary meeting between Atahualpa and Pizarro in Cajamarca, the incredible wealth of the Inca empire, the greed and ruthlessness of the Spanish, the resistance and cunning of Rumiñahui. Not for the first time, the legend struck me as fantastic, unbelievable even.

I began my letter by describing the background to Valverde's *derrotero* and the *cédula real*, explaining how the King of Spain had expressly ordered the governor of Latacunga to search for the treasure. I then gave a précis of the facts as they had appeared in *Ultimas Noticias* and cut to the chase. Did the bank have a record of Pastór's deposit, and if so, could they tell me what had happened to it? After all, £460 million in 1803 was a large sum of money. Even without interest, such a deposit would now be worth billions—enough, presumably, to buy both the Royal Bank of Scotland *and* the Bank of England many times over.

It was several weeks before I received a reply from the Royal Bank's London office. It was not encouraging. According to Jennifer Mountain—the officer who signed the letter—her colleagues in Edinburgh had consulted the bank's databases, but "unfortunately, no customer or general ledgers have survived for the Royal Bank of Scotland for the early 1800s." Ms. Mountain's letter continued: "I also searched the database for Sir Francis Mollison and Antonio Pastór y Marín de Segura, with no luck . . . so it would appear that we have no records relating to this case."

I wrote back immediately, insisting—politely—that her colleagues must be "mistaken." I pointed out that when the details of Pastór's will had emerged in the 1960s, the bank would have been besieged by inquiries from claimants in Ecuador and Peru. Could Ms. Mountain have another look, if not for Pastór's records, then for those of his wife, Narcisa Martínez, in whose name the money had supposedly been deposited?

This time Ms. Mountain was more forthcoming. There was still no trace of any customer ledgers for Pastór or Martínez, but she could confirm that between 1965 and 1968 the bank had been "swamped" with inquiries from their descendants. Officials had recruited a retired archivist, Robert Forbes, to look into the matter, and he had compiled a full report. An article about Mr. Forbes's report had appeared in the bank's staff magazine in 1984.

"In the hope that it will be of use, I am enclosing it with this letter," concluded Ms. Mountain helpfully.

With trepidation, I unfolded the faded newspaper cutting, unsure of what I would find. The headline read:

"DAY WHEN THE BANK FACED UP TO A CLAIM FOR £460M!"

The article explained that when the news of Pastór's deposit had broken in South America, the bank had been inundated with phone calls. It had also received visits from the ambassadors of Spain and Portugal and several South American consuls. According to Mr. Forbes, lawyers in Peru had subsequently forwarded the bank a copy of Pastór's will, laying out exactly how the treasure had been made up and packed in some ninety wicker baskets. The only document they had lacked was a safe-custody receipt. Unfortunately for the petitioners, this lacuna proved fatal.

Following the ambassadors' visits, Mr. Forbes had personally gone through the strong rooms in the basements of the bank's Edinburgh and Glasgow branches. The first thing he discovered was that the ledgers for the years 1795–1805 were missing—though whether they had been deliberately removed or accidentally lost, no one knew. Worse, from the petitioners' point of view, there was no record of a Sir Francis Mollison, only of a Sir Francis *Molison* of Errol, Dundee. Molison had been a director of the bank from 1864 to 1877—much later than the date of the supposed deposit. Also, there was no record in *Lloyd's Register of Shipping* of *El Pensamiento*, the ship that, under the joint captaincy of John Doigg and John Fanning, had supposedly set sail with the treasure in 1803 from Lambayeque. That did not rule out the possibility that *El Pensamiento* had been a captured Spanish bark sailing under the British flag. However, without knowing the vessel's new name, Mr. Forbes had been unable to trace it. Giving the petitioners the benefit of the doubt, he theorized that *El Pensamiento* could have been intercepted on its way to Scotland by a French privateer and the treasure diverted to Napoleon's armies. There was also another possibility—that Pastór had been the victim of a double cross. As Mr. Forbes put it: "My theory was that Antonio had diverted the treasure from the Spanish treasury into his own coffers and brought in Doigg, Fanning and perhaps Mollison to help him get it to a safer place . . . Unfortunately, Antonio may in turn have landed in bad company, resulting in the misappropriation of his treasure. Two wealthy Scottish sea captains may have been the end result of his machinations."

I didn't know whether to be pleased or disappointed by Mr. Forbes's wry conclusion. It seemed to suggest that there was little chance of tracing Pastór's deposit while leaving open the possibility that the story was an invention from start to finish. If so, that would mean of course that Andy and Roland were right and the treasure might still be hidden in the Llanganatis. On the other hand, the fact that the bank had not been able to corroborate the claimants' story cast doubt on Andrade's and Lou's theory that Pastór had found the treasure and had doctored the *derrotero*, leaving a forgery behind in the Latacunga archive.

In Ecuador, where everyone had an anecdote about someone who was descended from Pastór, the treasure had seemed palpable. Now I was no longer so sure. The key, as ever, was the *derrotero*. If the story was true, then there ought to be another copy in Seville, one containing different instructions as to how to proceed to the treasure cave. The Austrian explorer Thur de Koos had supposedly found it, and, if Lou's and my suspicions were correct, so had Padre Moreno. But where to begin looking? The Archivo General de Indias was huge, containing more than eighty million documents occupying more than five miles of shelving. Although Spain's Ministry of Culture had recently begun the mammoth task of compiling a database of the archive, the exercise was far from completed, and many documents still lay moldering, unexamined, in their original boxes. Without knowing which branch of government had dispatched the *cédula real* to Ecuador and a firm date, I could spend years examining the archives and achieve nothing.

For the time being, I decided to concentrate on Barth Blake. Who exactly was Blake, and who was his friend Albertson, the captain with whom Blake had been intending to return to the Langanatis? If Blake had been in the Royal Navy or merchant marine, as Dyott believed, then he ought to have a service record. And if he had fallen overboard or been murdered on his way to meet Albertson in New England, then there ought to be a ship's log containing the details of his demise. More important, if I could find an address for Albertson, I might be able to trace the family in Philadelphia who had written to Dyott and examine Blake's maps and letters for myself.

I made some inquiries and discovered that the old Admiralty service registers were kept at the Public Record Office in Kew. I knew the building well. The PRO was the repository for the government's most closely guarded secrets—some of which became available to the public every year in December when the civil service's arcane gagging orders expired. Generally, these documents made fascinating reading, revealing everything from the hushed-up infidelities of minor royals to corrupt deals with industrialists or the breathtaking incompetence of Britain's security services—information that, had it been known at the time, would almost certainly have prompted heads to roll. But as I contemplated the journey this time, my heart sank. The PRO was only a few hundred yards downriver from Kew Gardens. I had flown halfway around the world in search of adventure only to end up exactly where I had started.

Nevertheless, I told myself, the Admiralty records would repay study. Dating back to the seventeenth century, these registers contained the name and rank of every commissioned officer who had ever served in the Royal Navy. Not only that, but from 1814 the Admiralty had also published a quarterly *Navy List*, giving the basic outline of an officer's career, as well as the ships he had served on. I still didn't know the name of the four-masted schooner that had brought Blake and his colleague George Edwin Chapman to Guayaquil, but I did have a date: 1887. It was a long shot, but if either Blake or Chapman had been in the Royal Navy, then I ought to be able to find his service records and trace his vessels and the logbooks.

Built on a vast site overlooking the Thames at Kew, the PRO—now known as the National Archives—is not a particularly attractive building. Indeed, viewed from the Chiswick side of the river, it resembles nothing so much as an immense concrete bunker. Approaching from Kew station, the impression is little better. The first thing you notice is the PRO's gray ramparts looming over the suburban rooftops. Then, as you pass through a gap in the faux-Tudor terrace, a huge parking lot and piazza. In the center of the piazza is an artificial lake surrounded by willows and thickets of bamboo. But for all the attempts at softening the concrete lines, the lake might as well be a moat. The fortress-like appearance of the building reinforced my prejudices regarding the PRO's historical function—prejudices that were only in part dispelled by the airy glass atrium and helpful signs indicating where I could obtain a locker key and pencil and paper. To my surprise a large group of middle-aged men and women were already gathered at the registration desk. The week before, I learned, the Census Office's new Web site, which included a snapshot and access to records of every street in Britain in 1901, had crashed. As a result, the PRO was now besieged by eager groups of old-age pensioners, noses pressed keenly up against the microfiche readers, scanning the screens for clues to their family histories.

Thankfully, the issues of the *Navy List* lay in a secluded corner at the back of the room. I ran my fingers along the cracked leather spines until I arrived at the volume dated 1887. Would Blake's and Chapman's names be there? I turned the page to the alphabetical listing of serving officers and began scanning the closely typed columns.

"Black," "Blackburn," "Blackmore," . . . "Blake, Albert V."

Could this be my man? It seemed unlikely. His Christian names were wrong, and his rank was listed as "engineer." I turned to another section of the book listing the active vessels and their serving officers. This revealed that Albert Valentine Blake had been an engineer on the *Asia*, a guard ship of the reserve at Portsmouth, between April 1886 and February 1887. If the entry was accurate, he couldn't have been in Ecuador at the same time.

There were just two more Blakes listed as being on active duty in 1887: "Blake, George L.," a chaplain who'd served on the *Asia* at the same time as the aforementioned Albert Valentine; and "Blake, William H.," a gunner who'd been attached to a torpedo cruiser out of Sheerness between June 1886 and July 1887. Also not my man.

If Barth Blake had been in the Royal Navy in 1887, he could not have been a commissioned officer. Perhaps Andrade had been right after all; perhaps the rumors that Blake had been Dutch were true.

Next I turned my attention to his colleague Lieutenant George Edwin Chapman. As far as I knew, no one had disputed that he was anything but British.

There were no Georges listed, but there were seven Chapmans, three with either a first or a second initial *E.* The question was, did any of them stand for Edwin? There was nothing for it but to examine the ledgers one by one.

It was tedious, laborious work. PRO rules stipulate that you can only remove one microfiche at a time. Whenever I wanted another, I had to return the previous one to the drawer and retrace my steps across the reading room.

I looked for a quiet table where I could work in peace and knuckled down to the task. The first name on my list was "Chapman, E. S." I slid the spool into the reader, spilling the coils several times before they caught. Then, with trepidation, I advanced the film, straining to make sense of the spidery writing.

The ledgers were old and faded. Some officers' entries took up several pages, others merited no more than a few paragraphs. Finally I found the one I was looking for.

"Chapman, Edmund Stewart . . . midshipman on the *Bellerophon.*"

According to Chapman's record, the *Bellerophon* was a 7,500-ton iron ship that in 1885 had seen service in North America and the West Indies. Chapman had achieved his seniority on December 24, 1885. But he had later twice failed the exam for lieutenant and in February 1891 had been discharged from service.

Not my man.

The next Chapman had done rather better, graduating to the rank of major. Unfortunately, his middle initial stood for "Emerson." Not my man either.

I turned to the final Chapman, "Edward P.," and crossed my fingers. Edwin could be short for Edward. Moreover, the *Navy List* for 1887 had given his rank as lieutenant.

Revolving the spool, I ran my eyes along the faded microfiche entry until I arrived at the column containing his Christian names . . . "Edward Poore." Could this be Blake's mysterious companion, the man whose remains lay somewhere on the *paramo*?

His career looked promising. After enlisting in the Royal Marines at Portsmouth in 1872, Edward Poore Chapman had sailed to Gibraltar, Africa, and South America. In August 1878 he had been promoted to lieutenant. Then, in 1885, he had set sail from Halifax.

Better and better. Andy had told me that Chapman and Blake had been mariners from Nova Scotia. I advanced the spool, fully expecting to arrive at an entry for Guayaquil dated 1887. But when I reached the next page, the entry read "Clarke, George Edward." I spun the reader into reverse, returning to the previous page. Anxiously, I moved my finger to the last entry for Chapman. It was dated 1886 and read simply: "Found dead in bath."

I couldn't believe it. I had been sure that Edward Poore was my man, but in January 1887, when he should have been crossing the Ecuadorian Andes to Píllaro, he was already dead.

In frustration I double-checked the other Chapmans on my list. There were Charleses, Cuthberts, and Williams but no Edwins. If Lieutenant George Edwin Chapman had disembarked at Guayaquil in 1887, then he could not have been an officer in the Royal Navy. That didn't mean the story was a fabrication. Chapman could have been an officer in the merchant marine. But unfortunately, the marine kept records only of its captains.

I consulted *Lloyd's Register* anyway. There were forty-three Chapmans but none with the Christian name George or Edwin. There were fewer Blakes—twenty-seven—but none with the first name Bartholomew or the initial *B*. The only other way of tracing an officer in the merchant marine was via his vessel, but, unfortunately, Andy had never told me the name of the schooner that had brought the mariners to Ecuador.

Setting out for Kew, I had been uneasy. Now my gloom deepened. Had Andy been chasing an illusion all this time? Had Dyott simply been spinning him a yarn for his own amusement? The more I considered the story, the more convinced I was that Blake was a fiction. But if so, where had he come from? Despite Barth Blake's absence from the *Navy List*, Blake was a common enough name. Barth or Bartholomew, however, had a seafaring ring to it. Coupled with Blake, it brought to mind romantic images of cutlasses and daring exploits on the Spanish Main. Indeed, Bartholomew was a name that would probably have rung a very loud bell with seventeenth-century readers of John Exquemelin's chameleonlike book, *Bucaniers of America*. First published in English in 1684 and reprinted at least eight times by 1771, *Bucaniers of America* extolled the exploits of men like Lionel Wafer and William Dampier, whose audacious raids on Spanish shipping in the Caribbean had fed the imaginations of a public eager for far-flung stories of pirate plunder. Although the privateers' activities were illegal, their flouting of convention struck a popular chord and gave European literature a new kind of romantic hero—the bold, rough-hewn buccaneer. Most popular of all was the second volume of Exquemelin's book, "Containing," as the subtitle put it, "the dangerous Voyage and bold Assaults of Captain *Bartholomew Sharp* [my italics], and others, performed in the South Sea, for the space of two years."

Born in Stepney, east London, in 1680, Sharp, in the company of Wafer and Dampier, had marched across the Central American isthmus and seized a series of Spanish vessels in front of the city of Panama. With one of the boats, renamed the *Trinity*, Sharp launched a series of daring raids on Spanish possessions up and down the Pacific coast of South America, intercepting Spanish shipping at will and carrying off chests packed with silver and pieces of eight. Indeed, Sharp's exploits on the *Trinity* proved so popular that his journals were reprinted several times in different forms, most famously in a 1684 version by the master of the *Trinity*, John Cox, titled *The Voyages and Adventures of Capt. Barth. Sharp and Others, in the South Sea*. It was one of these versions that had inspired Stevenson to write his own classic tale of pirate adventure, borrowing from Sharp's, Cox's, and Wafer's narratives to create the memorable characters of Captain Flint and the diabolically complex Long John Silver. But now, as I read Sharp's account of his exploits in the South

Sea, it occurred to me that Stevenson might not have been the only one
to draw inspiration from Sharp's journal. Perhaps Uncle Sammy had
also been inspired by Exquemelin's second volume. Perhaps in reading
Sharp's account and the stories of the Spanish conquest, he had imagined a new character, Barth Blake, and his voyage around Cape Horn
to Ecuador. And perhaps, just as Stevenson had been inspired to write
Treasure Island after he found his stepson drawing a map of an imaginary isle, so Uncle Sammy had begun doodling his own maps of a lost
treasure, later hiding them in a whiskey bottle for the amusement of his
grandchildren.

Of course Uncle Sammy was not the only suspect. Blake and Chapman could just as easily have been figments of Dyott's or Andy's imagination—characters whose invention shored up their own febrile
obsession with Atahualpa's gold. Was this the real curse of the Llanganatis? Had Dyott, knowing the Ecuadorians' obsession with the treasure, conjured up the story of his commission to make himself more
interesting to Andy and anyone else who happened by his hacienda in
Santo Domingo de los Colorados? And had Andy—the impressionable
playboy, eager to find a cause worthy of his youthful athletic promise—
willingly bought into the fantasy?

I remembered how during our whiskey-fueled conversations at his
ranch Andy had drip-fed me information about Blake, recalling snip-
pets of Blake's letters from memory but never showing me the originals.
Instead, he kept them out of view, just as Dyott had done before him,
hinting at what more they might contain.

Andy's secrecy seemed mannered, an acquired tic. His volatile per-
sonality naturally tended toward the confessional, but by holding back,
he added to the intrigue. And without the final piece of evidence, who
could disprove his story? Was this what he had learned from the commander, the device by which he kept the obsession alive?

To get to the bottom of the mystery, I decided I needed to know
more about Dyott. I wanted to find out who the man behind the headlines about the "search for Percy Fawcett" had really been. Commander
Dyott seemed always to be on the cusp of history. I couldn't get it out
of my mind that as a pioneer of manned flight he claimed to have been
with the Orville brothers at Kitty Hawk. Then, during World War I,
the commander seemed to have enjoyed two heroic careers at once—

flying planes with distinction for the Royal Naval Air Service and heading up British intelligence activities in India. This love of adventure and secrecy was like a double motif running through his life. If he wasn't hacking through jungles in search of head-hunting Indians or lost explorers, he was chasing down Nazis in Bolivia. For the commander, it seems, there was never a dull moment. Or was there?

I felt the key lay in his later years in Ecuador, when he had retired from exploration and was occupied with various moneymaking schemes on his ranch. Between reading me tantalizing extracts from Dyott's journals, Andy told me how Dyott had patented a new method for extracting cacao and had experimented with the manufacture of ginger ale. Perhaps Blake's maps and letters had simply been another of his moneymaking ventures?

I obtained an address for Dyott's son, Mike, in California and wrote him a short note, explaining my interest in Richard Spruce and the *derrotero* and asking whether he could help me with the details of his father's two expeditions to the Llanganatis (I thought it politic to describe myself as a historian rather than a treasure hunter). Several weeks later an e-mail from Dyott dropped into my in-box. He began discouragingly, saying that he was "not that well-versed" in Llanganatis lore and that his father had never told him anything about the treasure. In any case, he continued, "I would myself resist any publicity about the treasure because every time a book or article comes out, several groups of people appear in the Llanganati that get themselves injured or killed."

Having got the moralizing out of the way, Dyott could not resist letting me know that he, too, had been into the Llanganatis—albeit, he claimed, in search of botanical specimens. According to Dyott, his father was "not a treasure hunter" but a "flora and fauna guy." He had had no interest in the treasure until the family in Philadelphia approached him. It was only after giving much thought to Blake's maps and letters that he had agreed to come out of retirement and undertake the expeditions to the Llanganatis.

"He saw it as a last hurrah in his love of nature and exploration after 15 years of farming," Dyott wrote me, adding almost in parentheses: "Although he never told me this, I can put it together from his papers and by reading between the lines."

I didn't believe Dyott for a moment. I felt sure he knew more than he was letting on. No one, with the possible exception of Spruce and my friend Lou, went to the Llanganatis purely to collect shrubs and flowers.

I wrote back immediately, explaining that while I did not question his father's motives I was curious to know what he had written about the Llanganatis in his private papers. Clearly he had believed that Barth Blake was a real person, but if that was the case, why was there no trace of Blake in the Admiralty records, the *Navy List*, or the merchant marine captain's register?

This time Dyott was a little more forthcoming. He, too, had looked for evidence of Blake's existence, but though he had found references to Barth Blakes and George Chapmans on various genealogy sites, there was "nothing that makes those guys merchant marine types."

As for his father's papers, while he had all the journals his father had written from 1935 onward, the pages for the fall and winter of 1947 to 1948—the months when Dyott had been in the Llanganatis— were mysteriously missing. All that was left were the negatives of the photographs his father had taken when he had been camped in the mountains—"and I wouldn't know I had those except, that when I made prints, I recognized the places."

Dyott thought the missing pages may have been "passed on to someone." The problem was he didn't know whom. "Everyone has a different version of who the recipient was," wrote Dyott. "A guy in Florida, one of my dad's young friends, now old, said that he had them and was going to send them to me. This was years ago and it got complex because he didn't have them physically in his possession. I did all I could searching one place and one person after another but all the trails went cold."

Dyott suggested that if I wanted to know more, I should get hold of a book by a writer from Bronxville, New York, titled *Sweat of the Sun, Tears of the Moon*. He said that after reading the book, he'd contacted the author, Peter Lourie, and they'd met in New York. According to Dyott, Lourie had led him to believe that he'd been to Seville and had found the *derrotero*, but from speaking to other treasure hunters he wasn't sure this was true.

"The more one hears, the more confusing it gets," he wrote. "It's that a story has a beginning, a middle, and an end, and all through those pieces there can be misinformation. If the listener knows, or believes, any of the pieces, it gives credence to the others and the misinformation gets passed on as 'fact.'"

For once, I believed him. Dyott's e-mail ended with the following advice:

> Let me say one more thing: These treasure guys are a real trip! It's like a spy novel, everyone's got a different story; there's danger, deceit and subterfuge; people get killed or die under peculiar circumstances; everyone lies and everyone tries to weasel information out of everyone else . . . If you're really doing what you say you're doing, you're going to have a great time.

I didn't have the heart to tell Dyott about my meetings with Andy and Roland—characters who fitted his description to a T. Instead, I looked up Lourie's book on Amazon.com. The hardback had been published in 1991, but there was now a paperback edition that Amazon could ship to me immediately. I clicked on the shopping cart. Four weeks later the book arrived in the post.

I opened the package with trepidation. The cover was illustrated with a familiar image—the Tolita sun mask, the very same mask I had studied in the Sala de Oro in Quito just months before. Above the jagged rays sprouting from the mythic gold face, the subtitle read: *A Chronicle of an Incan Treasure.*

I turned to the dedication page. "In memory of Eugene Brunner"— a German name, like Roland Glaser's.

According to the blurb, Lourie had first heard the legend of Atahualpa's gold in the early 1980s when he arrived in Ecuador to complete some anthropological fieldwork (he'd been hoping to discover a new species of monkey in the jungles of El Oriente). He at once abandoned his studies and devoted himself to organizing an expedition to the "forsaken Llanganati range." But the treasure hunters he approached in Quito kept him hanging around and eventually, "lured by the siren song of legendary gold," Lourie had had to mount his own expedition.

That was in 1982. Nine years later, to judge by Lourie's opening paragraph, he was still hooked. "I'm certain the gold is still there in those bewitching mountains, and someone will soon discover it," he had written in 1991 from his home in New York. "The history convinces me, the treasure hunters themselves convinced me, and I want to believe. I yearn for the mystery of this treasure tale."

Despite my discouraging correspondence with the Royal Bank of Scotland and my frustrating visit to the PRO, I still wanted to believe, too. Like Lourie, I was now hooked as much on the mystery and adventure of the treasure as on the promise of wealth. Could Dyott's account of the discovery of the Blake maps and letters be trusted? What was "fact" and what was "disinformation"? And how did this man Brunner fit into the story?

Over the next few days I worked my way through Lourie's book. Many of the passages resonated with my own investigation. Like me, Lourie had traveled to Guayaquil to meet Andy and ridden out to his ranch in his pickup. Sitting on the same veranda in the stifling tropical heat, Andy had fired Lourie's imagination with his descriptions of the riches of the Inca empire, the promise of Valverde's *derrotero*, and his own expeditions to the Llanganatis ranges. At one point between whiskeys Andy had even boomed, "Such is life in the tropics," the identical phrase he had used with me. The difference was that Andy had been younger and more vital then. Instead of demonstrating his bizarre push-up routine, he had challenged Lourie to an arm-wrestling contest and won. He had also told Lourie something he had never told me, namely that in the 1960s he and Dyott had recruited "a crazy Swiss-German" to mount expeditions on their behalf. This was Eugene Brunner, the man to whom Lourie had dedicated his book. Apparently, the three of them had gathered at Dyott's ranch in 1965 and drawn up a secret contract.

"Brunner had so much more spare time than any of us. Dyott had the new information about Blake. I had some money and Brunner could spend months in those mountains every year," Andy had said.

According to Lourie, Andy told him how Brunner subsequently climbed Cerro Hermoso and discovered a small square lake on top—as though fashioned by hand—with a wall or gate at one end, leading to a trench. Nearby was a cave angled at forty-five degrees. Convinced that this was the *socabón* and artificial lake mentioned in the *derrotero*, Brunner informed Andy, and with his help he returned to Cerro Hermoso to carry out further investigations. But without specialist equipment that could only be brought in by helicopter, he was unable to drain the lake, and the cave proved similarly impossible to penetrate beyond a certain depth.

Andy did not mention whether this was the same cave he himself had discovered in 1963 following his aborted helicopter flight over the mountain, or what information had led both him and Brunner to the conclusion that the gold was buried on Cerro Hermoso. Instead, he dropped the usual cryptic hints, suggesting that if Lourie was prepared to hang around he might be able to join his son-in-law Diego Arias on an expedition to the mountain later that year. Unfortunately, by the time Lourie caught up with Diego, he was no longer much use. Diego had invested all his money in a nightclub in Quito, but rather than knuckle down to the business, he spent his evenings propped up at the bar, drinking away his profits while bemoaning the recent breakup of his marriage to Andy's daughter Monica.

Lourie went on to recount how Brunner proved equally frustrating to deal with. Andy had long since lost touch with him—apparently, they had had some sort of falling-out in the 1970s—but Lourie managed to track him down to a tiny room in the colonial quarter of Quito. There, surrounded by treasure-hunting paraphernalia and maps of Ecuador showing the locations of sunken galleons and emerald mines, Brunner welcomed Lourie like a long-lost son.

Brunner explained, rather improbably, that he had come to Ecuador to escape the Nazis. According to Brunner, in the 1930s he'd been part of an organization that smuggled people out of Germany to Switzerland. On June 30, 1934, "the Night of the Long Knives," he'd been in Berlin when the Nazis killed seven of his close friends. He escaped by jumping out a window, but they caught up with him soon afterward and threw him into a concentration camp. It was when he got out, six months later, that he fled to Ecuador.

Like Andy, Brunner was guarded about revealing how much he knew. He had first gone into the Llanganatis in 1938 and by 1979 had made more than forty sorties. Every year he would aim to spend at least a month in the mountains, following the classic *derrotero* route and trying to make sense of Valverde's puzzling hieroglyph and locate Margasitas Mountain. But like every treasure hunter before and since, Brunner discovered the *derrotero* was little use after the fourth day. He traversed the Desaguadero de Yana Cocha, climbed Las Torres, explored Zunchu-Urcu and the Páramo de Soguillas, then veered north into the Roncadores region. But though he stumbled upon shards of Inca pottery and the remains of Indian constructions, the treasure cave and gold mine eluded him.

It was Dyott who gave Brunner's quest new direction. The two had met briefly at Dyott's camp at Zunchu-Urcu in November 1947. Brunner had gone there with a treasure hunter from Oregon named Gail Mendel, who had already crossed the Páramo de Soguillas once before and seemed to have his own information about where the treasure was hidden.

According to Lourie, Brunner said that Dyott's face had darkened when he saw Mendel and he had refused to speak to him. It was only later, when Mendel was off hunting deer with the Indian porters, that Dyott took Brunner to one side and warned him that Mendel was a "descendant of one of the mariners who threw Barth Blake into the sea."

At the time Brunner had not heard the story of Blake and Chapman and did not know what Dyott was talking about or that Dyott himself possessed copies of Blake's maps and was using them to guide his own exploration of the Llanganatis. But after that, Brunner kept a close eye on Mendel and noticed that whenever he thought no one was looking, he would secretly remove a notebook from his backpack and study the profiles of the mountains.

Just as Andy had been in awe of Dyott, so had Brunner. By the early 1960s he had begun to visit him regularly at his ranch. Together they would sit up late into the night as the commander regaled Brunner with anecdotes from his life of epic adventure. Then, one evening, to Brunner's amazement, Dyott told him about the "two officers in the British Royal Navy" and his commission from the family in Philadelphia. That was when Brunner put two and two together and realized that Mendel's notebook had probably contained the maps Blake had been carrying with him when he was pushed overboard. Brunner was incredulous. He had wasted nearly twenty years following the wrong guide! Then and there, it seems, he decided that Dyott was the oracle who could lead him to the treasure, and he set aside everything he had learned about the *derrotero* to concentrate on Blake's maps.

Just like Andy, Brunner had committed his conversations with Dyott to memory and was able to quote from Blake's letters verbatim. But as I read through Lourie's now-familiar description of the message in *Knapsack and Rifle* instructing Uncle Sammy's grandchildren to look in the "hollow tree on the island," I couldn't help smiling. According to Brunner, after discovering Blake's maps and letters, the children's parents had written to the British Navy to ascertain whether they had any records of Blake and Chapman. Apparently, the answer had come back that they did—a response I knew was impossible. Either Brunner's recollection was mistaken or Dyott had lied to him, knowing full well that he would be too lazy to check the information.

There were also several small but telling discrepancies between Brunner's and Andy's descriptions of the contents of Blake's maps and letters. In the version Brunner told Lourie, for instance, there was no mention of the code word on Blake's map containing the cryptic phrase "Look for the cross and 4 to L." However, other details—such as the Inca path and the spot marked "Gold in hidden cave here"—were exactly as they had been in Andy's story. Had Brunner deliberately omitted these important details, or had Dyott told him a different version of the story?

Some of the discrepancies were tantalizing. In Brunner's version, after Blake returned to England with samples of the gold and emeralds concealed in his backpack, the British Embassy in Guayaquil had messaged London: "By the merest chance he [Blake] found Atahualpa's hoard in a cave next to an extinct lake." However, Andy had told me it was Blake who had minted this phrase in the letter he had sent Uncle Sammy from Píllaro in May 1897.

More intriguing still, Brunner also appeared to have spoken to Dyott about the Reclining Woman. Andy had told me that Dyott thought the Reclining Woman lay to the east of Zunchu-Urcu, possibly in the region of Cerro Negro. But according to Brunner, the Reclining Woman was actually Cerro Hermoso when viewed from a particular angle. Brunner had first noticed this phenomenon when he climbed the mountain in 1965 and stumbled upon a large body of water that he christened "Lake Brunner." Since then, he had returned to Cerro Hermoso many times, making sketches and taking photographs showing the face and body of a woman lying in its contours. In short, Brunner's research had convinced him that the gold was buried on Cerro Hermoso and that he would be the one to find it.

"The treasure . . . I know where it is!" he had told Lourie theatrically.

Why was it that every treasure hunter thought that he alone would be the one to unlock the centuries-old riddle of the Llanganatis? Was it simply bravado, or was this what was required to keep going, the self-belief you needed when you were all alone on some craggy ridge far from civilization?

From Lourie's description of the frustrating time he had spent with Brunner in Quito, it seemed that Brunner prized his secret almost as much as the treasure itself. Everything he had discovered—the sketches, the photographs, Blake's maps and letters—was contained in a sixty-page manuscript titled "The Inca Treasure in the Llanganati Mountains and the Almost Unbelievable History of the English." The manuscript was Brunner's lifework. From time to time he would share portions of it with Lourie, but then—just as Andy had done with me—he would snatch it away at the last moment, as though it was the *real* treasure.

At one point Lourie admitted to being so maddened by Brunner's behavior that he considered stealing the document when Brunner's back was turned. "Forty-two years of searching had produced this sixty-page booklet," Lourie writes, "all of which—if he let me—I could read in a few hours."

However, Lourie never did steal it. Instead, he mounted his own expedition to the Llanganatis, recruiting one of Brunner's guides and two other men. Rather than set out from Píllaro, they decided to approach Cerro Hermoso from the south, trekking up the Río Muyo from El Triunfo.

For four days they scrambled and crawled up the mountain in the freezing fog. They reached the summit on the fifth day, but they couldn't find the *socabón* or the "lake, made by hand." However, by now Lourie had come to believe he had discovered something just as valuable. Standing on the edge of Lake Brunner on a rare crystal-clear night, Lourie had looked up to see Cerro Hermoso and the peaks of two other mountains perfectly silhouetted against the stars. Moved by the isolation and stillness, he wrote: "The three peaks, dark and lovely, stood out like noble gods way above . . . I sensed the treasure was that very bowl of stars in the cold wind ringed by the magic of the Incas who had come here to mine the metal that was so much more than money."

Were these the fabled Cerros Llanganatis in the "form of a triangle"?
Perhaps.

That was not the end of Lourie's story. In an intriguing epilogue he
revealed that Brunner had died suddenly in June 1984 at the age of
sixty-nine after admitting himself to the hospital for a routine checkup.
After Brunner's death his photographs and papers passed to his wife
and son-in-law. But when they came to examine the documents closely,
they realized that several key pages were missing. Brunner's son-in-law
suspected the culprit was Brunner's secretary, a woman whom the U.S.
State Department informed him had fled to Austria and was a suspected "Soviet/Peruvian spy." But nothing was ever proved, and the
fate of Brunner's precious manuscript remained a mystery.

There was one more tidbit. After his return from Ecuador, Lourie
had met Mike Dyott, who had told him the same story he had told
me—namely, that after his father had died, Dyott had gone through his
Ecuadorian journals only to discover that a large section, covering his
two expeditions to the Llanganatis, was missing. Soon after, however,
Mike Dyott had traveled to Ecuador to climb Cerro Hermoso, and
when Lourie next heard from him, he was guarded and secretive. "How
fast one becomes an expert on treasure," Lourie concluded wryly.

I put Lourie's book to one side. Mike Dyott was clearly keeping
something back. He'd directed me to Lourie's book, aware that it would
tell me little I didn't already know.

He was right about one thing, though: Brunner only confused the issue. What was it Dyott had written in his e-mail?

"All through those pieces there can be misinformation."

If Blake's maps pointed to the treasure being on Cerro Hermoso,
why hadn't Andy and Brunner found it? After all, their partnership
with Dyott had been formidable. Together, the three of them couldn't
have been better equipped to get to the bottom of the mystery.

The answers, I felt, lay with Andy, but I had little confidence he
would share them with me. Lourie had described him as an "agent
provocateur," and, to judge by my recent meeting with the old treasure
hunter, he had lost none of his flair for laying false trails. Andy had
been happy to let me believe that the *socabón* was on Cerro Hermoso
but had become evasive the moment I had pressed him about his sub-

sequent expeditions to the mountain. Perhaps the treasure wasn't on Cerro Hermoso at all. Perhaps that's why he had directed Lourie to Brunner—the "crazy Swiss-German fellow," as Andy put it—knowing that Brunner would lead Lourie into a cul-de-sac.

Then there was the mystery of Andy and Brunner's falling-out. What if it had had something to do with the original copies of Blake's maps and letters and the missing pages from Dyott's journals? I couldn't help but recall the folder Andy had suddenly produced during our drunken, candlelit talk, containing the dog-eared blotter and the thick sheaf of typewritten pages. Removing the blotter, he had run his fingers along the lines and reeled off exact dates and phrases.

"Wednesday, 22 October 1947: a nice quiet day with no discordant notes."

If this was an extract from Dyott's missing journals—the genuine voice of a veteran explorer in the Llanganatis—how and where had Andy obtained it? Was it, as he had claimed, contemporaneous notes made from his "conversations" with Dyott at his ranch? And what other secrets did Andy's folder contain?

I wondered whether any of these questions had occurred to Lourie, but was unsure how to approach him. After all, he had spent far longer than I had investigating the mystery. And just as Andy jealously guarded Blake's maps and letters, so Lourie might feel that the story was now his property and I a literary usurper.

In the end I decided to take the risk. At one point in his book Lourie had mentioned in passing how Blake and Chapman had been introduced to Spruce via his nephew, a young sailor who had been studying to be an officer in the Royal Navy. At this point, however, Lourie added a new detail: after meeting Spruce, the mariners—convinced of the derrotero's veracity—had presented the evidence to their superiors in the Admiralty and been given a "special license" to sail to Ecuador.

That nugget intrigued me. If true, it suggested a possible explanation for Blake's and Chapman's absence from the Navy List: namely, that they had been on a secret mission for the Admiralty.

I also wondered whether Brunner had ever spoken to Lourie about "Valverde's map." I had a theory that Spruce wasn't as disinterested a scientific observer as he made out but had deliberately held on to the map—making no mention of it in his paper to the Royal Geographical Society—as insurance against a penurious retirement. While in Ambato in 1858 Spruce had specifically mentioned his fear of returning to England without sufficient funds for his old age. "Poverty is such a positive crime in England," he wrote to his colleague George Bentham at Kew, "that to be there without either money or lucrative employment is a contingency not to be reflected on without dread."

I checked *Notes of a Botanist on the Amazon and Andes*. Spruce had posted the letter in September, just two months after his arrival in Baños. What if it was this fear of poverty that had spurred his hunt for Valverde's *derrotero*—a hunt that had resulted in his discovery not only of the guide but of another, even more precious document? This might even explain the mystery of Spruce's missing Ecuadorian journals—the ones Wallace had been so concerned to find when he came to write up Spruce's accounts of his travels in South America. What if Spruce had entrusted his Ecuadorian journals and "Valverde's map" to his nephew, and he in turn had shown them to his superiors in the Royal Navy? And what if the information they contained had been deemed so valuable by the Admiralty that Blake and Chapman had been dispatched to Ecuador posthaste?

It was a small but possibly significant detail. In all probability the information had come from Brunner and was no more reliable than anything else he had told Lourie. Nevertheless, it gave me the perfect pretext to write to him. I began my e-mail by explaining that I was a Spruce expert who had become fascinated with the *derrotero* while researching his travels in Ecuador in search of the cinchona tree. I was now looking further into his life and was intrigued by Lourie's reference to Spruce's nephew. As he would have been aware from reading *Notes of a Botanist on the Amazon and Andes*, Wallace had been fascinated with the "interesting problem of the Treasure of the Incas" and had considered an expedition to the Llanganatis "but a few months' holiday." Did Lourie know whether either Spruce or Wallace had ever sponsored an expedition to the Llanganatis, and could he shed any light on Spruce's supposed connection to Blake?

My e-mail was accurate—up to a point. My love of Spruce *had* fired my initial interest in the *derrotero*, but my own investigations were now

well advanced, and the truth was I was now obsessed with the treasure—
something I was certain Lourie couldn't fail to see.

Lourie responded within a matter of hours. I was right, Brunner had
been the source of the story about Spruce's nephew. Unfortunately,
Lourie could add little to what he had already written, because Brunner
was dead and Lourie was no longer investigating the story. However, after his book had come out, he had been approached by a man who
seemed to have more information about the treasure. According to
Lourie, this man claimed to be a direct descendant of the family from
Philadelphia who had commissioned Dyott's two expeditions to the
Llanganatis.

> He is very talkative. He lives in New Jersey and he has, he says—
> and I believe him—all the Dyott correspondence from those years
> in the Forties. He may easily have stuff about Blake and Spruce.

Lourie went on to "warn" me that the man was rather suspicious and
had insisted on dealing with him through an intermediary—a local veterinarian. Eventually Lourie had arranged a face-to-face meeting with
both men in New Jersey, and they had shown him a manuscript all
about the family's involvement with Blake and Dyott. But they had
been reluctant to give Lourie a copy, and in the end Lourie, tiring of
their secrecy—so reminiscent of Brunner's—had decided not to pursue
the matter. If, however, I was interested . . .

I e-mailed Lourie straight back, and he kindly sent me their details.
He couldn't remember the name of the man who claimed to be related
to Uncle Sammy, but the name of his veterinarian friend was Gordon
Stull.

"Last I heard Gordon was trying to get this fellow's book published
and he was acting a bit like the new book was a treasure . . . as we all do,
I guess."

If by now Lourie had divined my own obsession with the treasure, he
didn't let on. Instead, he appeared to be only too happy to pass the ba-
ton to another writer.

Nevertheless, I decided to err on the side of caution. Thanking
Lourie for his help, I replied that I would certainly "try" writing to

Stull, "though it sounds like he may be more trouble than he is worth." In fact, my e-mail was already on its way.

What was it Mike Dyott had written?

"Everyone lies and everyone tries to weasel information out of everyone else."

Now I knew what he meant.

2

SEVILLE

A COOL BREEZE BLEW OFF THE RÍO GUADALQUIVIR, INFUSING THE PATIOS and alleyways of Barrio Santa Cruz with the late-summer scents of jasmine and orange blossom. A light drizzle had fallen in the night, slickening the cobblestones of Seville's old Jewish quarter. Picking my way toward Plaza del Triunfo, I felt like a traveler out of time. Even at this early hour, I noticed, one or two hansom cabs were parked outside Seville's massive Gothic cathedral, their polished gaslights and buffed leather seats reminders of a world gone by.

The day before a gypsy fortune-teller had approached me at this very spot and thrust a sprig of rosemary into my hand.

"*Tenga confianza,*" she'd urged.

Fearing a trick, I'd rebuffed her offer. Now, gazing up at the Moorish minaret rising above the cathedral's ramparts, I regretted my earlier temerity.

To Sevillanos, La Giralda is a powerful symbol of religious tolerance. Built by the Almohads in the twelfth century as the minaret of the Great Mosque, the tower was incorporated into the cathedral following the Moors' expulsion from Seville in the fifteenth century. Then, in 1558, the Spanish architect Hernán Ruiz added several new kiosks and a belfry, finishing the structure off with a thirteen-foot-high bronze sculpture, known as the Triumph of Faith. However, the tower took its name not from the statue but from the weathervane, *el giraldillo* (literally "that which turns"), spinning at its feet. Wherever I went, the tower seemed to mock me, its bronze arrow twisting in the wind as if to say, "The gold went thataway."

For weeks I'd waited to hear from Lourie's veterinarian contact. Once again I had cloaked myself in the aura of Richard Spruce, writing that I was "intrigued" by the story of Barth Blake and was curious to know whether Dr. Stull, or his friend, could shed any light on the connection between the mariner and the botanist. But either Dr. Stull had seen through my ruse or he couldn't be bothered to reply. Finally, fed up with waiting, I had caught a plane to Seville. In all probability, I told myself, Blake was a red herring. The key was the *derrotero*.

On my first day in Seville, fizzing with excitement at my arrival in the treasure hunter's citadel, I had bounded to the summit of La Giralda, surmounting the thirty-five ramps inside the tower with long, easy strides. Looking out over the pretty Andalusian tiled roofs toward the Guadalquivir, I had tried to conjure up the scene when, on January 9, 1534, Hernando Pizarro's ship, the *Santa María del Campo*, had arrived from Panama with the first installment of Atahualpa's ransom. One of those watching on the quayside that day had been the young Pedro de Cieza. The experience changed the course of his life. A year later, setting sail for South America, he wrote: "I cannot stop thinking about those . . . opulent pieces brought from Cajamarca."

I couldn't stop thinking about them, either. What was it Padre Moreno had said? Loch and Dyott had been looking in the *wrong place*. Before being drawn even deeper into the labyrinth, I needed to know whether the *derrotero* Spruce had found all those years before in Latacunga was a real document or a forgery placed in the archives by Antonio Pastór to throw the king's men off the scent. In short, I needed to find the original.

On the opposite side of La Giralda, sandwiched between the cathedral and the picture-book turrets of the Alcázar palace, lay the squat outline of the Archivo General de Indias. A square two-story building in the Renaissance style, it seemed far too small to contain all the records of the New World, let alone anything as valuable as Valverde's *derrotero*.

Surely any treasure hunter lucky enough to have stumbled upon the document would have pocketed it or else secreted it where he could be confident no one would find it. I couldn't believe that after all these years it might still be lying there, burning a hole in some musty file.

Stealthily, I circled the building. The archive was enclosed in corrugated iron—the result of an ongoing program of building works—and all the entrances appeared to be boarded up. After asking the advice of a coachman in Plaza del Triunfo and receiving a blank stare, I noticed a smartly dressed woman dash up a narrow metal ramp and disappear through a small, studded wooden door. This appeared to be the way in.

On the other side of the door was a partition, behind which a security guard was dozing. Awoken from his nap, he rubbed his eyes sleepily and grunted. Didn't I know the archive was closed? If I wanted to consult the collections, I would need the permission of the head of the reference section. He scribbled a name, "Señora Pilar Lázaro de la Escosura," in my notebook and pointed to a building on the opposite side of the square. Crossing my fingers, I hurried across the cobblestones. I had come too far to be denied access now.

The annex to the archive was approached through a set of modern glass doors, behind which stood another security guard and, to his right, an X-ray machine. Over the years a number of the archive's documents had gone missing, and the Ministry of Culture was determined to stop further pilfering. The objects of this intimidating security included the vellum with Columbus's signature informing Ferdinand and Isabella of his discovery of the "Indies," Pizarro's announcement of the conquest of Peru, and Benalcázar's signature recording the foundation of Quito. These were all displayed in glass frames in the middle of the atrium together with other less well known treasures, such as maps of the coasts of Panama and Chile and a woodcut depicting Atahualpa's defeat at Cajamarca. There was even a watercolor of Tungurahua's eruption in 1773. To my increasingly superstitious way of thinking, it was an omen, an indication I had come to the right place.

"Can I help you, sir?"

I looked up to see a smartly dressed woman standing over me. Hesitantly, I presented Señora Lázaro with the letter of introduction from my publisher.

"So you're looking for the lost treasure of Valverde," she inquired condescendingly. "I suppose you want information on the *corregidor* of Latacunga, too?"

I nodded.

"Good luck. You're only the fourth person this year."

Showing me to a seat opposite her desk, she wearily explained that she had been the head of the reference section since 1977 and that in all that time "no one had ever seen this document."

She shoved a bundle of e-mails toward me.

"See. Every year we get hundreds of inquiries from people in the Americas asking the same thing. Believe me, if anyone had found the *derrotero*, I would know about it."

I didn't dare contradict her. With her sleek blond hair and pince-nez, Señora Lázaro was not a woman to be trifled with.

"No folders or notebooks in the reading room, only loose paper, okay?"

I nodded obediently.

"Good."

She stood up and strode across the atrium, her heels clicking bossily on the marble tiles. Hissing for me to follow, she led me to the first floor and ordered me to present my pass to yet another security guard, who handed me my seat assignment. The next thing I knew we were passing through another set of glass doors and into the reading room.

When I had tried to imagine this moment, I had envisaged rows of dimly lit oak desks with elderly retainers shuffling back and forth, but the room Señora Lázaro led me into couldn't have been brighter or more modern. Sunlight flooding through the tall windows overlooking Plaza del Triunfo turned the limestone flagstones a subtle shade of tangerine. Eight long wooden tables divided the room into a series of neat rows. Six computer terminals were arranged on each, alternating from one side of the desk to the other so as to give researchers plenty of room to work and make notes at the same time. Even at this early hour a number of readers were already ensconced behind stacks of papers, while others appeared to be taking notes directly from their screens.

"Two-thirds of the archive is now available on-line," Señora Lázaro told me proudly. "That's nearly sixty million documents."

The system was a revelation. The database was divided into sixteen sections, each one corresponding to a different branch of Spanish administration. Thus there was *Arribadas* (Arrivals), containing the records of every custom declaration made by ships arriving at Cádiz between 1674 and 1822; *Justicia*, containing the records of court proceedings and judicial appointments; *Contaduría*, the Council of the Indies' accounting department, which held financial records as far back as the sixteenth century; *Mapas y Planos*, maps and drawings; and *Correos*, containing a complete record of correspondence between the Spanish Crown and its officials in the colonies.

But these catalogs only represented the first level of the system's complexity. Each category also contained a series of subsections arranged hierarchically, so by clicking on a particular heading, you opened up a Pandora's box of cascading possibilities. Thus from *Gobierno* (Government) you could go directly to regional seats of government such as the Audiencia de Bogotá or, in the case of the *derrotero*, the Audiencia de Quito. Not only that, but by entering discrete search terms, you could also scan the system for keywords such as "Valverde" and *"cédula real,"* thus generating a list of hits across the entire catalog.

Padre Moreno was wrong. You no longer needed to be "young" to search for the *derrotero*. What had taken him a lifetime to discover I could accomplish with a few clicks of the mouse.

I began with what seemed the obvious section—*Mapas y Planos*— and typed in the phrase *"derrotero de Valverde."* An egg timer appeared in the top right-hand corner of the screen. Could it really be this simple?

The timer spun for nearly a minute. Then the icon suddenly disappeared, and another window materialized in my viewfinder: *"Resultado de busqueda: 0."*

A blank.

I widened the search to include the entire archive. This time the egg timer took even longer, but when the sand had drained from the glass, the result was the same: nothing.

Perhaps the system didn't recognize the search term "Valverde"? I tried *"derrotero"* on its own. This was much better—152 hits!

I moved my cursor down the list, looking for anything connected with the Audiencia de Quito or, failing that, *Correos* or *Contaduría*.

"Derrotero de Nuna da Silva," read the first item that caught my eye. I clicked on the entry, and a window appeared in the right-hand screen, describing the document's contents: "Notes of the *derrotero* made by the ship's pilot Nuna da Silva when his vessel was seized by the English privateer Francis Drake."

Nuna da Silva? Where had I read that name before? Then I remembered. A century before Bartholomew Sharp had crossed the isthmus of Panama with his buccaneers, Francis Drake had launched a series of audacious raids on the mule trains crossing the jungles of Darién with gold for the Spanish treasury. As the Spanish got wise to Drake's smash-and-grab techniques, however, he was forced to venture farther afield, sailing south along the coast of Brazil and Argentina and through the Strait of Magellan to raid Spanish shipping in the Pacific. In this venture, Drake was greatly aided by the navigational skills of a Portuguese, Nuna or Nunho da Silva. Formerly the pilot of the *Santa María*—a vessel Drake had seized off Cape Verde in 1578 and renamed the *Mary*—da Silva guided Drake's ships into secluded bays for revictualing and brought him safely back to the open sea when fog or bad weather threatened to ground him. Indeed, the Portuguese was responsible for much of Drake's subsequent success in terrorizing Spanish shipping off the coast of Peru, so much so that when they inexplicably parted company in Mexico, the Inquisition accused da Silva of having adopted the Englishman's religion and prosecuted him for heresy. In his defense, Nuna da Silva presented a lengthy deposition, recording the details of his voyage with Drake. This was the *derrotero* my search had called up. Needless to say, it was not what I had been looking for.

The next *derrotero* on my list looked more promising. "Delivery of gold and silver," read the heading. "Account of the gold and silver that was forwarded to Santo Domingo by Captain General Blasco Núñez Vela."

Blasco Núñez Vela had been in Peru at exactly the time the Spanish had been scouring the Andes and jungles of the Amazon for gold mines and lost Indian cities. In 1544, Carlos III had appointed him Viceroy of Peru with orders to enforce the New Laws, regulations designed to protect the Indians from the worst abuses of the *encomienda*—the system whereby Spanish settlers were granted Indian vassals to serve them rather than the Crown. The laws called for the abolition of slavery, the removal of Indians from any settlers who abused them, and a limit on the numbers of Indians who could be made to serve as vassals. But Núñez Vela had enforced the laws with too much vigor, upsetting the conquistadores who had fought hard for the right to exploit the natives, and his measures sparked a rebellion led by Pizarro's brother Gonzalo. On January 18, 1546, this rebellion culminated in a pitched battle at Anaquito, just north of Quito, in which Pizarro's forces routed the royalists and Núñez Vela was killed. Unfortunately, the *derrotero* I was looking at had nothing to do with this but referred to an earlier episode in Núñez Vela's career when he had been moving gold for Carlos III from Mexico to the Caribbean.

I scanned the other *derroteros* in my list. They all referred to similar footnotes in history—fascinating to the professional researcher but of little use if, like me, your object was a lost Inca treasure. I decided to abandon the term *"derrotero"* and try *"corregidor* of Latacunga" instead. It was a gamble, but if the King of Spain *had* sent the *derrotero* to Ecuador together with a *cédula real,* then a record of it might still exist in the catalog.

Again nothing.

With my faith faltering, I entered the name "Antonio Pastór." This time, to my surprise, I got three hits. Two referred to documents dating from the nineteenth century. However, one was headed "Quito" and dated 1796—exactly the time when Valverde's *derrotero* was thought to have first appeared in Ecuador. Could this be the infamous Antonio Pastór y Marín de Segura, Marqués de Llosa, the man who had supposedly murdered Padre Longo and spirited the treasure out of Ecuador without the King of Spain's knowledge? I double-clicked on the entry, bringing up a notation in the right-hand screen describing the document's contents:

> Samples of cinnamon from Quito. Letter from Juan José Boniche, Antonio Pastór, and Francisco Javier Sánchez de la Flor, the Duke of Alcadia, reporting the remittance of a case containing samples of cinnamon of the country together with their greetings to the Prince of the Peace.

Included with the document was a reply from said Prince of the Peace, Diego de Gardoqui, acknowledging the arrival of the cinnamon in Spain and thanking Pastór and his business colleagues for the spice's speedy delivery.

This had to be my *corregidor*. Hadn't Andrade written that after resigning as governor of Latacunga, Pastór had set up a cinnamon-export business? And hadn't Andrade speculated that it was under the cover of this spice business that Pastór had smuggled Atahualpa's gold out of Ecuador?

I clicked on the left-hand screen and called up the original document. Beside it was a camera icon, indicating that the document had been scanned. I highlighted the entry, navigating through the cascading tree of files until I arrived at the "book" containing the document. When I double-clicked again, a sheet of spidery writing materialized in the right-hand screen. At the top of the page I could just make out the dateline, "Quito, 21st of January 1796," and, underneath, "Permit for samples of cinnamon."

The document showed that in 1796 Pastór and his partners had loaded four containers of cinnamon onto the frigate *Minerva* and shipped the spice to Cádiz via Cartagena de Indias. Attached to the permit was a letter from Diego de Gardoqui acknowledging the cinnamon's arrival and saying he eagerly awaited further consignments. But when I searched for other documents bearing Pastór's name or those of his partners, there was nothing. Either the shipment had been a one-off or the records for the others had been lost.

I wondered what the term "Valverde" would turn up. I still had no idea what Valverde's Christian name was. I wasn't even certain when he had lived. All I knew was that a Valverde who had once been a soldier— possibly, although not certainly, a conquistador—had been married to an Indian princess from Píllaro. Like Núñez Vela, he must have been a royalist, otherwise why dictate the *derrotero* to the King on his deathbed?

This time my search yielded an astonishing 495 hits. Valverde was the Spanish equivalent of Smith or Jones. Cursing my luck, I reviewed the list. There were Juan de Valverdes, Francisco de Valverdes, Andrés de Valverdes—even my old friend the Dominican friar Vicente de Valverde.

I highlighted one of the entries, navigating through the hierarchy of titles as I ventured deeper and deeper into the system. Eventually I could go no further and double-clicked on the last page. As if by magic, an ancient parchment materialized before me. The words were barely decipherable. Written in a florid script, the crosses of the *t*'s had melded with the loops of the *g*'s and *y*'s of the lines above. For all I knew, it could have been Aramaic. I had to find some way of targeting my search, of narrowing the field to documents that were likely to have some connection with my Spanish treasure hunter.

I cross-referenced "Valverde" with *"cédula real"* and waited for the egg timer to run its course. This was better: only forty-five hits. I narrowed the field further to include only those documents with a "Quito" provenance and got six results. Two referred to a "Diego Valverde de Aguilar," a judge in the Audiencia de Quito in 1590, and two to a "Francisco Valverde de Alguilar," a notary who had been dispatched to Quito from the Indies in 1668. The final two referred to a "Pedro Valverde," the chief accountant of the Royal House of Quito from 1576 until 1579. The dates fitted: all three Valverdes had been present in Quito in the right historical period.

I called the sources up one by one, looking for great wealth or evidence that these Valverdes had taken Indian brides. But the documents were concerned exclusively with affairs of state. In order to know their family circumstances, I would need a *bien de difunto* (a death certificate) containing their last wills and testaments and next of kin.

I tried the military records instead, cross-referencing the Valverdes in my list with *Patronato* (Board). This time I got one hit, and it looked promising.

In 1568 Pedro de Valverde had been decorated for meritorious service during the conquest and pacification of Peru. According to the archivist's notes, he had fought for the royalists alongside Blasco Núñez Vela, later opposing the "tyrant" Pedro de Hinojosa, Gonzalo Pizarro's captain general. Two years later this same Valverde had been appointed accountant of the Royal House of Quito with responsibility for all the gold and silver in the King's treasury. By 1570, with Gonzalo's defeat and the repeal of the New Laws, the colonists were back on side, and again gold and silver began to flow to the Crown in large quantities. The sums were colossal. Page after page of the royal accounts attested to the riches of the Ecuadorian mines and the bounty being reaped by the King's servants. A typical entry read: "Fine gold: 22,672 pesos; Silver: 6,302 pesos." Beside each was a date, recording when the money had been received and what proportion had been shipped to Spain. And at the end of all these pages—what really amounted to a series of small books—was the same signature, "Pedro de Valverde."

I stared at the tail of his *r* where it joined the *o* of "Pedro." Was I imagining things, or did it resemble the hieroglyph in the *derrotero*? I recalled how Andrade had also found evidence of a Pedro de Valverde living in Quito in 1538. Were his Pedro and mine one and the same person?

The accountant Valverde had certainly been in the right place at the right time. Buried elsewhere in the Audiencia de Quito were letters bearing his signature, hinting at a far more intimate knowledge of the affairs of state than the mere title of "accountant" would suggest. Pedro de Valverde's responsibilities included the payment of government officials, the distribution of "alms" to the Iglesia de San Francisco and other convents, and, most interesting of all, the supervision of Indian labor in the mines. In one document, Valverde had responded to a *cédula real* concerning the alleged diminution of shipments of gold to the Crown (he had denied it). In another, he had blamed the loss of a shipment of gold on *"los ingleses"*—English pirates—adding, in parentheses, that he was having to pay royal officials in gold because there was insufficient *"plata labrada"*—worked silver—in the treasury. Most intriguing of all was a reference to his having "supervised a share-out to Francisco Atabalipa." Was this a son or nephew of *the* Atahualpa? And if so, what had Francisco done to deserve a share of the gold? The next line of the archivist's notes further deepened the mystery, referring to "works in the gold mines."

I scanned the collection for more information. If I could just find a *bien de difunto* for Pedro de Valverde, I might be able to establish his family position and ascertain whether he had left a substantial legacy. But in the year of his death, 1579, there was no record of a certificate or of a will. All I could find was a document with the tantalizing heading: "Testimony of the warrants received by royal officials of Quito concerning smelting." However, when I tried to call the document to my screen, I discovered it had not been scanned. If I wanted to read it, I would have to apply for the original records. But these could only be seen in person in the old archive building across the square, and the archive was closed for refurbishment for two years.

Padre Moreno had been right after all. Modern technology took you only so far. To discover more about Pedro de Valverde and his involvement in Quito's gold trade, I would have to resort to old-fashioned methods. But even if I waited two years, there was no guarantee the document would bring me any closer to a resolution of the mystery of the *derrotero*. I was beginning to understand why both Andy and Roland had steered clear of Seville. Their expertise lay in navigating rivers and mountains, not in probing yellowing ledgers. Far better to expend your energy and youthful enthusiasm on a physical quest than to see it turn to disillusionment in some dusty archive.

However, while I had failed to find the original *derrotero*, on the positive side I had found nothing to suggest that the copy Spruce had uncovered in Latacunga was a fake. On the contrary, I had confirmed that Pastór was a real person and that after resigning his commission as governor of Latacunga, he had set up a cinnamon-export business. Moreover, for proof that Quito had been awash in gold, I had only to look to the accounts bearing Pedro de Valverde's signature. In short, there was still every reason to believe in the treasure's existence.

I spent the rest of the afternoon exploring the cathedral. More than 180 yards long by 150 yards wide, it took the breath away. There was room for a football pitch in the orange garden alone.

When I entered via the Campanilla doorway from Plaza del Triunfo, my eye was immediately drawn along the central nave to the vast vaulted ceiling supported by thirty-two freestanding octagonal pillars. Next came the monument to Christopher Columbus crowned by four giant-sized mace bearers representing the four kingdoms of Castile, León, Aragon, and Navarre. Brought to Seville in 1899, Columbus's mortal remains were supposedly interred in the mausoleum in 1902, but historians had since cast doubt on these claims, arguing that the explorer had never left Santo Domingo.

For two hours I wandered through the cathedral's five aisles, nine transverse aisles, and thirty-four side chapels—each one more ornate and awe-inspiring than the last. The architects of Seville's cathedral had vowed to "erect a church so immense that everyone beholding it will take us for madmen." Basing their floor plan on that of the Great

Mosque, they had very nearly succeeded. According to *The Guinness Book of Records*, only St. Peter's in Rome and St. Paul's in London surpassed Seville in scale.

But it wasn't so much the memory of the cathedral that stayed with me as I left Seville as that of La Giralda. Walking from Plaza del Triunfo, I turned around for one last look at the arabesque friezes soaring above the cathedral's massive stone dome. Framed between the wrought-iron balconies and pretty Andalusian tiles of the buildings surrounding the square, the friezes naturally led one's eyes toward the tower's belfry and the inscription carved in its flanks: "TURRIS-FORTISSIMA-NOMEN-DOMINI." The quotation is from Proverbs 18: "The Lord is a strong tower: the righteous runneth it, and it is safe."

Was this the faith that had kept Andy going all these years, the true belief required of those who sought the treasure? Was this why Brunner had clung to Blake's maps and letters and the "almost unbelievable history of the English"? And was this why Roland had refused to give up his search for the lost Inca gold mine despite having made more than twenty expeditions to the Llanganatis—weeks and months of hardship and frustration?

3

"Gold, Ghosts, and Commander Dyott"

WHEN I GOT BACK TO LONDON, THERE WAS AN E-MAIL WAITING FOR ME from Dr. Stull. It was short and to the point. He was not an expert on the treasure, he said, but had merely "facilitated" his friend, Don Bermender, who had written a book about Blake and Dyott. Dr. Stull explained, "Don is a bit shy about speaking publicly of his knowledge of the Atahualpa treasure." But he had forwarded my e-mail to him "in hopes that you two have a chance to chat." At the end of his e-mail, Dr. Stull had helpfully included the phone number of his veterinary clinic. I checked the area code. It was in southern New Jersey, close to Philadelphia.

I waited several days to hear from Bermender. Finally, fed up, I called Dr. Stull's office. A cheery secretary answered the phone.

"Hi, V—Veterinary Clinic."

"Can I speak to Dr. Stull?"

"Oh, you mean Gordon. Just one moment."

There was a brief delay before a soothing male voice came on the line. Apologizing profusely for Don's failure to get back to me, Stull explained that Bermender lived in a retirement home and was suspicious of strangers.

"He's had all kinds of approaches from people claiming to be something they're not, you know."

I assured him I didn't fall into that category.

"Okay, I guess there's no harm in giving you his number. But make sure you call early. The only phone is in the canteen, and it's difficult to get a message to him otherwise."

I called Bermender at 1 p.m. the following afternoon, Greenwich mean time, catching him just as he was finishing breakfast. He was irascible and guarded. He knew little about Spruce, he said. His family's contact had been with Blake and Dyott. What possible use could that be to me?

Adopting my most superior, academic tone, I told him that "no one believes that old tale about the treasure." However, I was intrigued by the suggestion that Spruce had known Blake and Chapman and had recruited them for a mission to the Llanganatis. What evidence did he have that Blake and Chapman had served in the Royal Navy?

There was a long pause. Then, goaded by my devil's advocacy, Bermender responded: "Oh, Blake was a mariner all right. He found the treasure. He knew where it was buried!"

"In that case, why didn't Dyott find it?"

"Because Dyott made a mistake—he was looking in the wrong place."

Bermender's voice had a hard, seafaring crackle. He sounded like a man who had been around Cape Horn and could tell his mizzen from his mainsail.

My questions came thick and fast: What correspondence had passed between his parents and Dyott? Had Bermender met Dyott in person? Did he still have Blake's letters and maps?

Bermender paused. Had I been overenthusiastic?

"Yes, I have them," he eventually replied, "but the treasure belongs to the *indígenas*. If the Ecuadorian government gets their hands on the maps, the Indians won't see a cent."

"Can I see the maps? Can I read Blake's letters?"

Bermender hesitated. Then, like a crafty old seadog, he gave me a little more rope.

"I don't know. Why don't you call me when you're next in the States, or, better still, write to me."

Bermender dictated his address—the care home was in a place called Cinnaminson, New Jersey. Then he hung up.

I got out a map of the eastern United States. Cinnaminson was a tiny speck between Philadelphia and Atlantic City. The nearest main road was the New Jersey Turnpike, thirty miles to the west.

I waited several weeks before writing to Bermender. I needed time to think. There were so many holes in Blake's story. For instance, if Blake had indeed been acting for Spruce—or, as Brunner believed, the Admiralty—and he had returned to England with news of the treasure cave in 1887, why did he wait five years before launching a second expedition? And why hadn't Spruce or the Admiralty commissioned another treasure expedition when they learned of Blake's death?

Then there was the intriguing question of why Wallace hadn't mentioned Blake and Chapman's expedition in his introduction to Spruce's chapter on the Inca treasure. Had Spruce kept his colleague in the dark, too? Is this why Wallace had been so desperate to find Spruce's missing Ecuadorian journals?

Indeed, thinking about it now, I realized that the story of Blake and Chapman's expedition to the Llanganatis was a relatively recent addition to the history. Exploring the mountains in 1936, Erskine Loch had never once referred to the mariners. Similarly, Andrade had made no reference to Blake and Chapman in the 1936 edition of his book on the Llanganatis. It was only in the later, 1970 edition that he had mentioned the mariners, and then almost as an afterthought. Could it be that like everyone else in Ecuador Andrade knew nothing about Blake and Chapman until Dyott arrived on the scene?

The more I considered these questions, the more I realized that everything pointed to Dyott. It was only when Brunner had run into Dyott at Zunchu-Urcu in 1947 that Brunner had begun to suspect there might be another map. And it was only after Dyott began receiving Brunner and Andy at his ranch in the early 1960s that the two treasure hunters heard the details of Blake and Chapman's expedition for the first time.

So far Bermender was the only person I had found who lay outside this charmed circle. If he was really who he said he was, then he was in a unique position to corroborate Andy's and Dyott's stories. I would have to visit him in New Jersey.

Several weeks later, we rendezvoused at a neutral location—an Italian pizzeria Gordon knew about in Medford, New Jersey, close by the

Cinnaminson home. I had little difficulty spotting my lunch dates. Gordon and Don were already seated at a corner booth. A thick type-written sheaf lay on the table between them and, beside it, a large at-taché case with gleaming brass locks. If I hadn't known better, I would have taken them for a pair of local mafiosi.

I wandered over and introduced myself. Don stood up. He was smaller even than Andy—about five feet two inches—with wisps of shock white hair framing a liverish bald spot. I guessed he was in his early seventies. Dressed in a yellow-and-white tracksuit and sand-colored Timberland hiking boots, he did not look like the sort of man who had ever grasped a rope much less wielded a machete.

Gordon was more my kind of guy—not exactly an outdoorsman, but fortyish and fit looking, with a turquoise Lacoste shirt, curly brown hair, glasses, and a direct, easy manner.

He and Don had obviously been sitting there for some time. Don had taken the seat in the corner and had his back to the wall so as to af-ford himself a good view of anyone entering or leaving the restaurant. Gordon sat opposite, drumming his fingers on the table. Poking out of the corner of Don's attaché case was what looked like a map.

I slid into the seat beside Gordon and began engaging him in con-versation. I was curious to know how he and Don had met. Was Gor-don a treasure hunter, too?

"Oh, no, not at all," Gordon said with a chuckle. "Don and I met at the local video store. Don's an expert in Greek numerology, you know."

Quite what this had to do with anything was unclear, but I got the sense that Gordon had fallen into conversation with Don at the video store and was impressed with the old man's knowledge of classical liter-ature. They had soon struck up a friendship, and Gordon began visit-ing Don regularly at the home in Cinnaminson.

I wanted to ask Don what had happened to his family and how he came to be living in the home, but just then a large woman in a floral skirt dashed into the restaurant and sat down beside us.

"Ah, Pam," said Gordon. "Pam, Mark. Pam's another old friend of ours."

"And how do you two know each other?" I asked, genuinely curious.

"Oh, I cured Pam's cat of cancer."

"Yes, he extended her life by five years," Pam interjected cheerily.

"And then I introduced Pam to Don, so I guess you could say we're all one big happy family," Gordon added.

I studied Gordon's beaming face. Then I looked across the table at where Pam was shooting me an identical grin. They were serious. Had I wandered into the Medford chapter of the Cat Appreciation Society by mistake?

It was Don who brought the conversation back to reality—if that was the correct word for his obsession with Blake and the Inca treasure.

"This is the manuscript of my book. Would you like to have a look?"

Don pushed the typewritten sheaf toward me. I studied the title page. It was headed "Gold, Ghosts, and Commander Dyott."

For a moment I thought of grabbing the manuscript and making a run for it. Then I realized that Pam and Gordon had me hemmed in. Was this why Don had invited them?

I turned the pages nonchalantly, trying not to appear too keen. The manuscript was neatly typewritten and double-spaced. Judging by its bulk, it was more than three hundred pages long.

Here and there, I caught sight of a familiar phrase—"the ransom of the Inca," "Atahualpa's curse," "the Cerros Llanganati"—and names like Valverde, Pizarro, and Rumiñahui. Then my eye fell on what appeared to be an extract from a letter dated 1889. I just had time to read the first sentence before Don yanked the manuscript out of my hands: "My dear old Captain, You will remember that when I visited you three years since, I remarked that I had learned through an ancient Spanish map of the existence beyond doubt of a vast amount of Indian treasure buried to escape the greed of the Spaniard."

"An ancient Spanish map." Did this refer to Valverde's legendary chart? Was this one of Blake's famous letters to Albertson, the letters that Andy had recited to me from memory?

I longed to put these questions to Don, but first I had to convince him that I wasn't here to wheedle information out of him, which of course I was.

I decided to play devil's advocate again. At the risk of betraying my own obsession with the treasure, I explained that I'd been to the Public Record Office in Kew in search of information about Blake and Chapman but had found nothing to suggest that either man had been in the

Royal Navy. How could Don be sure Uncle Sammy hadn't made the whole thing up?

Don's eyes narrowed, then flickered with amusement.

"Uncle Sammy didn't serve with Blake in the Royal Navy. They met in the American merchant navy."

He paused, letting the penny drop.

"You mean Blake was a captain in the U.S. merchant marine?"

"Exactly."

No wonder I hadn't found Blake's service record in the *Navy List*. If Don was right, I had been looking in the wrong place. Either Dyott made a mistake when he told Brunner that Blake and Chapman had been sailors in the Royal Navy and had been dispatched to Ecuador by the Admiralty, or Brunner had got his wires crossed. There was another possibility, too, given Dyott's background in espionage: disinformation.

Don explained that Sam Albertson had been his maternal grandfather (his mother had taken the name Bermender when she married Don's father). Like Blake, Albertson had been a captain in the American merchant marine, though within the family he was known affectionately as Uncle Sammy.

One day, Don's parents had been arguing over Uncle Sammy's birthday and asked Don to fetch the family's King James Bible, recalling that it contained the date of Uncle Sammy's confirmation. According to Don, he had found the Bible in the attic of their home in Philadelphia—not on a shelf in their summer house in Maine, as Andy had told me.

"When I opened it, a sheet of paper came loose from the binding," said Don.

Although he didn't realize it at the time, that paper was one of Blake's maps of the Llanganatis. According to Don, it was his father—not Dyott—who had first noticed the faint pinpricks under the passages in the Book of Judges spelling out the message "Atahualpa's gold in the lake of Marcasitas," and the note telling them to look in *Knapsack and Rifle*. Don said his father remembered the book well because, shortly before he died, Uncle Sammy had made a present of it to him, saying—pointedly—that it was "something to remember me by." It was in the flyleaf of *Knapsack and Rifle* that Don's father had discovered Blake's letters and the second map.

"But I thought you and your brother found Blake's map on the island near your summer home?"

"That's Mr. Lourie's version," said Don.

"So, his version is untrue?"

Don refused to affirm or deny it. "That's his version," he repeated, mysteriously.

According to Don, the second map was much larger than the first. "Ten and eleven-sixteenth inches by seven and three-sixteenths." Don recited the dimensions precisely.

"What was on it?"

"Valverde's map of the Llanganatis of course, the one that accompanied the *derrotero*."

"Is that what Blake means when he refers in his letter to the 'ancient Spanish map'?"

Don nodded.

"Do you still have it?" I asked, scarcely able to believe what I was hearing.

Don reached into his briefcase and handed me the piece of paper I had spotted earlier.

"This is a photocopy."

I held the paper in my hands. On it was a small grid—a fragment from the original. To my surprise it looked nothing like either of the maps Andy had drawn. Here and there I could make out what appeared to be the profile of a mountain and a small cross. There was also some writing. But the photocopy was so poor and indistinct it was impossible to read what was written on it or to determine what part of the Llanganatis the map referred to.

Don apologized for the poor quality of the reproduction. "On the original you can see that this line has been traced in red ink."

He indicated what appeared to be a faint pencil mark contouring around the foot of a mountain.

"Do you have the original with you?" I asked. "Can I see it?"

"I'm afraid not. It's in a safety-deposit box," he replied. Then, eyeing me suspiciously: "The deposit box isn't in my name." He snatched the map out of my hands and returned it to his briefcase, snapping the lid shut with a firm clump. Had I asked too many questions? Should I have been more guarded?

Thankfully, at this point Gordon, who had been following our exchange intently, interceded. "A few years ago there was a break-in at Don's office, and someone stole two of Blake's letters," he explained. "Since then, Don has had to be very careful."

Gordon glanced at Pam for support, and they both shot Don a grave look.

"That's right," said Pam. "Luckily, the letters weren't the most valuable ones."

She paused, looking at Gordon to check she hadn't spoken out of turn. Gordon smiled at her reassuringly.

His intervention seemed to do the trick: Don relaxed his grip on the attaché case and began studying the menu.

"How about we order lunch?" he suggested.

The adjoining tables were now packed, and the pizza chef was working overtime, theatrically swirling balls of dough into floppy Frisbee-shaped pies. A pretty young waitress with long dark hair wandered over to take our order. We must have looked a bizarre group: Don, hunched in the corner gripping his outsize briefcase; me with my notebook, trying not to glance at the manuscript; and Gordon and Pam, the local veterinarian and his jolly client.

I ordered a pepperoni pizza, while Gordon and Pam ordered pasta. Despite studying the menu longer than anyone, Don couldn't make up his mind. Eventually he ordered a chef's salad and a glass of milk. It was hard to believe that this frail old man had once discussed the treasure with Dyott. To embark on a treasure hunt was every boy's fantasy. I would have loved to have been a fly on the wall at that meeting. How had his parents contacted Dyott, and why hadn't Don joined his expedition to the Llanganatis?

My questions seemed to placate him. His parents had got Dyott's name from the National Geographic Society in Washington. His mother had taken the lead in writing to Dyott, and after an exchange of letters the commander had visited them at their home in Philadelphia. (I wrote "Philadelphia" in my notebook and underlined it twice: hadn't Andy told me that Dyott had been contacted by a family from Philadelphia?)

Don, then eighteen, was enthralled by the "great man's" stories. "I was dying to be the commander's right-hand man," he acknowledged.

But Dyott had deemed the expedition too risky, and Don's parents were against it.

"What about later? Surely when you were older . . ."

Don looked at me sheepishly. He had never been to Ecuador, he admitted.

"Dyott said the government would make all sorts of promises, but if we found the treasure, we would be out on the sidewalk. In any case, gringos have caused enough problems in that country."

I thought of Pizarro and Benalcázar and all the treasure hunters who had lost their lives in the Llanganatis. Nothing but misery had come from the obsession with the gold. Don was right: if it was ever found, it ought to be returned to the Indians. As laudable as I found Don's sentiments, however, I wasn't entirely convinced by his answer. Even if he had no intention of removing the treasure, he must have been curious. After all, finding the gold would have provided the perfect ending for his story. He was leaving something out, I was sure of it.

Tentatively, I asked whether he would let me read the manuscript—or, better still, make a copy. I still had so many unanswered questions: not least, who had introduced Blake to Spruce and whether it was Spruce who provided Blake with Valverde's map. Then there were the enigmatic clues on Blake's own maps. I was eager to compare the drawings Andy had given me with the originals and to find out what conclusions Dyott had come to. Did he think the *socabón* lay on Cerro Hermoso, Cerro Negro, or some other mountain? And which area of the Llanganatis had he been exploring during his expeditions in 1947 and 1948?

Don took a slug of milk while he thought about my request. Then he pushed the manuscript toward me.

"I can't allow you to make a copy, but if you want, you can read it here," he said.

It was frustrating, but I didn't have a choice. For the next half hour I tried to absorb as much of the manuscript as I could, furiously scribbling in my notebook while exchanging lighthearted cat banter with Gordon and Pam.

I began by turning to the page where I had left off. Blake had written that he had visited Uncle Sammy "three years since." Although this may not have been his last visit, as the letter was dated 1889, that meant

1886—in other words, the year before his and Chapman's expedition to the Llanganatis. The rest of the sentence made it clear that this was also the year in which he had first studied the "ancient Spanish map," the map that, according to Blake, proved the "existence beyond doubt of a vast amount of Indian treasure buried to escape the greed of the Spaniard."

The next few paragraphs recounted Blake's journey across the *paramo* and the death of his colleague Chapman, who "succumbed to a tropical maldie on the return." Then he discussed the discovery of the treasure cave. Blake had written, "It is impossible for me to describe to you the wealth that now lies in that distant cave marked on my map."

Wasn't that the same phrase Andy had recited to me from memory?

Having explained that he had to go back to sea "for a while," Blake begged Albertson "to keep for me my map which of course I dare not take with me." He would return for Albertson the following year, he said, when they would travel together to South America "to recover the gold."

"I can think of no man with whom I would rather share it . . . The amount believe me is enormous," he wrote, before imploring Albertson to keep the matter "in the greatest confidence."

I scribbled the phrases in my notebook and turned the page. Don had finished his chef's salad and was staring at me intently.

The second letter was also dated 1889. In it Blake must have enclosed a second map; his letter differentiated between "my own chart" and "my own hand-copied Valverde chart, with my notes and additions."

That must be the larger chart, I thought—the one hidden in the binding of *Knapsack and Rifle*. So Blake had never possessed the original but had copied it from another source, just as some forty years previously Spruce had copied Guzmán's map in Baños. What had happened to the original? I wondered. Was it with Spruce's Ecuadorian journals, the ones that Wallace had been at such pains to find, or was it gathering dust somewhere?

These reflections soon paled into insignificance, however, when I read the next paragraph:

> You must be acquainted with this all-important detail: Valverde's written guide and his map do not indicate the same thing. The former instructs on how to locate the hidden treasure of the

Incas. The latter shows the location of the mine that the Incas worked.

So there it was—the confirmation I had been looking for. The map and the guide were different. It was Valverde's map that had led Blake to "probably the world's biggest gold mine," and, presumably, it had been while making sense of the Inca path marked in red on the map that he and Chapman had also stumbled upon the treasure cave mentioned in the guide. The question was, where was it?

Don had ordered a coffee and was making noises about leaving. A literary miner now, I speed-read Don's manuscript, hoping to extract further information from the precious text before he took it back.

On the next page was an extract from one of Dyott's letters to Don's mother. Dated May 17, 1947, the letter was addressed to "Mrs. Bermender" and acknowledged the receipt of a letter she had sent Dyott a week earlier:

> Your letter of May 10th arrived this morning and afforded me much interest in view of the fact that I was instrumental in getting Captain Loch to come to Ecuador some years ago on a similar mission. Captain Loch however had nothing to base his search on except Valverde's guide which always seemed to me to be very inadequate.

So Dyott had claimed credit for Loch's expedition, too. But what were the points Mrs. Bermender had raised in her previous letter?

Dyott didn't say. Instead, the remainder of his letter was taken up with a diatribe against the Ecuadorian authorities:

> I cannot enter into reasons in this letter but to have anything to do with the government is absolutely fatal to almost any plan . . . you will never get a cent of your enterprise even if you should find what you seek.

I was wasting time. Don had already told me Dyott's opinion of the Ecuadorian authorities.

Suddenly Gordon stood up and announced he had to leave. He kissed Pam on the cheek. Then, turning to me, he said: "I hope you enjoyed Don's manuscript."

"It's f-fascinating," I stuttered distractedly. Out of the corner of my eye I noticed that Pam was looking at her watch.

"I need to get Don back to the home," she said. "Are you almost finished?"

Don made a move toward the manuscript. I put my hand out to stop him. "One moment. Just let me finish this note." My eyes had alighted on another extract—what appeared to be another fragment from one of Blake's letters:

> The true Path to Treasure Cave . . . runs south from Marcasitas . . . The treasure in the cave at the S. is of pure worked GOLD, many pieces inlaid with Emeralds, and more than a thousand men could carry . . .

The next thing I knew Don had whipped the page out of my hands. Glaring at me suspiciously, he stuffed the manuscript into his attaché case and turned to Pam.

"I think you'd better take me home."

"Is everything okay?" I asked.

Don didn't respond.

"It's been a long morning," Pam said apologetically. "Don isn't used to all this excitement."

I stood up and shook Pam's hand. I wanted to ask about the possibility of our meeting again, but Don was already halfway to the door. Instead, I wished Don luck with his manuscript and whispered to Pam to tell Gordon that I would write to him shortly. Pam nodded noncommittally and picked up Don's bulging attaché case. Then she took Don by the arm and led him outside.

I watched as they hobbled across the parking lot, Don's tracksuit gleaming yellow in the bright winter sunlight. Then they got into Pam's car and drove off.

So many questions were racing through my mind I barely registered the drive back to New York. Uppermost was why Don had never been to

Ecuador. "Nothing like this has happened to me before or since," he had told me at one point. "I could have left my bones in the Llanganatis." Yet unlike all the other treasure obsessives, Don had chosen to remain at home. Why?

Then there was his claim that Dyott hadn't found the treasure because he had been looking in the wrong place. Is this something Don had worked out from Blake's letters, or did he have a partner—someone who, unlike him, had been into the Llanganatis and could make sense of the mariner's correspondence? Someone, in short, like Andy?

Finally, there was that tantalizing last fragment from Blake's letter. Don had clearly been annoyed that I had spotted it. Treasure hunters had puzzled over the hieroglyph in Valverde's guide for centuries, but if Blake was to be believed, the "true Path" to the treasure cave ran "south from Marcasitas." Presumably this was something he had been able to work out from Valverde's map. However, without knowing which mountain was Margasitas, I realized that Blake's insight was of little use, for hadn't Roland told me that the Llanganatis abounded in pyrites? You could hike for weeks through those mountains without ever finding it.

No, the only way to make sense of Don's story was to persuade him to let me examine the map and manuscript at my leisure. But judging by his angry reaction to my note taking, this would be a difficult, drawn-out process. Lourie had been right: Don had guarded the manuscript as if it *were* the treasure. And perhaps he was right to do so. Perhaps Don hadn't been to Ecuador precisely because he didn't want to run the risk of having his illusions shattered. After all, to launch an expedition to the Llanganatis was to court the possibility of disappointment. Why should Don do that when he already had his treasure at home?

I DECIDED NOT TO CALL DON IMMEDIATELY. I WANTED TO GIVE HIM A chance to forget our meeting, to let his memory of my frenetic note taking subside. Instead, I decided to follow up the new leads. I wrote to the National Archives in Washington, which keeps a register of former officers in the American merchant marine, requesting information on

Barth Blake, George Chapman, and Sam Albertson. A week later I received a disappointing reply. None of those names appeared in the lists of the U.S. merchant marine. If I knew the names of the vessels the men had served on, then it might be possible to check the ship's logs. Otherwise, I was out of luck.

Despite all my research I still had no idea of the name of the schooner that had brought Blake and Chapman to Ecuador. It didn't appear in Lourie's book, nor had I noticed it in Don's manuscript—though, given the restrictions that had been placed on me, I could easily have overlooked it. It was possible that Andy remembered the name of the vessel, but when I tried calling his office, his secretary informed me that the *"señor"* was away on business and she did not know when he would be back. That just left Don.

I was tempted to call him again at the home in Cinnaminson, then thought better of it. I didn't want to risk antagonizing him further. Instead, I wrote to Gordon, saying that I had a number of "unanswered questions" and looked forward to continuing our correspondence when I got back to England and had had a chance to do some more research. Gordon's reply was sufficiently friendly to give me hope. Wishing me a "safe trip across the pond," he wrote that anything that I could "find out about Barth Blake and share with Don would be greatly appreciated."

That Don wasn't prepared to risk his life for a treasure that might well prove fictional or, if not fictional, unattainable made perfect sense to me. But such thoughts never seem to have occurred to Dyott or Brunner, or to Roland and Andy for that matter. On the contrary, the more elusive Atahualpa's hoard became, the more they lusted after it. It wasn't so much the size of the cache that obsessed them—after all, neither Andy nor Roland needed the money—as the mystery, the challenge of solving a riddle that had defeated men for centuries.

"What can be more enthralling," wrote Fawcett, shortly before he disappeared into Mato Grosso, "than penetration into the secrets of the past, and throwing light upon the history of civilization itself?"

Perhaps it was a weakness of character or a fault in their genetic makeup that attracted explorers like Fawcett to these mysteries. Fawcett's hunt for "Z" wasn't the first time he had become obsessed with

unearthing archaeological treasures. As a subaltern in the Royal Ar-
tillery, Fawcett had served for seven years in Trincomalee, Sri Lanka,
during which time he spent all his available leave and money on a fruit-
less search, carried out with the aid of a cryptic map, for the buried treasure of the Kandyan kings.

There was also a streak of mysticism to his obsession, a willingness to
set logic aside and, at the crucial moment, indulge in magical thinking.
Fawcett had long been persuaded of the need for an expedition to Brazil
by the report of a group of Portuguese explorers who in 1743 had supposedly stumbled upon the ruins of the lost city while exploring a high
plateau in Mato Grosso. But what convinced him to return to Brazil a
second time was a black basalt figure given to him, oddly enough, by
Rider Haggard. Haggard had obtained the figure from a dealer in Brazil
and could tell Fawcett nothing about its origins. But when Fawcett
took it to a psychometrician for "testing," the "vibrations" from the
basalt induced visions of "elaborate temples" beneath erupting volcanoes
in a continent stretching from Africa to South America—a vision that
helped convince Fawcett his lost city might be Atlantis!

Neither Roland nor Andy had gone so far as to suggest that Valverde's
derrotero might point to a similar lost city—an Ecuadorian Machu Picchu perhaps—but in their willingness to read significance into particular formations in the ranges, I had detected similar magical thinking.

I SPENT THE FEW DAYS I HAD LEFT IN NEW YORK CHASING UP LOOSE
ends. I was particularly intrigued by Dyott's reference to Erskine Loch.
In his letter to Mrs. Bermender, Dyott had written that he had been
"instrumental in getting Captain Loch to come to Ecuador some years
ago on a similar mission." This surely was a reference to Loch's 1936
Andes-Amazon expedition and suggested that Dyott had known about
the Llanganatis treasure long before Mrs. Bermender had contacted him.

I decided to visit the Explorers Club in New York to see if I could shed
further light on Dyott's comments. After all, both he and Loch had been
members of the club in the 1930s, and it was to there that Loch had retired in 1938 to complete the manuscript of *Fever, Famine, and Gold*.

An old-fashioned Upper East Side mansion with a twin-arched facade of brick and limestone, the Explorers Club looked like an unlikely location to plot incursions into the Amazon. It was difficult to believe that once upon a time men such as Theodore Roosevelt, Roald Amundsen, Charles Lindbergh, and Thor Heyerdahl had filled this building to capacity. This impression of an institution out of time was reinforced by the club's wood-paneled interior, complete with stone arches leading to dark banquet rooms. If I hadn't known better, I would have thought I had been transported to a Tudor mansion in the middle of the English countryside.

I introduced myself to the librarian and was ushered into a cramped, book-strewn room on the second floor. What was the purpose of my research, she asked? Once again I found myself hesitating. Should I write "Valverde's gold"? I decided against it and wrote "Erskine Loch."

The librarian disappeared behind a bookcase. There was a metallic whoosh and clang. Then she reappeared from behind the stacks and plopped a thin cardboard folder onto the desk.

"I'm afraid this is all we have," she muttered apologetically.

Inside was Loch's original membership application, together with a brief curriculum vitae and the letters of his seconders.

"Captain Loch is unusually qualified by long field experience [and] a keen desire to contribute to the knowledge of mankind through exploration, education and gentlemanly conduct," began one praising note.

Loch's application had been accepted on August 7, 1935—three days before he left New York for Ecuador. He had given his address as the Alpha Delta Phi Club on Forty-fourth Street. On the form, Loch had also listed his exploration achievements: "Travelled alone from Takum to Banyo West Africa at a time when there was no record of a white man having traversed that region." Then, in 1932, he had joined Dyott's expedition to the Jivaro Indians in eastern Ecuador—"I was second-in-command."

Was it during this expedition that Loch and Dyott had first discussed Valverde's gold? Was this when Dyott had suggested that Loch return someday and lead an expedition to the Llanganatis? And what had become of Loch after he emerged from the Llanganatis? Had he gone on to other feats of exploration?

I found the answers to these and other questions in a series of letters stuffed in the back of the folder. The letters were from another member of the club, Herbert Spencer Dickey, and were addressed to the club's secretary, Donald B. Upham.

A trained physician and ethnologist, Dickey was the first man to trace the Orinoco River to its source in the Parima Mountains of Brazil (a feat he accomplished in 1931 in the company of his wife, Elizabeth). This had been followed by several similarly impressive journeys through Colombia, Peru, and Ecuador, where Dickey became the first white man to live among the Jivaros.

When Loch arrived in Ecuador in 1936 at the head of the Andes-Amazon expedition, Dickey had observed his preparations. He had not been impressed. Writing to Upham, Dickey said that Loch's expedition had been a "debacle" from start to finish. Indeed, a number of youths had gone home "swearing that they were going to put the gallant captain in jail." When Loch emerged from the Llanganatis for the second time in 1937, Dickey himself had been approached by a friend of the captain's asking for money to help pay his fare back to the United States (apparently Loch was broke and owed $500 to a Quito hotel). Dickey refused, and Loch had to find another way to pay his debts.

By July, Loch had returned to New York. It took him the rest of the year and most of 1938 to complete the manuscript of *Fever, Famine, and Gold*. Then, in 1939, he went back to Ecuador.

On this occasion he went straight to El Oriente to prospect for gold, returning to Quito a few months later with five kilos of what Dickey described as "the most beautiful gold nuggets you have ever dreamt of." Once again Loch flew to the United States, where he persuaded a "poor, gullible stock-broking millionaire" to sink $100,000 into the prospecting venture. Hundreds of pits were dug at Scasa-Yacu near the Río Anzú in El Oriente, but Dickey reported "not one solitary nugget, not even a grain of gold, was discovered." The reason, suggested Dickey, was that the original nuggets had actually been collected from the Río Verde, some two hundred miles from where Loch said his mine was located. It seems that the original owner of the nuggets was one José Gabriel Maldonado—presumably the mysterious "Señor X" mentioned in Loch's book. Loch had agreed to pay Maldonado for the right to mine on his land, but somewhere along the way Loch had reneged on the deal or else failed to give Maldonado a sufficiently large cut. Whatever the case, Maldonado was "singing plenty," wrote Dickey.

Meanwhile, even though Loch had long since given up on the mine and, to assuage his disappointment, had gone on an epic drinking "jag," he continued to "hoodwink" the American investor into sending him regular checks.

Writing to Upham in September 1943, Dickey warned that Loch was now ensconced at the Hotel Savoy in Quito, drinking a bottle of Scotch a day. The British legation wanted nothing more to do with him, and once he'd exhausted the goodwill of his U.S. investor, Dickey predicted, the Ecuadorians would deport him.

"Now if you lads, with a pretty chance to get rid of him, want to continue the captain as a member of the club, all right," Dickey wrote. "But be prepared for the consequences . . . I spill this stuff for the club's benefit. I have no axe to grind, nothing to gain nor to lose. Loch is of a type that I don't care for it is true, but I certainly would not turn him in as I am doing were I not positive of my facts." Upham must have taken Dickey's warning seriously, because a month later—in October 1943—he wrote to Loch, expelling him from the club "for non-payment of dues."

I could find nothing in the archives to suggest that Loch had contested the club's decision or had felt compelled to respond to the slight. Perhaps by this point he had become so riddled with self-loathing he no longer cared.

According to Dickey, Loch continued fleecing his American investor and drinking epically—six cases of Californian claret and two cases of Scotch in fifteen days. "There is no percentage in writing more about a lost case," Dickey bluntly told Upham.

True to his word, Dickey did not refer to Loch again for several months. Then, in January 1944, he wrote to inform Upham that Loch had died. Apparently, the gallant former infantry captain had shot himself in the head with his service revolver. The picture Dickey painted of Loch's suicide suggested that while he may have lost his mind, he retained his sense of melodrama to the end.

Loch had not had a haircut or a "beard trim" for months and "had neglected a bath for some time," wrote Dickey. He died "on the floor of a tumble-down house he was occupying, surrounded by lighted candles with his [yellow fever] vaccination certificate stuck in his belt, and in almost indescribable squalor."

It subsequently emerged that Loch had been diagnosed with an intestinal cancer "as big as his head." It was this that, together with the boozing, had probably tipped him over the edge.

"*Sic transit gloria mundi,*" commented Dickey sardonically. "Thus passes the glory of the world."

I returned the letters to the folder and stared out the window at the icicles forming on the sills. I couldn't help thinking that Dickey's verdict was unfair. Yes, Loch's Andes-Amazon expedition had been marred by accidents and loss of life, but it had also been an incredible feat of organization and endurance. In seventy days Loch had crossed the Llanganatis from west to east—something that no other explorer had ever managed before. It was only afterward that he had run into financial difficulties and his character flaws were exposed.

Then there was that intestinal cancer. Coming on top of his money woes, it was rotten luck—almost as if Loch really had been cursed.

I made a list of all the explorers whose obsession with Atahualpa's hoard had ended in similarly tragic fashion. Not counting the numerous porters and soldiers who had died transporting equipment for gringos, there were ten: Padre Longo, Anastacio Guzmán, George Edwin Chapman, Barth Blake, Isabela and Colonel Brooks, Paul Thur de Koos, Erskine Loch, Eugene Brunner, and Diego Arias. As far as I knew, only two had survived to enjoy their old age: George Miller Dyott and Andy Fernández-Salvador.

Perhaps that was the real reason Don had stayed at home. Perhaps he was afraid.

As soon as I returned to my hotel, I dialed the number of the Cinnaminson home. Either Don would allow me to read Blake's letters and maps in full or he wouldn't. I had to find out.

The phone rang several times before a nurse answered. I asked to speak to Don, and she agreed to see if he had finished dinner. In the background I could hear the hollow scrape of chairs and the clatter of dishes being cleared.

"Hello, this is Don."

His voice was tense and cautious. I introduced myself and asked whether Gordon had passed on my message.

"Look, Mr. Ho-nigs-baum"—Don spat the syllables as if he had just swallowed something distasteful—"I've told you everything I know about Spruce. What further interest could you have in my manuscript?"

I hesitated before answering. It was time to admit my obsession, to come clean about my months of travel and research.

"I've been to Zunchu-Urcu," I stuttered. "The cross . . . it's the Southern Cross. I think I can help you find the gold."

Don harrumphed indignantly. "I thought I already told you, Mr. Honigsbaum, I'm not interested in the gold. It belongs to the *indígenas*. Goodbye."

"No, wait . . ."

But it was too late. Don had already hung up.

I stared at the receiver in disbelief. I had been prepared for resistance but not for this. Don's abrupt dismissal left me feeling angry and foolish. I had felt sure I could make him see my point of view, that in the interests of scholarship and history I could persuade him to part with Blake's maps. Now I had to face the fact that for all my cajoling and cunning, I was still no closer to knowing the truth of Blake's story. Don had played me like an expert fly fisherman, showing me only as much of the manuscript as he needed to hook me. Then, when I took the bait, he severed the line, leaving me floundering on the point of my obsession.

A FEW DAYS AFTER MY ABRUPT CONVERSATION WITH DON, I E-MAILED Roland. We had spoken briefly after my hike to Zunchu-Urcu but had had no other contact since my return to Europe. Judging by Roland's response, however, Don Segundo had given me a glowing report.

"Everything is ready for our expedition," he reassured me by return e-mail. "I have only two questions. Are you prepared to walk through extreme terrain for twenty-one days, and can you finance the costs of the porters and food?"

In all we would need eleven men, seven to carry our food and provisions as far as the junction of the Parca Yacu and the Río El Golpe and four more to continue on to El Mundo Nuevo. After that we would attempt to exit the ranges via the Sacha Llanganatis, emerging on the Río Napo just as Erskine Loch had done nearly forty years earlier. If I wasn't up to a three-week expedition, Roland said we might be able to hire a helicopter to drop us on the Río Mulatos, thus saving seven days on the outward-journey time. The only catch was the cost: $5,000 for an hour's helicopter ride.

Mindful of Andy's accident on Cerro Hermoso and my dwindling bank balance, I responded that I would rather walk. If I was to perish in the Llanganatis, I preferred to do it in the traditional manner.

Part Six

BEYOND THE RANGES

There's no romance to this, nor to a battle—while one takes part in it. Great physical effort and discomfort are one's sole companions.

—ERSKINE LOCH, *Fever, Famine, and Gold*

1

ROLAND AND ANDY REDUX

IT WAS EARLY JANUARY WHEN I RETURNED TO ECUADOR. BELOW THE wing Quito was a latticework of electric light, an orange-and-yellow filigree teased and stretched between the Andes. Swooping low over Pichincha, the plane seemed to graze the statue of the Virgin on El Panecillo. Then we were stepping out of the pressurized cabin, and I experienced that sudden gasp of recognition, that realization of where I was and what I had come to do. This time there could be no turning back.

On my previous visits to Quito I had stayed in the backpacker district, but the Mariscal, with its brightly painted hostels offering organic breakfasts, no longer held the attraction it once did. I didn't want to swap notes with tourists any longer over where to exchange money or the best way to acclimatize for Chimborazo. Instead, I rented a small apartment near the old town and breakfasted in cafés where the menus were in Spanish and the coffee had the harsh, gritty taste of the sierra. Here the ocher skins and haughty profiles of the Incas far outnumbered those of the descendants of the conquistadores. Wandering the narrow backstreets, I could well imagine the city as it must have been before Benalcázar destroyed it: the magnificent polygonal stone block walls with their trapezoidal doorways and recesses; the low, thatched houses and rectangular plazas teeming with people and fresh produce; and at the center of it all—where the Iglesia de San Francisco now stood—Atahualpa's palace, perfectly aligned on the solstices and equinoxes. If it had been anything like the Temple of the Sun in Cuzco, it must have been a magnificent sight. "All the plate, the ornaments . . . were of gold or silver," wrote the historian William Prescott.

> The censers for the perfumes, the ewers which held the water for sacrifice, the pipes which conducted it through subterraneous channels into the buildings . . . were all of the same rich materials . . . If the reader sees in this fairy tale picture only the romantic colouring of some fabulous *El Dorado*, he must recall what has been said before in reference to the palaces of the Incas and consider that these "Houses of the Sun" were the common reservoir into which flowed all the streams of public and private benefaction throughout the empire.

Now, at last, I was going to trace one of those streams to its source, to the Llanganatis, the place where Roland believed the Incas had mined and smelted their gold. I couldn't bear the thought of another delay, another disappointment.

I had expected to find Roland poring over maps and provision lists, the floor of his office piled high with the detritus that marks the beginning of a treasure expedition, but the Roland who greeted me on my return had one more surprise in store. The rope and tarpaulin, the rubber jackets and tanks that had littered the floor of his office when I last visited him were gone. In their place he had built a partition wall and installed a pair of expensive matching leather sofas.

That was not the only alteration. Beside his desk, where previously there had been only a phone and a typewriter, glowed a new computer monitor complete with scanner and fax.

Roland embraced me and ushered me into his subtly transformed lair. He had had a beard trim and smelled of expensive cologne.

"So, Marcos, you are in good health, jah?"

I nodded.

"Good. This is not going to be a, how you say, a breakfast."

"A picnic," I corrected him.

Roland laughed heartily at his mistake and offered me a seat on the sofa.

"Jah, it won't be a picnic, that's for sure. But don't worry, in the mountains I always eat very well. What would you like, some salami, a nice Bavarian ham perhaps?"

Roland grabbed a piece of paper and began making an impromptu shopping list. This was not what I had been expecting. From my seat I could see that Roland's desk was littered with glossy brochures. On the cover of one was a picture of a helicopter. Perhaps I was wrong. Perhaps Roland was taking our expedition more seriously than I thought.

"Your office is looking very smart," I said.

"Yes, I have an important business meeting coming up."

I wondered what meeting could be so important as to have warranted this sudden transformation. Until now I had assumed that Roland's income came from his farm in Tena and his gold-mining activities. But he had sold his mine in Zamora in southern Ecuador some time ago, and as far as I knew, the Canadian company to which he had leased exploration sites on his farm had yet to strike a similarly lucrative vein.

Then there was the cost of his expeditions to the Llanganatis to consider—$100,000 over fifteen years—and the upkeep of his apartment here in Quito and the new house he was building for his wife in Los Chillos. Even if he had invested the profits from his mine wisely, that was an awful lot of expenses.

Sensing my confusion, Roland walked over to his desk and picked up the brochure and a ring binder bulging with documents. He hesitated before handing them to me. "I'm not sure you'll approve," he said sheepishly.

I studied the cover of the brochure. Up close I could see that it was illustrated with a police helicopter. Inside there were pictures of batons, pepper sprays, and bulletproof vests—everything in fact that a modern law-enforcement service might need. The contents of the ring binder were even more shocking: Heckler & Koch MP5 submachine guns, armored personnel carriers, patrol boats, even a page devoted to jungle-warfare equipment. At the end of the list of military paraphernalia was a letter from an arms company in Miami detailing the costs of the weaponry. After this came a sample contract and another letter from the Fuerzas terrestres—the Ecuadorian land forces. The letter, I noticed, contained a figure followed by several zeros.

It took me some time to absorb the information, but the conclusion was inescapable: Roland had set himself up as an arms dealer.

"I know what you're thinking," he said apologetically, "but believe me, I have done everything very properly. If it wasn't me, it would be somebody else."

"But how . . . when?" I spluttered.

"You remember this painting?" He pointed to the portrait of Rumiñahui in the entrance hall. It was the only thing in his office he hadn't changed.

"Of course, you told me it was painted by a friend of yours in the army." I stared at the signature to remind myself of the artist's name. "Gallo, wasn't it?"

"Yes, but what I didn't tell you is that Colonel Gallo is the head of Ecuadorian military intelligence."

Roland explained that the army, concerned about guerrilla activity along the Colombian border, was looking to place a big order for rocket launchers and automatic machine guns. At the same time the navy was hoping to acquire a new fleet of fast patrol boats, while the Quito police, worried by a recent surge in bank robberies, was planning to buy two new helicopters.

Roland said he had learned of the contracts the previous spring through a family friend—a general in the Ecuadorian Army—but it was Gallo who had suggested he get in touch with the arms firm in Miami and offer to broker the deals.

Suddenly I realized why Roland had been so reluctant to set a date for our expedition: he had been plotting with Gallo all along. The story about his parents' being ill had been an excuse. Worried that I might not approve of his new venture, Roland had sent me to Zunchu-Urcu with Don Segundo. After all, what better way of getting rid of someone than to send them on a wild-goose chase to the Llanganatis?

Roland was right: I didn't approve of his new sideline, but I couldn't find it in my heart to judge him either. Compared with Valverde's gold, the arms deals were a far more palpable treasure. In fact, had Roland closed the deal then and there, I wouldn't have objected. My real fear was that Colonel Gallo and his cronies would string Roland along for

weeks, sabotaging my hopes of getting into the Llanganatis before the
onset of the rainy season.

But I didn't say any of this. Instead, I joked that perhaps before selling the helicopters to the police, Roland could persuade them to make
a test run over the Llanganatis.

Roland smiled, then knit his brows seriously. "You know, only last
week I was approached by some rich Americans. They already have a
helicopter standing by." He let this thought settle for a moment. "But
don't worry, I told them I couldn't guide them. I don't want my valley
overrun by crazy gringos."

He explained that he had invested too much time and money to risk
a gold rush now. Better to return to "El Mundo Nuevo" with a small
team. That way, if he found the mine, he would be able to protect his
discovery.

"But enough of me," said Roland suddenly. "How did your research
in Europe go?"

I gave him a précis of my investigations, choosing my words carefully. Although Roland liked to think of himself as a scientist of the
treasure, I knew that his obsession with the history and geology of the
Llanganatis was also a deeply held faith. To undermine it now could be
a disaster.

So, I played up the significance of Pedro de Valverde, the accountant
in the Royal House of Quito whose letters I had discovered in Seville.
Although I had been unable to find any trace of a *derrotero* in the
archives, I explained that the documents bearing Pedro de Valverde's
name had contained tantalizing references to the "works in the gold
mines." I also told Roland about the intriguing document referring to
Antonio Pastór's role in the export of cinnamon. However, I said there
was nothing to indicate that the governor of Latacunga had smuggled
the treasure out of Ecuador or, indeed, that he had invested the profits
in the Royal Bank of Scotland.

Roland absorbed my report calmly—I decided not to bother him
with the details of my research into Blake and Chapman or my meeting with Don Bermender. Then he reached into a drawer and handed
me a bundle of photocopied pages from an old library book. I studied
the title page; it was a monograph of the canton of Píllaro. On the first
page was a picture of the author, a priest and member of the National

Academy of History named Dr. José María Coba Robalino. Next to his picture was the date of publication: 1929, twenty-one years *after* Spruce's *Notes of a Botanist on the Amazon and Andes*.

"Quick, turn to page 255," urged Roland. "I think you'll find it interesting."

I flicked forward until I found the page in question. Roland had underscored several passages in thick pencil, including one that read "Minas del Llanganate" (Mines of the Llanganatis).

I scanned the entry, scarcely able to believe what I was reading. According to Coba Robalino, in 1812, at the height of Ecuador's war of independence, a "good man named Valverde" had been on the point of death when he called for the local curate, a Dr. Don Manuel de los Reyes. Before absolving Valverde of his sins and administering the last rites, Don Manuel had asked him whether he had anything on his conscience. According to Coba Robalino, Valverde had immediately handed the curate a map of the Llanganatis, telling him he wished to reveal something "very important." The map described an "abundant deposit of gold nuggets" hidden deep in the ranges. Valverde said the deposit had been left to him by his grandfather, who had gone there many times and grown very wealthy. One day, however, the authorities— noticing that his grandfather was without work—had arrested him and accused him of being a thief. Faced with imprisonment, his grandfather confessed his secret, but so far no one had succeeded in finding the mine. Nevertheless, now that Valverde was dying, he wanted to bequeath his grandfather's map to the curate so that the gold would go to the Church.

The curate thanked Valverde for his gift and immediately formed an exploration company. But though he succeeded in opening a trail into the Llanganatis, the original path marked on Valverde's map was gone— destroyed, most likely, by a huge earthquake that had rocked the region in 1797.* In the end the only thing the curate discovered was the remains of an old copper mine. Nevertheless, wrote Coba Robalino, Píllaro still abounded in legends of lost gold and treasure. One of the most popular stories, current in 1929, told of an enchanted cave in the

---

* The earthquake was caused by the eruption of the Sangay volcano.

Llanganatis containing an altar with a golden statue of an Indian princess. The altar and walls of the cave were said to be lined with gold and precious stones, but the cave was protected by a powerful spell, and so far no one who had entered it had returned to tell the tale.

I flicked through the remaining pages of Coba Robalino's monograph. There were references to Mariano Enríquez de Guzmán, the Píllaro curate who in 1793 had also mounted an expedition to the Llanganatis (this was the same curate whose map had interested the Ecuadorian historian Andrade). But, oddly, there was no mention of Anastacio Guzmán, the botanist whose map had fascinated Spruce, or of Antonio Pastór. Indeed, except for his reference to a "good man named Valverde," Coba Robalino could have been describing another *derrotero* entirely. But Roland wasn't concerned about these anomalies. He was interested only in the points where Coba Robalino's version of the *derrotero* and Spruce's intersected.

"Don't you see, if what Coba Robalino writes is true, it's further evidence for the existence of the gold mine. The only reason the curate couldn't find it was because the road had been destroyed."

I recalled what Jorge Anhalzer had told me before our hike to Zunchu-Urcu: how he, too, had seen Roland's channels and the rectangular pools in the Sacha Llanganatis, but when he had tried to return to the constructions a second time, a series of landslides had transformed the valley beyond recognition. Did Roland know about Jorge's attempts to reach the valley? What if the constructions had been destroyed?

Roland's face darkened.

"Ach, Jorge is a photographer, not a geologist," he scoffed. "Do you think the Americans are offering him a free ride in a helicopter? No, they know there is only one person who can lead them to the valley."

Once again the veiled threat that another group of treasure hunters was waiting in the wings if I didn't come up with the money for the expedition.

Until now I had seen Roland as an antidote to Andy, a teetotaler to Andy's whiskey priest. But now I was beginning to realize that in his own way the German geologist could be just as obsessive and manipulative. If for Andy the key to Valverde's gold lay in decoding Blake's maps and letters, for Roland it was his obsession with the mine. Convinced it lay somewhere near his valley in the Sacha Llanganatis, Roland had searched for evidence to support his prejudice. Coba Robalino's *derrotero* certainly pointed to the existence of a lost gold mine, but it also raised uncomfortable questions, not least the complete absence of any mention of the three *cerros* or the "lake, made by hand"—a clue Roland had considered crucial because it fitted his theory about the rectangular pools and channels. Were these lacunae that could safely be ignored, or were the discrepancies between the two *derroteros* evidence of what John Hemming had argued all along: namely, that Valverde's gold was an invention like El Dorado, a myth that came in as many versions as there had been people to transcribe it?

I needed to focus, to remember what had brought me back to Ecuador. I asked Roland to show me the route he planned to take to the valley. It had been so long since I had studied a map of the Llanganatis I could hardly recall where it was.

Roland unfurled the maps from the Instituto Geográfico Militar—the same maps we had pored over a few months before. There was the road running alongside Pisayambo—the road I had driven along with Jorge, Rómulo, and Don Segundo—and there, midway between the Spectacle Lakes and Mesa Tablón, was the point where we had parked our pickup and started walking. But this time Roland indicated that instead of heading southeast toward Auca Cocha, we would cleave to the classic Way outlined by Valverde.

"We will follow the trailhead as far as we can, then we will cut northeast across the *paramo* to Yana Cocha." He placed his finger on the dark pool of the black lake. Having contoured up and around the southern shore of the lake, we would then proceed east along the left bank of the Desaguadero—in reality a narrow ravine that dropped to join the Río El Golpe. Just beyond the point where the *quebrada* met the river was a hut belonging to a local farming cooperative that corresponded roughly to Valverde's second sleeping place.

"It's drafty but very comfortable," Roland assured me.

The following day we would continue "through the forest in the same direction"—just as Valverde's guide stipulated—until we reached the Parca Yacu. Roland shifted his gaze to the second map, labeled "Río Mulatos." The Parca Yacu emerged from the divide in the left-hand corner, snaking east and north. On some of the ridges to the south of the river I could see that Roland had drawn circles in a yellow marker and scribbled the abbreviations of different metals from the periodic table.

"Here we have a possibility for Margasitas Mountain," said Roland, prodding a hill marked "Fe" and "FeS$_2$," (iron and pyrites), "and here we have another. But on this trip we won't be concerned with pyrites. We will be panning the river for gold. Our aim is to reach this canyon here."

Roland indicated a point where the river suddenly narrowed before dropping to the north. Immediately to the south was a fearful summit, labeled "Gallo-Urcu"—Rooster Mountain.

"I believe this could be the area Valverde refers to in the last lines of the *derrotero*." Roland removed a copy of the guide from his drawer and recited the lines to refresh my memory:

> If thou lose thyself in the forest, seek the river—follow it on the
> right bank—lower down take to the beach, and thou will come on
> a deep ravine such that although thou seek to pass it thou wilt not
> find where; climb therefore the mountain on the right hand and
> in this manner thou canst by no means miss the way.

"This is the point where we will send most of the porters back to San José de Poaló. I don't know if Jorge told you, but when he came this way, his porters deserted him."

I recalled Jorge's description of how he had woken up to find the porters gone, and how after breakfast he had had to abseil up a sheer rock wall on the right bank of the Parca Yacu—just as the *derrotero* described—dragging the Wall Street broker and his fiancée's possessions after him.

Rather than climb out of the gorge, however, Roland planned to build a series of bridges. This would enable us to follow the Parca Yacu beyond the gorge to the opposite side of Gallo-Urcu. From here we would be able to cut directly across country to the Río Mulatos to emerge upstream of the valley containing the constructions.

"If everything goes according to plan, we should reach 'El Mundo Nuevo' in ten days."

"How much will it cost?" I asked.

Roland took a pencil from the drawer and began scribbling figures on a piece of paper.

"Let me see. We will need seven men to carry our food and provisions, and it will take us at least four days to reach the canyon—that's eight days there and back. At a rate of $10 a day that makes $560."

Roland wrote "$560" on the paper.

"Then we will continue on with Don Segundo and three other men for sixteen more days. But they are more experienced than the rest, so we will have to pay them a little more, say $12 to $15 a day."

Roland multiplied four by twenty by twelve.

"That makes $960. Then there's the cost of a pickup to drop us at the trailhead and food for eleven men—thirteen counting you and me." Roland wrote down the figures $40 and $400. "Have I left anything out?"

I shrugged my shoulders. I had no idea what an expedition of this size required.

"No? Good. That makes $1,960—let's say $2,000 to be safe."

I stared at the figure in disbelief. It was a stupendous sum, far more than I had budgeted for. But I had invested too much to turn back now.

"When do we leave?" I asked.

"In one week. I just have one or two things to sort out first."

Was Roland awaiting a shipment of submachine guns from Germany? I decided I would rather not know.

We shook hands and promised to talk again over the weekend. As I left his office, the phone rang. Roland picked up the receiver and began talking animatedly in hushed tones.

It sounded like a business call.

IN THE DAYS THAT FOLLOWED, I BEGAN TRAINING SERIOUSLY FOR OUR expedition. I recalled how my legs had felt like lead on the hike to Zunchu-Urcu, how with each footfall I had sunk deeper into the mud while Don Segundo had skipped over the bogs like a Boy Scout on a seaside outing. I was determined that this time I would do better.

Fortunately, there was a park not far from my apartment with a sand running track. The track boasted its own boot-camp-style training circuit and was a magnet for the local Quitenian jocks—men who, to judge by their reversed baseball caps and the ripped sleeves of their sweatshirts, had seen one too many *Rocky* movies. As I attempted a circuit, my lungs screaming for oxygen, they would launch into bizarre calisthenics on the crude equipment, diving headfirst through tires suspended on ropes or having a "buddy" sit on their legs while they did thirty sit-ups on a plank of wood stuck into the ground at a forty-five-degree angle.

To add to the unreality of the scene, beside the track was an adventure playground boasting an abandoned plane, a tank and several rusting armored vehicles. The hardware looked as if it had had to be abandoned in a hurry, as if the recruits had fled the scene following a misguided coup attempt by their superiors. In one spot there was even a heavy gun with a revolving magazine (I assumed the bullets had been removed, but in Ecuador you could never be sure). The riskiest part of the exercise, however, was simply getting there. At 6:30 a.m. the park was a desert. To reach the track, I had to cross a wild scrubland populated by rabid strays and leering drunks. Not surprisingly, I usually sprinted.

It was the sort of routine I imagined Andy would have reveled in in his heyday as Mr. Ecuador—he probably still had the ripped sweatshirt in his bottom drawer—and I decided to use the little time left before my expedition to reestablish contact. Before my own attempt on the treasure I wanted to see if I could pry more information out of him about his experiences in the Llanganatis and hoped that my meeting with Don would provide the lever. I was also curious to know what had really transpired between him, Brunner, and Dyott in 1965. At our meeting Andy had never mentioned Brunner or the contract the three of them had signed at Dyott's ranch. I had had to discover that in Lourie's book. Did he still think of Brunner as that "crazy Swiss-German fellow," or had old age brought a grudging respect?

I dialed Andy's number in Guayaquil and spoke to his secretary. As I waited for her to put me through, I felt a sudden apprehension. How would Andy react to the news of my own treasure-hunting ambitions? The last time we had met he had belittled my physical prowess, saying that judging by the way I handled a horse I would be "cursing every second" in the Llanganatis. Only small, tough guys like him and Dyott had what it took to survive in the ranges, he had boasted. But that was before I had climbed Mesa Tablón and seen the moon rise above Zunchu-Urcu.

I was worrying unduly. From Andy's voice I could tell immediately that I had got Dr. Jekyll this morning, not the monster who sometimes appeared at night.

"Ah, Marcos, welcome back to Ecuador. How goes your research?"

I gave him a summary of my progress, explaining that I had made a trip to Zunchu-Urcu and was about to go deeper into the ranges.

"¿Ah, sí?" he replied, disinterestedly. "Did you see Diego's grave?"

"Yes, we said a small prayer and left flowers."

"Thank you, that was a nice gesture. I was just there, you know, in December."

"At Zunchu-Urcu?"

"No, no, no, we were deep inside the mountains."

"Really?"

This was astounding news. For all his bravado, I had assumed Andy was too frail to contemplate another expedition to the Llanganatis.

"But your knee—I thought you said it gave you too much pain."

"My knee is a bloody nuisance," Andy agreed. "Luckily, I was able to get a lift."

Andy explained that a few weeks before Christmas he had persuaded his son-in-law to lend him the company helicopter. Accompanied by three trusted guides, he had flown deep into the ranges—he wouldn't say exactly where—returning twenty-one days later.

"I found the dried-up crater lake just where Blake described it. I am sure the treasure cave is close by, but the terrain is very hard. If it wasn't for my damn knee . . ."

Andy trailed off, contemplating what might have been had he been younger and fitter. What did he mean by a "dried-up crater lake"? Was this the "extinct lake" Uncle Sammy had referred to in the message he had pinpricked in the King James Bible, the lake where Blake had supposedly found Atahualpa's hoard?

I was desperate to question Andy further but realized there was little point in interrogating him over the phone. I had to lure him to Quito, but how?

I decided to play my trump card.

"Did I tell you I met Mrs. Bermender's son? He has Blake's maps, the same ones you showed me."

"¿Ah, sí?"

This time it was Andy's turn to be surprised.

"But he also has something else." I paused, choosing my words carefully. "You were right, Andy. Valverde not only left a guide; he drew a map. Don has it."

The old treasure hunter could hardly contain his excitement.

"Have you seen it? Did he let you make a copy?"

"No, he keeps it in a safe. But he showed me a letter in which Blake talks about the map, one that I don't think even you have seen."

The phone fell silent.

"Andy, are you still there?"

"*Sí*, Marcos, I was just thinking, I have a business meeting in Quito on Friday. When did you say you were leaving on your expedition?"

"Next week."

"Give me your number. I'll have my secretary call with the time of my flight."

Andy's secretary called me that very afternoon. Andy would be arriving first thing Friday morning on a private jet from Guayaquil. I was to rendezvous with him by the side entrance of the airport, where his chauffeur would be waiting to meet us. The *"señor"* had booked a table for lunch at the Swissôtel. We would have all morning to talk.

I trained harder than ever those next few days. I wasn't only racing to get physically fit; I was preparing myself psychologically. I had little expectation that Andy would tell me where Blake's treasure cave was—in any case, I figured that if he really knew, he would have removed the gold long ago. Instead, I set my sights on Dyott's letters and journals—the ones from which Andy had read me extracts at his ranch. As far as I knew, no one other than Andy and perhaps Don Bermender had ever read Dyott's account of his two expeditions. (Hadn't Mike Dyott told me that when he inherited his father's journals the pages covering the years 1947 and 1948 were mysteriously missing?) Together with the fragments from Don's manuscript I hoped they might enable me to complete the puzzle.

On Friday morning I rose at 8 a.m. and caught a taxi to the airport. Andy's flight wasn't due in until 9 a.m. but he was a stickler for punctuality and I didn't want to risk being late.

It was a beautiful sunny morning. Even though it was winter in the sierra, it hadn't rained in Quito for weeks—the total opposite of the

situation on the coast, where the flooding had continued unabated—
and to the south Cotopaxi shone majestically over the city, its summit
clearly visible through the haze.

I had no difficulty spotting the arrival gate. SUVs and limousines were
already parked two deep by the curbside, the drivers leaning casually on
the fenders, smoking Larks. In their identical black suits and mirrored
sunglasses, they looked like extras in a Tarantino movie. You could tell
they, like most Ecuadorians, were imagining themselves somewhere else.

I joined them in the road, plane-spotters all. The first flight to arrive
was an American Airlines Boeing from Bogotá, then a tiny Air Icaro
Fokker, its twin propellers spinning noiselessly in the wind.

The next plane was Andy's. I knew it was his flight because a group
of soldiers suddenly appeared from the hangar and formed a welcome
cordon.

First off were a pair of army colonels, their brass buttons glinting
brightly in the sun, then a thin man in an Italian suit—from the chauf-
feurs' whispers I gathered he was someone high up in government. Then
came a stream of businessmen and, bringing up the rear, Andy.

Dressed in a light blue blazer and slacks, he looked older and smaller
than I remembered. In his right hand he carried a bulging overnight
bag while in his left he gripped a thin attaché case. As he crossed the tarmac, he wobbled unsteadily in his cowboy boots.

The chauffeur rushed forward to meet him, and Andy grumpily
handed him the overnight bag. I noted, however, that he kept a tight
grip on the attaché case.

We shook hands warmly, and Andy introduced me to a smart young
man walking beside him.

"This is my son-in-law. He manages the family water business now."

A Latin Richard Gere shook my hand perfunctorily, then took a call
on his mobile phone. From his dismissive manner I gathered that he
considered me another of his father-in-law's indulgences.

We climbed into the company SUV and wended our way south—
past Plaza de Toros and Parque la Carolina—toward the city center.
Andy's dark eyes twinkled with recognition at the familiar sights. This
was the city where he grew up, he explained, the city where his father
built Tesalia and Güitig into household names. It was only later that
they had transferred to Guayaquil.

"In those days the weather here was terrible," he joked. "My father used to say there were only two seasons in Quito: *"la estación de las lluvias y la estación de tren"* (the season of rains and the train station). Andy slapped his thighs, cackling like a small boy. It was a dreadful pun on the Spanish word for both "season" and "station" (*estación*), but I couldn't help laughing with him. For all his vanity and egotism, Andy was a charming raconteur, and I found myself wondering whether, had we met a few years earlier, I might now be contemplating an expedition with him to the Llanganatis instead of with Roland.

I asked him how his latest expedition had gone.

"*Como siempre*—the usual. We had clear blue skies only on the first day and the last. In between it rained continuously."

He had left on December 14, he explained, flying from Shell Mera, the oil station below Baños where he had landed his crippled Cessna thirty-five years earlier. The helicopter had dropped him on a beach in the heart of the ranges and had picked him up at the same spot three weeks later.

He handed me a snapshot showing his men erecting a tent in a clearing between huge boulders. It could have been anywhere.

"Is this the Mulatos?" I asked, fishing.

Andy wagged his finger admonishingly. "That, my friend, is a secret."

All that he would tell me is that he had been looking for signs of volcanism. "Here we found a carbonated spring," he said, handing me another picture showing water bubbling from beneath some rocks. "Then, a little farther on, we stumbled upon this."

Andy handed me a picture showing a valley bare of vegetation. At the center was a large, bowl-like depression.

"We tested the rocks. They were very calcareous!" Andy declared triumphantly. "Don't you see? It's Blake's crater lake, the one he mentioned in the Bible."

I studied the photo, trying to see his point of view. A viscid mist clung to the higher slopes, giving the valley an impenetrable, unknowable quality. Aside from the absence of *flechas* and *frailejones*, it looked like any other valley in the Llanganatis.

I changed the subject.

"I have a theory about Blake's clue 'Look for the cross.' I think he meant the Southern Cross."

I explained how, when I had stood at Zunchu-Urcu, I had seen the moon and the distinctive four-pronged constellation reflected in the waters of Cable Lake and how, if you measured four degrees to the left, the constellation appeared to point toward Cerro Negro.

Andy looked at me with renewed interest.

"Many years ago I reached a similar conclusion, Marcos."

Andy explained that shortly before Dyott's death, he had chartered a helicopter to fly over Zunchu-Urcu.

"I aligned the nose of the helicopter with the mountain to the south, and then instructed the pilot to turn a few degrees to the east. That's when I saw the silhouette of Topo Mountain exactly as it appears on Blake's map."

Andy wouldn't say exactly where this Topo Mountain was—"Perhaps later, Marcos, when we have had a drink." (I gathered it was not Cerro Hermoso or Cerro Negro but another mountain farther to the east.) But apparently, when he had told Dyott, the commander had been "ecstatic."

"Andy," he had said, "I think you've got it."

Had Andy really identified Topo Mountain, or was this just another ruse to keep me interested? And why did he always have to place himself at the center of the story?

I was getting tired of his games. It was time for him to lay all his cards on the table. Clearly my meeting with Don had intrigued him, otherwise he wouldn't have agreed to see me again. If he wanted to know more, I resolved, he would have to give me something in exchange.

We pulled into the forecourt of the Swissôtel. Andy's son-in-law, who had spent most of the drive on the phone, briefly broke off his conversation to remind Andy that there was a Tesalia board meeting at 3 p.m. He would return promptly at 2:30.

I glanced at my watch; it was just after ten. That gave us nearly four and a half hours together.

We found a table in the bar, and Andy ordered a whiskey. I waited for the barman to serve him, then asked about Brunner. What had transpired between them at Dyott's ranch in 1965?

"Eugenio was a dreamer, that is all. Dyott and I sponsored him— until we got bored."

I said that was not the impression I had got from reading Lourie's book. There Brunner made out that it was he, not Andy, who had been Dyott's main partner.

Andy scoffed. "Another fantasy! I was the one who sent him to Cerro Hermoso, but Eugenio became fixated on the mountain. He wouldn't consider any other possibility. Dyott thought he was a fool."

It was my turn to be incredulous. Dyott might well have had his doubts about Brunner, but that didn't necessarily mean he trusted Andy more. I suspected the truth was that Dyott had played one man off against the other, showing them different parts of Blake's maps and letters but never allowing either to get the whole picture. Presumably, that was why Andy was so interested in my meeting with Don.

I cast Andy a dubious look. How did I know that he wasn't trying to mislead me? After all, I told him it wasn't as if I could speak to Dyott.

Andy opened his attaché case and pulled out a folder—the same folder I had seen at the ranch. "Yes, you can," he said, handing me a bunch of crumpled documents.

I stared at the documents in disbelief. On the first page was a photocopy of a typewritten letter, followed by what appeared to be a series of handwritten notes. The letter was addressed to "Mrs. Bermender" and had been sent care of the British legation in Quito on February 28, 1949. Although the signature at the end of the letter was indistinct, there was little doubt whom it was from as the subsequent notes were headed "Personal thoughts of Commander Dyott" and "Llang. esp. Gen. Report 1948–1949. G. M. Dyott."

I read the first line of Dyott's report:

> When looking at Blake's maps or reading his brief letters in your comfortable home, everything looked so simple and easy, but somehow or another when on the spot things take on a different complexion.

"But this is incredible. Where did you get this?"

"They were sent to me after Dyott's death—I don't know by whom."

"Can I read them?"

Andy thought about this for a moment. "It depends. What do I get in return?"

I decided to give him a brief summary of my meeting with Don and

Gordon in New Jersey: how Don had been seated in the farthest corner of the pizzeria grasping his manuscript (I wanted to say, much as Andy was grasping Dyott's notes now, but thought better of it); how he had allowed me to read fragments of Blake's letters and had shown me part of a map—not sketches like the ones Andy had drawn for me but another map entirely, Valverde's map.

"How did you know it was Valverde's map?" Andy interrupted excitedly. "What was on it?"

"Oh, it was Valverde's map all right," I lied (in truth the copy had been so poor it could have been a child's scrawl, but Andy didn't need to know that). "There were letters and symbols on it and a trail marked in red ink. Besides, Don showed me a letter from Dyott addressed to his mother, just like the one you have here."

I explained that Dyott had visited the Bermenders in Philadelphia and told them not to mention the map to the Ecuadorian authorities, warning that if they did they'd "never get a cent" from the treasure.

Andy smiled. "The commander often told me the same thing. 'Andy,' he used to say, 'you and I must be like squirrels. If we find the treasure, we must bury it and return for it another day.'"

He paused, lost in reverie. Had Andy really been Dyott's acolyte? I wondered. Had they been close, or was this just how Andy preferred to remember it?

"It's a pity Don didn't let you copy the map," Andy said wistfully. "That really would have been something. Was there anything else? What about these other letters you mentioned?"

"Blake's letters?"

"Yes."

It was time to call his bluff.

"If I tell you, will you let me read Dyott's journals?"

Andy thought about my offer for a moment. It was against his nature to concede anything, but he could see this was my sticking point.

"Okay," he said finally. "You can read them here and take notes. But when I leave for my meeting, that's it." He thumped the table, glaring at me to let me know this was his final offer. Under the circumstances I had little choice but to accept.

For the next two hours I read Dyott's journals, scribbling furiously. At the same time Andy ordered lunch, and I told him what I had

gleaned from Don: how in one of his letters Blake had drawn a vital distinction between Valverde's guide and his map, saying that the first indicated the path to the treasure cave and the second the path to the
mine; and how in another letter Blake had written that the "true Path
to treasure cave [ran] south from Marcasitas."

Andy seemed pleased with the information. "I knew it," he muttered. "It's just as I thought." But by now I had become too immersed
in Dyott's journals to care about his theories.

The first entry, dated September 27, 1947, read:

> I have set into some curious quests in my time but this is cer-
> tainly by far the most strange . . . Neither do I think Bermen-
> der's grandfather was the kind of man to stage a hoax . . . Besides
> he knew nothing about the subject to have worked out what
> he did.

So Dyott *had* believed Uncle Sammy's messages in the Bible. That was
encouraging. But Dyott's entry appeared to be incomplete. Where was
the rest of it?

The next entry was already familiar to me:

> Wednesday, 22 October 1947: a nice quiet day with no discordant
> notes . . . Sometimes I give up hope of being able to do anything
> worthwhile in this *cursed region*. Not the singlest description
> which I have read gives the slightest idea of the nature of the
> country and Loch's account is the most misleading of all.

This was the comment Andy had read to me at his ranch, chuckling at
the commander's turn of phrase. But where in the Llanganatis had Dyott been when he made the entry? What had he been looking for?

I turned to Andy for enlightenment.

"Oh, I'm sorry, Marcos, this must be very confusing for you. I forgot, you know nothing about Dyott's two expeditions."

Andy explained that the majority of the notes were from Dyott's first
expedition to the Llanganatis in 1947. Andy claimed he had copied them
out in his own hand some years ago from the original set that had been
sent to him anonymously in the post. The extracts were incomplete

because he had only noted down those comments that had struck him as relevant and interesting at the time. Also, he had sometimes added his own commentary in parentheses, pointing out where he disagreed with Dyott over the correct interpretation of Blake's maps.

On his first expedition, from September 1947 to February 1948, Dyott had followed the Parca Yacu as far as a dry ravine known as the Pava-Micuna (the Turkey). The ravine led Dyott smack into the side of Las Torres. There he found two peaks and a cave that he thought might correspond to the drawing on Blake's second map. But the cave was empty, so Dyott continued south, thinking he had made a mistake and had not gone far enough.

According to Andy, Dyott's route had led him down the gorge marked "Encañada de Sacha Pamba" on Guzmán's map. But when he reached the spot where Guzmán had marked "Gran Volcán del Topo," he found himself staring up at the ramparts of Cerro Hermoso.

"That expedition convinced Dyott that both Guzmán's Gran Volcán del Topo and the Topo Mountain of Blake's map were false," said Andy. "See here."

He pointed to two entries I had yet to come to. The first, dated November 1, read, "Guzmán's Volcán del Topo is I am sure completely false." The second, dated November 5, 1948—in other words, the November of the following year—was even more explicit:

> Briefly I can say with a good deal of certainty that I have established some very important facts. First, Blake's no. 2 map which shows "the true path to the treasure cave" is completely false. Second, that the first map, while it was quite clear to Blake, has absolutely no meaning to others.

I scratched my head. Blake's maps false and meaningless? If Dyott had reached this conclusion in 1948, then what had been the point of Andy's secrecy? Had he been wasting my time?

"I don't understand: Dyott didn't think Blake's first map made any sense either?"

Andy explained that after reaching Cerro Hermoso, Dyott had headed northwest to Zunchu-Urcu, or, as he referred to it, Pan de Azúcar.

Convinced that the mountain closely resembled the peak on Blake's first map, Dyott established a camp there and began exploring the area, trying to make sense of Blake's clue: "Look for the cross and 4 to L."

"Dyott told me he poked around that mountain for weeks. First he looked for a cross—a wooden cross, that is—on the north side of the ridge. Then he pondered the meaning of '4 to L.'"

According to Andy, Dyott decided Blake must have meant four *ridges* to the left of Zunchu-Urcu, so during clear spells he began counting the ridges to the east. He eventually spotted one on Las Torres that resembled the profile on Blake's second map, but when he reached it, there was once again no trace of the treasure cave.

The following year Dyott had returned to Zunchu-Urcu and contoured around Soguillas to the valley of Isabela Brooks at the foot of Cerro Negro. By now he had decided that Blake's maps were of little use. He had resolved to concentrate on the coded messages in Uncle Sammy's Bible, "Atahualpa's gold in the lake of Marcasitas" and "treasure in dead volcano by extinct lake."

"Dyott thought that by 'extinct lake' Uncle Sammy could have meant a dried-up lake bed or an old volcanic crater. See this entry here."

He pointed to an entry dated October 30, 1948. Dyott had written: "Could the old sea captain have meant a dried up lake when he pinpricked the message 'extinct lake'? It opens up a new field of thought."

Then, two weeks later, on November 12, the commander had written, "Yesterday when on the north ridge of this valley I saw something of the Cerro Negro's black head. So far as I could see there are three smallish crests, not very high, and a depression in the center which is probably an extinct crater."

Andy fell silent, waiting for me to absorb the significance of Dyott's comments.

"What happened?" I asked finally. "Did he find the extinct crater?"

"No," said Andy. "Soon after he wrote that, he fell and hurt his knee. He had to give up and return to Píllaro."

Even if Dyott hadn't injured himself, Andy said he doubted the commander would have continued searching much longer. He had already spent more than $1,000 of his own money—a colossal sum in 1948—and was heartily sick of the quest. Andy pointed to Dyott's last entries.

"I must admit it will be with no regrets that I leave this inhospitable region of cold, fog and rain," the commander had written on November 15. Then, two weeks later, on December 1: "The chances of finding the treasure seem to become daily more and more remote . . . my brain is quite worn out trying to find logical answers to Blake's many ways of concealing the whereabouts of his treasure cave."

I thought of my own brief foray to Zunchu-Urcu and how exhausting the climb had been. But the fatigues of the Llanganatis were nothing compared to the riddle of Blake's maps and letters. If Dyott, who had possessed a complete set of documents, had been unable to make sense of the mariner's coded references, what chance did I have, armed only with the fragments from Andy and Don?

Besides, by now it had become clear to me that whatever Andy said about his relationship with Dyott, the commander had kept the most important document from him. I knew from Don that Blake had sent Uncle Sammy a copy of Valverde's map and that the Bermenders had given Dyott a copy to take with him to the Llanganatis. Yet nowhere in the extracts from Dyott's journals and reports was Valverde's map mentioned. The reason, I suspected, was that contrary to Andy's claim that Dyott's journals and letters had been sent to him after the commander's death, Andy had copied the extracts while Dyott was still alive. Most likely, Dyott had read him the extracts by candlelight—just as Andy had first done to me—editing his journals as he went along. That explained why the notations were incomplete and, with the exception of one typewritten letter addressed to Mrs. Bermender, they were all in Andy's hand.

It was nearly 2:30 p.m. I looked across the table at Andy. He was on his third glass of whiskey and had hardly touched his food.

Suddenly I felt a wave of sympathy for this courageous but misguided old man. Andy had spent nearly forty years musing over his conversations with Dyott, convinced that if he studied his notes long and hard enough he would decode the puzzle the commander had left him. But the more Andy pored over Blake's maps, the more confused he had become. The tragedy was that Dyott had already given him the answer—Blake's maps were indecipherable or at least of no use to anyone but him—but Andy had refused to accept that verdict. Obsessed with the mystery, Andy had convinced himself that only he, Andrés Fernández-

Salvador, a descendant of the conquistadores and a former Pan-American sprint champion, had what it took to cross the finish line.

As we got up to leave, Andy told me that he believed Dyott had been on the right lines when he turned his attention to the "extinct lake" but had not penetrated the ranges far enough. The lake lay farther to the east, behind Cerro Negro. That is where Andy had been looking on his last expedition and where he would continue looking in the future.

"Dyott was wrong about Blake's second map," he said, suddenly grabbing my arm. "The treasure cave exists. Just one more push and I will prove it!"

I nodded. I was too tired to contradict him. Let him keep his delusions, I thought. They weren't harming anyone; indeed, at this point they might be the only things keeping him alive.

I walked him back to the lobby and wished him luck. A few minutes later his son-in-law returned in the company SUV and Andy climbed in. As he sped off with his precious attaché case still balanced on his lap, I realized he hadn't asked me one question about my own expedition.

2

ORO ES TRABAJO

"TWENTY DAYS IN THOSE MOUNTAINS IS A LONG TIME," ROLAND WAS warning me. "It's not the weather so much as the conversation. Every evening I ask Don Segundo the same question, 'Do you think it will rain tomorrow?' and every evening he gives me the same answer"—Roland pulled a face, mocking Don Segundo's singsong country accent—"*'Parece que sí, parece que no, señor'*—perhaps yes, perhaps not, sir. It's enough to drive you crazy."

As he said this, Roland began stuffing bags of powdered potatoes and rice into his specially designed carrying tanks. There were ten blue tanks lined up on the floor of his office, one for each of the porters who would be accompanying us (Don Segundo was excepted on account of his age and seniority). In addition Roland had laid out cookware, tarpaulin, and three tents. We would be sharing one of the tents, he explained, while Don Segundo and the porters would divide themselves equally between the two others.

After so many false starts it was a relief to see Roland focusing on our expedition at last. As the date of our departure neared, I had worried that he would find another excuse to cancel, but when I called him the day after my meeting with Andy, he was all business. "Bring some money," he said, "we're going shopping."

On Saturday afternoon we drove to a local supermarket and filled two large shopping carts to overflowing. Roland's approach to expedition planning was haphazard to say the least. Although he'd written out a long list of provisions, he seemed to grab anything that took his fancy as he maneuvered the carts between the aisles.

"The Llanganatis are a very hungry place. The worst thing is to bring too little," he said.

For breakfast, he explained, we would eat a hot gruel made from powdered oats, condensed milk, water, and pinole—barley flour mixed with sugar and cinnamon. During the day, when we were hiking, we would snack on bread and cheese. Then, in the evenings, we would build a fire and prepare pasta soups or rice with tuna and lentils. However, while the porters could survive for weeks on such monotonous fare, we would need to vary our diets.

"You won't believe how boring it can be," said Roland, scooping ten salamis and several cans of anchovies and sardines into the cart. "Every night the same thing, tuna and rice, tuna and rice."

Roland stopped in front of a shelf stacked with brightly colored desserts and held up a packet decorated with a smiling cartoon character.

"Do you like powdered gelatin? In the tent I will make us a hot drink from this every night." Roland punched me on the shoulder. "It is very good for cramps."

Now that he had finally made up his mind to go, I detected a subtle change in his attitude. Previously Roland had done his best to dissuade me, peppering me with questions about my resolve to undertake such a grueling expedition. Now he was concerned only with my comfort and survival.

"Let me see your backpack," he said when we returned to his apartment. I handed him the backpack I had brought on the last expedition. It was a Lowe Alpine. Made from the latest water-repellent fabric, it had kept my belongings perfectly dry on the hike to and from Zunchu-Urcu.

Roland emptied the contents onto the floor. "This bag is a rain trap," he scoffed. "Take this one instead."

He handed me a blue rubber backpack of his own design. It had a single opening at the top with a simple clasp locking mechanism. To close the bag, you had to fold the rubber over twice, making a seal that was completely airtight. I noticed there were no outside pockets or straps to catch on branches.

I filled the backpack with my belongings, added several bags of gelatin for good measure, and hoisted it onto my back. I winced. The straps dug painfully into my shoulders. I tried shifting the bag to a different position, but the harness was rudimentary, and there was no way of making the load comfortable.

Roland smiled and offered me one of the blue tanks. "Perhaps you would prefer one of these instead?"

I grabbed the tank by its H-frame and tried to lift it, but it wouldn't budge. The tank was packed to the brim with rice, pasta, and canned tuna—dead weight.

"But how . . . ?"

Roland held out his hand to silence me and crouched down, feeding his arms through the straps of the H-frame. Then he tilted forward, gradually easing the tank onto his back.

"For the porters this is nothing, believe me. I've seen them carry twice as much."

He put the tank back on the floor and removed a set of small padlocks from his trouser pocket. Then he placed a lid on top of the tank, checked to make sure it was watertight, and locked it.

"Never make the mistake of thinking the porters are your friends. If they see an opportunity to steal something, they will take it." Roland looked at me sternly. "I trust no one in the mountains. Do you understand? No one!"

I nodded, fearful of contradicting him. Was I included in that statement?

He fished a card from his wallet. "Here, look at this," he commanded.

I turned the card over. On the front was a picture of Roland dressed in a smart suit and tie. Next to it, in bold type, was written, *"Guardián de vida silvestre, Parque Nacional Llanganates,"* and below it in smaller print, *"Ministerio del Medio Ambiente."*

"You're a wildlife warden?" I asked incredulously.

"Jah, the minister of the environment is a good friend of mine. If I catch anyone hunting bears or treasure in my valley, I can have them arrested."

Truly Roland was full of surprises. I realized that for all the time we had spent discussing the treasure, I still knew little about him. What if we succeeded in finding the gold? Would he have *me* arrested, too?

Once again Roland must have read my mind. Why, he suddenly demanded, was I so interested in the history of the treasure? What was I hoping to get out of the expedition?

I chose my words carefully. If I was too enthusiastic, if I told Roland I was hoping to find the gold—clearly the answer he was expecting—I risked stoking his paranoia further. But if I told him the truth, that my doubts about the treasure's existence had deepened, I risked undermining his confidence in me entirely.

In the end I decided to be economical with the truth. Leaving out my recent meetings with Don and Andy, I told him that the hike to Zunchu-Urcu had whetted my appetite. Standing on top of the mountain, gazing across the landscape that had so long occupied my dreams, I had realized I could never know the truth of Valverde's guide or Blake's maps and letters unless I entered the steaming canyons of the Río El Golpe and Parca Yacu. I didn't want to have to depend on someone else's memories to inform my narrative. I wanted the authentic Llanganatis experience.

My reply seemed to placate Roland without entirely convincing him. "You know, Marcos, no one has attempted to cross the Llanganatis from west to east since Erskine Loch. If we succeed, it will be something to tell our grandchildren about. But you must understand, this represents twenty years of my life. If we find the gold, you must let me decide what percentage you get. Okay?"

Once again I nodded.

"Good. Now show me your boots."

Despite his suspicion that I was out to rob him, I think Roland was looking forward to having a companion in the mountains. To keep up his motivation, Roland needed someone with whom he could share his obsession; the last thing he wanted to hear was *"parece que sí, parece que no."* But the truth was, although I was relieved to finally be leaving, a part of me remained deeply apprehensive about what we would—or would not—find in Roland's valley. I was also uncertain about my ability to endure twenty days in the ranges. This was a question not of stamina— physically I had never felt fitter—but of psychology.

Andy had told me that the Indians considered the Llanganatis bewitched, and from reading Loch's account, I knew this was no idle su-
perstition; the isolation, the silence, the "perpetual mists and biting,
never-ceasing rains" could undermine the resolve of even the most battle-
hardened expeditionary. Even Dyott, the veteran of Mato Grosso, had
come close to giving up hope in that *cursed region.*" In such circumstances, I realized, a talent for self-delusion might be useful. Wasn't that
how Andy had been able to keep going all those years, and why he kept
coming back for more? For Andy, Blake's treasure cave wasn't just a
story, it really existed; moreover, he was going to be the one to find it.
Similarly, from his analysis of the geology and his reading of the two
derroteros, Roland had convinced himself that the fabled lost mine of
the Incas had to be near the valley of "El Mundo Nuevo." What was it
he had said to me? "I am close; I can feel it. Just one more push and we
will be there."

In order to survive three weeks in the ranges, I had to rediscover that
sense of childish wonder and awe I had felt on first reading *Treasure Island*, the thrill of the games with my friends in the quartz caves beneath
Atlantis, my trepidation on opening Spruce's notebook at Kew and
alighting on his mysterious entry "Derrotero de Valverde." In short, I
had to suspend disbelief just a little longer.

I SPENT SATURDAY NIGHT CURLED UP ON ROLAND'S SOFA, THE SAME SOFA
on which he had entertained police and military officials only weeks
before. To be sure of making it to our first campsite beside Yana Cocha
by sundown, we had to rise early, leaving Quito before dawn. I slept
soundly, knowing it would be the nearest thing to a mattress I would
enjoy for weeks.

Instead of going via Ambato, we took a shortcut, following the Pan-
American Highway south as far as Salcedo, from where we could take a
back road to Píllaro. It was a dark gray morning filled with foreboding.
Huge thunderheads clung to the heart-shaped peak of El Corazón,
obliterating the sun. Every now and then a kamikaze truck driver, his
headlights blazing, hurtled toward us, straddling the central reserva-
tion. Then, as we entered Cotopaxi National Park, we plunged into a

fine silvery mist. "When the weather here is bad, it is usually a good sign for the Llanganatis," said Roland optimistically.

A dusty, fume-filled village perched just below the highway, Salcedo at first sight seemed to have little to recommend it. I was all for driving straight through, but Roland insisted we get out and take a look. It was just south of here, in Panzaleo, he explained, that the Spanish had captured Rumiñahui, and it was in Laguna de Yambo, the lake beneath Salcedo, that many believed the Inca general had hidden Atahualpa's treasure.

I climbed out of Roland's Toyota and crossed to the lip of the highway for a better view. There, directly below us, was a deep chasm filled with choppy gray water.

Atahualpa's gold, here? It seemed unlikely. But was the belief that Rumiñahui had taken the gold deep into the Llanganatis any more credible?

According to Roland, it was. "How could Rumiñahui have drained a lake such as this?" scoffed the German. "In order to recover the treasure someday, he needed an artificial lake, like the ones in my valley."

From Salcedo the road led down through a sunny valley planted with swaying fields of maize and then up the other side to Píllaro. Approaching the ranges this way, from the west, I saw few signs of industrialization, and I tried to imagine the country as it must have looked in Guzmán's day—the red-painted haciendas and the wide *estancias*, the *peones* toiling in the fields and the *señor* on his horse, the glassy black lakes and the curling plumes of ash on the horizon—but the images wouldn't come. Once again I found myself questioning my decision to undertake this expedition. Why couldn't I be more like the blind Boston historian William Prescott, who, drawing on eyewitness accounts of the conquest, had described the scene at Cajamarca without ever leaving home? "It was not long before sunset, when the van of the royal procession entered the gates of the city," Prescott had written.

> Elevated high above his vassals came the Inca Atahualpa, borne on a sedan or open litter, on which was a sort of throne made of massive gold of inestimable value. The palanquin was lined with the richly coloured plumes of tropical birds, and studded with shining

plates of gold and silver . . . Round his neck was suspended a col-
lar of emeralds of uncommon size and brilliancy. His short hair
was decorated with golden ornaments . . . The bearing of the Inca
was sedate and dignified; and from his lofty station he looked
down on the multitudes below with an air of composure, like one
accustomed to command.

Prescott's descriptions of the confrontation between Atahualpa and
Pizarro at Cajamarca and the looting of Cuzco had never been bettered.
Moreover, in his imagination Prescott had conjured up such vivid images of the gold sculptures in the royal Inca gardens that, years later,
other lesser writers had turned to him for inspiration. But the imagination, I now knew, was an unreliable guide, and in the case of the Llanganatis mine was all used up. To know that forsaken landscape, I had to
enter it and see it.

We arrived at San José de Poaló at 9:30 a.m. just as the thunderheads
dissolved. Don Segundo was waiting for us by the football pitch, his
machete glinting grimly in the sun. Beside him, sitting on the grass
verge, were eight men ranging in age from eighteen to fifty. Wearing
loose-fitting cotton shirts and identical black rubber boots, they looked
as if they had just returned from picking potatoes in the fields.

After greeting us warmly, Don Segundo made the introductions.
This was Efraín, his son, and his good friend Antonio. Efraín was taller
and lighter-skinned than his father, but he had the same wide, Asiatic
cheekbones and dark eyes. Antonio's features, on the other hand, were
pointier and more Spanish looking. Like Don Segundo, both men were
wearing baseball caps.

Next came Manuel, an Indian George Clooney look-alike. Manuel
was a singer and the village's leading goal scorer. Broad-shouldered and
easygoing, he was also the only porter wearing yellow boots. Next to
him sat a second Antonio—a stocky, tough-looking Indian with curly
black hair and a large mole just below his left eye.

Don Segundo continued down the line, the introductions becoming
a blur. To put names to faces, I concentrated on the clothing: Iván, a
young man in a Guess shirt; José Luis, another teenager wearing a
leather hunting cap; his friend Rigoberto in a green woolen hat; and
Mario, another teenager with a long, curving Inca nose and a baseball

cap turned back to front. Counting Don Segundo there were nine in all. We were two short.

Roland cast around for additional men. Our arrival had caused quite a stir. Half the village was now gathered around his Toyota. We were willing to pay *"buena plata"*—good money—he announced. At $10 a day anyone joining us for the first part of the expedition—four days there and four back—would make $80.

Roland's announcement did the trick: two teenagers suddenly came bounding from a nearby bungalow to offer their services. A late riser, the first was still struggling into his dungarees; the second was barefoot and was wearing a hunting cap with the wings flapping comically in the wind.

"What's your name? Do you have boots?" Roland demanded of Wing Tip.

"My name is Julián," he replied, and, "No, sir, but I can borrow them."

We hired the pair on the spot. Julián was only sixteen—his friend, Luis, in the dungarees, barely a year older. Born and raised in San José, they had worked in the valley all their lives. This would be their first trip over the ranges.

"HAVING GONE THROUGH THE JUCÁL, THOU WILL SEE TWO SMALL LAKES called Los Anteojos (the spectacles) from having between them a point of land resembling a nose.

"From this place thou mayest again descry the Cerros Llanganati, the same as thou sawest them from the top of Guapa."

Pisayambo was exactly as I remembered it: gray and drizzly with a curtain of fog clinging to the higher banks. We skirted the reservoir's southern shore, then crossed the Río Milín as before, parking at the beginning of the trailhead. Roland instructed me to put on my boots and hand my shoes to his driver. I wouldn't need them again, he said, until we returned to Quito—with any luck in twenty days.

We unloaded the tanks—eleven in all—and Roland checked the lids to make sure they were secure. Then he distributed chocolates and sweets to the porters, and we were off. Don Segundo led the way with his son Efraín and Roland immediately behind. It was 10:30 a.m. From our arrival in San José it had taken us exactly one hour to launch our expedition.

Although the Ecuadorians refer to the Llanganatis as the "beard of the world," the treeless, wet *paramo* is better characterized as a giant "living sponge." Because of the cold and altitude, dead vegetation takes a long time to decompose. The sumptuous blend of grasses, mosses, cushion plants, lichens, and shrubs form peat-like depressions, trapping the mineral-rich rains that condense on the ranges in myriad bogs and underground streams. Eventually these streams filter through the bedrock to form pristine torrents and dramatic cascades. But when you are alone on the *paramo*, there is little sense of this gathering hydrologic force, just the squelch of your boots, followed by the slurp of the sapping mud.

For the first half hour we danced over spongy lichens and cushion plants, the fog rolling in off the hills like a school of angry sperm whales. But as we contoured around the rim of the black lake, the terrain grew steeper and boggier, and I increasingly had to keep my eyes focused on the ground to maintain my footing. If the three Cerros Llanganatis were visible through the mist, I didn't see them.

Although my pack was considerably lighter than it had been on the hike to Zunchu-Urcu, by the end of the first hour I was sweating profusely, and by the end of the second I was cursing my decision to return. What had I been thinking of? If I felt like this on day one, how would I get to day twenty?

I glanced at Roland. His pack was twice the size of mine, yet he looked to be in his element. Despite the altitude he had a cigarette clamped permanently between his teeth. Watching him move with loose, easy strides, using his machete as a walking stick, I found it easy to believe he was a wildlife warden. Before setting off, he had shown me a laminated sign he planned to pin to a tree when we reached the Río El Golpe. The sign read, "Protected Area. It is strictly prohibited to fish, hunt, or cut wood"—rules that in due course we would break one by one.

The next thing I knew I had stepped on a rotten branch. To my alarm the wood gave way and I sank into the mud. Wing Tip, squelching freely under a much heavier load, reached out a hand to aid me.

"*¿Se va a los Llanganatis, señor?*"—Are you headed for the Llanganatis, sir? he joked.

I couldn't muster the breath to answer.

We continued climbing, up, up, into a thin veil of drizzle. Every now and again a quick, small bird would flit across the sky, screeching furiously. At any moment, I thought, the weather could suddenly change and I could find myself lost in a hailstorm. To survive here, on the roof of the world, you had to be as fierce and determined as the flora.

By now Roland and the porters had disappeared into the mist, and I had to concentrate to make sure I stuck to their trail. Every hill looked just like the one before. It was a mystery how anyone could navigate in this boggy wilderness, much less locate a lost treasure.

Then I emerged on a high bank. Directly below me was a mass of still dark water: Yana Cocha—Black Lake. It was here that Valverde had left his horses, unable to take them farther; here that a few years later the governor of Latacunga had come, accompanied by the King's soldiers in their heavy Castilian armor and Padre Longo in his priestly robes; and here that Blake and Chapman had passed with their primitive leather backpacks containing the *derrotero* and Valverde's map.

"FOLLOWING NOW ON FOOT IN THE SAME DIRECTION, THOU SHALT COME on a great black lake, which thou must leave on the left hand, and beyond it thou shalt seek to descend along the slope of the hill in such a way that thou mayest reach a ravine."

We found the *quebrada* of Yana Cocha at 1 p.m., climbing through a thicket of thornbushes to emerge in a narrow gully through which crystalline mountain water spouted freely. The *derrotero* spoke of a waterfall here and, a little farther on, "a bridge of three poles." According to Roland, the bridge was long gone, but just beyond the point where we were seated now, the *quebrada* turned and dropped steeply, producing a brilliant cascade. However, to reach the "remains" of the "hut" that would serve as our first sleeping place, we would need to stick to the higher slopes, leaving the *quebrada* far below us, before climbing back down to rejoin the Golpe later.

Although we were still some 10,500 feet above sea level, the fierce winds that whipped across the *paramo* did not penetrate the *quebrada* and the vegetation was more jungle-like: palms and bamboos and knotted trees with brilliant red bromeliads nestling in their branches. Taking advantage of the microclimate, Don Segundo and the porters had removed their packs and were warming their faces in the sun. It was the end of January, perilously close to the start of the rainy season, but so far our luck seemed to be holding. Behind us, over the lip of the *quebrada*, directly to the south, lay Zunchu-Urcu and a different world.

The rest of the afternoon passed in a daze. Despite my training on the track in Quito, I continued to slip and stumble. The tangled roots lurking beneath the surface of the mud were a particular nuisance, tripping me every time, and I was soon far behind the others. Eventually Roland and Don Segundo took pity on me and relieved me of my pack, but by the time I limped into the agricultural cooperative at 4 p.m., I was exhausted.

The hut consisted of two rooms, divided by loose, rough-fitting planks. In one Don Segundo had already built a fire and was busy preparing the evening meal—soup followed by tuna and rice. Roland and I took the other room and studied our maps. We had covered four miles in a little over five and a half hours. Tomorrow, with luck, we would reach the Parca Yacu and in another day the *quebrada* where Blake claimed he had found the gold mine.

Darkness fell and we gathered around the fire, listening to Don Segundo's stories. When he had been a young boy, he said, his father had also set off with some *"norteamericanos"* to the Río Mulatos. But the gringos never made it. Instead, they took a detour north up the Quebrada de las Tundas—the place Blake had labeled as "probably the world's biggest gold mine" on his map. Like Blake, the Americans had noticed that the ravine abounded in glittering rocks and filled their pockets with stones, hoping it was valuable ore. So convinced were they that they had stumbled upon the mine they even cordoned the *quebrada* off and forbade Don Segundo's father and the porters to follow them. But the rocks were pyrites, and on their way back one of the Americans slipped and fell into the river.

"What happened?" I asked.

"The man drowned," replied Don Segundo. "He couldn't swim and the rocks weighed him down."

Efraín, who had been listening intently to his father's story, grunted as if there was some lesson here—the greed that always got the better of the white man. I studied the faces of the porters: those of the younger ones were like teenagers the world over—eager and mischievous—but those of the older porters were furrowed and careworn. I wondered what these men really thought of us. Did they resent the fact that Roland and I had come to their land with maps and documents that pointed to the location of gold that was rightly theirs, or were we just another pair of gringos with more money than sense?

I studied the second Antonio. In the flickering light of the fire the lines on his face cast deep shadows, valleys, and peaks that told of a life of hard agricultural labor. Directly above him, scored in charcoal on the cross beam of the hut, was the cooperative's motto: *"El trabajo es oro"*— Work is gold.

"HAVING PASSED THE NIGHT THERE, GO ON THY WAY THE FOLLOWING day through the forest in the same direction, till thou reach another deep dry ravine, across which thou must throw a bridge and pass over it slowly and cautiously, for the ravine is very deep."

When I was reading the *derrotero* in the comfort of my hotel room, everything had looked so simple, but now, as we crawled along mud banks, clinging to the tendrils of mossy lianas for support, I began to re-alize that time in Valverde's guide was a relative concept. It wasn't so much that the distances were greater than they appeared on the map—they weren't—it was that none of the old trails existed anymore. Instead, we had to fight for every yard, slashing at the matted, sinewy vegetation with our machetes and, where the forest proved too dense, getting down on all fours and slithering through the tangled green crawl spaces like the tapir whose trails we sometimes came across in the hollows.

Every now and again, where the river flattened out, we were able to descend from the forest and follow a wide rock-strewn beach, but this was no easier. While the porters delighted in hopping from boulder to boulder, their blue tanks balanced precariously on their backs, I found the mossy rocks a menace. After placing my foot on top of one boulder, only for it to suddenly give way, I became more and more cautious: a moment's lapse of concentration, I told myself, and I could fall into the river or, worse, slip and break a leg. What would become of me then? As Roland continually reminded me, we were now far from civilization.

We passed many deep, dry ravines but, by the end of the second day, none that we had had to throw a bridge across. Roland reckoned that the ravine Valverde had spoken of was actually a two to four days' journey farther downriver, but in the Spaniard's day there were ready-made trails and the Indians had been able to travel much faster.

"You see up there?" he said, pointing by way of explanation to a faint undulation in the tree line high above us. I squinted, unable to make out anything definite. "It's the remains of an Inca Way. I've walked it many times."

"Shouldn't we be following it?" I asked, incredulous that we were cutting a path along the riverbank when there might be a ready-made trail nearby.

"There's no point. You can follow it only as far as Pava-Micuna, and then, kaput!"—Roland raised both arms in the air resignedly—"destroyed by a landslide. If we went that way, we would be stranded."

The third day was the hardest yet. We broke camp at 8 a.m., following the course of the Parca Yacu east. For the first hour we contoured above the right bank at elevations of between 7,500 and 7,800 feet. Then we dropped down onto a wide beach. Almost immediately Roland spotted some bear tracks, but a few yards farther on the tracks, and the beach, suddenly disappeared.

We were now directly below Pava-Micuna—the so-called Turkey ravine. On the map it was a mass of tightly spaced contour lines, but looking at it now, I realized it was a vertical wall of solid rock. To reach the other side, we would have to hack a path through the forest and emerge on its flanks higher up.

For the next hour we crawled and scrambled up a sheer slope, grasping at the stems of plants and the gnarled roots of trees for support. In places the only thing between us and a fifty-yard drop to the river was a thin layer of vegetation. At one point I rested my foot in a nest of branches only for the wood to crack and give way. Feeling myself slipping into oblivion, I reached out a hand and found Roland's just in time.

"¡*Cuidado!*—Be careful, Marcos. Before planting your feet, you must always feel like this first"—Roland pointed his toe, probing the ground with the tip of the boot. "Otherwise . . ."

There was no need to finish the sentence.

That afternoon we emerged on a wide sun-kissed beach littered with white and yellow quartz and greenish black granite. Roland knelt down, picked up a large egg-shaped rock, and brought it down on a boulder with a loud crack. The rock split in two, revealing a mosaic of yellow octahedral crystals.

"Pyrites," said Roland. "See how the crystals glitter in the sun. Gold is much duller." Tomorrow we would arrive at the Quebrada de las Tundas, he said, and I would see it was the same.

That evening we camped in a clearing beside the river. By now the routine had become second nature. After pitching the tents, the two Antonios would cut reeds for the bedding while Efraín and the younger porters scoured the beach and forest for firewood. Sometimes the first Antonio would get lucky and catch a trout, but more usually we had to content ourselves with the soups and tuna mixtures prepared by Don Segundo. The old man was meticulous. Between servings every bowl and cup was thoroughly washed. Then, after a dessert of hot chocolate, he would retire to his tent, leaving the younger men smoking and cracking jokes by the fire.

Roland and I had our routine, too. Before bed Roland would prepare a brew of gelatin. Then, after I had downed the syrupy liquid, he would hand me a glass of rum and commiserate with me over the travails of the day. "The Llanganatis are *muy duro*"—very hard. "You must keep your strength up."

Then by torchlight we would unfurl the maps and swap theories, about where Blake had been and what he had really found, and about what lay ahead of us in "El Mundo Nuevo." A few years before, Roland revealed, he had ascended the Quebrada de las Tundas to its source. There he had found a green lake and a vintage bottle of cognac—abandoned perhaps by the two mariners—but no sign of a gold mine.

"I checked the *quebrada* from one end to the other; everything was pyrites. But then, Blake was a sailor; he knew nothing of geology."

If the mine lay anywhere, insisted Roland, it was in his valley. "I will pan the rivers and you will see."

"GO ON THY WAY, AND THOU SHALT SEE A MOUNTAIN WHICH IS ALL OF *Margasitas (pyrites) the which thou must leave on the left hand, and I warn thee that thou wilt have to go round it thus: ☞. On this side thou wilt find a* Pajonal *(pasture) in a small plain, which having crossed thou wilt come on a strait passage between two mountains, which is the way of the Inca."*

Days four and five passed as the first three had, with us hopping across lichen-covered rocks and, where the beach ran out, hacking trails through the forest. I marveled at Don Segundo's stamina. He handled the machete as if it were an extension of his body, swinging and cutting with his right arm and then, when that tired, switching effortlessly to his left. Sometimes he would let Roland or one of the Antonios take a turn, but whenever the undergrowth became dense or the way forward became unclear, he would insist on taking the lead. He did not carry a compass or a GPS, relying instead on the sun and his instinct for the lay of the land to divine the best route east.

By now we had passed Blake's *quebrada* and had descended to 6,500 feet. Directly to our south lay Las Torres and Cerro Negro, but we were too deeply embedded in the river to make out any of the peaks, let alone the three *cerros* in the shape of a triangle. At one point, resting after the ascent of a near-vertical bank, Roland gestured to the mountain directly in front of us and asked, "How can you look for a treasure cave here?" Like every mountain that had preceded it, it was covered in dense forest. It would take several days just to cut a trail to the top of the ridge, several weeks to conduct a systematic search of one of its flanks.

Margasitas Mountain was equally problematic. Nearly every ravine we passed was littered with glittering pyrites like the ones Roland had shown me before. Even if we had known the correct way to contour around the mountain, there were too many candidates to choose from. No, the only approach that made sense was Roland's.

On the afternoon of day five I removed $560 from my billfold and paid off the seven younger porters. We had covered more than eighteen miles since Sunday—roughly a third of the total distance we had to travel—and had reached a wide, mist-enshrouded beach. It was here, said Roland, that Jorge's porters had deserted him, knowing that a little to the south the Parca Yacu plunged precipitously through a narrow gorge. Depending on the height of the river, it might take several days to cross. Under the circumstances it was better to camp here and investigate the gorge tomorrow.

Wing Tip and his colleagues seemed delighted with the money. Each was now $80 richer, and as I watched them retrace their steps along the beach, I couldn't help but feel a pang of envy. In four days—less if they walked quickly—they would be reunited with their families in San José, while we still had at least two weeks of hard marching ahead of us.

Since leaving Yana Cocha, I had seen little evidence of any of the landmarks or "signs" in the *derrotero*, but now, as we approached the gorge, the clues began to make a peculiar sense. On reaching a deep, dry ravine, the traveler, according to the *derrotero*, was to look for a bridge with three poles or, if it was no longer there, to put another "in the most convenient place." Then, a little later, if you missed the Way of the Incas and the entrance to the *socabón*, the *derrotero* urged you to continue along the right bank of the river until you came upon another "deep ravine such that although thou seek to pass it thou wilt not find where." This was exactly the situation that faced us now. After we hiked some hundred yards farther along the beach, the river fell sharply and the mud banks on either side abruptly disappeared. We were faced by a series of dropping cataracts bounded on either side by narrow walls of glassy rock, and it was impossible to see what lay beyond them. We tried inching to the edge of the gorge, but the water was too deep and the current threatened to sweep us off our feet.

For an hour we sat on a boulder above the cataracts weighing our options. Valverde had been right. The gorge appeared impassable. "Climb therefore the mountain on the right hand and in this manner thou canst by no means miss the way," advised the last line of the *derrotero*. This was what Jorge had done, using ropes to guide the Wall Street broker and his fiancée up the rock face in order to rejoin the river on the other side. But examining the map now, we considered this option unattractive. The gorge was at the foot of Gallo-Urcu—Rooster Mountain. In order to reach the river again, we would have to not only haul ourselves up a sheer rock wall but also ascend the mountain to ten thousand feet and contour around the summit.

There was nothing for it but to build a bridge. On the opposite side of the river was a large boulder. If we could fell a tree in the right place, we might just be able to pin it against the huge rock and crawl across.

All that afternoon and the following morning, Don Segundo and Roland took turns hacking at trees. The first three fell short, their

canopies bobbing uselessly near the shoreline, but eventually Don Segundo found a monster in exactly the right place and brought it crashing down with a sickening groan. This time the branches caught on the
side of the boulder, and, using the current to aid us, we managed to
wedge the trunk into a secure position. However, the tree was too
flimsy to support our weight on its own, and it took the demolition of
two more before we had our "bridge of three poles."

That evening on the way back to camp I thought I identified another
sign. In the morning, the ridge above the valley in which we were
camped had been obscured by cloud. But now, as the sun sank in the
west, I could see that directly above us were two peaks and, to their left,
a long, high ridge. As the ridge swelled and shifted in the fading light, a
torso appeared and a gentle protuberance where a woman's breasts might
have been. Then, a little to the right, was a jagged pinnacle in the shape
of a nose.

"Look for the Reclining Woman and all your problems are solved."

Had Blake stood in this very spot? Was this the sign Dyott had been
looking for?

Perhaps.

*"TO ASCEND THE MOUNTAIN, LEAVE THE BOG AND GO ALONG TO THE
right, and pass above the cascade, going round the offshoot of the mountain."*

The thunder of the cataracts the next morning was deafening. As I
inched across the bridge, a rope looped around my wrist in case I slipped,
it took all my willpower not to look down. Daggerlike rocks rose in the
seething water, like sharks waiting to devour their prey. It was on just
such a river crossing that Roland had nearly lost one of his porters two
years before.

We now found ourselves on the left bank of the Parca Yacu, but sixty
yards farther on we came upon another set of cataracts and were forced
to improvise a second bridge. For two hours the only sounds were the
chime of Don Segundo's and Antonio's machetes, then a series of
wrenching groans and the slow-motion descent of a majestic green sen-
tinel. In the end I lost count of the number of trees we felled—seven?
eight? Whatever the number, it was too many.

If anything, the river dropped even more precipitously here. Roland was taking no chances. After wedging the felled trunks between a pair of boulders as before, he had Efraín cross to the right bank with a cable. Then, with the cable secured to some trees high above the river, the porters winched the tanks across one by one.

We were now on a narrow beach on the opposite side of the gorge. Beyond it the forest reclaimed the river in a low tangle of green limbs, forcing us to crouch on bent knees until we were no bigger than hobbits. No light penetrated here, and as we felt our way over the rotted stumps and musty half-fermented vegetation, I had the impression we were crossing to another world—Isengard, perhaps, or the lost realm of Arnor.

We made good progress that day, following the corkscrewing course of the river down, down, over immense white boulders made less perilous by the heat of the midday sun. We were now poised between the cloud forest and the jungle, and where once there had been only buzzards circling high above us, we began to hear the squawk of macaws and the tap of toucans.

That afternoon—day seven—it was warm enough to swim, and after finding a campsite beside the river, we retired to bed early. This was the time I liked best. The shadows and laughter of the porters seated around the campfire, the roar from the rapids below, and Roland in his woolen hat, smoking and reading by torchlight.

By now we had fallen into an easy routine. Once Don Segundo and the others had bidden us *buenas noches*, Roland and I would crawl into our sleeping bags and light the portable gas burner we kept by the bedroll. Then, having heated the water for our hot gelatin restorative, Roland would break out the lemon brandy and mull over the extraordinary history of Llangantis explorers. I don't know if it was the exhilaration of fording the cataracts or the fact that we were now only days from our goal, but tonight Roland was in a particularly expansive mood.

"Did I ever tell you about Stellan Moerner?"

The name rang a bell, but I couldn't place it.

"Count Moerner he called himself. He was the Swedish collector who acquired the papers relating to General Toribio Montes's expedition in 1812. You remember, the ones Andrade Marín tried to get his hands on."

According to Roland, in the late 1960s, armed with the general's papers, Moerner had secretly journeyed to the Llangantis to look for the

Inca gold mine. Whether he succeeded in finding it no one could be sure, but in 1970 he'd been photographed on the Río Topo holding what appeared to be two massive rocks of gold ore. On his return to Europe, Moerner sent the photograph to *The Times* of London, telling the newspaper he had found the Inca mine and was planning to go back to Ecuador shortly to recover the treasure. To finance the expedition, Moerner established an investment vehicle, The Llanganati Treasure Society, and issued two thousand shares valued at 500 Swedish kronor each. Subscribers, promised Moerner, stood to make back "ten times" the value of their investment.

The Times obligingly published Moerner's fantastic story, together with a picture of the share certificates, and within the year he was back in Ecuador. But Moerner never launched another expedition, taking a suite at the Hotel Quito instead, where he drank away his investors' money.

"What became of him?" I asked.

"The last thing I heard he was running a hotel in Gran Canaria," replied Roland matter-of-factly.

I asked Roland to describe "El Mundo Nuevo" again. How exactly had he stumbled upon the constructions? What would we find there?

Roland unfurled the map and followed the twisting course of the Parca Yacu with his torch. Then he found the Mulatos and directed the beam to a mass of knotted contour lines just above the point where he'd indicated the channels and pools all those months ago in his office in Quito.

"Don Segundo and I were trying to find a way back to the Mulatos via this ridge"—Roland stabbed the contour lines with his cigarette finger, spilling ash onto the sleeping bag—"when we suddenly stumbled right into them. The wall was completely overgrown with trees and creepers, but once we'd cleared them, we could see that it must once have stood twenty yards high."

According to Roland, the wall had a channel running along the top, like an aqueduct, and, though broken in several places by landslides, measured about 130 yards in length.

The construction of the wall, he said, "was ingenious." The stones were huge, with smooth, close-fitting joints, like those found in Cuzco and at other Inca sites. Then, at the end, built into the rocks, he had found the *piscinas*—the rectangular pools. According to Roland, the largest had measured ten feet by four and, like the channels, seemed to have been carved by hand.

"And you think they were for washing gold?"

"*Seguro*—certainly," Roland replied. "There's no other possibility."

Until now I had taken the Parca Yacu for granted. Since the descent from Yana Cocha the river had been our constant companion, its tumbling waters a subliminal soundtrack speeding us east toward our rendezvous with the Inca gold mine. But now, in order to reach Roland's valley, we would have to leave the Parca Yacu and cut straight across mountain and jungle to find the river Roland had been groping for in the dark: the Mulatos.

Day eight was the hardest yet. From our camp we had to scramble up a steep, scree-covered slope, then haul and wrench our way another five hundred yards up a muddy cliff face. A landslide had destroyed part of the mountain, and in places we had to revert to ropes again, passing the tanks up behind us. By now both Efraín and the two Antonios had begun to sweat profusely. Since the other porters had gone back and the loads had been redistributed, the tanks had become even heavier, but Efraín and his colleagues seemed to know exactly where to place their feet in order to gain maximum traction. Even so, as we began contouring in zigzag fashion through dense forest to the summit of the mountain, the three of them fell steadily behind.

For a while I concentrated on the swish of Roland's and Don Segundo's machetes. Then I heard a cry of "*¡Avispas!*" and looked up to see Roland stumbling over a rotten tree stump. Angry yellow jackets swarmed from a hollow in the wood, making a beeline for their attacker. Thinking Roland had drawn the majority of the wasps after him, I decided to follow him over the nest as quickly as possible.

It was a mistake.

No sooner had I reached the stump than a cloud of wasps rose up to meet me, stinging me about the face and ears. I beat a hasty retreat down the trail, nearly colliding with Efraín on the way up. He raised a finger to his lips to silence me and calmly brushed the wasps from my clothes. My screams, he joked, could be heard "as far back as Píllaro."

For the rest of the morning we continued on and up, thrusting through the cloud forest, the sodden trees tearing and rasping at our packs. At midday we arrived at the summit and strained our necks to see what lay on the other side. Before us, silhouetted against an azure sky, lay a palisade of gently rising rock and, below it, a steaming green valley. Here and there we could make out violent white-and-yellow gashes in the canopy where landslides had carved pistes in the valley's flanks. A craterlike bowl defined the valley's southern limits, while to the east and north the ridgeline dropped gently toward a wide beach and a tense glitter of water.

"The Mulatos," murmured Roland, then, pointing to three shadows on the horizon, "the Cerros Llanganatis."

I strained my eyes to see. There, just behind the valley, were three undulating peaks. Puffy white clouds, like drifting snow, swam about their feet, giving them a dreamy, ethereal quality. The summits were nothing like the jagged peaks of the *paramo* but gentle and rolling. They looked close enough to touch.

Were these really the three *cerros* or a testament to Roland's powers of suggestion? For months he had been promising to show me his valley, building up my expectations only to dash them at the last moment. In my frustration I had spent hours poring over his maps, trying to imagine myself surmounting Gallo-Urcu and looking east toward the Sacha Llanganatis. But now that I was actually standing on the summit of that long-desired mountain, I found my judgment had deserted me. The peaks certainly appeared to form a triangle, but so had many of the other formations we had passed.

I decided I would have plenty of time to think about it later. For now, I had to concentrate on the *bajada*—the knee- and joint-wrenching endurance test that was the descent. Navigating the Parca Yacu the day before, I had slipped and bruised my left ankle. Climbing to the summit of Gallo-Urcu, I had not been bothered by the discomfort, but in descending I found I couldn't put any weight on the foot without wincing. To ease the pressure, I leaned on my walking pole, using it as a second leg, but my progress was painfully slow. Once again I cast envious glances at the porters. Using gravity to full advantage, they were already sliding effortlessly in and out of the trees, the tanks perfectly balanced on their backs, like commandos racing in the giant slalom.

At around 3 p.m. we heard the distant rumble of the river, but by four we had still not reached it, and by five I was growing desperate.

Roland's saying we were following in Loch's footsteps was all very well, but Loch had crossed to the Sacha Llanganatis via the Páramo de Soguillas and Las Torres with seventy men. We were pioneering an entirely new trail and with only six men to raise the alarm should anything go wrong.

Finally, shortly before six, we jumped free from the forest and landed in a bamboo grove. Hacking feverishly at the thorny wood, we thrust forward, expecting to find the river at any moment, but the grove just stretched on and on. Exhausted and bleeding from myriad scratches, we paused, summoning all our energy for one last push. Moments later, as if by magic, the branches parted and we fell onto a wide, boulder-strewn beach.

"AND ON THE LEFT HAND SIDE OF THE MOUNTAIN THOU WILL SEE THE 'Guayra' *(for thus the ancients called the Furnace where they founded metals) which is nailed with golden nails. And to reach the third mountain, if thou canst not pass in front of the* socabón, *it is the same thing to pass at the back of it, for the water of the lake falls into it."*

Roland crouched beside the stream, cradling the rusty pan in his machete-worn hands. Slowly, deliberately, he lit a cigarette, savoring the moment. Then he sluiced some water into the bowl and began rocking the sediment gently from side to side.

Liberated by centrifugal force, dark lumps of granite, mottled feldspars, and shards of orange quartz swam in the muddy water. Roland teased the rocks to the edge of the bowl, flicking them back into the stream one by one. Then he sluiced some more water into the pan and resumed his rocking motion. Finally, when all that was left at the bottom of the bowl was a fine gray sediment, Roland cupped some more water in his right hand and drizzled it over the material, tilting the pan to see if any grains caught the light. Roland repeated this process several times before he was satisfied. Then he emptied the pan into the water, and we moved on up the ravine.

We had been exploring "El Mundo Nuevo" for three days now. It was not at all how I had imagined it. In my mind's eye the constructions Roland had described to me in his office had morphed into a second Machu Picchu, complete with walls of perfectly cut polygonal stones. Once Roland had identified the first channel, I told myself, it would be a simple matter to follow the Inca masonry up into the valley, clearing the jungle as we went along, until, like the Yale archaeologist Hiram Bingham, we emerged at the sun gate and the entrance to Valverde's fabled *socabón*. But when we reached the *quebrada* where Roland claimed he had seen the pools and channels all those years before, there was only jungle and shattered rocks—the result, it would seem, of a recent series of landslides.

On the first day we had walked the entire length of the *quebrada*, slipping and sliding on sharp gravel, expecting to come across the pools and channels at any moment. The next day, thinking that the landslides had shifted the *quebrada* and that the forest might have reclaimed the constructions, we had returned to cut a trail parallel to the *quebrada*'s right bank. But though we came across what looked like a series of sunken trenches, there was no evidence of Inca stonework, let alone of the *socabón* or the "lake, made by hand."

On the third day we split into two teams, and while Efraín and the two Antonios climbed to the rim of the valley, Roland, Don Segundo, and I concentrated on the *quebrada*'s left bank. For hours we climbed through the forest as mosquitoes and wasps buzzed annoyingly about our heads. The vegetation here was more jungle-like, and every now and again we would catch sight of a howler monkey observing us from high in the canopy. We also came across stands of limes and tree tomatoes— the remains of what could have been ancient agricultural terraces—but while the fruit quenched our thirst, the absence of the man-made constructions was disheartening.

"They were right here, I swear it," said Roland, drawing a line in the earth with his machete to explain where he and Don Segundo had first stumbled upon the pools and channels. "I can't understand how they could have just disappeared."

It was around this time, I noticed, that Roland's gold panning became increasingly obsessive. Since arriving on the banks of the Río Mulatos, we must have tested gravel from more than twenty different locations. In ascending the ravine leading up to the valley, we had had to stop repeatedly for Roland to dig beneath rocks, looking for evidence of gold placers. So far, all he had to show for his efforts, however, were a few measly grains.

By the fourth day I was beginning to question Roland's judgment. Had he really seen the constructions, or had he only imagined them? Studying the maps in his office in Quito, he had seemed so certain. Now I began to wonder whether he might have lost touch with reality.

One evening, for instance, after a particularly sunny day when we had hiked to the top of the *quebrada* for a fourth time, I found him sitting beside the river, muttering to himself in German. I asked him what he was doing, and he pointed to a ravine on the opposite side of the Mulatos.

"Do you see that hillside?" he said. "I am sure I saw a ball of flame there earlier."

Roland explained that during the day gold and other metals buried in the ground conducted heat from the sun; at night, when the ground cooled, the trapped energy escaped, appearing as an orangy red light on the horizon. He claimed that he had seen the phenomenon—known as electro-phosphorescence—once before at his mine in Zamora and that it was "well known" to the ancients. "Tomorrow I will cross the river and you will see. The vein of gold is very near, I can feel it!"

But when he crossed the river and panned the ravine the next morning, there was only more frustration.

In Quito, Roland had insisted that he was not like Andrés Fernández-Salvador and all the other treasure hunters. "I am a prospector first and a treasure hunter second," he had told me. But now I wondered whether I would have done better to go with Andy. It wasn't that Roland wanted to deceive me; it was that, like old Q—the elderly Spanish *peón* who had accompanied Loch on his first expedition in 1936—he couldn't face "undeceiving himself." Fifteen years of study had convinced him that the gold mine lay somewhere near his valley in the Sacha Llanganatis. To give up now would be to admit that all those years of effort had been wasted.

Until now I had resisted soliciting the porters' opinion. Like Roland, I didn't want to hear Don Segundo say, *"Parece que sí, parece que no."* However, since the incident with the wasps, Efraín and I had formed a bond, and one afternoon, when the others had gone panning for gold, he asked if he could take a photograph of me by my tent.

Efraín was fascinated with my camera, a Canon. Grasping it firmly in two hands as if it were the most precious thing he had ever seen, he twisted his head to get a better view of the focus ring, asking me to explain the meaning of each of the symbols and functions. After he had taken the shot, I allowed him to wander off on his own and experiment with the viewfinder while I made some notes in my journal. Twenty minutes later I glanced up to see Efraín standing over me with a quizzical look on his face.

"Excuse me for disturbing you, *patrón*, but how much does one of these cost?"

"That depends," I answered. "You could probably pick up a model like that for about a hundred dollars."

"A hundred dollars!" Efraín exclaimed. For him and his friends, he explained, that was a fortune. "Perhaps if we found the gold I could afford it."

"Efraín, if we found the gold, you could buy Canons for the whole village. In fact," I added, "you could probably buy the whole company."

"Really?" he replied. "You really think the treasure is worth that much?"

His innocence threw me. Clearly Efraín had no conception of the size of Atahualpa's hoard, but the way he had phrased it made me question whether the treasure was worth any of our efforts. I had spent two years and God knows how much money trawling archives and traipsing through bogs with nothing to show for my efforts but a sore head and a lot of notes. But my camera, now there was something worth having.

It was shortly after my conversation with Efraín that I made my decision. Taking Roland to one side, I explained that I only had sufficient funds to pay the porters for twenty days. We had now spent fifteen days in the mountains and faced at least another four- to five-day hike before we reached the banks of the Río Napo. We could spend all month exploring "El Mundo Nuevo" and still not find anything. Wouldn't it be better to cut our losses and return another day, perhaps with a local Indian guide who knew the exact location of the pools and channels?

Roland looked at me in confusion. "B-but, Marcos," he stammered, "we've only just got here. If we keep looking, we'll find them, I'm sure of it."

What could I say? That like every explorer before us we had failed, that my faith was all used up, and that in my heart of hearts I had never truly believed we would find the gold—that that was something which only happened in treasure stories.

I had desperately wanted to bring back some evidence: a shard of Inca pottery perhaps or a gold nugget or a photograph of one of the channels, anything to give the naysayers pause and make them reconsider their dismissive verdict of Valverde's *derrotero*. But now I had to admit that I had failed and that in all probability John Hemming had been right. I had allowed my admiration for Spruce and my infatuation with Guzmán's map to cloud my judgment. There had been numerous warning signals, but I had ignored them all. The chroniclers' disagreement over the size of Atahualpa's hoard had been the first clue (in retrospect, even Cieza's conservative estimate of the treasure's size seemed to beggar belief). Then there was the peculiar story about the deposit in the Royal Bank of Scotland and the absence of any record of Blake and Chapman in the registers of the Royal Navy or the American merchant marine. Finally, there was Andy's pathological secrecy and the discrepancies between Dyott's and Bermender's versions of how the mariner's maps had come to light.

Rather than acknowledge the truth, I had twisted the facts to fit the story I wanted to hear. I could not face the possibility that Valverde's gold might be a fiction. Instead, like all the other seekers after legendary treasure, I had allowed myself to be swept up in the mystery and excitement of the quest, convincing myself that if I gathered together all the documents and spread the facts in an orderly and logical fashion on the table, the solution to Valverde's riddle would suddenly emerge.

But the hieroglyph had remained as impenetrable as ever. Like Raleigh, Fawcett, and the Wall Street investors who'd convinced themselves they'd solve the mystery of the Oak Island treasure, I'd been indulging in wishful thinking. And after all, wasn't that what all treasure hunters did, how they kept going? My rational mind had always doubted the treasure's existence, but my unconscious mind refused to accept it. Instead, I'd permitted Andy's and Roland's obsession to become my own. I had to. I couldn't have embarked on an expedition to the Llanganatis otherwise. For me the Llanganatis had become an end in themselves, a goal that, having set myself, I was unwilling to retreat from. Andy's taunts had been the spur; vanity and bravado had done the rest.

But now I realized I had been hooked not only on the treasure but also on its very elusiveness. How had Andy put it? "A story to astound the world." Yes, it was that, but it was also something more. Valverde's gold represented both the possibility of myth and the promise of youth. It was the thrill of the unknown, the chance to inhabit Stevenson's childish realm. It was an escape from the humdrum, the opportunity to be part of something bigger, something out of the ordinary. And in the final analysis, wasn't that what everyone wanted? In my heart of hearts I might have been courting failure all along, but at least I gave it a go, and in an increasingly cynical world that had to count for something.

Looking back on my ordeal now, however, I realized how naive I had been: the topography was remorseless, my knowledge of the geology and botany too scanty to compensate for the physical deprivations. But worst of all was the fact that I had allowed Roland to lead me to "El Mundo Nuevo" knowing that the constructions had almost certainly been destroyed (Jorge had told me that prior to our hike to Zunchu-Urcu).

What I wanted to say to Roland now but couldn't was that I was heartily sick of the Llanganatis. I had had my fill of vertiginous peaks, humid forests, and quaking bogs. I no longer cared to divine the meaning of Valverde's hieroglyph or the location of the three *cerros*. I just wanted to exit the ranges as quickly as possible.

But of course I couldn't say any of that. So I told Roland I was tired of our repetitive diet of tuna and rice and wanted to get home. He urged me to sleep on it. For someone as inured as Roland was to disappointment, it was inconceivable that I could abandon our search just like that. But when we awoke the next morning and he saw I was as determined as ever, he acquiesced.

Sheepishly, he explained my decision to Don Segundo, Efraín, and the two Antonios. Don Segundo smiled briefly, then nodded. I think it made little difference to him what we did. For Don Segundo ours was just one more in a long line of misguided expeditions.

IT SEEMED TO TAKE US FOREVER TO EXIT THE RANGES. WHEREAS BEFORE the valleys and peaks had been imbued with secrets and mysteries, now they were simply barriers. For a while we continued along the beach of the Mulatos—no longer a sacred current but just another river tumbling east. Then we crossed to a river Roland called the Verde Yacu and began climbing up and over a series of rolling *cerros*.

It was day seventeen now, and we had reached the extreme limit of Guzmán's map and also of our endurance. Here, beyond the Gran Volcán del Topo—a mountain we had never seen—the Spanish botanist had shown a range of low hills covered with trees and forest. But though the ascents were longer and gentler than the terrifying drops of the *paramo*, in their own way the Sacha Llanganatis were to prove just as grueling.

On day eighteen, for instance, we left the river early, hoping to take a shortcut through the forest, only to find that by lunchtime we had still not reached the summit of the mountain we had begun climbing shortly after breakfast. Then, sometime around mid-afternoon, the slope began to point downward. However, by 5 p.m. we had still not reached the bottom, and with no telling how far we would have to walk before finding the river again, we had no choice but to stop and camp in the forest.

It was a long, thirsty night as we had forgotten to fill our water bottles and had to make do with a trickle from a nearby spring. To add to my discomfort, my right foot had swollen badly and I was finding it difficult to walk again. Even Roland seemed disheartened. This would be the last time he would attempt to cross the Llanganatis on foot, he said. "The next time I will come by helicopter or not at all."

The following morning we arose early and continued down, emerging almost immediately in a wide cutting. It was the first proper path we had come across since entering the mountains, and Don Segundo stopped to examine its construction. Rather than follow the contours of the mountain, the cutting seemed to run more or less in a straight line east. We followed it for a while, marveling at its levelness. Cinnamon trees, their bark pungent with spice, grew above and below the cutting, leading us to believe that it might be the very trail the governor of Latacunga had used to smuggle the treasure out of Ecuador. But after half an hour we reached a deep gash and looked down to see that the path had fallen away. All around us were broken trees and huge boulders—more evidence of the region's propensity to tectonic activity. No wonder we hadn't been able to find the Inca constructions. It wasn't just that the guide and maps were unreliable; the land itself was against us. Perhaps the Indians were right. Perhaps Atahualpa did watch over the treasure still, conspiring with the earth deity, Pachamama, to frustrate those who sought to steal his inheritance.

On day twenty we finally left the forest and began descending to the jungle. Here the air was thick and dreamy. Huge mangoes and bananas ripened in the trees. Any moment, we thought, we would arrive at the first *finca*, knock on the door, and be offered a bowl of *chicha*—the fermented cassava-root drink given as hospitality throughout El Oriente. Instead, we found ourselves on another river—the Jatun Yacu—and a wide sandy beach. We kicked off our boots, oblivious to the sand flies nipping at our ankles, and cooled our aching feet in the water. Then, after cooking up the last of our powdered pinole, we continued east along the river's right bank, hoping to find a ferryman.

By now we were desperate for deliverance. We could see the road to Tena winding high above the bank on the opposite side of the river, but without a boat we couldn't reach it. Normally, the water would be full of fishermen, but today was a Sunday and the river was deserted.

We walked for an hour, the plastic tanks warping in the heat. Then, just as we were about to give up, we spotted a woman on the opposite bank spreading some brightly colored sheets on the rocks to dry. Surrounded by her children, she was the first person we had seen since leaving Pisayambo.

Six unwashed men with beards waved at her in unison. The woman disappeared into the trees. We thought we had scared her away, but moments later she reappeared with her husband, and through a combination of shouts and hand gestures we explained our predicament.

Dragging a small dugout from the bushes, her husband punted across to continue the conversation. "Where have you come from?" he asked.

We pointed west, to the steaming summits rising above the jungle, proud at last of what we had achieved. The man's jaw dropped. "But that's impossible," he mouthed. Then he eyed our tanks and disheveled appearance and saw we were telling the truth.

After crossing the river, we hailed a taxi to Tena. There I treated Don Segundo, Efraín, and the two Antonios to a celebratory dinner of chicken and chips and paid them the money I owed them. Eager to return to the *paramo*, they boarded a bus to Píllaro that very night. Roland and I, however, checked into a hotel, enjoying a much-needed wash and shave before leaving the following morning.

We spoke little on the return journey to Quito. After twenty days in each other's company we were all talked out. Only when we began the long, grinding ascent of the cordillera did Roland regain something of his old spirits.

"What we have just done, you know, is no small thing. Not even Loch could have crossed the Llanganatis in three weeks!"

Then he grabbed my arm, and with the old urgency returning to his eyes, he insisted: "The constructions are there, believe me. In a few months I will return with a guide from El Oriente and take pictures. I will send them to you, I promise!"

But I was no longer listening. I could already see Pichincha and El Panecillo on the horizon. The next thing I knew we were pulling into the Terminal Terrestre. As far as I was concerned, this time it really was the end of the line.

EPILOGUE

ROLAND NEVER SENT ME THE PICTURES OF THE INCA CONSTRUCTIONS.
Instead, a few months after our expedition to "El Mundo Nuevo," I received an e-mail from him. Roland informed me that Don Segundo had been urging him to return to the Sacha Llanganatis to explore the old cinnamon route (had Don Segundo finally been bitten by the treasure bug?) but that he was preoccupied with a new gold-mining venture in northwest Ecuador and couldn't spare the time. However, if I was willing to wait until he struck gold, Roland would hire a helicopter and we would fly to his valley together. "This time I will pay for everything," he promised.

FOLLOWING MY RETURN TO LONDON, I SENT ANDY A LETTER IN WHICH I attempted to clarify various details on Blake's maps and other discrepancies in his story. I couldn't shake the suspicion that Blake and Chapman were fictions. If only Andy could tell me the name of the schooner that had brought them to Ecuador, I might be able to find the ship's log and verify their service in the U.S. merchant marine. But if he knew the ship's name, he wouldn't tell me.

"I cannot say any more," he wrote. "Just as you have your little secrets, so I have mine."

Instead, he sent me a faded newspaper cutting, detailing the highlights of his athletic career. The article was illustrated by a series of photographs taken in California in the 1940s showing Andy striking he-man poses on a Santa Monica beach. The article said that in 1939, at the age of fifteen, Andy had lifted a 1,500-pound weight on his shoulders, prompting the California Athletic Commission to declare him "the strongest boy in the world."

IN THE SPRING OF 2003 I WROTE AGAIN TO DON BERMENDER AT THE Cinnaminson home to ask if he would send me the original copy of Valverde's map, but my letter was returned unopened. I later learned that the home had closed. There was no forwarding address.

A FEW MONTHS AFTER I RETURNED TO LONDON, I RECEIVED AN E-MAIL from Lou Jost. He was still living in Baños and still making collecting trips along the Río Pastaza in search of new varieties of orchids. His foraging had led him over the steep, forested hillsides that abut the gorge, up the Río Topo, and deep into the Sacha Llanganatis. In some areas the forests had been unusually dry—it was hard to find fresh water anywhere—and on one trip, Lou wrote, he'd stumbled upon a hollowed-out tree where someone—presumably a treasure hunter—had hidden some bottled water. He'd also heard an intriguing story about an "Inca wall" on the Topo. The wall had been unearthed by a landslide, but Lou had learned of it only recently when he fell into conversation with a Swiss hotelier from Baños. The hotelier, Olivier Currat, claimed to have discovered the wall by chance in 1997 when he was exploring a trail near the Topo with a friend, and he had not been back to it since.

According to Lou, the wall was forty yards high by twenty long with several "nice footholds carved in strategic places on the otherwise flat rocks." Although Currat had found no evidence of a *socabón* or of Valverde's "lake, made by hand," Lou wrote that the find was "exciting" and could be the proof I was looking for that the Incas really had passed through the Llanganatis in search of gold.

"My friend will take me there soon. I hope it's true!!! Adiós, Lou."

A few weeks later, just as this manuscript was on its way to the typesetter, I received another communication from Lou. He and Currat had been back to the Topo to look for the wall but, finding the trail "completely abandoned and overgrown," had been forced to give up their search. Nevertheless, Lou had asked Currat to dig out the photographs he'd taken in 1997—pictures that Lou had thoughtfully attached to the e-mail.

They did not disappoint. The wall was immense, with more or less rectangular and close-fitting rocks that could only have been man-made. Oddly, it was not freestanding but appeared to have been built into the hillside at a forty-five-degree angle. In one picture, Currat was shown perched halfway up the wall, beaming at the camera. In another he was bent over a large rock, running his fingers along its plane-like surface.

According to Lou, the wall was in a "totally random location" and did not appear to serve any strategic purpose. Intriguingly, Currat had also found a small brook to one side of the wall and, flowing over it, a sheet of water, "making a sort of artificial waterfall."

SINCE RETURNING FROM ECUADOR, I HAVE BEEN ASKED BY A NUMBER OF people whether I still think the treasure exists. My answer is that in London it is hard to believe in anything very much but that in the wilds of Ecuador, where you can still indulge childish dreams, it seems to me that anything is possible. Were Roland, Andy, or Lou, even at this late date, to provide me with firm evidence for the existence of the mine and the treasure lake, I would probably be off like a shot.

Having said that, I will admit that part of me is ambivalent about whether the gold ought to be found and who would benefit if it were. The more I think about it, the more convinced I am that Don

Bermender is right. The treasure is the birthright of the indigenous people of Ecuador, and to spend time and money pursuing it is a sort of obscenity. For this reason, perhaps we should be thankful that Rumiñahui hid it well and that so far no one has succeeded in decoding Valverde's *derrotero*. After all, why spoil such a perfect mystery?

Appendix

DERROTERO DE VALVERDE

(Guide, or Route, which Valverde left in Spain, when death overtook/seized him, having gone from the mountains of the Llanganati, which he entered many times and carried off a great quantity of gold; and the King commanded the Corregidors of Tacunga and Ambato to search for the treasure: which order and guide are preserved in one of the offices of Tacunga)

"Placed in the town of Píllaro, ask for the farm of Moya, and sleep (the first night) a good distance above it; and ask there for the mountain of Guapa, from whose top, if the day be fine, look to the east so that thy back be towards the town of Ambato, and from thence thou shalt perceive the three Cerros Llanganati, in the form of a triangle, on whose declivity there is a lake, made by hand, into which the ancients threw the gold that they had prepared for the ransom of the Inca when they heard of his death. From the same Cerro Guapa thou mayest also see the forest, and in a clump of *Sangurimas*, standing out of the said forest, and another clump which they call *Flechas* [arrows], and these clumps are the principal mark, for which thou shalt aim, leaving them a little on the left hand. Go forward from Guapa in the direction and with the signals indicated, and a good way ahead, having passed some cattle-farms, thou shalt come on a wide morass, which thou must cross, and coming out on the other side thou shalt see on the left hand a short way off a *Jucál*, on a hill-side, through which thou must pass. Having gone through the

---

The spelling, italics, punctuation, and grammar are as per Spruce's original, as are the translations of the terms contained in parentheses. Thus Spruce's translation of *Pajonal* is "pasture," rather than "scrubland" (Collins). Similarly, Spruce, after Valverde, writes, *Jucál*, a now-obsolete form for *juncal*, meaning "place of reeds" or, simply, "reedy." In the version published in the *Journal of the Royal Geographical Society*, some of the terms, such as *Pajonal, Jucál*, and *Margasitas*, which had a capital in Spruce's original, were lowercase (*jucál, margasitas*). In the interests of authenticity I have reinstated the capitals, as they appear in Spruce's notebook. Similarly, where the RGS typesetter wrote *cañon*, I have reinstated Spruce's "strait passage."

Jucál, thou will see two small lakes called *Los Anteojos* [the spectacles] from having between them a point of land resembling a nose.

"From this place thou mayest again descry the Cerros Llanganati, the same as thou sawest them from the top of Guapa, and I warn thee that thou must leave the said lakes on the left, and that in front of the point or 'nose' there is a plain, which is the sleeping-place. There thou must leave thy horses, for they can go no further. Following now on foot in the same direction, thou shalt come on a great black lake, which thou must leave on the left hand, and beyond it thou shalt seek to descend along the slope of the hill in such a way that thou mayest reach a ravine, down which comes a waterfall, and here thou shalt find a bridge of three poles, or if it do not still exist thou shalt put another, in the most convenient place, and pass over it. And having gone a little way in the forest seek out the hut which served to sleep in, or the remains of it. Having passed the night there, go on thy way the following day through the forest in the same direction, till thou reach another deep dry ravine, across which thou must throw a bridge and pass over it slowly and cautiously, for the ravine is very deep; that is if thou succeed not in finding the pass by which it may be crossed. Go forward and look for the signs of another sleeping-place, which I assure thee thou canst not fail to see, in the fragments of pottery and other marks, because the Indians are continually passing along there. Go on thy way, and thou shalt see a mountain which is all of *Margasitas* [pyrites] the which thou must leave on the left hand, and I warn thee that thou wilt have to go round it thus:

On this side thou wilt find a *Pajonal* [pasture] in a small plain, which having crossed thou wilt come on a strait passage between two mountains, which is the way of the Inca. From thence as thou goest along thou shalt see the entrance of the *socabón* [tunnel] which is in the form of a church porch. Having come through the passage and gone a good distance beyond, thou wilt perceive a cascade which descends from an offshoot of the Cerro Llanganati and runs into a *Tembladal* [quaking bog] on the right hand; and without passing the stream in the said bog there is much gold, so that putting in thy hand what thou shalt gather at the bottom is grains of gold. To ascend the mountain, leave the bog and go along to the right, and pass above the cascade, going round the offshoot of the mountain. And if by chance the mouth of the *socabón* be closed with certain herbs which they call *Salvaje*, remove them and thou wilt find the entrance. And on the left hand side of the mountain thou will see the '*Guayra*' (for thus the ancients called the Furnace where they founded metals) which is nailed with golden nails. And to reach the third mountain, if thou canst not pass in front of the *socabón*, it is the same thing to pass at the back of it, for the water of the lake falls into it.

"If thou lose thyself in the forest, seek the river—follow it on the right bank—lower down take to the beach, and thou will come on a deep ravine such that although thou seek to pass it thou wilt not find where; climb therefore the mountain on the right hand and in this manner thou canst by no means miss the way."

FURTHER READING

GEOLOGY AND BOTANY

Acosta Solís, Misael. *Naturalistas y viajeros científicos que han contribuido al conocimiento florístico y fitogeográfico del Ecuador*. Quito: Casa de la Cultura Ecuatoriana, 1968.

Bromley, R. J. "The Llanganatis of Ecuador." *Explorers Journal* (1972), pp. 141–48.

Kennerley, J. B., and R. J. Bromley. *Geology and Geomorphology of the Llanganati Mountains, Ecuador*. Instituto Ecuatoriano de Ciencias Naturales, Contribución no. 73. Quito: Minerva, 1971.

Kunstaetter, Daisy, and Robert Kunstaetter. *Trekking in Ecuador*. Seattle: Mountaineers Books, 2002.

Vázquez, Miguel, Mario Larrea, and Luis Suárez, eds. *Biodiversidad en el Parque Nacional Llanganates: Un reporte de las evaluaciones ecológicas y socioeconómicas rápidas*. Quito: EcoCiencia, 2000.

TREASURE FICTION

Conrad, Joseph. *Nostromo*. London: Penguin, 1980.

Dumas, Alexandre. *The Count of Monte Cristo*. Translated with an introduction and notes by Robin Buss. London: Penguin, 1996.

Haggard, H. Rider. *King Solomon's Mines*. Edited with an introduction and notes by Dennis Butts. New York: Oxford University Press, 1998.

Stevenson, Robert Louis. *Treasure Island*. Edited with an introduction and notes by Emma Letley. New York: Oxford University Press, 1998.

St-Onge, Daniel. *Llanganati; ou, La Malédiction de l'Inca*. Montreal: Triptyque, 1995.

CHRONICLES AND HISTORIES OF CONQUEST

Cieza de León, Pedro de. *The Discovery and Conquest of Peru: Chronicles of the New World Encounter*. Edited and translated by Alexandra Parma Cook and Noble David Cook. Durham, N.C.: Duke University Press, 1998.

———. *The Incas of Pedro de Cieza de León*. Translated by Harriet de Onís and with an introduction by Victor Wolfgang Von Hagen. Norman: University of Oklahoma Press, 1995.

Fernández de Oviedo y Valdés, Gonzalo. *Historia general y natural de las Indias.* Edited by Juan Pérez de Tudela. Madrid: Biblioteca de Autores Españoles, 1959.

Garcilaso de la Vega, El Inca. *Royal Commentaries of the Incas, and General History of Peru.* Parts 1 and 2. Translated by Harold V. Livermore. Austin: University of Texas Press, 1966.

Hemming, John. *The Conquest of the Incas.* London: Macmillan, 1970.

Markham, Sir Clements. *The Incas of Peru.* London: Smith, Elder, 1910.

Prescott, William H. *History of the Conquest of Peru.* London: Allen and Unwin, 1913.

Salazar, Ernesto. *Entre mitos y fábulas: El Ecuador aborigen.* Quito: Corporación Editora Nacional, 2000.

LLANGANATIS: EXPEDITIONS AND LORE

Andrade Marín, Luciano. *Viaje a las misteriosas montañas de Llanganati.* Quito: Imp. Mercantil, 1936, 1970.

Anhalzer, Jorge. *Llanganati.* Quito, 2000.

Blomberg, Rolf. *Buried Gold and Anacondas.* London: Allen and Unwin, 1959.

Brunner, Eugene K. "El tesoro de Atahualpa en las montañas de Llanganati y la casi increíble historia de los ingleses desde 1857 hasta hoy." Quito, 1979. Unpublished manuscript.

Loch, Erskine. *Fever, Famine, and Gold.* London: William Heinemann, 1938.

Lourie, Peter. *Sweat of the Sun, Tears of the Moon.* Lincoln: University of Nebraska Press, 1998.

MacInnes, Hamish. *Beyond the Ranges: Five Years in the Life of Hamish MacInnes.* London: Victor Gollancz, 1984.

Spruce, Richard. *Notes of a Botanist on the Amazon and Andes.* Edited by Alfred Russel Wallace. London: Macmillan, 1908.

———. "On the Mountains of Llanganati, in the Eastern Cordillera of the Quitonian Andes." Illustrated by a map constructed by the late Don Atanasio Guzmán. *Journal of the Royal Geographical Society* 31 (1861), pp. 163–84.

PIRACY, TREASURE, AND ADVENTURE

Cleator, P. E. *Treasure for the Taking.* London: Robert Hale, 1960.

Dyott, George Miller. *Man Hunting in the Jungle: The Search for Colonel Fawcett.* London: Arnold and Co., 1930.

———. *On the Trail of the Unknown in the Wilds of Ecuador and the Amazon.* London: Thornton Butterworth, 1926.

Exquemelin, A. O. *Exquemelin and the Pirates of the Caribbean.* Edited with an introduction and additional material by Jane Shuter. Oxford: Heinemann, 1993.

Howse, Derek, and Norman J. W. Thrower, eds. *A Buccaneer's Atlas: Basil Ring-rose's South Sea Waggoner: A Sea Atlas and Sailing Directions of the Pacific Coast of the Americas, 1682.* Berkeley: University of California Press, 1987.

Verrill, Alpheus Hyatt. *Lost Treasure: True Tales of Hidden Hoards.* New York: D. Appleton and Co., 1930.

———. *The Found Gold: The Story of Successful Treasure Hunts.* New York: G. P. Putnam's Sons, 1936.

Wilkins, Harold T. *Modern Buried Treasure Hunters.* London: Philip Allan, 1934.

———. *Secret Cities of Old South America.* New York: Rider, 1950.

ACKNOWLEDGMENTS

There were several occasions during the writing of this book when I came close to questioning my sanity. For encouraging me to persevere with the quest for *Valverde's Gold*, even when it seemed hopeless, and for providing me with a much-needed reality check when my fantasies about striking it rich threatened to get the better of me, there are a number of people I wish to thank. First and foremost, my gratitude goes to Stuart Evans, my editor at Macmillan, whose enthusiasm and belief in the story never flagged, even when it seemed doubtful that I would return from the Llanganatis alive or at least with a publishable manuscript. Ditto John Glusman, my editor at Farrar, Straus and Giroux in New York; his tireless assistant, Aodaoin O'Floinn; and my agent, Derek Johns, without whom I would never have had the courage or wherewithal to embark on a treasure hunt in the first place.

For planting the seed of this book and tending it through its long and sometimes arduous gestation in Ecuador, my thanks to my fellow Llanganatis enthusiasts Robert and Daisy Kunstaetter and Lou Jost. Your comments on the text were invaluable (as was your advice on keeping dry) and saved me from many embarrassing errors. On the same note, I must also thank John Hemming for his comments on the historical passages and my sharp-eyed copy editors at Macmillan, Talya Baker and Nick Blake (no relation to Barth).

A number of people read the manuscript at different stages in its development and provided invaluable comments on the structure and pacing, not least Eric Baldauf, who also took the photograph of me that appears on the British book jacket, and my wife, Jeanette. My thanks to her also for agreeing to put her studies on hold for three months so that we could move to Ecuador and for tolerating my long and often unsettling absences in the mountains. Finally, my thanks to my sister Claire for her spiritual support in Lisbon; to my Spanish teachers in London and Quito; to Giles and the gang at the London Library; to my parents, Naomi and Frank; and to my children, Olivia and Max, whose faith in their father's madcap adventures kept me in touch with my own "child's" imagination. This book is also for them and all the other *pequeños buscadores*.

INDEX

A

Agamemnon, 72

Albertson, Captain Sam (Uncle Sammy), 261, 282, 291, 292; Blake's letters to, 9–10, 98, 101–104, 252–57, 259; story of, Fernández-Salvador's version, 98–101, 103, 104, 108, 138, 143, 217; story of, Lourie's version, 229, 234, 254; treasure tale possibly invented by, 222, 253, 289

Almagro, Diego de, 80, 81, 202, 204, 205, 227

Alvarado, Pedro de, 122

American Bank Note Company of New York, 39

Amundsen, Roald, 263

Andrade Marín, Luciano, 130, 145, 179, 188, 250, 311; on Blake and Chapman, 137–39, 219; on Dyott's commission, 138; and etymology of Llanganatis, 132, 139; existence of multiple *derrotero* versions proposed

by, 133, 134, 136, 137, 277; forgery of *derrotero* by the governor of Latacunga suggested by, 153, 216; on governor of Latacunga, 134–37, 143, 243; Moreno as possible informant to, 156, 168, 169, 172–73, 179; on murder of Padre Longo, 136, 153; scholarly investigation of *derrotero* by, 129–32, 153, 245; and Valverde's identity, 131, 133–34

Anhalzer, Jorge, 160, 162, 163, 187–91, 195–97, 199, 200, 206–8, 277, 279, 309, 320

Anselmo, Don, 117–18

Archivo General de Indias, Seville, 137, 145, 155, 156, 169, 217, 237–46

Argosy (magazine), 50, 51

Arias, Diego, 107–9, 151, 266, 282

Arias, Monica, 108, 227

Atabalipa, Francisco, 245

Atahualpa, 11th Inca, 119; beliefs of, 143; defeat of, 77–79, 81–82, 214,

Atahualpa, 11th Inca (*cont.*)
238, 300; execution of, 82; imprisonment at Cajamarca, 7, 25; Montezuma, parallels with legends of, 117, 118; palace of, 272; ransom of, 7, 25, 79–80, 124–26, 237; tomb of, 169–72, 178, 179; treasure hunters and the horde of, 51, 123, 261, 266; treasure of, 23–24, 26, 37, 41, 46, 100, 121, 122, 126–28, 214, 229, 282, 291, 299, 318, 319
Atis, 132
Atlantis, 262
Aztecs, 78, 117, 118, 121

B

Bahía people, 142
Banco Central del Ecuador, 130
Benalcázar, Sebastián de, 25, 122–25, 162, 165, 169, 256, 271
Bentham, George, 233
Bermender family, 292
Bermender, Don, 251, 260, 283, 326; on discovery of Blake's letters and maps, 253–55; distinction drawn between Valverde's guide and map by, 289; Dyott and, 255–56; manuscript of, 248, 252, 256–59, 261; phone conversations with, 249, 266–67
Bermender, Mrs. (Sam Albertson's daughter), 262, 287, 292
Bingham, Hiram, 316
Blake, Albert V., 218
Blake, Barth, 6–10, 13, 20, 26, 63, 109, 194, 203, 303, 307, 308, 310; Albertson and, 9–10, 98–104, 138, 229, 252, 253, 256–57; Andrade's version of the story of, 137–39, 219; author's research on, 158, 209,

217–22, 260–61, 275, 319, 325–26; Bermender and story of, 247–49, 253–55, 260, 267, 282, 288; Brunner's version of story of, 229, 233, 250; and Chapman's death, 9, 102, 204, 205, 207, 257; and clue of the cross, 102, 181, 189, 201, 207–8, 285; death of, 10, 109, 138, 228, 250, 266; discrepancies between versions of story of, 15, 138, 139, 229, 232, 250, 254; Dyott and, 97–98, 105, 138, 160, 223–24, 226, 258, 262, 287, 288, 293; Fernández-Salvador's possession of documents of, 73–74, 84, 89, 99; gold mine discovered by, 304; maps and letters of, 107, 120, 143, 177, 180, 183, 184, 201, 231, 277, 290, 291, 297; as possibly fictional character, 221–22, 250; Spruce and, 33, 233–34, 250; treasure cave discovered by Chapman and, 9–10, 14, 36, 63, 101–2, 119, 127, 141, 182, 204, 257, 259, 282, 292, 298; and Valverde's map, 21, 29, 254, 256, 257–58, 283, 289
Blake, George L., 219
Blake, William, 219
Blavatsky, Helena, 128
Boschetti, Guido, 88, 129
Boschetti, Tullio, 129, 131
British Museum, 10
Brooks, Colonel Edward C., 39, 40, 41, 45, 87, 125, 155, 266
Brooks, Isabela (née de Troya), 39, 40, 41, 109, 266, 291
Brun, Georges, 52, 55
Brunner, Eugene, 225–34, 247, 250, 261, 266, 281, 286
Bucaniers of America (Exquemelin), 221–22
Butler, Ben, 88

C

Canaris tribe, 123
Cantuña, 162, 163
Capitana, La (ship), 6
Carlos I, King of Spain, 27, 81
Carlos III, King of Spain, 134, 135, 241, 242
Carlos IV, King of Spain, 134, 136, 214
Catholic University, 119, 151, 159
cédula real (royal certificate), 27, 137, 214, 217, 244, 245, 329
Chapman, Edmund Stewart, 219
Chapman, Edward P., 220
Chapman, Lieutenant George Edwin, 6–10, 13, 20, 26, 98, 194, 233, 303; Andrade's version of the story of Blake and, 137–38; author's research on, 158, 218–20, 224, 252–53, 261, 275, 319, 325–26; death of, 9, 102, 109, 181, 204, 205, 207, 257, 266; Dyott and, 228, 229; as possibly fictional character, 222, 250; Spruce and, 15, 29, 33, 232, 250; treasure cave discovered by Blake and, 9–10, 14, 36, 63, 101–102, 143, 204, 258; and Valverde's map, 100
Charles V, Holy Roman Emperor, *see* Carlos I, King of Spain
Charles I, King of Spain, 27, 81
Charles III, King of Spain, 134, 135, 241, 242
Charles IV, King of Spain, 134, 136, 214
Chinchorro people, 128*n*
Cieza de León, Pedro de, 83, 119, 121, 122, 124, 171, 237, 319
Cocos Island, 115
Comercio, El (newspaper), 74, 145
Conquest of the Incas, The (Hemming), 124
Conrad, Joseph, 43, 47, 73

Coricancha (Temple of the Sun), 119, 123–24, 141, 143, 272
Cortés, Hernando, 78
Cotopaxi National Park, 298
Count of Monte Cristo, The (Dumas), 47, 48, 65
Cox, John, 221
Cuauhtémoc, 117
Currat, Olivier, 326–27

D

Dampier, William, 221
da Silva, Nuna (Nunha), 241
Days of My Life, The (Haggard), 118
de Koos, Paul Thur, 155, 216, 266
derrotero of Valverde: Anhalzer and, 161, 188, 189; arrival in Ecuador of, 134; author's expeditions using, 42, 194, 303–22; Hemming's dismissal of, 121, 278; governor of Latacunga's use of, 26, 32, 118, 123; Guzman's use of, 133; Lourie and, 224, 226; Moreno and, 160, 164–66, 168–70, 171–73, 178, 179; multiple versions of, 133, 152–53, 155, 156, 173, 298; text of, 20, 33–36, 91, 117, 301, 329–31; research into authenticity of the, 144, 158, 214, 237, 239, 246, 297, 319, 328
Dickey, Elizabeth, 264
Dickey, Herbert Spencer, 264–66
Discovery and Conquest of Peru, The (Cieza), 119
Doigg, Captain John, 135, 139, 216
Drake, Sir Francis, 241
Dumas, Alexander, 47, 48, 65
Dyott, Commander George Miller, 96–97, 106, 110, 169, 201, 205, 209, 217, 260, 266, 286, 293, 298, 310, 319; Bermender family

Dyott, Commander George Miller
  (*cont.*)
  and, 234–35, 237, 248–50, 252,
  255–56, 258; biography of,
  96–97; Blake possibly invented by,
  221–22, 250; Brunner and, 226, 228,
  229, 250, 253, 281, 287; and clue of
  the cross, 181; expeditions by, 96,
  97, 107, 138, 290–91; journals of,
  109, 223, 224, 232, 283, 287–89, 292;
  and location of Valverde's treasure
  cave, 102; Loch and, 262–63, 289; in
  possession of Blake's papers,
  97–100, 103–5, 108, 138–39
Dyott, Mike, 223–25, 231, 235, 283

E

Eco, Umberto, 113
Ecuador: Air Force, 14; Army, 170,
  179, 274; Instituto Geofísico, 146
Ecuador minero, El (Andrade), 130
Edison, Thomas, 96
El Dorado, 23, 72, 122, 272, 278
encomienda, 241
Entre mitos y fábulas (Salazar), 151
Espinosa, Gaspar de, 169
Explorers Club, 57, 262–63
Exquemelin, John, 221–22

F

Fanning, Captain John, 135, 139, 216
Fawcett, Colonel Percy Harrison, 72,
  96, 97, 105, 222, 261, 262, 319
Fawcett, Jack, 96
Fernández de Oviedo, Gonzalo, 83,
  121, 124, 137
Fernández-Salvador, Andrés "Andy,"
  143, 246, 261, 262, 266, 268, 277,
  298, 317, 319, 325; and Andrade's

version of events, 139; author's
  meetings with, 74–111, 151, 180, 225,
  282–93; on Blake and Chapman,
  98–102, 220; and Blake's maps and
  letters, 73–74, 84, 89, 99, 120, 183,
  202, 229, 256, 257; and Bermender's
  version of events, 253–54; Dyott
  and, 96, 97, 103–110, 160, 221, 222,
  228, 287, 288; expeditions by,
  87–94, 282; life of, 75, 85–87, 94–95,
  326; Lourie and, 226–27, 231–32; on
  Pizarro and Atahualpa, 76–83; on
  treasure cave, 119, 141, 170, 181, 182,
  205, 216
Fever, Famine, and Gold (Loch), 51, 57,
  262, 264, 269
Findlay, A., 30, 31, 61
Fitzgerald, Sylvia, 15, 16, 17, 21, 29
Flynn, Errol, 73
Forbes, Robert, 215
Freire, Alina, 159, 161, 164
Freire, Señor, 164, 167

G

Gallo, Colonel, 274
Gardoqui, Diego de, 243
Glaser, Roland, 130, 68–69, 187, 204,
  274–76, 325, 327; and Andrade's
  theories, 130; author's impressions
  of, 61, 65, 73, 154–55, 261–62;
  author's meetings and conversations
  with, 57–70, 74, 129, 160–61,
  177–85, 225; Don Segundo and,
  191–93, 198; and Guzman's map, 64;
  expeditions of, 60–61, 69, 143, 144,
  160, 177, 179, 180, 182–85, 247,
  267–68, 272–73, 278–80, 285,
  294–323; Loch and, 65; and lost
  gold mines, 67, 100, 216, 247, 272,
  277–78; man-made pools discovered

by, 66, 188–89, 277–78;
photographs by, 60, 62–64, 208;
system of, 51, 139, 246; and
Valverde's *derrotero*, 62–65, 67–70,
160, 181–82, 276–79
Gold Waiting to Be Found, 68
Grist, Stan, 46, 49, 50, 51, 61, 65, 69,
144, 165
Guzmán, Anastacio (Atanasio), 64,
118, 133, 134, 151, 152, 266, 277, 299;
Brooks's use of the map of, 40;
death of, 266; death of Padre Longo
recorded by, 27, 168; expeditions in
search of treasure by, 28–29, 31, 34,
133; map of, viii–ix, 17, 21, 22, 29,
30–31, 33–38, 42, 61, 69, 70, 87–89,
100, 102, 127, 137, 154, 194, 197, 198,
201, 208, 209, 257, 290, 319, 321;
mining ventures of, 28–29, 38
Guzmán, Mariano Enríquez de,
132–33, 277

H

Haggard, H. Rider, 11, 22, 103, 115–18,
139, 175, 195, 205, 262
Haggard, Jock, 118
Haggard, Louisa, 117, 121, 125
Harvard University, 120
Hemming, John, 23, 24, 56, 77, 121,
124, 143, 278, 319
Herrera, Antonio de, 124
Heyerdahl, Thor, 263
Hinojosa, Pedro de, 244
History of the Conquest of Peru
(Prescott), 119
Holt, Bob, 109–10
Homer, 71
Hooker, Sir William, 30
Huáscar (Atahualpa's half-brother), 77,
79, 81, 119

Huayna Capac, 10th Inca, 77, 119, 140,
162
Humboldt, Alexander von, 29, 133,
134, 151, 152
Hunter's Wanderings in Africa, A
(Selous), 116

I

Incas, 4, 53, 228, 321, 326, 327; Blake's
discovery of the treasure of, 101;
Canaris tribe as enemy of, 123;
Catholic culture's conflict with, 163;
empire of, 4, 77, 119, 214; government protection of artifacts, 84; lost
mines of, 28, 34, 57, 65, 130, 155,
247, 258, 298, 312; lost treasure of, 9,
15, 16, 24–26, 31, 50, 97, 118, 119, 163,
242, 250, 257; Pizarro's conquest of,
76–83; roads, trails, and ways of, 8,
29, 36, 37, 63, 64, 99, 101, 170, 181,
189, 306, 309, 330; value of gold
and silver in society of, 23, 142–43;
see also Atahualpa, Huáscar,
Huayna Capac, Rumiñahui, Temple
of the Sun
Incas of Pedro de Cieza de León, The
(Von Hagen), 171
Indians, pre-Columbian, 54
Inquisition, 171, 241
Instituto Geográfico Militar, 181, 278

J

James I, King of England, 72
Jebb, John, 117, 118
Jijón y Caamaño, Jacinto, 134, 151
Jivaro tribe, 56, 264
Jost, Lou, 144–48, 150–58, 160, 164,
168, 169, 172, 173, 187, 216, 224,
326, 327

Journal of the Royal Geographical Society, 8, 329

Jung, Carl, 42

K

Kandyan kings, 262

Kidd, Captain William, 68

King Solomon's Mines (Haggard), 11, 22, 116, 117, 175

Klamroth, Bill, 52, 54

Knapsack and Rifle, 98, 229, 253, 257

L

LaBeach, Lloyd, 75

Lasso, Galo Plaza, 198

Latacunga, Governor of, 27, 32, 123, 132, 239, 303, 321, 329; *see also* Pastór y Marín de Segura, Don Antonio

Lázaro de la Escosura, Pilar, 238, 239

Legarda, Bernardo de, 167

Lewis, C. S., 22

Lindbergh, Charles, 263

Llanganati (Anhalzer), 161–63

Llanganati Treasure Society, 312

Llanganatis, derivation of word, 131, 132

Lloyd's of London, 97

Lloyd's Register of Shipping, 216

Lloyd's Register, 220

Loch, Erskine, 51–57, 65, 100, 125, 147, 169, 237, 250, 269, 315, 323; death of, 266; descriptions of Llanganatis by, 157, 177, 298; Dickey's letters regarding, 264–66; Incan gold works discovered by, 56–57; Dyott and, 104–5, 258, 262, 263, 289; Fernández-Salvador and, 87; as inspiration for Grist, 50;

Llanganatis expeditions of, 51–55, 131, 188, 191, 198, 267, 297, 317; membership in Explorer's Club of, 262–64

Longo, Padre, 109, 133, 153, 156, 185, 266, 303; accompanies governor of Latacunga on expedition, 27, 38, 118, 132, 303; death of, 22, 40, 63, 134, 136, 152, 266; Moreno's disbelief in the existence of, 168, 178; possible murder by Pastór, 136, 152, 242

Los Angeles Examiner, 87

Lost Treasure: True Tales of Hidden Hoards (Verrill), 125

Lourie, Peter, 224–35, 254, 260, 261, 286–87

Luque, Hernando de, 169

M

Machu Pichu, 262, 315

Maldonado, José Gabriel, 264

Man Hunting in the Jungle (Dyott), 97

Marín de Segura, Doña Rosa, 135

Markham, Sir Clements, 122

Martínez, Doña Narcisa, 135, 215

Mendel, Gail, 228

Mercantil Press, 131

metalurgy, pre-Incan, 101, 130

Minerva (ship), 243

Missouri Botanical Garden, 159

mitimaes, 4

Modern Buried Treasure Hunters (Wilkins), 127

Moerner, Stellan, 134, 311, 312

Mollison, Sir Francis, 135, 214, 215, 216

Montes, General Toribio, 134, 311

Montezuma, Aztec Emperor, 117, 118

Moreno Proaño, Padre Agustín, 158–61, 171, 237, 240, 246;

Andrade's acquaintance with, 168–69, 172–73, 179; author's contact with, 164–73; claims to have location of Atahualpa's, 169–72; rumored to have copy of original of Valverde's *derrotero*, 144–45, 155, 156, 178, 217

Mountain, Jennifer, 214–15

Museum of the American Indian, 52

Mysteries of Ancient South America (Wilkins), 127

N

Name of the Rose, The (Eco), 113

Narnia series (Lewis), 22

National Archives in (Washington), 260

National Geographic, 96

National Geographic Society, 255

New Laws, 241–42, 244

New York Public Library, 51

North American Newspaper Alliance, 97

Nostromo (Conrad), 43, 47

Notes of a Botanist on the Amazon and Andes (Spruce), 15, 21, 29, 31, 61, 74, 87, 147, 233, 276

Núñez Vela, Captain General Blasco, 241–44

O

Oak Island treasure, legend of, 68, 72, 73, 319

On the Trail of the Unknown in the Wilds of Ecuador and the Amazon (Dyott), 96

Orellana, Francisco de, 122

Ortiz, Fernando, 159

Osbourne, Lloyd, 116

Owens, Jesse, 75, 84

P

Pachamama, 322

Paititi (fabled lost city), 128

Pastór y Marín de Segura, Antonio (Marqués de Llosa), Governor of Latacunga, 153, 242, 243, 246, 277; Andrade's research on, 136; possible altering of Valverde's *derrotero* by, 156, 173, 237; rumor of deposit to the Royal Bank of Scotland by, 135–37, 157–58, 213–16, 275

Pastór, Don Bartolomé, 135

Pensamiento, El (ship), 135, 139, 216

Philip II, King of Spain, 27

Pizarro, Francisco, 25, 68, 76–83, 121, 122, 124–26, 214, 237, 238, 242, 256, 300

Pizarro, Gonzalo, 242, 244

Pizarro, Hernando, 78

Power, Tyrone, 87

Prescott, William H., 119, 120, 272, 299, 300

Public Records Office (Kew), 226, 252

Q

Quichua people, 132

Quinteros, Señor (Old Q), 52, 53, 54, 317

Quito, Archaeological Museum of, 140

Quito, Royal House of, 244, 275

R

Raleigh, Sir Walter, 72, 319

Raleigh, Walt, 72

Ré, Humberto, 131
Reagan, Ronald, 87
Reiss, Wilhelm, 89, 90
Rimmel, Raleigh, 96
Rique, Fray Jodoco, 159
Robalino, José María Coba, 276–78
Rómulo (Jorge Anhalzer's assistant),
    190, 195, 196, 199, 200, 207, 278
Roosevelt, Franklin D., 73
Roosevelt, Theodore, 263
Royal Bank of Scotland, 135–37,
    139, 157–58, 213–16, 226, 275, 319
Royal Botanic Gardens (Kew), 15, 16,
    29, 38
Royal Commentaries of the Incas (Vega),
    119
Royal Geographical Society (RGS),
    27, 30, 37, 61, 117, 122, 153, 154, 233,
    329*n*
Royal Marines, 220
Royal Navy, 7, 14, 138, 217, 228, 229,
    249, 250; Air Service, 96, 99; *Navy
    List*, 218–21, 224, 232, 233, 253
Ruiz, Hernán, 237
Rumiñahui (Atahualpa's half-brother),
    119, 126, 178, 190, 214; Andrade's
    research on, 132; Atahualpa's
    treasure hidden by, 25, 49, 66, 121,
    137, 139, 169, 328; burial of
    Atahualpa by, 169–70; in Cantuña
    narrative, 162–63; and Spanish,
    81–83, 122–25, 139, 299; tortured by
    Benalcázar, 25

S

Salazar, Ernesto, 151
Santa María del Campo (ship), 237
Sauer, Walther, 90
Scarloch Mines Incorporated, 57, 65

Schliemann, Heinrich, 71, 72
Segundo, Don, 197–98, 202–3, 205; on
    Llanganatis expedition, 280, 300,
    301, 303–4, 307–13, 316, 320, 321,
    322, 325; on Zunchu-Urcu expedi-
    tion, 184, 186, 187, 189–209, 267,
    274, 278
Segundo, Efraín, 300, 304, 307, 311,
    313, 316, 317, 318, 320, 322
Selous, Frederick Courteney, 116
Sharp, Bartholomew, 221–22, 241
Slater, Matthew B., Esq., 17, 30
Spain: King of, 8, 18, 21, 25, 26,
    32, 118, 132, 136, 168, 214, 242, 244,
    329 (*see also names of specific mon-
    archs*); Ministry of Culture of, 217,
    238
Spanish, 5–7, 142, 146, 170; *see also*
    Benalcázar, Pizarro
Spanish-American War, 39
Spruce, Richard, 13, 46, 74, 119,
    122, 125–27, 134–36, 145, 223, 224,
    237, 267, 329; Blake and Chapman
    and, 7–10, 14, 15, 33, 101, 103, 232,
    234, 249, 250, 256; death of, 138;
    Dyott contacted by grandson of,
    138, 139; Ecuadorian travels of, 24,
    26, 30, 147; and etymology of Llan-
    ganatis, 132; and Guzman's map, 17,
    21, 27–31, 37, 133, 152, 257, 277;
    journals and notebooks of, 16–17,
    20, 21, 24, 29–30, 61, 168, 233, 298;
    nephew of, 233–34; Royal Geo-
    graphical Society (RGS) report of,
    27, 30, 37, 61, 117, 154, 233, 329*n*;
    and Valverde's *derrotero*, 7–8, 18,
    24, 27, 37, 38, 69, 133, 144, 151–53,
    156, 173, 246, 319, 329; and
    Valverde's map, 8, 20, 21, 22, 101,
    233, 256

Stevenson, Robert Louis, 20, 103, 115, 116, 125, 139, 221–22, 320

Stull, Gordon, 234–35, 237, 248, 250–52, 255, 256, 259, 261, 266, 288

Suárez, Hernán, 162, 163

Summer Institute of Linguistics, 92

Sweat of the Sun, Tears of the Moon (Lourie), 224

T

Tacunga, Governor of, *see* Latacunga, Governor of

Tahuantinsuyo (Incan empire), 4, 77, 119, 214

Temple of the Sun (Coricancha), 119, 123–24, 141, 143, 272

Theroux, Paul, 166

They Found Gold: The Story of Successful Treasure Hunts (Verrill), 125, 211

Times of London, 312

Tolita culture, 141–42, 225

Tolkien, J.R.R., 22

Treasure Island (Stevenson), 20, 115, 116, 221, 222, 298

Trinity (ship), 221

Troy, 71

Troya, Alonso de, 41

Troya, Isabela de, *see* Brooks, Isabela

U

Ultimas Noticias, 134–36, 139, 153, 213, 214

U.S. Army, 39

U.S. Merchant marine, 253, 260, 319, 326

Upham, Donald B., 264, 265

V

Valverde, 122; Andrade and, 129–39; Atahualpa and Rumiñahui not mentioned by, 122; Blake and Chapman and, 100–101, 138, 181; Brooks and, 39, 40; Brunner and, 227; Cantuña legend's parallels with, 162–63; Coba Robalino and, 276; Dyott and, 223, 258; Fernández-Salvador and, 87–88, 91, 99, 100; Glaser and, 51, 62–65, 67–70, 182, 306; and Guzman's map, 33–38, 61, 87, 100, 137, 198; identity of, 119, 121, 133–34, 243, 276; Jost and, 147, 151, 327; legends of, 7–8, 25, 74, 124, 126, 127, 133–34, 143; Loch and, 51–55, 152–56, 191; Spruce and, 7, 8, 15–18, 21, 24, 26, 27, 74, 154, 233; map of, 8, 9, 21, 99–103, 127, 128, 209, 232, 252, 254, 256–58, 283, 288, 292, 303, 326; Wallace and, 31; *see also derrotero* of Valverde

Valverde, Felipe de, 133

Valverde, Isidoro de, 133

Valverde, Jerónimo de, 133

Valverde, Joaquín de, 133

Valverde, Pedro de, 133, 275

Valverde, Pedro, 244, 245, 246

Valverde, Father Vincente de, 81, 82, 133, 143, 156, 243

Valverde de Aguilar, Diego, 244

Valverde de Aguilar, Francisco, 244

Vega, Garcilaso de la, 83, 119–21, 124, 127

Verrill, Alpheus Hyatt, 125–26, 211

Viaje a las misteriosas montañas de Llanganati (*Voyage to the Mysterious Llanganati Mountains*) (Andrade), 130

Von Hagen, Victor Wolfgang, 171
*Voyages and Adventures of Capt. Barth.
Sharp and Others, in the South Sea,
The* (Cox), 221

W

Wafer, Lionel, 68, 221
Wallace, Alfred Russel, 21, 29, 30, 31,
33, 37, 38, 39, 119, 125, 127, 188, 233,
250, 257

Wilkins, Harold T., 127–28
World Health Organization, 95
World War I, 96, 97
World War II, 97
Wright Brothers, 96

Z

"Z" lost city of gold, 96, 261
Zoologicial Society, New York, 52
Zope-Zopahua, 122, 124, 125